FRANZ SCHUBERT AND HIS WORLD

OTHER PRINCETON UNIVERSITY PRESS VOLUMES PUBLISHED IN CONJUNCTION WITH THE BARD MUSIC FESTIVAL

Brahms and His World
edited by Walter Frisch (1990)

Mendelssohn and His World
edited by R. Larry Todd (1991)

Richard Strauss and His World
edited by Bryan Gilliam (1992)

Dvořák and His World
edited by Michael Beckerman (1993)

Schumann and His World
edited by R. Larry Todd (1994)

Bartók and His World
edited by Peter Laki (1995)

Charles Ives and His World
edited by J. Peter Burkholder (1996)

Haydn and His World
edited by Elaine R. Sisman (1997)

Tchaikovsky and His World
edited by Leslie Kearney (1998)

Schoenberg and His World
edited by Walter Frisch (1999)

Beethoven and His World
edited by Scott Burnham and Michael P. Steinberg (2000)

Debussy and His World
edited by Jane F. Fulcher (2001)

Mahler and His World
edited by Karen Painter (2002)

Janáček and His World
edited by Michael Beckerman (2003)

Shostakovich and His World
edited by Laurel E. Fay (2004)

Aaron Copland and His World
edited by Carol J. Oja and Judith Tick (2005)

Franz Liszt and His World
edited by Christopher H. Gibbs and Dana Gooley (2006)

Edward Elgar and His World
edited by Byron Adams (2007)

Prokofiev and His World
edited by Simon Morrison (2008)

Brahms and His World (revised edition)
edited by Walter Frisch and Kevin C. Karnes (2009)

Richard Wagner and His World
edited by Thomas S. Grey (2009)

Alban Berg and His World
edited by Christopher Hailey (2010)

Jean Sibelius and His World
edited by Daniel M. Grimley (2011)

Camille Saint-Saëns and His World
edited by Jann Pasler (2012)

Stravinsky and His World
edited by Tamara Levitz (2013)

FRANZ SCHUBERT
AND HIS WORLD

EDITED BY CHRISTOPHER H. GIBBS
AND MORTEN SOLVIK

PRINCETON UNIVERSITY PRESS
PRINCETON AND OXFORD

Published by Princeton University Press, 41 William Street,
Princeton, New Jersey 08540
In the United Kingdom: Princeton University Press,
6 Oxford Street, Woodstock, Oxfordshire OX20 1TW
press.princeton.edu

For permission information, see page xvii

Library of Congress Control Number: 2014940720

ISBN: 978-0-691-16379-6 (cloth)
ISBN: 978-0-691-16380-2 (paperback)

British Library Cataloging-in-Publication Data is available

This publication has been produced by the Bard College Publications Office:
Ginger Shore, Project Director
Karen Walker Spencer, Designer
Anita van de Ven, Cover Design
Text edited by Paul De Angelis and Erin Clermont
Music typeset by Don Giller

This publication has been underwritten in part by grants from
Roger and Helen Alcaly and Furthermore, a program of the J. M. Kaplan Fund

Printed on acid-free paper. ∞

Printed in the United States of America.

1 3 5 7 9 10 8 6 4 2

Contents

Preface

Dein Freund Schubert. These were probably the last words the composer ever wrote, about a week before he died on 19 November 1828, at age thirty-one. They were the conclusion to a heart-wrenching letter to Franz von Schober, his closest friend, that began: "I am ill. I have eaten nothing for eleven days and drunk nothing. And I totter feebly and shakily from my chair to bed and back again."[1] He then made the simple request that Schober send him some novels by James Fenimore Cooper.

Schubert's last letter points to some defining dimensions of his all-too-brief life: that friends and family were at its center (he was living at the time with his older brother Ferdinand, having recently moved from Schober's place); that literature was a consuming passion; and that serious illness led to early death. An obituary a few weeks later observed that the composer "lived solely for art and for a small circle of friends."[2] To this constellation of friendship, art, and a life of seemingly endless potential cut short, we should add another crucial element: Vienna. Unlike great predecessors who moved to the gloried "city of music," Schubert was born and remained there, with only infrequent excursions not far away.

An understanding of the music Schubert wrote during his brief career benefits enormously from awareness of the social, cultural, intellectual, and political context in which he lived and worked. This book, the twenty-fifth in the Bard Music Festival series published by Princeton University Press, aims more than ever to be true its title: to explore a particular composer's world, a world that in Schubert's case proved quite limited in duration, geography, and professional opportunities, but that nonetheless nourished astounding creative achievements, not only from contemporaries in music, such as Beethoven, but in the other arts as well.

One of the many enduring myths about Schubert is that he was largely unrecognized during his lifetime, a sad situation allegedly allayed to some extent by a devoted circle of friends who embraced his music. The reality seems to have been much more complex. He enjoyed considerable success, both in Vienna and beyond, with his songs and small-scale pieces, most intended for domestic consumption. A culture of intimate music-making is epitomized by the Schubertiades of the 1820s, evenings devoted to his music at which Schubert and others played for friends and invited guests. Schubert's ambitions, however, went much farther, extending to what he once described to a publisher as his "strivings after the highest in art."[3] He ultimately produced a staggering quantity of music, although most of it remained unpublished during his time. Already as a teenager he composed a large number of chamber, orchestral, sacred, and dramatic pieces, but it was in his twenties that he claimed real ownership of these genres. (Had he been of the mindset of Johannes Brahms, he probably would have destroyed much of his early instrumental music.) Many of these large-scale works were never performed in his lifetime and some were therefore unknown even to certain friends who viewed him, as did the public in general, principally as a composer of Lieder. Franz Grillparzer, Austria's leading writer and an acquaintance, captured contemporaneous perceptions in the epitaph he crafted for Schubert's grave: "The Art of Music Here Entombed a Rich Possession, But Even Far Fairer Hopes."[4]

The idea of an unfinished career finds expression in Schubert's most popular instrumental work, his Symphony in B Minor—the "Unfinished"—composed in 1822, and actually just one of a handful of his unfinished symphonies. When the work was finally premiered more than forty years later, in December 1865, critic Eduard Hanslick noted the "excited extraordinary enthusiasm" of the audience and how after hearing only a few measures "every child recognized the composer, and a muffled 'Schubert' was whispered in the audience . . . every heart rejoiced, as if, after a long separation, the composer himself were among us in person."[5] Three years later Schubert's close friend Moritz von Schwind created his famous sepia drawing of a Schubertiade at Josef von Spaun's house (see Figure 1 on page 68). Schwind also worked on a version in oils, which appears on the cover of this book, but it was not yet completed when the artist died in 1871.[6] The unfinished state of both the symphony and painting helps remind us of Schubert's unfinished life, suggesting a figurative "program" to various pieces that have none declared, not just the "Unfinished" Symphony, but also the "Quartettsatz," "Reliquie" Piano Sonata, and other marvelous torsos.

The span of Schubert's active public career lasted less than fifteen years, from 1814 to 1828. It is fitting that this book should appear in 2014, and that the Bard Music Festival honors Schubert during its twenty-fifth season, as the year marks the bicentennial of his miraculous masterpiece *Gretchen am Spinnrade*, whose composition on 19 October 1814 is often hailed as the "Birthday of the German Lied." In political history, the year also had profound consequences for Schubert and his contemporaries, as it saw the convening of the Congress of Vienna, held between September 1814 and June 1815 to negotiate borders and balances of power in the wake of the Napoleonic Wars. A period of reaction in Austria under the powerful Prince Clemens von Metternich led to censorship and repression that crucially defined aspects of Schubert's world.

A better appreciation of this time and place reveals matters that contemporaries, especially close friends, would have understood but that have since been obscured or forgotten. Despite the focus of much recent Schubert scholarship on ahistorical analytic matters, there have nonetheless been enormous strides in advancing archival and documentary knowledge of Schubert's world, all building on the pioneering work of the great Schubert scholar Otto Erich Deutsch (1883–1967). The publications of the Internationales Franz Schubert Institut between 1987 and 2005, the journal *Schubert: Perspektiven*, abundant conference reports, contributory volumes, and monographs continue to enlarge our historical understanding of the composer.

One result is that the image of Schubert has changed considerably, from the familiar one of a poor, shy, largely unappreciated figure, surrounded by merry friends, who composed "clairvoyantly," to a darker portrait of one who struggled valiantly with health, depression, career, and political repression.[7] The revisionist portrait is built on a firmer documentary basis and is surely more nuanced, although of necessity it is still often speculative and hampered by large holes in the historical record, not least because so few verbal documents survive from Schubert himself. The most sensational repositioning of Schubert, which generated the most heated debates, concerns his sexual life, an issue still far from resolved (and probably unresolvable) that is not much discussed in this book.[8] What has proved salutary is the more skeptical and subtle examination of Schubert's own writings and of those about him, which helps construct a much more psychologically complex and professionally confident figure than the clueless one earlier trivialized in sentimental fiction, operettas, films, and biographies.

There remain large gaps to fill, facts to find, and secrets to solve, a project this book seeks to advance. The order of the chapters presented here combines the roughly chronological with the thematic. The first three in various ways consider Schubert's social sphere, his famous "circle of friends." In some of the book's essays, scholars revisit, revise, and expand their own earlier work. Twenty years ago Rita Steblin, a Canadian scholar living in Vienna whose formidable archival work on Schubert and Beethoven has yielded fascinating finds (and sometimes controversial interpretations), discovered newsletters of the so-called Unsinnsgesellschaft (Nonsense Society). Schubert participated in this secret society, made up largely of artists and poets, along with some familiar friends, notably Leopold and Josef Kupelwieser, but also with individuals previously not known to have had any contact with him. The Unsinnsgesellschaft was active from April 1817 to December 1818, when Schubert was in his very early twenties. The surviving newsletters—the *Archive of Human Nonsense*—reveal a subculture in which code names, secrets, playfulness, and irreverence were paramount values. They shed new light on some of Schubert's compositions and contain marvelous illustrations, a few included here, that add to the limited supply of contemporaneous images of the composer.

Schubert had graduated a few years earlier from the Vienna Stadtkonvikt, an elite boarding school to which he had won a scholarship because of his musical gifts and where he began to forge lasting friendships. His somewhat older school friends (and then friends of these friends) initially guided his career, suggested (and sometimes wrote) poems for him to set to music, and helped to facilitate various career opportunities. Most of these young men were musical, but not professional musicians. David Gramit, in his presentation of three translated articles from *Beyträge zur Bildung für Jünglinge* (Contributions to Education for Youths), offers another window into Schubert's early social milieu, an altogether more serious one than that associated with the Unsinnsgesellschaft. This short-lived annual appeared for just two years (1817–18) and contained essays, poems, translations, dramatic scenes, and other edifying offerings. Today we might think of it as akin to a literary journal put together by smart graduate students at a good university. One encounters earnestness, ambition, and idealism, a search for virtue, truth, and the good—all appropriate to the age of the contributors.

As these two opening chapters show, Schubert was engaged with different social networks, but posterity has nevertheless loosely lumped them all together as a monolithic "Schubert Circle," the individuals who populate Schwind's composite Schubertiade illustrations. John M. Gingerich demonstrates that this was not the case and examines overlapping spheres in which Schubert participated, sometimes at the periphery or, with Schober, at its center (leading Schubert to coin the name "Schobert").[9] In the fall of 1824 a major conflict divided the circle around Schubert and Schober over an issue that superficially seems a mere test of loyalty. But the subsequent paths of various members reveal fissures that mirror divergences between early and late Romanticism, or more precisely, between the Friedrich Schlegel of 1799 and the same Friedrich von Schlegel of the 1820s, which means that they were also profoundly divided over religious and political issues. Gingerich traces the connections various members of the group had to both early and late Schlegel, some of them intense and personal, as well as the varied involvement of the painters in the circle with the so-called Nazarenes, a movement in German painting also influenced by the Romantic writer. The essay reveals a Schubert circle profoundly divided over some of the central ideological, social, and artistic controversies of the time, and to a surprising extent personally engaged with some of the main actors in those controversies.

The next three essays touch on Schubert's engagement with dramatic works, each from a very different vantage point. In the first, coeditor Morten Solvik explores the Liederspiel, a form of semi-dramatic, domestic music-making associated with simple strophic songs. He lays out for the first time in English a case he has made in earlier work concerning Schubert's 1815 settings of twenty poems by Gotthard Ludwig Kosegarten, demonstrating that they form a group of Lieder for three singers portraying the tragic tale of an amorous adventurer and his forlorn mistresses. Schubert's path-breaking later song cycles to poems by Wilhelm Müller, *Die schöne Müllerin* (1823) and *Winterreise* (1827), are much more familiar today and have obscured this earlier practice, a type of song performance in private salons involving amateur acting and multiple characters. In what emerges as something of a detective story, Solvik examines Schubert's manuscripts for the Kosegarten songs, as well as musical evidence based on tonal planning, head motives, and other compositional devices, to make the case that the composer conceived these Lieder as a unified set telling a Biedermeier story of love gone astray.

In addition to such domestic spheres, including the Schubertiades, Schubert regularly attended a reading group that discussed contemporary authors including Goethe, Heinrich Heine, Heinrich von Kleist, and Ludwig Tieck. Theater was a preoccupation for the Viennese in general and an area in which Schubert also hoped to succeed as a public figure—he wrote more than a dozen theatrical works, from brief Singspiele, to incidental music, to full-scale operas. Anselm Hüttenbrenner described his friend's typical day: Schubert would get up early and compose from six to one, he "never composed in the afternoon; after the midday meal he went to a café, drank a small portion of black coffee, smoked for an hour or two and read the newspapers at the same time. In the evening he went to one or other of the theaters."[10] Even if Hüttenbrenner exaggerated the frequency of Schubert's theatrical attendance, there is little doubt he and his friends went to a great many plays, folk theater, and operas. Lisa Feurzeig considers how the Volkstheater tradition, plays by Ferdinand Raimund and Adolf Bäuerle with music by Wenzel Müller and Joseph Drechsler, may have found echoes in pieces by Schubert, including the "Wanderer" Fantasy, *Winterreise*, and *Der Hirt auf dem Felsen*.[11]

Schubert's theatrical aspirations are most apparent in his full-scale operas *Alfonso und Estrella* (1822) and *Fierabras* (1823), neither of which was staged during his lifetime. In the midst of the Rossinimania that captivated Vienna in the late teens and early 1820s, Schubert held out hopes that German opera might succeed. The triumph of Carl Maria von Weber's *Der Freischütz* in 1821 made this seem reasonable, just as the failure two years later of the same composer's *Euryanthe* is partly responsible for dashing those hopes. Schober wrote the libretto for *Alfonso*; the two friends enjoyed a secluded period in the fall of 1821 working together on the project, which was completed in January. Decades later Schober brought the opera to the attention of Franz Liszt, with whom he was closely associated at the time in Weimar. Liszt adored Schubert's music—he once called him "the most poetic of musicians"—and although he harbored reservations about *Alfonso*, he nonetheless mounted its much belated premiere in 1854.[12] He also wrote an extended essay about the work, which Allan Keiler introduces and translates here. Liszt does not pull his punches, pointing to the faults in the opera, but also to its many marvels.

The final three chapters explore the intersection between intention and reception, Schubert's goals as a composer and the manner in which he has been understood by posterity. Schubert won his first and most enduring fame with Lieder, the genre in which he produced his initial masterpieces to texts by Goethe and that engaged him to the very end (the playfully serious *Die Taubenpost*, on a poem by the Viennese poet Johann Gabriel Seidl about an esoteric mode of communication employed by both lovers and spies, was apparently the last piece he wrote). His songs have invited an astonishing range of scholarly attention and approaches. Recent German-language scholarship in particular has become attuned to political imagery in numerous poems that he chose to set in the repressive post-Napoleonic chill that came over Vienna just as his career was starting up. The hopes of so many in his generation for a spring-like renewal after the war were frustrated by an interminable winter. Kristina Muxfeldt's essay explores how Schubert's music deftly reshaped words and allowed unsuspected meanings to resound in the changing political climate. In a time of censorship, music with words, such as songs and operas, had to receive official approval, but Muxfeldt argues that Lieder nonetheless offered Schubert an expressive realm for political thought, "freedom of song, if not speech," as she puts it.

Beethoven was the commanding musical presence in Schubert's world and the composer he most revered. Coeditor Christopher Gibbs returns to a topic broached in earlier writings to propose that Schubert composed the Piano Trio in E-flat Major, Op. 100, in honor of Beethoven. We know Schubert was deeply affected by the master's death and participated in his funeral on 29 March 1827. The following November, just as Beethoven's gravestone was dedicated, he began composing the trio, which premiered publicly on 26 March 1828, the first anniversary of Beethoven's death. Various strains of biographical and musical evidence converge to suggest that Schubert wrote the piece as a *tombeau de Beethoven*, which may explain why many listeners have perceived a ghost haunting the work ever since.

Schubert died less than eight months after the premiere of the E-flat Piano Trio and a few days later he was buried, supposedly at his expressed request, near to Beethoven. The two composers became increasingly united in death, their graves a pilgrimage site, and the musical values embodied by their compositions compared and contrasted. The continual posthumous discovery of ever more of Schubert's music meant that his achievement seemed more in line with Beethoven's.

With Schubert's premature passing he entered not only a realm of myth making, but also of contest for his legacy, a subject Leon Botstein considers in the final chapter. Among the posthumous careers of the great Classical and Romantic composers Schubert's is unprecedented and extraordinary: most of his significant instrumental, dramatic, and religious music was released in the decades following his death, a steady stream of masterpieces that surprised and delighted many. The discovery of new marvels—Hanslick commented that it appeared Schubert was "composing invisibly"[13]—made it seem as if he were still alive, a contemporary not only of Mendelssohn and Schumann (both of whom died well before the premiere of the "Unfinished" Symphony), but also of Wagner and Brahms. Thus Schubert could be enlisted or dismissed as a continuing presence in the contested musical politics of the century, and not simply invoked as a departed master. His close identification with Vienna accelerated, and choral groups such as the Wiener Männergesangverein and Schubertbund claimed him as a native son. Botstein takes the story into the twentieth century, including the 1928 centennial of Schubert's death, when he continued to be extravagantly celebrated and condescendingly diminished by individuals and groups with larger ideological agendas.

Great historical figures are, of course, always ripe for reassessment, provoking studies that can reveal, with the benefits of hindsight, new perspectives on the distant past while also inevitably reflecting current concerns and attitudes. Anniversary years add impetus, as shown by *Schubertjahre* in 1897, 1928, 1978, and 1997. As the Bard Music Festival and this book series celebrate their silver anniversary, we are halfway now from the Schubert bicentennial to the next big anniversary in 2028. Among leading composers of the past two and half centuries Schubert, with his largely uneventful and poorly documented life, and his extraordinary posthumous career, turns out to be a fascinating and unusually inviting figure for continual reappraisal.

— Christopher H. Gibbs

NOTES

1. Otto Erich Deutsch, *Schubert: A Documentary Biography*, trans. Eric Blom (London, 1946), 819–20.

2. Otto Erich Deutsch, *Schubert: Memoirs by His Friends*, trans. Rosamond Ley and John Nowell (London, 1958), 10.

3. Deutsch, *Schubert: A Documentary Biography*, 740.

4. See Ernst Hilmar, "Zu Grillparzers Inschrift auf Schuberts Grabdenkmal," *Schubert durch die Brille* 29 (2002): 125–28.

5. *Hanslick's Musical Criticisms*, ed. and trans. Henry Pleasants (New York, 1978), 102.

6. For more about Schwind's drawing and painting, see Maurice J. E. Brown, "Schwind's 'Schubert-Abend bei Josef Spaun,'" in *Essays on Schubert* (New York, 1966), 155–68.

7. Christopher H. Gibbs, "'Poor Schubert': Images and Legends of the Composer," *Cambridge Companion to Schubert*, ed. Christopher H. Gibbs (Cambridge, 1997), 36–55.

8. Maynard Solomon first raised the issue of the composer's possible homosexuality in "Franz Schubert's 'Mein Traum,'" *American Imago* 38 (1981): 137–54. His argument achieved wide notoriety with the article "Franz Schubert and the Peacocks of Benvenuto Cellini," *19th-Century Music* 12 (Spring 1989): 193–206; and responses in "Schubert: Music, Sexuality, Culture," a special issue of *19th-Century Music* 17 (Summer 1993).

9. Deutsch, *Schubert: A Documentary Biography*, 98.

10. Deutsch, *Schubert: Memoirs by His Friends*, 183.

11. Concerning possible influences of popular theater on Schubert's own dramatic music, see Mary Wischusen, "Franz Schubert and Viennese Popular Comedy," in *The Unknown Schubert*, ed. Barbara M. Reul and Lorraine Byrne Bodley (Aldershot, 2008), 83–97.

12. Janita R. Hall-Swadley, ed. and trans., *The Collected Writings of Franz Liszt*, vol. 2: *Essays and Letters of a Traveling Bachelor of Music* (Lanham, 2012), 327.

13. Deutsch, *Schubert: Memoirs by His Friends*, 383.

Acknowledgments

With *Franz Schubert and His World* the Bard Music Festival series, published each year by Princeton University Press, reaches its twenty-fifth volume. Many of the individuals deserving thanks for their efforts with this book have long been involved with the series, some going back to *Brahms and His World* in 1990. First and foremost is Leon Botstein, who when he founded the festival was determined that performance and scholarship should exist in fruitful dialogue and that a lasting legacy of each year's explorations would be a volume of essays and documents.

Ginger Shore has overseen the process since 1996 and retires this year; our thanks to her for dedication to these volumes, for always keeping things moving forward, and for her sensitive oversight of design issues. Irene Zedlacher, executive director of the Bard Music Festival, brings her keen editorial eye to reading the book and deals with many other matters to make things run smoothly. Don Giller has set the musical examples since the series began and we thank him for his careful work. We are grateful to Erin Clermont for copy-editing, Karen Spencer for the layout, and Ruth Elwell for indexing.

Our special thanks to another veteran of the series, Paul De Angelis, who oversees the production of the book from start to finish. His generous help and support as well as his terrific editorial comments and suggestions are what editors, authors, and contributors crave but so rarely receive in publishing ventures these days. We count ourselves very lucky.

We would also like to thank our families for their patience and support as we put together this book in countless email exchanges, Skype calls, trans-Atlantic trips, and long nights of editing. We are grateful for their care and understanding.

Finally, when a publisher asked Schubert about the dedication of one of his pieces, the composer responded: "The work is to be dedicated to nobody, save those who find pleasure in it. That is the most profitable dedication." In that spirit we wish to thank and dedicate this book to that most precious and endangered group in classical music, the generous music-loving patrons and benefactors who have made the Bard Music Festival possible year after year.

Christopher H. Gibbs, Annandale-on-Hudson, New York
Morten Solvik, Vienna, Austria

Permissions and Credits

The following institutions and individuals have graciously granted permission to reprint or reproduce these materials:

Erich Lessing/Art Resource, New York, for the front cover image by Moritz von Schwind; and for Figure 3, p. 224.

Handschriftensammlung, Wienbibliothek for Figure 1, p. 2; Figure 5, p. 9; Figure 7 (and 7a–7b), pp. 18–19; Figure 4, p. 127 (from the album "Stammbuch Karl Haslinger. Herrn Karl Haslinger zur Erinnerung an den 25-jährigen Bestand seiner musikalischen Abende gewidmet 1862"); and Figure 4, p. 235.

Musiksammlung, Wienbibliothek for Figure 2, p. 123.

Wien Museum Karlsplatz the copyrighted © images reproduced in Figure 2, p. 4; Figure 3, p. 5; Figure 4, p. 6; Figure 6, p. 12; Figure 8, p. 24; Figure 10, p. 28.

Kunsthistorisches Museum, Vienna/The Bridgeman Art Library, for Figure 9, p. 25.

Lebrecht Music & Arts for Figure 1, p. 55 and Figure 3, p. 98.

Wien Museum Karlsplatz, Vienna, and Erich Lessing/Art Resource, New York, for Figure 1, p. 68; Figure 2, p. 69; and Figure 2, p. 186.

Goethe House and Museum, Frankfurt, Germany/Art Resource, New York, for Figure 4, p. 103.

Irving S. Gilmore Music Library, Yale University, for Figure 3, p. 124.

Austrian National Library (ÖNB), Bildarchiv und Grafiksammlung, for Figure 5, p. 133; Figure 6, p. 134; and Figure 1, p. 168.

Staatsbibliothek zu Berlin, Musikabteilung, Stiftung Preussischer Kulturbesitz/Art Resource, New York, for Figure 7, p. 144.

Beinecke Rare Books and Manuscripts Library, Yale University, for Figure 8, p. 150.

National Gallery, London, U.K./The Bridgeman Art Library for Figure 1, p. 214.

The Metropolitan Museum, New York for Figure 2, p. 216 (From *Galerie du Palais royal, gravée d'après les tableaux des differentes ecoles qui la composent : avec un abrégé de la vie des peintres & une description historique de chaque tableau, par Mr. l'abbé de Fontenai / par J. Couché*, vol. 2 [Paris: Chez J. Couché, J. Bouilliard, 1786–1808], held by the Metropolitan Museum).

Archiv, Bibliothek und Sammlungen der Gesellschaft der Musikfreunde in Wien, for Figure 2, p. 256; Figure 3, p. 257; Figure 4, pp. 265–66; Figure 5, p. 285.

The authors and publishers have made every effort to trace holders of copyright. They much regret if any inadvertent omissions have been made.

FRANZ SCHUBERT AND HIS WORLD

Schubert: The Nonsense Society Revisited

RITA STEBLIN

Twenty years have now passed since I discovered materials belonging to the Unsinnsgesellschaft (Nonsense Society).[1] This informal club, active in Vienna from April 1817 to December 1818, consisted mainly of young painters and poets with Schubert as one of its central members. In this essay I will review this discovery, my ensuing interpretations, and provide some new observations.

In January 1994, at the start of a research project on Schubert iconography, I studied some illustrated documents at the Historisches Museum der Stadt Wien (now the Wienmuseum am Karlsplatz), titled "Unsinniaden."[2] The documents comprise forty-four watercolor pictures and thirty-seven pages of text recording two festive events celebrated by the Nonsense Society: the New Year's Eve party at the end of 1817 and the group's first birthday party on 18 April 1818.[3] The pictures depict various club members, identified by their code names and dressed in fanciful costumes, as well as four group scenes for the first event, including *Vivat es lebe Blasius Leks* (Long live Blasius Leks; Figure 1), and two group scenes for the second event, including *Feuergeister-Scene* (Fire Spirit Scene; Figure 6 below).[4] Because of the use of code names—and the misidentifications written on the pictures by some previous owner of the materials—it was not initially possible to interpret these documents correctly.[5]

A few months later, in April 1994, I discovered a second set of papers, housed in the manuscript collection of the Wiener Stadt- und Landesbibliothek (now Wienbibliothek) in Vienna's City Hall, and these made it easier to unravel many of the society's secrets.[6] This second set of materials had been purchased in 1937 from a descendant of the club's vice-editor, code-named Zeisig (a type of finch).[7] It consisted of handwritten newsletters titled *Archiv des menschlichen Unsinns* (Archive of Human Nonsense). One numbered issue of the newsletter was apparently produced each week, although the collection contained only twenty-nine newsletters, those between 17 April 1817 and 10 December 1818 (nine from

Figure 1. *Vivat es lebe Blasius Leks: Zur Unsinniade—5ter Gesang* (Long Live Blasius Leks: For the 5th Song of Nonsense), 31 December 1817. Watercolor by Carl Friedrich Zimmermann (Aaron Bleistift).

1817 and twenty from 1818). Each issue, penned in *Kurrentschrift* (German running script) and usually eight pages long, begins with a motto and ends with a watercolor picture; in between are humorous and rather off-color texts spoofing contemporary politics, social mores, scientific discoveries, art, drama, and literature, each signed with the writer's code name. At the beginning of the first issue, in Zeisig's hand, is a key headed "Namen der Unsinnsmitglieder" that identifies most of the club members—twenty-two in all. This is what made it possible to link the newsletters to the documents in the Wienmuseum and, after intensive biographical research on the club's participants, establish Schubert's important role in the secret society.

Most of the members were young painters—students at the Vienna Art Academy—with code names that reflect their profession: for example, August Kloeber (1793–1864), famous for the portrait he sketched of Beethoven in 1818, was called Goliath Pinselstiel (Giant Paintbrush) and Johann Nepomuk Hoechle (1790–1835), who would paint Beethoven's studio a few days after the composer's death, was called Kratzeratti Klanwinzi (Little Scratcher). Three Kupelwieser brothers are also clearly identified on this list: Blasius Leks (Josef), Chrisostomus Schmecks (Johann), and Damian Klex (Leopold).[8] Not all of the club's members are initially listed; Schubert's name, for example, is missing. Moreover, various code names that occur in the newsletters or on the individual portraits, for example that of Quanti Verdradi (Totally Mixed-Up), whom I have identified as Schubert's friend Franz von Schober, are also not on the initial list. Compounding this, at least two-thirds of the newsletters originally produced by the club are now missing (including the twenty-three issues immediately after the first one), a loss that makes a definitive interpretation of all the complicated allusions difficult.

Schubert's connection to the society was referred to in at least two memoirs by his friends but was misinterpreted by the great scholar Otto Erich Deutsch (1883–1967), who was only aware of another group, the so-called Ludlamshöhle (Ludlam's Cave). The first reference comes from Heinrich Anschütz (1785–1865), a famous Burgtheater actor, who delivered Franz Grillparzer's celebrated oration at Beethoven's funeral. He wrote in his memoirs:

> I had spent my first Christmas in Vienna at the end of 1821.... This Christmas was of special interest to me because it brought Schubert to my house for the first time. Franz Schubert was one of the most active members of the late Nonsense Society. In this my brothers had been most intimately associated with him for years and it was through my [brothers] that he came to my house.[9]

There is no reason to doubt Anschütz's assertion about Schubert's active participation in the "late" Nonsense Society—"late" meaning that the group no longer existed in 1821. Moreover, the first two names on the list of Nonsense Society members are the actor's two brothers: "Anschütz Eduard . . . Schnautze, Redacteur" and "Anschütz Gustav . . . Sebast^{n} Haarpuder" (see Figures 2–4).[10] Eduard Anschütz (ca. 1797–1855) was actually the club's leader, as well as the main editor (*Redacteur*) of the newsletters; most of the texts were written in his hand. His code name Schnautze, meaning (big) snout, is an anagram of Anschütz.

The second reference to the Nonsense Society, although the group was not mentioned by name, appears in an obituary for Schubert by Eduard von Bauernfeld (1802–1890):

> At the time Schubert came out into the world several young men in his native city, mostly poets and painters (e.g. the

Figure 2. *Die Redaction: Herr Schnautze* (The Editorial Board: Mr. Snout), 31 December 1817. Watercolor by Ernst Welker (Kritzli Batzli).

Figure 3. *Schnautze Redacteur* (Snout Editor), 18 April 1818.
Watercolor by Johann Nepomuk Hoechle (Kratzeratti Klanwinzi).

Figure 4. *Sebastian Haarpuder* (Sebastian Hairpowder), 31 December 1817. Watercolor by Franz Goldhann (Ultimus).

> esteemed [Leopold] Kupelwieser), gathered together, whom genuine striving after art and similarity of views soon united in sincere friendship, and into whose circle Schubert too was drawn. The mutual communication between these youths and their artistic conversations had a great effect on him and stimulated him, if not so much to talk, at any rate to the most varied musical productivity. To several of these friends he was most cordially devoted to the end of his life, and he often expressed regret, in letters as well as conversation, that the friendly union of so many worthy young men, as will happen, became disrupted by their pursuing different careers and by other chances.[11]

Bauernfeld's mention of "other chances" having led to the disruption of this circle of poets and painters was probably a hint that the increasingly strict police measures against club formations in Prince Clemens von Metternich's Vienna made it too dangerous for the Nonsense Society to survive. One of the friends to whom Schubert "was most cordially devoted to the end of his life" was Franz Goldhann (1782–1856), the society's oldest member—aged thirty-five—and thus code-named Ultimus. His father had helped Mozart out financially, and he himself would become a member of Ludwig Mohn's reading circle in late 1823, using the new euphemism "Dr. Faust." His family name Goldhann actually means golden rooster, and the portrait painted of him for the club's first birthday party depicts him holding a shield displaying a barnyard fowl of this color. The pictures are full of such hidden clues to the members' real identities. Fortified by the references from Anschütz and Bauernfeld regarding the importance of this society for Schubert and his musical output, I began the search for his presence in this extremely secretive, encoded material.

Iconographic Evidence

The most immediately compelling evidence for Schubert's participation in the Nonsense Society could be gleaned from the many illustrations that accompanied the various issues of the newsletter. One particularly striking example is *Zur Unsinniade—5ter Gesang* (For the 5th Song of Nonsense) a watercolor containing the banner "Vivat es lebe Blasius Leks" (Long live Blasius Leks) and illustrating the last poem or song that Josef Kupelwieser wrote to describe the New Year's Eve party on 31 December 1817 (see Figure 1). The term *Unsinniade* suggestively resembles a later, far more famous word-creation: *Schubertiade*. Could the former have served as the inspiration for the latter?

Standing in the middle of the scene is a short man with curly sideburns and wearing eyeglasses, dressed in a brown suit, whom I have identified as Schubert. He is accompanied by two young women attired in formal white dresses and blue accessories, arriving at the end of the party, perhaps after attending another festivity elsewhere. The little man on the left, wearing a hat with fancy feathers, is the still-life painter Johann Carl Smirsch (1793–1869), whose code name was Nina Wutzerl. He is mentioned in the Schubert literature for having provided the composer with the opportunity to send the deeply moving letter of 31 March 1824 to his close friend Leopold Kupelwieser in Rome.[12] The man on the right, dressed as a roughneck from Berlin and offering a toast to the two female guests, is Carl Friedrich Zimmermann (1796–1820), the one Jewish member in the club. He painted this picture, which is signed with his code name Aaron Bleistift (*Bleistift* meaning pencil, used by a *Zimmermann*, meaning carpenter). The two women are most likely Babette and Therese Kunz, sisters with whom Schubert gave concerts in March 1818 and for whom he arranged, in December 1817, his two Overtures in Italian Style as four-hand piano works (D592 and D597). The person playing the violin at the left of the complete picture is the amateur painter Ludwig Kraißl (1792–1871), code-named Pinselmo Schmieraliri (Brushy Smearup). He was also a friend of Leopold Kupelwieser and played the violin in the well-known picture *Ball Game at Atzenbrugg* (dating from 1823), in which Schubert sits on the grass, smoking a pipe.[13] Kraißl's prominent position at the forefront of the Unsinniade scene means that he serves as a kind of musical herald, announcing the arrival of his superior: the musical genius Schubert—who is placed so prominently in the center of the picture.[14]

Other illustrations also point to Schubert. The caricature in Figure 5, *The Kaleidoscope and the Draisine*, was painted by Leopold Kupelwieser (signed with his code name Damian Klex) and is attached to the newsletter of 16 July 1818.[15] It spoofs the composer as a portly schoolteacher, holding a stick and peering through a kaleidoscope, and the artist himself as a young student riding the newly invented draisine, a forerunner of the bicycle. The picture's meaning is explained in the accompanying article "Zum Kupfer" credited to the editorial board—that is, Eduard Anschütz:

> The latest example of contemporary history proves just how dangerous the new invention of ice-slides is in Paris. But even the seemingly harmless inventions of the kaleidoscope and the draisine have their dangers, as the accompanying

Figure 5. *Das Kaleidoskop und die Draisine* (The Kaleidoscope and the Draisine), 16 July 1818. Watercolor by Leopold Kupelwieser (Damian Klex).

> picture illustrates. The stout gentleman is absorbed in the contemplation of the kaleidoscope's wonderful play of colors—the dark glass makes him even more nearsighted than usual. He is about to be knocked to the ground by a passionate draisine rider, who likewise has his eye fixed only on his machine. Let this be a warning for others. There is already supposed to be a police order in the works on the strength of which every blockhead is strictly forbidden, on account of the danger, from using both new inventions.[16]

The nearsighted Schubert was habitually associated in the newsletters not only with eyeglasses, but with other optical devices as well, such as the kaleidoscope.[17] This new invention was patented by Sir David Brewster in 1817 to create inexhaustible forms of symmetrical geometric patterns; the draisine was likewise invented in 1817, by German Baron Karl Christian Ludwig Drais von Sauerbronn.

These illustrations provide vital clues for unlocking coded references to Schubert in the newsletters. Once a word or object was associated with a member, subsequent issues developed the association in other creative ways, which in turn could lead to further associations. Thus Gustav Anschütz, using the kaleidoscope as a coded allusion to Schubert, writes as follows in a newsletter dated 10 September 1818:

> The undersigned has the honor of faithfully informing the venerated public that he has for sale a kind of kaleidoscope (also known as looking-through-tube) with the unique property that one can use it to see through all kinds of clothing. The great benefit of this optical device should be apparent to everybody since it discloses some items that are at present carefully kept hidden. Especially for young men who like to go walking on the Graben.

Today the Graben is filled with expensive shops, but in Schubert's time it was associated with prostitutes, the notorious "Graben nymphs." In another account, Josef Kupelwieser warns that the kaleidoscope can have a strong effect not only on the eyes, but also on the nose. He may be alluding to an advanced stage of syphilis in which the nose is eaten away. It is known that Schubert eventually contracted this disease, most likely in late 1822—probably through contact with a prostitute. The exact nature of Schubert's illness was hushed up by his contemporaries, but Wilhelm von Chézy, whose mother, Helmina, in 1823 penned the text to the drama with incidental music *Rosamunde* (D797), came close to revealing this in his recollection of the composer, published in 1841: "Schubert adored women and wine. Unfortunately this taste had caused him to stray into wrong paths from which he could no longer find his way back alive."[18] Indeed, as we shall see, there is enough evidence provided by the surviving Nonsense Society materials to suggest strongly that Schubert was already using prostitutes in 1817.

Kupelwieser's caricature also alludes to Schubert's work as an assistant at the school where his father was headmaster, for it shows him carrying a stick. This attribute—associated with the disciplining stick used by teachers, sometimes known as a "Spanish rod"—occurs repeatedly in the newsletters, again pointing to the composer. For example, the issue dated 24 September 1818 describes the invention of a new machine called the *Hiebeidoskopf*—a play on the words *Hiebe* (blows, strokes) and *Kaleidoskop*—whereby a quantity of installed Spanish rods could give out the desired number of blows.[19] The machine could also be used to beat the dust from clothing. Directly following is a newsletter article by Josef Kupelwieser describing the search for a theater librettist and the conditions under which he is to serve. The article closes as follows: "A composer is also required, under similar terms, except that he must also clean the boots and clothes of the director."[20] Thus, in this encoded manner, a composer (Schubert) is associated with both the kaleidoscope and the stick. The stick occurs again in connection with "Ritter Zimbal" (Knight Cimbalom), in a newsletter dated 5 November 1818: here Schubert's code name follows the phrase "25 blows with a stick on the backside of a Hungarian soldier." What is more, a long serial drama by Schnautze Redacteur that appeared in the last five surviving newsletters (dated 12 November to 10 December 1818) satirizes Schubert as a *Genie* (genius) who flies out of a *Schublade* (a drawer) to the sound of music. After being transformed into a stick, this *Genie* warns about how dangerous it is to consort with a prostitute, disguised as a seductive woman in white.

Der Feuergeist

These allusions to Schubert in 1818 all refer back to an article in the second surviving newsletter, dated 25 September 1817, in which Schubert's role as composer emerges in a context completely unknown to music historical accounts. Under the rubric "Theateranzeige" (Theater News), Eduard Anschütz announces that the Nonsense Society was about to begin rehearsing a drama in four acts with choruses and stage machinery called *Der Feuergeist* (The Fire Spirit). The text was written by Blasius Leks (Josef Kupelwieser), and Schnautze himself was to play the role of the fire demon.[21] Schubert must have composed the music for this work; this is attested by the watercolor titled *Feuergeister-Scene*, painted to document a production of the drama that took place at the club's first birthday party in April 1818 (see Figure 6). This picture is remarkably similar to a scene in Schubert's three-act melodrama *Die Zauberharfe* (The Magic Harp; D644), a work he supposedly composed in a mere few weeks in the summer of 1820. Although the libretto to *Zauberharfe* is lost, the program for the 19 August 1820 premiere at the Theater an der Wien names such characters as Sutur, an evil fire demon; Count Arnulf; his estranged wife, Melinde; and their son Palmerin, who plays the magic harp. The plot, as reconstructed on the basis of Schubert's music and the first newspaper reviews, contains a scene in Act 3 that unfolds as follows: Arnulf is happy and wants to reconcile his differences with Melinde, but the demonic Sutur appears and reminds her of

Figure 6. *Feuergeister-Scene* (Fire Spirit Scene), 18 April 1818.
Watercolor by Franz Goldhann (Ultimus).

an oath she had made to him earlier. With the help of his fire demons, Sutur tries to destroy her. Palmerin flies in to the rescue, playing on his magic harp. His music overpowers the evil forces and saves the true love of his parents. This is exactly the situation depicted in the illustration. In keeping with the nonsense theme of the society, Arnulf is portrayed here as a *Bierhäuselmensch* (a beer-house person) and Melinde—the role played in 1817 by Schnautze—is a barmaid.

In Eduard Anschütz's prose description of the birthday party—"Il giorno di nascitá"—he identifies the players and their parts, and we learn that they were assigned roles different from the original production. Schnautze concludes: "The fire demons drank everything up. All the actors competed honorably with each other, the choruses fell apart beyond all expectation and the piece disintegrated marvelously. What a wonder therefore that the performance ended with much laughter, art's beautiful reward."[22] Role reversal, that is, spoofing the identities of other members, was one of the defining features of the club, and the exchanged parts no doubt led to the performance's disintegration.

An additional clue pointing to Schubert's involvement with *Der Feuergeist* is Schnautze's use of the word *Schub* (push, thrust) in describing the birthday performance. This is how he begins the introduction to his prose account: "When a woman gives birth, a human being is born and this is a *Hauptschub* [major event]. But, if an exceptional person is born, this is a little bit more, and if a God of Nonsense is born, this is still two bits more."[23] Thus, by using the word *Schub* and referring to an "exceptional person," Anschütz gives an encoded allusion to Schubert's important role in this celebration, although the composer himself was not present at this particular event. Later, in a newsletter dated 15 October 1818, Schnautze builds on this analogy in a children's ballet titled *Insanius auf Erden* (Insanius on Earth). Schubert is featured here as the ABC (primary school) teacher called Hymen Halbgott (Hymen Half-God); the God of Nonsense "Insanius" appears as a "3/4 Gott"—three-quarters being "a little bit more than half," and also alluding to dances in 3/4 time.

In the summer of 1820, when Schubert was under great time constraints, he must have reused some of the music of *Der Feuergeist* for *Die Zauberharfe*. Other evidence supports this supposition. The overture to *Die Zauberharfe* contains music that he had already composed in November 1817. Much comes from the introduction and coda for the Overture in the Italian Style in D Major (D590) that Schubert arranged in December 1817 in a four-hand piano version (D592) for the Kunz sisters. An earlier dating of the music to *Zauberharfe* would also explain the great confusion that exists in the numbering of the scenes in the manuscript material. When Schubert's *Zauberharfe* was staged for the first time in August 1820 at the Theater an der Wien, its librettist remained officially anonymous. A diary entry by Josef Karl Rosenbaum names him as Georg von Hofmann, who usually wrote for the Kärntnertortheater. I suspect that Rosenbaum may have been mistaken. Moreover, one of the newspaper reviewers of the *Zauberharfe* production, "B. S.," generally thought to be the poet and Schubert-friend Baron von Schlechta, called the librettist "ein ehrlicher Kämpfer für den Unsinn" (an honorable fighter for nonsense).[24] Perhaps Schlechta was here admitting his inside knowledge that the real librettist was Josef Kupelwieser. Schubert's melodrama was criticized by contemporary reviewers for its many drinking choruses. Since the picture from 1818 shows the ensemble of fire demons behind a table loaded with drinks, Schubert must have written many such choruses for the Nonsense Society. The early collaboration between Schubert and Kupelwieser is important in light of their later joint venture, *Fierabras* (D796), usually considered Schubert's best opera.[25]

The Knight of the Keyboard

It should come as no surprise that Schubert's ingenious talents as a composer found their way into a wide range of allusions in the newsletters. In fact, his primary code name in the Nonsense Society was Ritter Juan de la Cimbala (Don Giovanni of the Keyboard), *Cembalo* being the German—actually Italian—word for harpsichord.[26] This name, although not found on the list of members attached to the first newsletter, is the only code name for any of the members with a musical meaning. It occurs in the issue dated 13 August 1818, written by the vice-editor at a time when Schubert was away from Vienna serving as music master in the home of Count Johann Esterházy at his summer residence in Zseliz, in what is today southeastern Slovakia but what was then part of Hungary:

> According to reports from Spain, the inquisition has arrested the famous painter Juan de la Cimbala because, owing to his own admission, he has been occupied with black magic in addition to his usual duties. Nevertheless, we hope that he will get out of this alive, in that even before his arrest he had severely burned himself.

Zeisig, the author of this extremely encoded entry, has in typical nonsensical fashion turned Hungary into Spain and the musician Cimbala into a painter. The passage "owing to his own admission" probably indicates that Schubert had recently sent a letter to his friends in the Nonsense Society, relating his activities in Zseliz. This must have been similar to the well-known account addressed on 8 September 1818 to Schober and six of Schober's friends in which he describes in great detail the people at the Esterházy estate, including "the chambermaid very pretty and often my companion . . . the manager my rival."[27] Other letters make it clear that the composer had two groups of Viennese friends at this time—"the city friends" and the Schober circle.[28] (It goes without saying that many of Schubert's letters are lost.) I interpret the "black magic" in Zeisig's account as referring to the compositional activities of the Spanish Don Juan (Schubert), in addition to his usual teaching duties for the Esterházy family in Zseliz, where he was "confined" for about five months. He had "burned" himself earlier by writing a secretive 19-bar palindrome for *Feuergeist*. When musicologist Brian Newbould discovered this amazing feat in its later version in *Die Zauberharfe*, for music associated with the fire spirit Sutur, he described this achievement as the "product of intellectual manipulations, the willful reversal of values, as in the 'black mass.'"[29]

There may also be a double meaning in the word *burned*. Since Schubert had hinted in his correspondence that he was having a love affair with the maid-servant (Pepi Pöckelhofer), he was again "playing with fire"—having severely burned himself earlier in his relations with prostitutes.

Another newsletter, written on 5 November 1818 while Schubert was still in Zseliz, uses the name "Ritter Zimbal," an appropriate reference to cimbalom, the Hungarian hammered dulcimer. The next newsletter, one week later, is headed with the motto "Heidideldum! Heidideldum! Hopsasa hopsasa Heidideldum!" and opens with an article by Blasius Leks (Josef Kupelwieser) about the Spanish nobleman "Hans from the Hinterland" riding back to Austria on a *Hanselbank* (sawhorse). The words "Hans in Wien" are underlined for emphasis. Hans, of course, is the diminutive for Johannes, the German form of (Don) Juan, hence another allusion to Schubert as Ritter Juan de la Cimbala. Kupelwieser elaborates on the name to announce that Schubert is about to arrive back in Vienna from his long stay in the "hinterland" of Hungary.[30]

A remarkable observation regarding Schubert's sojourn in Hungary is his composition there of a work that explicitly refers to his moniker in the club: Variations on a French Song (D624). This is the four-hand piece consisting of eight variations on *Le bon chevalier* (*Der treue Ritter* or The Good Knight) that Schubert later dedicated to Beethoven as Op. 10. It seems highly likely that Schubert chose this particular song about a faithful knight relating the tale of hopeless love (no doubt with autobiographical elements as well) as a tribute to his role as Ritter Juan in the Nonsense Society.

The code name Cimbala/Zimbal is clear in its reference to his musical instrument, the keyboard. But what about the Spanish nobleman—Don Juan? There are, in fact, many jokes in the newsletters about Ritter Juan's pursuit of women.[31] In the same month that Schubert composed his piano duet variations—September 1818—we find the following tale about "Chevalier Touchetout" in the newsletter:

> *L'observateur curieux* [The Curious Observer] has reported—that in the dilemma in which *Madame Culronde* [Roundbottom] has felt herself placed as the ardent *Chevalier Touchetout* [Touches Everything], who casually undertook some physical-anatomical investigations with her, and his hand, to the misfortune of the lady and the great astonishment of the *Chevalier*, instead of the assumed natural curves pulled out some socks—nothing further other than that her dilemma was without end.

There are numerous clues that point to Schubert in this passage. The immediately preceding newsletter item mentions *Schuhe* (shoes)—*Schubert* actually means "shoemaker"—and the item directly following discusses a "Caleidoscop." The French word *touche* (German *Tasten*) means not only "touch," but also piano keys. *Chevalier* is the French word for *Ritter* (knight), Ritter Juan is the only code name with this title. In the newsletter dated 12 February 1818, the poem "Impromptu"—which dealt with a sock—follows an article about "a fortepiano for sale." The poem also jokes about Ritter Cimbala's lack of expertise as a painter—obviously an inside joke among the many visual artists in the society.

From such passages we can already begin to see the value of this material in uncovering details about Schubert. A close look at the text and illustrations of the Nonsense Society reveals something of a running commentary on what scholarship has been able to piece together from other sources regarding these twenty-one months of Schubert's life. By April 1817, Schubert, having passed his pedagogy exams in 1814, had been working for some time as an assistant teacher at his father's school in the district of the Rossau, and the major event of 1818 was his appointment working for Count Esterházy in Zseliz. This remarkably detailed chronicling, or rather spoofing, of the main activities of Schubert's life during his membership in this club sheds light on other events as well.

The Rossau

According to Deutsch, Schubert moved to the Rossau—the suburb closer to the inner city than the parish of Lichtental, where he grew up—at the end of 1817, after his father was appointed director of the new schoolhouse there.[32] Interestingly, the Rossau is mentioned in two Nonsense Society newsletters from November 1817, the very month that the school year began.[33] The suspicion therefore looms large that there was already a connection to the Rossau in the newsletters from this month and that these texts contain hidden messages involving Schubert. The fifth surviving newsletter, dated 6 November 1817, begins with the following item, titled "Politisches Allerley" (Political Miscellany), and is signed by Schnautze:

> According to reports from the Rossau, a ship is being built there, but we have not yet been able to discover its purpose. However, it is not to be used for war, and one suspects, on account of its build, that it will not at all serve as a transport or

> merchant ship. But, from its interior furnishings, we believe we may conclude that it will function as it had previously—as a place of eating and drinking [*Einkehrwirthshaus*]—especially as a man who has already shown himself to be a good host is supposed to be appointed as its commander.[34]

On 28 October 1817 a petition had been made by the parish priest in the Rossau to appoint Schubert's father as the new school director. He is praised for having raised all of his sons to be worthy schoolmen. Moreover, he had promised that his sons would provide the music services for the Rossau church for free, thus amounting to a savings for the parish of several hundred Gulden annually. Schubert's activities for the Nonsense Society, however, help to explain the lack of any substantial sacred music dating from 1818 and suggest that he was now more interested in writing theater music for his friends. The petition was submitted to the higher authorities for approval on 5 November 1817 and one day later the Nonsense Society was already joking about how a ship in the Rossau—meaning the newly built schoolhouse, which would also have included the home of the Schubert family, the only new building constructed in that suburb—would serve them as a place of refreshment. The next item, also written by Eduard Anschütz, begins:

> The Klosterneuburger ship's captain Blaser has safely arrived at the Schanzel this morning with his ship, called Herr Dekan. But, according to his own report, he had to withstand a great deal of adverse wind which he attributes to the load carried by his vessel, since it consisted mainly of garlic and green beans.

The rest of the article is about a rather obscene battle with women selling fruit at the Schanzel, a marketplace alongside the Danube Canal. The ship's captain "Blaser" is obviously Blasius Leks, that is, Josef Kupelwieser, and his ship—with its name meaning a school dean (*Dekan*)—is Schubert. Since Josef had a short time earlier written the text to *Feuergeist*, which the club had begun rehearsing in September 1817, it makes sense that the two friends—librettist and composer—would then have been in close contact.

This ship's tale, with its mention of wind created by eating gassy foods, probably inspired the story of the voyage through Vienna's suburbs that appeared in the next surviving newsletter, dated 20 November 1817, illustrated by the picture *Windhosen: Der sechste Welttheil in Europa* (Wind Trousers: The Sixth Area of the World in Europe; see Figure 7). There

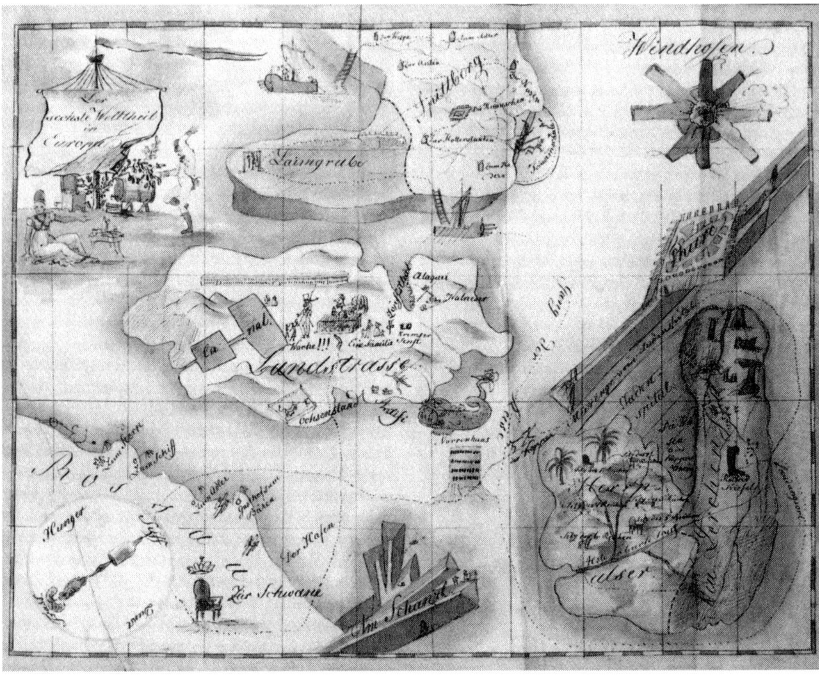

Figure 7. *Windhosen: Der sechste Welttheil in Europa* (Wind Trousers: The Sixth Area of the World in Europe), 20 November 1817. Watercolor by Johann Carl Smirsch (Nina Wutzerl).

are many clues pointing to Schubert here, including his profile on the section of the map labeled “Rossau”: his snub nose and cleft chin are especially visible on the shoreline (to the lower left). The round glass on Schubert’s cheek, with its compass pointing to *Frass* (gluttony) and *Suff* (boozing), harks back to the previous mention of eating and drinking. The long text, signed by Blasius Leks, contains the following passage:

> Now we sailed to the <u>Rossau</u> where we thought we could fix our foremast which had suffered significantly during the Spittelberg storm and which we, because we lacked help [*Hülfe*], were in danger of losing completely. The Rossauers might have already noticed us from afar because we saw clearly how they brought wood onshore from the timber rafts in the harbor, in order to defend themselves as we drew closer. Thus we did not find it advisable to land directly at

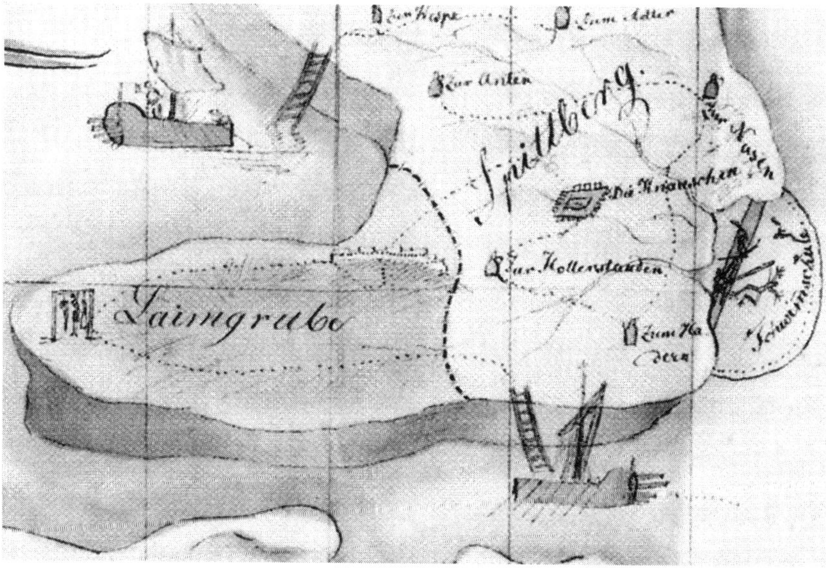

Figure 7a. Detail from *Windhosen*, showing the suburb of Spittelberg, with Leopold Kupelwieser's nose middle right.

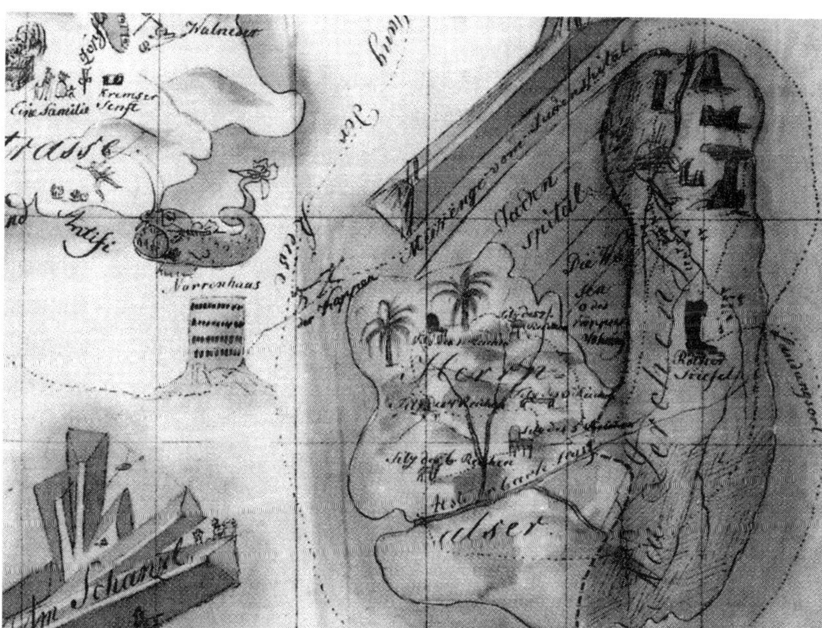

Figure 7b. Detail from *Windhosen*, showing the suburb of New Lerchenfeld.

> the harbor, but disembarked at a place some distance away, next to the Schanzel bath. There we snuck around via some detours, undergoing cannon fire from the Bear, Eagle, Ship and Star (forts skirting the harbor), deeper into the countryside and finally arrived at the main goal, the Swan, where we—unrecognized—had some refreshments and then continued on our journey.[35]

Spittelberg was a Viennese suburb notorious for its prostitutes. The foremast seems to be Schubert, who as we have seen is often associated in the newsletters with sticks, but also with wood—and, of course, with the Rossau, which was a place where piles of wood were stored. An additional clue is the word *Hülfe* since Schubert's official profession at this time was that of a *Schulgehülf* (assistant school teacher). The word *Swan* in the text, and the prominent inscription "Zur Schwane" next to the throne (or armchair) topped by a crown and the letter *S*, was probably added because of the association of Schubert with a "singing swan" (desiring a euphemistic death). The prominent stack of wood labeled "Am Schanzel" next to Schubert's face has a tiny drawing on it: of a couple making out behind the woodpile. Since Schubert's first teacher was named Michael Holzer, this may have been a source of the many jokes associating him with wood (*Holz*).[36]

The boot at the top of the map, resembling Italy (see Figure 7a), contains the names of various inns—some real, some nonsensical—located in the suburb of Spittelberg, including the made-up name "Zur Nasen" (At The Nose), written on a drawing of Leopold Kupelwieser's nose.[37] Next to his mouth is the sign "Schwimmschule" (Swimming school)—referring to Leopold's noted skill in swimming. Next to the fortress of "Thuri"—the small suburb directly adjoining Schubert's birthplace—is a green "tower," obviously pornographic, labeled "Neu Lerchenfeld" (see Figure 7b). This was the suburb where Josef Kupelwieser—a notorious womanizer—lived, in the house "Roter Stiefel" (Red Boot), as is indicated by the caption "Die Wiesen des Koppers Wohnung" (The Meadows of Kopper's Residence), with its wordplay on his name, *Koppel* meaning a fenced-in grazing meadow. *Fortress* was a term used for a prostitute in Schubert's (and Beethoven's) Vienna, and the erect green tower indicates the promised land next to the Egyptian desert of Hernals, another of Vienna's suburbs. I suspect that Schubert's Lied *Auf der Riesenkoppe* (D611), which translates as "On the giant peak" and which he set to a text by Theodor Körner in March 1818, may have been inspired by this map. The song begins: "High on the summit / Of your mountains / I stand and marvel

/ With glowing fervor, / Sacred peak, / You that storm the heavens."[38] Schubert may have been spoofing Josef's prowess with women here. (Later, in 1823, Josef would suddenly abandon his Court Theater position to run after the actress Emilie Neumann, with disastrous results for the planned production of *Fierabras*.)

Swimming from the Spittelberg next to the "Narrenhaus" (House of Fools, the Viennese insane asylum), is a fish wearing eyeglasses—Schubert. He is about to swallow the name "Antifi," which as we will see has musical significance. The island in the middle of the map is labeled "Landstrasse" and contains a cage with a rooster on top—the regular meeting place of the Nonsense Society. Under the cage is a beckoning finger. This clue, together with the throne topped by a crown and the letter *S* already mentioned, again point to Schubert's important role in the society. The newsletters often parodied the works of the popular Viennese theater writer Joachim Perinet (1763–1816), whose hit piece at the time was the travesty opera *Aschenschlägel*, a Cinderella story with the genders reversed. Schubert, perhaps not surprisingly, was the club's Cinderella. One of the lines in Perinet's play reads: "Aschenschlägels Ebenbild ist ein unschuldiger Schwann" (Cinderella's image is an innocent swan). He sits at the hearth baking buns—hence the necklace of buns which Schnautze wears in his second individual portrait, the one with the gesturing finger (Figure 3). But, instead of losing a slipper, this male Cinderella finds a glove (lost by Insanius, the club's God). This story line is especially evident in the children's ballet *Insanius on Earth* featuring the half-god Hymen (Schubert). Scene 6 contains this passage:

> Hymen and the children as geniuses. They have ABC books in their hands and are supposed to learn how to read. They refuse and Hymen gets mad. The children throw their books at his head. Hymen runs around the theater like a fool [*Narr*] and looks for his stick. He finds Insanius's glove and dances a minuet with the children who are so astonished that they run away. Hymen alone. He studies the glove and recognizes it. He is happy that *Insanius* is also here.

An armchair (like the throne on the map) also makes an appearance in the play about Hymen; it is transformed into a tree trunk (that is, wood).

Returning to the map and another favorite writer parodied by the club, Friedrich von Schiller, in particular his poem "Der Handschuh" (The Glove): among its opening lines are the phrases: "Saß König Franz / Und wie er winkt mit dem Finger, / Auf tut sich der weite Zwinger" (King

Franz sat / And as he gestured with his finger, the distant prison cell opened). Thus, in this cleverly encoded way, the club joked that Schubert was their "King Franz." The upper left-hand corner of the map shows a woman sitting in front of a three-legged object that looks remarkably like a spinet. Next to a keg of wine is a man dancing the Austrian "Schuhplattler"—a courtship dance in 3/4 time in which the man slaps the sole of his shoe. Thus, we have here the nonsensical version of "wine, women, and song"—with "song" being replaced by "dance."[39]

A similar scenario to the Rossau map is suggested by a two-part tale written by Eduard Anschütz, "Die Fee Musa oder Die verwandelten Jünglinge" (The Fairy Musa or The Transformed Youths) that appeared in the newsletter on 10 and 17 September 1818.[40] This fairy tale relates that two members of the Nonsense Society had been so mesmerized by the sensuous charms of the water-nymph Aqualine that they abandoned the virtuous Musa for damp, swampy regions. The two youths were transformed into a fat singing frog (Schubert) and a tall, eloquent carp (Schober), and were so delighted with catching flies in the water that they refused to be rescued by their draisine-riding friends (led by Leopold Kupelwieser). The serialized tale was accompanied by two illustrations: the first one, showing the frog and carp diving into the swamp, was painted by August Kopisch (1799–1853). This young painter and poet from Breslau, whose code name was Galimathias Hirngespinst (Gibberish Headspinner), would later become famous for discovering the Blue Grotto of Capri (in 1826) and for penning the tale about the "Heinzelmännchen of Cologne" (in 1848)—the elves who worked secretly in the night for the tailor, the baker, etc. The second illustration is by the landscape painter Tobias Raulino (1785–1839)—code name Bubone di Stivali (Bubo of the Boots)—and depicts the frog and carp cavorting in an accurate representation of the swimming pool in Vienna at the time. Both pictures also show the incensed Musa and the enticing Aqualine. This illustrated tale is actually a moral message presaging the upright Josef Kenner's later report to Ferdinand Luib about Schober's "lasting and pernicious influence over Schubert's honest susceptibility," and how this "false prophet, who embellished sensuality in such a flattering manner" helped to drag the composer's "soul down to the slough of moral degradation."[41]

The illustrations that accompany Schnautze's tale about Musa and the transformed youths are full of sexual innuendos. Clever wordplay clearly identifies Schubert and Schober as the frog and the carp. For example, such words as *écossaise*, *Posaune*, *Flötentöne*, and *Genius* are used in connection with the fat singing frog, while the carp is described with such terms as *alles Reden* (full of talk) and *Krümmungen seines Schweifes* (his crooked tail)—referring to Schober's reputed eloquence and bowed legs. The mysterious appearance in the tale of an antagonist—the coach-driver "Sepperl" (the name is a diminutive of Josef)—is probably a reference to Josef Kupelwieser and his rivalry with Schober. In my opinion, many other words—some of which are associated with Schubert elsewhere in the newletters—point to the composer: *Auge* (eye), *Zedernholz* (cedar wood), *Fuß* (foot), *Musik*, Aqualine's enticing singing "mit bezaubernder Laubfroschstimme" (with a spell-binding tree frog voice), *Stiefel* (boot), *ein dummer Spitzbub* (a silly rascal), *Zauberstab* (magical stick), and so forth. And, the words *Persian* and *Chinese* in the subtitle of the tale "Fragment eines persischen Mährchens aus dem chinesischen übersetzt" (Fragment of a Persian Fairy Tale, Translated from the Chinese) point to the exotic lady's man: Schober. Since wordplay was such a favorite pastime in the Schubert circle, in particular, the making up of poems or short stories on a set number of given words, I believe that Schubert's later allegorical tale "My Dream" (1822) may have been written as part of such a game.[42] Indeed, it is not hard to determine what might have been the given words, for example: *Bruder*, *Vater*, *Liebe*, *Lustgelage*, *Speise*, *Schmerz*, *Tod*, *Leiche*, *Augen*, *Garten*, *Jungfrau*, *Seligkeit*.

Schubert's Friends

Franz Schubert is not, of course, the only person of interest in the pages of the *Archiv des menschlichen Unsinns*. We have already seen open allusions to two friends well known to Schubert research, Leopold Kupelwieser and Franz von Schober, but there are others whose presence in the composer's life was previously unknown and who add to our picture of the Viennese cultural scene in sometimes surprising ways. Carl Friedrich Zimmermann, who had come to Vienna from Berlin in 1816 to study at the Art Academy and who roomed with August Kloeber, likewise from Berlin, painted the final group scene for the New Year's Eve's party in 1817, signed with his code name Aaron Bleistift.[43] As mentioned, this image (Figure 1) shows Schubert in a brown suit next to two young women and the artist himself as a duel-fighting roughneck. Earlier in the evening, however, Zimmermann had worn a different costume and, in my opinion, had come disguised as Schubert (see Figure 8). This double portrait, painted by Kloeber, shows Aaron Bleistift on the left as a fine gentleman with curly hair, clad in a brown suit and peering through double glasses at Leopold Kupelwieser. A conspicuous handkerchief hangs from the gentleman's suit tail—similar to the piece of linen wrapped around the tail of the fish with eyeglasses

Figure 8. *Play with Double Glasses*. Carl Zimmermann (as Schubert) and Leopold Kupelwieser, 31 December 1817. Watercolor by August Kloeber (Goliath Pinselstiel).

Figure 9. *Franz Schubert.* Oil portrait attributed to Josef Abel, ca. 1814

swimming toward the Rossau in the *Windhosen* map—and he wears exaggerated signet rings at his waist.

I believe these valuable items were meant to parody Schubert as he was depicted in the oil portrait attributed to Josef Abel (1764–1818),[44] which shows the nearsighted composer, gripped by inspiration while seated at a fortepiano, with a number of signet rings at his waist (Figure 9). The dress, the glasses, the hair reproduce the Abel portrait with stunning accuracy. Perhaps the pencil (*Bleistift*) placed so prominently on the piano even became an inside joke, associating Aaron Bleistift—whose father in Berlin was actually a "Holz-Inspector"—with Schubert, who as we have seen is often connected with wood in the newsletters. In the Abel portrait, a name is inscribed on the fortepiano with the decipherable letters reading "[?]enie."[45] I now believe that the artist, who was famed for incorporating symbolic attributes in his paintings, meant the name-plate to indicate: *Genie*, a designation that finds prominent mention in the newsletters in association with Schubert.

Zimmermann, who painted four surviving pictures for the society, was a popular member, praised for his artistic talent and teased for his pursuit of women. One of the newsletter reports, titled "Psychologische Beobachtungen" (Psychological Observations) and dated 2 April 1818, begins with an obscene spoof on pretentious intellectual writing, using passages in pseudo-Yiddish, and then describes Zimmermann proudly riding a horse down the Rotenturmstrasse. The article ends with the following passage mentioning a shoemaker apprentice named "Hansel"—that is, Schubert:

> But let us consider a small group of shoemaker boys, full of innocence. . . . He [Zimmermann] stops suddenly in front of a house in the Rotenturmstrasse and his whistling mouth closes in silence. His eyes are directed upwards and he smiles gently. What is the object of his fixed gaze? It is a maid, washing the windows on the second floor. To balance herself, she has stretched out her right leg rather carelessly into the street. The shoemaker apprentice, absolutely delighted, calls to one of his comrades: Hansel, stop! Here you can see the whole city of Paris!

The double mention here of shoemaker and Hansel, implying Ritter Juan, reinforces the connection made in the double portrait between Zimmermann and Schubert. The artist's unexpected death in 1820 in a drowning accident, soon after he had married a member of the extended Mendelssohn family, was a tragic loss to art: his stunning illustrations of Goethe's *Faust* are the visual counterpart to Schubert's 1814 masterpiece in song: *Gretchen am Spinnrade* (D118).[46]

Since Eduard and Gustav Anschütz have scarcely been mentioned previously in the Schubert literature, it is worth devoting a few lines to them here.[47] Among the pictures in the Wienmuseum are individual portraits of the brothers, showing how they were dressed for each of the celebratory events. Figures 2 and 3 depict the younger brother, Eduard, the club's leader and newsletter editor. In each portrait he holds a staff or scepter topped by a rooster. The club's *Stammlokal* (regular haunt), where the members met every Thursday evening, was the inn called the Roter Hahn (Red Rooster)—still standing today as a hotel with that name—in the suburb of Landstrasse just southeast of the inner city. (Although Schubert was working at his father's school in 1817, he would normally have had Thursday afternoons and evenings free.) Eduard was a poet—in 1816 the Vienna *Theaterzeitung* published a poem by him criticizing the Italian prima donna Angelica Catalani for her vanity—and he later pursued a career as an actor.

Gustav Anschütz (1793–1839) used the code name Sebastian Haarpuder. In the portrait depicting his costume for the New Year's Eve party, he wears a late Baroque outfit, including a wig from which a sign hangs reading "Extra fein Haarpuder" (Extra fine hair powder), and he is deep in discussion with a portrait of Pythagoras (see Figure 4). Since he grew up in Leipzig, his code name probably had some connection with Johann Sebastian Bach, especially since the "mathematical" Bach wore a powdered wig. It has also been argued that Bach composed the *Art of the Fugue* to display Pythagorean principles, including mirror images.[48] Was Gustav aware of this inside information? Gustav later worked as a jeweler and was a passionate dancer. At his death in 1839 he was survived by his wife, who taught singing, and his two young children. Since his brother Eduard died unmarried, the question arises: Who inherited the still-missing Nonsense Society materials? Perhaps they will be found one day, owned by descendants of either Gustav or Heinrich Anschütz.

In the context of this predominantly male society of close friendships it would be remiss to disregard the question of sexuality, especially in light of the plethora of contributions to this topic in recent Schubert literature. Indeed, even a casual glance at the newsletters and watercolors at times suggests feminine allures and cross-dressing among some of the members of the club. Closer inspection, however, reveals a rather more heterosexually oriented form of banter. A case in point is Smirsch, alias Nina Wutzerl (see Figure 10).[49] Although this member took on a woman's role in the club and was teased for his "tender" traits, the hat he wore decorated with peacock feathers represented his teaching specialty at the Polytechnical Institute: painting flowers and feathers. (Smirsch later sang with the Wiener Männergesangverein, amassed a huge fortune as a financier, and married his longtime cook at the age of seventy-seven.) He is featured in a picture, *Nina's Triumph*, attached to the newsletter dated 12 November 1818. This sacrilegious triptych spoofs a barbershop scene in which Nina introduces an untutored new member to culture.

Figure 10. *Nina Wutzerl*. 31 December 1817.
Watercolor by Johann Nepomuk Hoechle (Kratzeratti Klanwinzi).

This member, named "Alebrand," as well as a witness to the scene named "Mordschlag" are still unidentified. The text describing the picture explains that it was painted by Rafaele van der Riso di Zaardam (Carl Peter Goebel, a prize-winning student at the Vienna Art Academy) as a form of penance for his having produced bad art for the society. In an earlier newsletter, Riso di Zaardam had been punished by Zeisig with a disciplining stick for being lazy in his creative efforts. The stick would seem to be an allusion to Schubert and his high artistic ideals.

An earlier picture, attached to the newsletter dated 23 July 1818, shows another sacrilegious scene: a parody of Da Vinci's *The Last Supper*, with the club gathering for their Thursday meeting in a shed topped by a huge red rooster, thus representing their *Stammtisch*. This picture was painted by Goldhann, who included himself, his wife, and two young daughters as a family of golden chickens in the left foreground. A chicken in a fancy hat decorated with colorful feathers—Nina—stands in front of a music stand and sings. Goldhann, who also wrote the accompanying text, explains that we see in this pretty bird "the unfortunate capon [eunuch] whose single pleasure is in singing and whose only listener is the splendidly dressed-up gallus galinaceus or turkey." This turkey, who judges the singer, is obviously meant to represent Schubert. He is placed right in the middle of the picture, directly under the huge red rooster, but faces in the opposite direction, thus suggesting a "verkehrte Welt" (topsy-turvy world), another favorite theme, in addition to the "ship of fools," that characterized this society.

There is also the case of the super-macho former soldier Ferdinand Dörflinger (1790–1818), the author of many unsavory articles in the newsletters about cooking and prostitutes.[50] He had adopted the persona and dress of the notorious actress Elise Hahn, who had cuckolded her husband, the famous poet Gottfried August Bürger. Dörflinger's hasty marriage on 14 September 1817—his bride was already pregnant—served as the butt of many jokes, including Schnautze's literary parody of Schiller's poem "Hektors Abschied" with the travestied title "Lisels Abschied, als sie Mariage machte" (Lizzy's Farewell, as She Got Married), and Nina Wutzerl's painting of a Parisian fashion plate of fancy hats dedicated to "her" disreputable girlfriend "Elise Gagarnadl von Antifi." The *Windhosen* map (dated 20 November 1817) shows the voyage of a fish wearing eyeglasses—Schubert—swimming from Spittelberg, with its loose women, toward the Rossau with its piles of wood. The fish, with a piece of (dirty?) linen wrapped around its tail, is about to swallow the name "Antifi." In December 1817 Schubert composed the original (longer) version of *Das Dörfchen* (The Little Village, D598) for four unaccompanied male voices in what I believe is the musical counterpart to the earlier literary and painterly jokes on "Elise." Schubert must have chosen this text—the author of the poem is none other than Bürger—not only because of the connection to Elise Hahn, but also because of the wordplay (*Dörfchen*) on Dörflinger's name. The absolute giveaway is Schubert's selection of several verses mentioning "Elise"—for example, "Schön ist die Flur; / Allein Elise / Macht sie mir nur / Zum Paradiese"; that he omitted these humorous verses, with their private message, when he published the work later in 1822, in the shorter, better-known version of the work in Op. 11, No. 1 (D641) is itself revealing.

Schubert likely composed other works "für Elise," including the Lied fragment *Entzückung eines Lauras Abschied* (Delight at the Departure of Some Laura, D577), on a text by Schiller, in August 1817. The title is not a mistake, as Deutsch had thought, but a deliberate attempt to spoof "some kind of woman's" pending farewell. The Schiller text "Elysium" (D584), which Schubert set in September 1817, ends with the celebration of an eternal wedding feast: the word *ewig* (eternal) is stretched out in an exaggerated word parody for an incredible ten bars. Since it is set for high tenor voice, I suspect that Schubert sang this himself at a wedding party for Dörflinger, hosted by the club.

Johann Nepomuk Hoechle became famous as the painter of battle scenes for Emperor Franz—and is still remembered today for his Beethoven depictions: these include an ink wash drawing of the composer walking in the rain, the well-known music-studio scene painted on 30 March 1827 with the bust of Schubert in the window, and a quick sketch of Beethoven's funeral procession.[51] Under his code name Kratzeratti Klanwinzi, Hoechle drew eleven surviving pictures for the Nonsense Society, including the group scene *Zur Unsinniade—2ter Gesang*, an "action shot" of the New Year's Eve party, and the illustration *"Zebedäus" in His Studio* in the newsletter dated 8 October 1818. This image makes fun of the extremely old director of the Vienna Art Academy, Martin Fischer (1741–1820), identified in the double wordplay: "Mr. Zebedäus from Fisher Alley." The name of the biblical fisherman Zebedee is reinforced by the name of the street where he lives. A similar kind of wordplay points to Schubert: for example, in the reports about a musician who lives in the "ABC house" or a curly-headed "Jean" who lives at Erdberg (where Schubert stayed with the Watteroth family in 1816).[52] Hoechle's picture shows old Fischer making some anatomical investigations of a woman's bottom, the same theme found in the tale about Chevalier Touchetout pulling out some socks. This in turn reflects the mention of

Ritter Cimbala in the poem "Impromptu" about a sock, in the newsletter dated 12 February 1818. The poem follows immediately a tale about a fortepiano signed by Quanti Verdradi (whom I assume to be Franz von Schober), and which reads as follows (note the double wordplays):

> *Fortepiano to play out*. A completely new played-out *Fortepianoforte*, fitted with many notes and provided with a quantity of fine and coarse [*grob*] strings, as one would wish to have it, and which in addition has already been admired by many admirers, is to be had by a certain gentleman for playing purposes—because the drums and trumpets produce tones by themselves when one presses the so-called Turkish Turkish [!] music stops up and down with one's foot. The beginning of this play is on the third of this [month] in the house of the person playing. *Quanti verdradi*.

The mention of *grob* here was probably a deliberate reference to Therese Grob (1798–1875), Schubert's beloved singer, whom he had hoped to marry in 1816.[53]

In mid-November 1818, after Schubert returned to Vienna from his five-month stay in Zseliz, he abandoned his teaching position and moved into an apartment with the older poet Johann Mayrhofer (1787–1836).[54] A lengthy account written by Josef Kupelwieser for the newsletter dated 26 November 1818 spoofs Mayrhofer's daytime job with the government police office as a censor of books. Here are a few excerpts:

> Advertisement. The following prohibited and permitted works are on public sale at the editor's publishing house:
>
> 1. Prohibited
> Multiplication tables from 1 to 1000 and back again in reverse order.
> ABC book with pictures by a priest of the Jacobin order. . . .
> 2. Permitted Books
> Introduction to the art of revolution. Paris 1792
> On the art of deceiving the course of nature, for the benefit of the population, by a misanthrope. . . .
> Introduction to the art of defrauding people, along with thorough instructions on how to declare a false bankruptcy. Vienna, Police House, 1818.

Among the clues pointing here to Schubert and his roommate are "ABC book" and "Jacobin order"—the house where Schubert now lived, Wipplingerstrasse 2, had originally been occupied by the Jacobins.[55] In addition, there is the reference to a "misanthrope," a word used to describe Mayrhofer's character.[56] There is no evidence that the poet himself belonged to the Nonsense Society—membership in such a secret society would have been extremely dangerous for someone working for the police—but his biographer, Ernst von Feuchtersleben, reported that "every morning [Mayrhofer] entered into his diary the jokes of one such instinctive, humorous, natural person [Schubert], who was the soul of wit of a merry evening society."[57]

Conclusion

Although the episodes recounted in this overview point to the presence of the composer, one should keep in mind that there are many other passages where we are left, at best, to interpret. Certain words appear over and over again in what I believe are encoded references to Schubert. One of these is *Schuh* (shoe)—also found in combinations, such as *Handschuh* (glove)—as well as various appearances of *Auge* (eye), *Brille* (eyeglasses), or *Glas*. The words *Fest* (festival) or *Festung* (fortress/prostitute) also seem to be associated with the composer. I have already discussed such words as *Holz* (wood) and various items made of wood, including sticks—*Stab*, *Stock*, etc. I assume that the many references to music, to dance (especially the *écossaise*), and to musical instruments (especially the *Posaune*) refer to Schubert. Since he most likely composed the music for *Feuergeist*, the many jokes about *Feuer* (fire) probably involve him as well—as do the frequent occurrences of *ABC* (standing for the primary school class that he taught). A wonderful example of word combinations pointing to Schubert is the expression "handfester Holzhacker" used to describe the person who lives "beym goldnen A B C" (at the golden A B C) and who is studying Beethoven's fantasies and variations (newsletter of 23 October 1817). I also believe that variants of the name *Juan*—for example, Johannis, Hans, Hansel, Jean, etc.—may as well refer to Schubert. Other members are also associated with particular words or concepts: Leopold Kupelwieser, for example, is represented by the draisine, swimming, and comets. And, if I am correct in assuming that Schubert's close friend Franz von Schober was regarded as the enemy—or at least as a rival to Josef Kupelwieser (in writing librettos for the composer)—then he appears everywhere in the newsletters not only as the evil Turk, Arab, or Chinaman, but also as the stupid traveler to the topsy-turvy world, "Ulf Dalkensohn," the dumbbell with a Swedish sounding name. Schober, who was born in Sweden, is thus the "Dummkopf" (blockhead) who leads the "Narr" (innocent fool), that is, Schubert, on sexually promiscuous adventures, for instance to Aqualine's swamp, as told in the long tale about Musa and the transformed youths.

We can only also guess at the extent of the direct impact of this social circle on Schubert's musical output, although some works in particular suggest a strong connection to his participation in the Nonsense Society: *Der Feuergeist,* an early version of *Die Zauberharfe* (D644); *Entzückung eines Lauras Abschied* (D577); *Elysium* (D584); *Das Dörfchen* (D598); *Auf der Riesenkoppe* (D611); Variations on a French Song, Op. 10 (D624).[58] There is also much more to discover in the annals of the Nonsense Society beyond Schubert: how a young generation of Viennese artists understood their world in the late 1810s, their awareness of current events and scientific discoveries, their view of morality and sense of humor, their artistic talents and mutual admiration. That Schubert was an integral part of this circle only adds to the richness of this discovery in the history of art and social interaction. As I expressed in 1997 in "Schubert Through the Kaleidoscope," my first English-language article describing this new material:

> This documentary find will not only open up new perspectives for research on the composer, it will also give new impetus to the fields of literature, art and theater, in particular as they relate to the sociological and cultural study of the Biedermeier period. I hope then that the future collegial work on this material by serious scholars in many fields will add innumerable splendid colors—kaleidoscope-like—to our current picture of Schubert and his Viennese circle of friends.[59]

The time is still ripe for other scholars to be enticed by this rich and fascinating material and award it serious attention.

NOTES

This is a heavily edited version of the article I wrote in November 2012 for the Bard Music Festival of 2014. That article provided a more detailed account of how my research progressed and highlighted my new, unpublished ideas on this topic and was published, in its original form, in late 2013 as "New Thoughts on Schubert's Role in the Unsinnsgesellschaft," *Schubert: Perspektiven* 10/2 (2010): 191–223. It can be consulted there for comparative purposes.

1. All the surviving materials created by the Nonsense Society, including seventy-three watercolor pictures, have been interpreted and published in my book *Die Unsinnsgesellschaft: Franz Schubert, Leopold Kupelwieser und ihr Freundeskreis* (Vienna, 1998), 490 pages. As yet, little of this material has been examined by other scholars. The present article, in English, summarizes my findings.

2. My project to conduct new research on Schubert iconography was initially suggested by Ernst Hilmar, founder of the International Franz Schubert Institute in Vienna, and was later supervised by Gerhard Stradner, director of the Collection of Ancient Musical Instruments in Vienna. Funding was provided by the Austrian National Bank, Jubiläumsfonds, with two research grants, 1994–97.

3. These documents had been purchased by the museum in 1943 from the Viennese antiquarian dealer Gilhofer but were mistakenly identified as belonging to the Ludlamshöhle, a different club—with older members—that was also founded in 1817. For a discussion of this second club, which was raided by the police in April 1826 just as Schubert was about to become a member, see Alice Hanson, "The Significance of the Ludlamshöhle for Franz Schubert," in *Essays on Music and Culture in Honor of Herbert Kellman*, ed. Barbara Haggh (Paris, 2001), 496–502.

4. For the record, these illustrations do not have titles. I devised the titles referred to here from the captions on the individual portraits and group scenes, as well as from the written explanations in each newsletter, titled "Zum Kupfer" (About the Copperplate).

5. Rupert Feuchtmüller made a valiant attempt to explain this material in his book *Leopold Kupelwieser und die Kunst der österreichischen Spätromantik* (Vienna, 1970), 14–15, but he confused the Nonsense Society with the Ludlamshöhle. He also published two of the costumed portraits on pages 84–85 with the following identification: "Josef Kupelwieser/als Mitglied der Unsinnsgesellschaft/Blasius Lecks/1818" and "Leopold Kupelwieser [*sic*] / als Mitglied der Unsinnsgesellschaft/Gallimatias Hirngespinst/1818." The second picture shows August Kopisch, not Leopold Kupelwieser, whose code name was Damian Klex.

6. I wish to thank Morten Solvik for showing me the book by Gerhard Renner, *Die Nachlässe in der Wiener Stadt- und Landesbibliothek: Ein Verzeichnis* (Vienna, 1993), that led me to make the discovery of Nonsense Society materials located in Vienna's City Hall. These items, divided according to year, have the call numbers Jb 86.125 (for 1817) and Jb 86.126 (for 1818).

7. The vice-editor's real name was Franz Zöpfl (ca. 1791–1871), a bookkeeper who later became an official at the Austrian National Bank. I wish to thank Michael Lorenz for establishing the biographical connection between Zöpfl and Marie Schuster, the person who sold the twenty-nine newsletters to the Vienna City Library in 1937 (see Steblin, *Die Unsinnsgesellschaft*, 8). These surviving issues make up only about one-third of the original number of weekly newsletters that must have been created (between April 1817 and the end of 1818), and it may be that Eduard Anschütz, the editor, took the other two-thirds (about 58 issues). These newsletters are still missing. The material in the Wienmuseum apparently once belonged to Josef Kupelwieser, who penned the poems called "Unsinniaden" for the New Year's Eve celebration in 1817. However, both the poem and the picture belonging to the third "Unsinniade" are missing.

8. In 1997 I read a paper at the American Musicological Society Meeting in Phoenix titled "*Leks, Schmecks* and *Klex*: Three Kupelwiesers and Franz Schubert in the *Unsinnsgesellschaft*" devoted to these three brothers: Josef Kupelwieser (1791–1866), Johann Kupelwieser (1794–1856), and Leopold Kupelwieser (1796–1862).

9. Heinrich Anschütz, *Erinnerungen aus dessen Leben und Wirken* (Vienna, 1866), 264–65, cited in Otto Erich Deutsch, *Schubert: Memoirs by His Friends*, trans. Rosamond Ley and John Nowell (London, 1958), 222–23; translation amended by Christopher Gibbs. Deutsch commented that by the Nonsense Society "Anschütz probably meant 'Die Ludlamshöhle' to which Anschütz, though not Schubert, had belonged" (224).

10. For a facsimile of this list of Nonsense Society members, see Steblin, *Die Unsinnsgesellschaft*, 9.

11. Deutsch, *Schubert: Memoirs*, 32.

12. Otto Erich Deutsch, *Schubert: A Documentary Biography*, trans. Eric Blom (London, 1946), 338–40. The letter is discussed in Christopher Gibbs's essay in this book as well as in John Gingerich's.

13. See ibid., plate 18, *Game of Ball at Atzenbrugg*, facing page 465.

14. According to my research on Ludwig Kraißl, funded in 2000 by a Social Sciences and Humanities Research Council SSHRC grant administered by the University of Victoria, B.C., Canada, this member of the Schubert circle was christened on 11 December 1792 (Vienna, Pfarre Maria Rotunda, Taufbuch Tom. I, fol. 125). He died on 10 February 1871 in Klagenfurt, where he had lived since 1824 as a painter employed by the wealthy family of the industrialist August von Rosthorn.

15. See Steblin, "Schubert durch das Kaleidoskop" (Schubert Through the Kaleidoscope), *Österreichische Musikzeitschrift* 52/1–2 (Schubert Special Issue 1997): 52–61.

16. For the original German, see Steblin, *Die Unsinnsgesellschaft*, 335–36, which reprints the newsletter dated 16 July 1818. Since such information can readily be found in my book under the date of the newsletter (as well as through the footnotes of my articles), I will dispense with further references here.

17. The kaleidoscope could now be associated with Schubert's music, as I suggested in "Schubert Through the Kaleidoscope" in 1997: "The inexhaustible variety of his melodic invention and in particular the sudden, abrupt changes between harmonic motives and keys have a kaleidoscopic effect about them" (56). My idea was then further developed by Brian Newbould in his article "Schubert im Spiegel," *Musiktheorie* 13 (1998): 101–10, esp. 105. I later expanded this thought, connecting it with Donald Tovey's term "star clusters" and Richard L. Cohn's discussion of this term, in my article "Schubert's Pepi: His Love Affair with the Chambermaid Josepha Pöcklhofer and Her Surprising Fate," *The Musical Times* 149 (Summer 2008): 47–69, esp. 52–53.

18. This passage by Wilhelm von Chézy was discovered by Till Gerrit Waidelich and published in his book *Rosamunde: Drama in fünf Akten von Helmina von Chézy. Musik von Franz Schubert. Erstveröffentlichung der überarbeiteten Fassung* (Tutzing, 1996), 53–54.

19. Franz Lachner told the following anecdote about Schubert's strict discipline: "Once, when with a group of friends, Schubert told of a sweetheart, who left him for the reason that she wanted to avenge herself for the beatings he had given her in the ABC class when he was a schoolteacher. He added: 'It is quite true; whenever I was composing, this little gang annoyed me so much that the ideas always went out of my head. Naturally I gave them a good hiding then.—And now I have to suffer for it!'" See Deutsch, *Schubert: Memoirs*, 292.

20. Steblin, *Die Unsinnsgesellschaft*, 375.

21. Ibid., 214–15. The theater announcement is signed with another code name for Eduard Anschütz: "Michael Karthaunerknall Schauspieler." *Knall* (bang, explosion) refers to the meaning of his real name *Schütz* (shot), and *Schauspieler* (actor) refers to his profession.

22. Steblin, *Die Unsinnsgesellschaft*, 195.

23. Ibid., 190.

24. See Otto Erich Deutsch, *Schubert: Die Dokumente seines Lebens* (Kassel, 1964), 106; and the discussion in Steblin, *Die Unsinnsgesellschaft*, 29. The long review by B. S., which appeared in the *Wiener Konversationsblatt* on 29 August 1820, is given in its entirety in Deutsch's 1964 German edition of Schubert's documents but only in truncated form in his translated *Schubert: A Documentary Biography*, 148.

25. For a lengthier discussion of *Der Feuergeist* as the forerunner to *Die Zauberharfe*, see Steblin, *Die Unsinnsgesellschaft*, 26–30.

26. See Steblin, *Babette und Therese Kunz: Neue Forschungen zum Freundeskreis um Franz Schubert und Leopold Kupelwieser* (Vienna, 1996), which is dedicated to the memory of my harpsichord teacher in Vienna, Isolde Ahlgrimm (1914–1995).

27. Deutsch, *Schubert: A Documentary Biography*, 100. Deutsch identified the chambermaid as Pepi Pöckelhofer (102). For new biographical information on her, see Steblin, "Schubert's Pepi."

28. From Ferdinand Schubert's letter from mid-October 1818: "Your city friends could not be sought out, as they were all in the country." See Deutsch, *Schubert: A Documentary Biography*, 106; and from Schubert's reply to Ferdinand, dated Zseliz, 29 October 1818: "The city friends are the limit!" (109). The German word actually used by Schubert here *liederlich* (lewd) is much stronger. See also Steblin, *Die Unsinnsgesellschaft*, 362, for my discussion of how Schober, disguised as a carp with a crooked tail, sings the words: "Ich bin liederlich, du bist liederlich" (I am lewd, you are lewd) in Schnautze's tale "Die Fee Musa" about the transformed youths (Schubert as the frog, Schober as the carp).

29. Brian Newbould, "A Schubert Palindrome," *19th-Century Music* 15 (1992): 209–10.

30. For a detailed analysis of all the clues pointing to Schubert in this message, as well as a facsimile of this newsletter page, see Steblin, *Die Unsinnsgesellschaft*, 20–22. Josef Kupelwieser would later write the libretto for Schubert's most important opera, *Fierabras* (D796), composed in 1823.

31. See Steblin, "Schubert's Relationship with Women: An Historical Account," in Brian Newbould, ed., *Schubert Studies* (Aldershot, 1998), 159–82.

32. Deutsch, *Schubert: A Documentary Biography*, 82.

33. See Steblin, "Schubert and the Pfarre Roßau: New Documents from the Diözesanarchiv Wien and the Servite Priory," *Studien zur Musikwissenschaft* 46 (1998): 153–73.

34. Steblin, *Die Unsinnsgesellschaft*, 236.

35. For the original German, see ibid., 249–50.

36. See Steblin, "Michael Holzer, Schubert's Music Teacher in Lichtental: A New Genealogical Study," *Schubert: Perspektiven* 10/1 (2010): 10–44.

37. See Steblin, "Schubert's Role in the *Unsinnsgesellschaft* as Revealed by Clues from Schiller and *Aschenschlägel*," in *Franz Schubert und seine Freunde*, ed. Eva Badura-Skoda, Gerold W. Gruber, Walburga Litschauer, and Carmen Ottner (Vienna, 1999), 238–45.

38. Richard Wigmore, *Schubert: The Complete Song Texts* (London, 1992), 61. Schubert's setting of this Körner text has puzzled scholars; the standard explanation is that he was thinking of his mother, since a mountain peak called Riesenkoppe was located in Silesia, although it was nowhere near the area where she grew up.

39. On 28 November 1822 Schubert wrote the traditional saying "Wer nicht liebt Wein, Mädchen und Gesang, Bleibt ein Narr sein Lebenlang" (Who loves not wine, maidens and song, remains a fool his whole life long) on an album leaf for Albert Schellmann. See Deutsch, *Schubert: A Documentary Biography*, 246.

40. See Steblin, "Schubert's Pepi."

41. Deutsch, *Schubert: Memoirs*, 86. See Steblin, "Schober's Love Affair with Marie von Spaun and the Role Played by Helene Schmith, the Wife of Mozart's First Violinist," in *Schubert: Perspektiven* 8/1 (2008): 49–87, in which I take issue with Susanne Eckstein's interpretation of the pictures that accompany Schnautze's tale about Musa and the transformed youths. Also, see the discussion of Schober in John Gingerich's essay in this volume.

42. For the German text of "Mein Traum" see Deutsch, *Die Dokumente seines Lebens*, 158–59; English translation in *Schubert: A Documentary Biography*, 26–28

43. See Steblin, "Schubert's Hidden Past as Caricatured by the *Unsinnsgesellschaft*: The Painter Carl Zimmermann and the Jewish Connection," in *The Past in the Present: Papers Read at the IMS Intercongressional Symposium, Budapest & Visegrád, 2000*, ed. László Dobszay (Budapest, 2003), 263–86.

44. See Steblin, *Ein unbekanntes frühes Schubert Porträt? Franz Schubert und der Maler Josef Abel* (Tutzing, 1992), for my authentication of this oil portrait. Abel was a highly regarded member of the Vienna Art Academy and an artist praised by Schubert in his diary of 1816.

45. Ibid., 48n22. No fortepiano maker could be identified with these letters.

46. Two of Zimmermann's illustrations, which he made in 1819 and 1820 in connection with the musical setting of Goethe's *Faust* by the Polish Prince Anton Radziwill, are included in my article "Schubert's Hidden Past," on 283 and 285.

47. My book *Die Unsinnsgesellschaft* devotes a brief chapter to each of the members of the Nonsense Society, summarizing their biographies and the roles they played in the society. I have since conducted further research on the two Anschütz brothers and the three Kupelwieser brothers, and I provide some of this new information here.

48. See Hans-Eberhard Dentler, *Johann Sebastian Bachs "Kunst der Fuge": Ein Pythagoreisches Werk und seine Verwirklichung* (Mainz, 2004).

49. Steblin, "Schubert's 'Nina' and the True Peacocks," *The Musical Times* 138 (March 1997): 13–19.

50. Steblin, "Schubert's Elise: *Das Dörfchen* and the 'Unsinnsgesellschaft,'" *The Musical Times* 140 (Spring 1999): 33–43.

51. See Steblin, "Hoechle's 1827 Sketch of Beethoven's Studio: A Secret Tribute to Schubert?" *Beethoven Forum* 8 (2000): 1–23. For a discussion of the Beethoven funeral procession in front of the Alsergrund Church, which is still virtually unknown, see my article "'Höchle zeichnete mir diesen Leichenzug': Anton Gräffer, Johann Nepomuk Hoechle und die verschollene Zeichnung von Beethovens Begräbnisfeier," *Wiener Geschichtsblätter* 58/4 (2003): 299–315.

52. Steblin, *Die Unsinnsgesellschaft*, 233–34. For Schubert's remarks at the opening of a manuscript of six écossaises that he wrote for Marie von Spaun, Schober's beloved at the time: "Composed while confined to my room at Erdberg, May 1816," see Deutsch, *Schubert: A Documentary Biography*, 59.

53. For a comprehensive discussion of Schubert's relationship to this woman, see Steblin, "Schubert's Beloved Singer Therese Grob: New Documentary Research," *Schubert durch die Brille* 28 (January 2002): 55–100.

54. See Steblin, "Schubert's Problematic Relationship with Johann Mayrhofer: New Documentary Evidence," in *Essays on Music and Culture in Honor of Herbert Kellman*, 465–95.

55. I explain that the house at Wipplingerstrasse No. 2 where Schubert lived with the poet Mayrhofer had been "originally the place of rendezvous of the Jacobins" in ibid., 474. Citation from Heinrich Kreissle von Hellborn, *The Life of Franz Schubert*, trans. Arthur Duke Coleridge (London, 1869), 1:48.

56. For a reference to Franz Gräffer's 1844 mention of "misanthropic" in connection with the poet's character, see Steblin, "Schubert's Problematic Relationship with Johann Mayrhofer," 480.

57. Johann Mayrhofer, *Gedichte*, ed. Ernst von Feuchtersleben (Vienna, 1843), 23.

58. See Steblin, "Schubert und die 'Unsinnsgesellschaft': Musikbezogene Ergebnisse," in *Schubert neu entdeckt*, ed. Erich Benedikt (Vienna, 1999), 37–44.

59. Steblin, "Schubert Through the Kaleidoscope," 61.

Excerpts from *Beyträge zur Bildung für Jünglinge*, 1817–1818

ANTON VON SPAUN AND JOHANN MAYRHOFER
TRANSLATED, INTRODUCED, AND ANNOTATED
BY DAVID GRAMIT

The *Beyträge zur Bildung für Jünglinge* (Contributions to Education for Youths) appeared in two volumes in Vienna in 1817 and 1818. Although the publication does not mention Schubert and he took no part in the project, this collection of pedagogical essays, translations, literary excerpts, and poetry nonetheless reveals important aspects of the literary, intellectual, and relational world that the young composer encountered through a number of his friends. He met most of them during his service as a choirboy in the Imperial Chapel Choir from 1808 to 1813, which brought with it enrollment in the Vienna Stadtkonvikt. This boarding school attracted students from relatively well-heeled families from other provinces, including a number with whom Schubert established lasting relationships—and it was those students, members of their families, and their friends who spearheaded the *Beyträge*: Anton von Spaun (1790–1849), leader of the project and brother of Schubert's lifelong friend Josef von Spaun; Anton Ottenwalt (1789–1845) who, like Spaun, was a native of Linz and a former student at the monastic school in Kremsmünster; and Johann Mayrhofer (1787–1836), the Steyr born poet whose long relationship with Schubert led to more settings of his poetry by the composer than of any poet except Goethe.[1]

A number of scholars have drawn attention to the *Beyträge* and the impact of the friends whose activities inspired it and brought it into being.[2] Most recently, Ilija Dürhammer has analyzed the League of Virtue (Tugendbund) and its ideals of friendship, patriotism, and freedom, each of which took forms deeply influenced by the intellectual and political climate of Austria in the Napoleonic and Restoration eras.[3] Dürhammer's tracing of the roots of this group gives rise to a more nuanced view of Schubert's introduction to literary culture than has previously been available. It also makes clear that this group represents only a part of Schubert's social and intellectual world—it is not only far removed from the lighthearted and satirical world of the Unsinnsgesellschaft (Nonsense Society) that Rita Steblin explores elsewhere in this book, but it is also distinct from the sphere of professional musicians active in Vienna. Indeed, Josef von Spaun would later feel compelled to argue that "living among this circle of people was far more advantageous to Schubert than if he had lived among a circle of musicians and professional colleagues, though he did not neglect these either."[4] At the time of the *Beyträge*, however, any such need to defend the activities of a great composer among them was well in the future; here the group of friends seeks rather to defend itself and its own intellectual and social world.

Still, the *Beyträge zur Bildung für Jünglinge* can orient readers to aspects of Schubert's world more directly than virtually any other source. An overview of the two volumes reveals their characteristic blend of classical learning, Germanic history and Austro-German patriotism, and didactic and sentimental poetry and literature, both excerpted and original (see Tables 1 and 2, showing the contents of each volume). The ordering of selections seems almost random, but both volumes attest to a determined effort to blend received wisdom with personal experience, in the hope that the former would beneficially shape the latter. As the three selections below reveal, the *Beyträge* can provide insights into what it meant to be devoted to classically grounded self-cultivation as practiced not only among the friends of Schubert's youth but also by countless others in the German-speaking world of the early nineteenth century. Furthermore, the volumes give expression to the sentimental, affective world in which those intellectual goals were pursued, and to the tensions that could arise as a result. Such an orientation would hardly have been necessary for Schubert's own audiences, many of whom had grown up with the values and practices inculcated by such an upbringing. Indeed, the contents of the journal were unremarkable enough to receive at best lukewarm reviews at the time of its publication, and its existence was largely forgotten until scholars drew attention to it after World War II.[5] For today's readers and listeners, however, especially for English speakers without a grounding in Austro-German history and literature, the idea of self- and national development through reflective reading and earnest discussion, as well as the culture of sentimentality that characterized these intense male friendships, are likely to be foreign enough that simply to describe them conveys little of the spirit and power they held, whether in Wilhelm von Humboldt's Prussia or in Schubert's Vienna and its environs. But for all their pedantry and awkwardness—indeed, in part because of them—the *Beyträge zur Bildung für Jünglinge* convey those ideals powerfully, along with the distinctive tensions that accompanied this group's efforts.

Table 1.
Contents of Volume 1 of the *Beyträge zur Bildung für Jünglinge* (1817).
Italicized notes below titles are editorial additions to indicate the nature of each item. Unless otherwise noted, contributions are unattributed.

Table 1. continued

The Warrior and his Son *Poem by Johann Mayrhofer*	161
Clever and Insightful Sayings of the Germans, from Zincgref's *Deutsche Apophtegmen* *Excerpts from the German proverbs of Julius Wilhelm Zincgref*	164
Kunigunde *Legend by Johann Mayrhofer*	171
Thoughts on Various Topics *Aphorisms by Anton von Spaun*	196
Epimeleia *Verse dialogue by Josef Kenner*	201
Ortwin and Edgar *Dialogue—"Sch." (further identity unknown; perhaps Franz von Schober)*	205
Summer Birds *Fable by Joseph Kreil*	217
The Guardian Spirit *Poem*	220
Excerpts from Jean Paul Friedrich Richter's Works *Excerpts from Jean Paul's novels,* Titan *and* Hesperus	224
Praise of the Divinity *Poem by the Persian poet Sadi, translated in Herder's* Zerstreute Blätter	235
To the Highest God *Poem by Cleanthes*	239
Callicratidas *History of the Spartan naval commander (after Plutarch)*	243
A Scene from *The Phoenician Women* of Euripides *Translation*	255

Table 2.
Contents of Volume 2 of the *Beyträge zur Bildung für Jünglinge* (1818).
Italicized notes below titles are editorial additions to indicate the nature of each item. Unless otherwise noted, contributions are unattributed.

Table 2. continued

Foreword
(vol. 1, iii–viii)

Anton von Spaun's foreword to the first volume of the Beyträge zur Bildung für Jünglinge *outlines the aim and scope of the project, as well as setting its tone. Characteristically, he begins not with abstraction, but with the circle of friends of which the volumes present a public record. The apparent motivation for making that record public, however, goes unmentioned: a need to present the activities of the circle as above all virtuous and patriotic. As Josef von Spaun wrote on 9 October*

1815 to Franz von Schober (1798–1882), the younger friend whose behavior occasioned a great deal of consternation among the circle's leaders, the entire group was under investigation as an illegal secret society.[6] *Ilija Dürhammer cites a newly discovered letter that provides a lengthier discussion of the matter; the document makes clear that the incident took place before the summer holiday of 1814 at the Kremsmünster Monastic School that many of the friends attended, and that it revolved around a figure whose name has been partially expunged but began with "Sch." Dürhammer plausibly argues that the most likely identity for "Sch" is Schober, and also that the suspicion was likely moral rather than political—for love of freedom and fatherland were, at the time of the Congress of Vienna, not yet values under political repression, as they would be within a few years.*[7] *Sincere though the collection's expressions of loyalty to the Austrian authorities may have been, then, they also had value as implicit reassurances of innocence. The intense male friendship that was one of the circle's highest values was also one of its greatest liabilities, so the way that the journal presents both the friends' activities and the concept of friendship itself can be read, in part, as an apologia.*

The foreword begins with "shared, cheerful diligence" and "pious, quiet hope." It then proceeds to describe what the reader will encounter within: translations and excerpts from exemplary authors, essays written under the influence of those authors, and poems. Only in the case of the last does Spaun allow an emotional motivation: they were inspired, he writes, "by the exalted mood of some lovely moment." If the correspondence of the friends suggests that such moments were as valued and sought after as the philosophical thought and exhortations to "manly civic virtue" on which Spaun dwells, we may suspect that among the reasons for this difference is not only the desire of an elder leader of the group to maintain values threatened by its younger participants (always most prominently including Schober), but also a constant awareness of the need to project the intellectual and civic utility of the group rather than its often sentimental tone of interaction.

The present collection arose among a circle of young friends in the course of their youthful education. Accordingly it can and should make claim to nothing less than the title and the merit of a learned work, which, granted, consists of more than can be acquired in the brief years of youth. In it, what was acquired during a time of youth spent in shared, cheerful diligence, and several memories dear to us, are laid out with feelings of gratitude, in the quiet, pious hope that it may be a friendly encouragement to others. To that and nothing more do these pages wish to make their claim.

Here are excerpts from good authors of ancient and modern times as we collected them from the beginning of our acquaintance with them; translations which we undertook among ourselves for practice; larger and smaller essays, in which we attempted to express our thoughts and views about various things from the inner and outer world of youth, and to present historical developments; and finally, such poems as were brought into being by the exalted mood of some lovely moment.

The whole collection contains perhaps less of our own than that of others; but the reader will not lose anything thereby. With the latter, we are certain of providing everyone with contributions to cultured education. Beyond this, should the smallest part of our own work be unique to us, it is only a demonstration that we learned from those others, that we too drew cultivation from them. May it be counted to our credit that we set down alongside the thoughts of our great teachers that which we have thought in following their example.

There is much in these pages that belongs to philosophy; too much, it might seem, for such a publication and for young people, our readers. But there is so much talk these days about such matters in life and in books—talk often so dangerously superficial, and often so dangerously deep and captious—that this tendency of the *Zeitgeist* must not be overlooked in pages for the cultivation of youth; it is thus far from a worthless effort to oppose this by bringing to mind the simple, powerful teachings of wise men concerning the True, the Good, and the Beautiful, which are alone suited to develop character and a manly, noble, and generally useful life. Their wisdom speaks comprehensible words and is the serious but intimate friend of youth.

More emphatic and elevating to us than any teaching, however, is a great deed, a great life—most forcefully as expressed by a man who has his own sense for great things. Thus we gladly choose such pieces from the famous historians, presenting in their own words that which cannot be said more strongly or worthily. History is the teacher of manly civic virtue; when a young man reads of men who lived and died for their Fatherland, he learns to feel what a Fatherland is, and that he too has duties toward his own. May these pages contribute to making this feeling, which has in our own day accomplished such splendid things, alive and active in a good many youths—for true cultivation derives only from activity for the common good.

We hereby set the tone of these pages rather seriously, and on the whole they are and shall remain so; may the support of the friendly Muses keep them from becoming strict and dry. Is there any noble young spirit who does not feel himself more touchingly addressed and inwardly moved by warm words about the True and the Good, by great men and their life and work, by ancient history, the Fatherland, its heroes and its history, than by any sort of mere recreational reading? No, we want to provide something better—something, however small it may be, in return for all that is great and invaluable that we received from the beloved Fatherland. Were we not aware of the power of this desire, greater than all timidity and caution, these pages would never have left the small circle that gave them their existence; for we know well enough how slight these contributions are and what a great matter education is. But our times are a great summons for every man to do what he can in working together toward the greatest good; and so we give as well the best that we can, hesitant yet happy that we are able to give something. May the Fatherland not scorn this small offering, and may it be an inspiration and guide to some youth, that one day he may himself be able to accomplish something better in word or in deed! That alone is our wish and, because the smallest seed of the Good flourishes easily and powerfully in a youth's warm heart, also our quietly rewarding hope.

On Friendship
(vol. 1, 4–17)

The anxieties that underpin the high-minded project of education become apparent early in the collection's first essay. The essay, Anton von Spaun's consideration of the phenomenon of friendship, which is preceded only by a brief dedicatory and patriotic poem, represents the activity of collective cultivation at its most reflexive: it applies the practice of reading the classics and modeling behavior to the phenomenon of the circle of friends itself, going to great lengths to build a securely virtuous basis, not so much for intellectual activities themselves as for the relational context in which they take place.[8] *Beginning with a paean to the value of friendship among the Ancients and stressing its civic and public value, yet warning against their "sad aberrations"—for the intellectually respectable grounding in Socratic philosophy brought with it precisely the risk of association with homosexual interaction that the publication needed to avoid—Spaun proceeds to explore his topic enthusiastically, if unsystematically. What we love in others, he posits, is an ideal "which we suppose to exist even within ourselves," but that internal ideal is threatened by repression, which brings about a longing that "rages through the breast with tormenting flames—or, breaking out somewhere, often drags us into errors or vices." Mutual recognition of that ideal between two beings who "have recognized each other in truth, penetrated one another, and united in spirit," is friendship.*

Having defined friendship in such highly charged terms, with love as its basis, Spaun then finds it necessary to draw a distinction between (spiritualized) friendship and (sensual) love. But the language Spaun uses to approach the issue immediately undermines the distinction: "For do we not find illustrated in the purest models of manly friendship that same anxious longing, that quietly admiring rapture as *the tender, playful, rhapsodizing essence that otherwise tends to characterize feminine love?" Grappling with sentimental and often physical expressions of closeness among male friends, Spaun reaches for the biblical example of David and Jonathan and hesitantly posits the additional quality of "love in the narrower sense" as "the addition of external beauty, and with the help of that, of feelings raised to a certain degree of ecstatic enthusiasm." That is, the ancient association of the Good and the Beautiful is itself a danger—but only if it leads to the loss of self-control that Spaun's term for that enthusiasm (*Schwärmerei*) often connotes. But the cure itself is perilous. Citing the example of Theages, for whom the presence of and physical contact with Socrates was restorative, Spaun considers the prospects for a youth determined to overcome deeply rooted deficiencies while constantly threatened by relapse. For such a youth—and it is difficult not to hear echoes of the friends' long history of exhortations to Franz von Schober in this context—the only hope is if "he throws himself into the arms of a friend and reveals to him his innermost self."*

From this climactic moment, the essay recedes first to more abstract reflection on the connection of inner essence to the divine, followed by an exhortation to share this vision of purified relationship, and finally an assurance that, Montaigne to the contrary, such intense relationships can indeed exist among a group of individuals and not only a pair. By the end, there is no doubt that Spaun is determined to maintain virtue by transcending the physical and emotional, but it is equally clear that to do so brings about a struggle not only with literary sources grounded in very different norms but also with the individuals engaged in the process.

There is no doubt that people would be better if more true friendship existed among them. But it is just as certain that we would encounter more friendship among them if they were better.

The ancient states, whose preeminent focus was to use the combined strength of individuals and upbringing to strive for an improved, more perfect state of affairs, regarded friendship as one of the most effective motivators of virtue, as is shown by the laws they issued about it as well as the many images of the most exalted friendship that shine forth from that distant place, both to our shame and our encouragement. It was friendship that animated those sons of the gods who first freed the earth from monsters and crude violence, friendship that taught youths civic virtue and inspired them to victory or death. Friendship was always the terror of tyrants. The bond of closest friendship was to bind together those who, Pythagoras wished, would enliven declining states with fresh spirit; love of friends was the essence of Socratic wisdom. Without denying that their friendship, too, was not completely pure and unblemished but encompassed many aberrations, let us trust the truth at the root of both those splendid pronouncements and their sad aberrations, and reflect on what true friendship consists of, and how we can attain virtue through friendship or friendship through virtue.

Every person in whom the human element is even somewhat active bears something higher within himself that he aspires to reach, something he loves and marvels at; and even the villain bears in his breast the image of a more consistent, happier villain.

Accordingly, it is not ourselves whom we love in our beloved, as many claim, but that which we demand of ourselves and which we love and venerate with that demand. It lies in our nature to want to find this ideal embodied outside us, because captive longing, feeling endlessly repressed within, rages through the breast with tormenting flames—or, breaking out somewhere, often drags us into errors and vices. The joy or illusion of finding this higher ideal, envisioned always only within, realized as well outside of us, is the feeling of friendship. Friendship in the strictest sense, however, occurs only when two such beings have recognized, penetrated, and spiritually joined one another in truth.

But who among us can in this sense say that he has found a friend, or is someone's friend? As little as we despair in our struggle for virtue when we fail to achieve it in its pure and perfect form, so little must we disdain friendship when we fail to carry it to such heights.

It violates the basic laws of eternal justice to demand of others that which we lack. We should therefore certainly not take the realization of our ideal as the basic condition of our friendship, but rather only a faithful respect for and pursuit of that ideal. But selfishness, and the delusion that things we can behold only vaguely in our most far-reaching thoughts, when elevated by the wings of our imagination, are vitally present within us, that we are one with ourselves—in friendship these things make us measure with standards we ourselves cannot meet.

If a higher being were to hear humans' quiet laments, how so many complain at once that they cannot find their ideal, that their love is not requited, that friendship here on earth is a dream that only they dream—and saw therewith their distracted, idle, and loveless activity; how, mutually desiring and misunderstanding, they pass by one another so coldly and antagonistically—he would have compassion on us and, were he not compelled to scorn us, would surely want to help us, opening our eyes and arms. Thus when we choose a friend let us not close our heart against anyone who struggles with a shortcoming of which our ideal is free—but rather ask ourselves modestly and probingly whether one who, like us, has this or that weakness; who was highly strict toward others yet indulgent toward himself, letting himself be carried away by passions and habitual behaviors; whether someone who in his life and his dealings was completely like us could be embraced as a friend? He who does not deserve a friend will never win one—and that is why complaints and vain wishes are so abundant, but friends so rare.

Aristotle already said* that living together and closer association among people is always a dangerous precipice for friendship; most such friendships break up, largely on account of accumulated annoyance over provocations that are insignificant but recur constantly.

Who does not remember from childhood years how busy we were at filling out as beautifully as possible the image of that boy or youth we had yet to meet; with what impatient longing, what joyful expectation we looked forward to those moments when we imagined we would find everything our heart desired, while we neglected those whom habit and daily interaction had brought nearer as nothing more than empty, hollowed-out shells of our hopes; both with equal injustice. The reason is that we envisioned one as the inner essence, free of all that is trivial and coincidental and thus all the greater and more splendid, whereas with the other, confused by the many external circumstances and often most insignificant weaknesses and habits, we failed to perceive the spirit that works within—just as at the foot of a small hill we fail to see the mountain behind it that rises into the clouds.

Let us therefore never lose sight of the essential on account of the inessential, and take care always to conduct all outer affairs so that no one can misjudge our ever creative, thinking spirit; and let us practice what is right with steadfast attention, even in the smaller, inconspicuous relations of life. The most difficult thing, said Plutarch, is to affirm one's dignity in familiar, daily interaction—but with true virtue the most visible also seems to us the most beautiful, and with the truly great, strangers find nothing more remarkable than the way they conduct themselves daily with their acquaintances.

The question is often posed whether love and friendship differ. But if we wanted to try to separate true friendship from love, we would soon find that both are in essence one, but as they express themselves differently, have been given different names. To make this distinction nonetheless along the lines of gender would be quite incorrect; for do we not find illustrated in the purest models of manly friendship that same anxious longing, that quietly admiring rapture as the tender, playful, rhapsodizing essence that other-

Politics, vol. 2, chap. 3. [Here and throughout, footnotes are those provided in the *Beyträge*.]

wise tends to characterize feminine love? And did not David once say of his friend Jonathan, "His love was more to me than the love of women"?*[9]

I believe, then, that the difference between friendship and that which is called love in the narrower sense consists only in the addition of external beauty, and with the help of that, of feelings raised to a certain degree of ecstatic enthusiasm [*Schwärmerei*].

Indeed, it lies deep within our nature to think of the highest ideal of the Good as also beautiful. Yet how often this drive, which flows through the thinking spirit with premonitions of delight, has disappointed and misled the hearts of mortals in the partial, broken, confused relations of earthly life! Let us never forget, then, how much more substantial is the signified than the sign, that the beauty of virtuous souls is as superior to the beauty of external forms as the eternal immutable is above the corruptible blooming of the body—and neither immoderately crave nor selfishly and stubbornly forgo the beauty of forms. So many people always remain only on the outermost surface of things, and it is not unusual that the most unworthy objects—showing barely the faintest reflection of deeper meaning of the last, highest sensation—exhaust all the feelings of their deluded hearts. There are people who praise, with all the enthusiasm available to their vapid nature, the beauty of a foot. If only they knew how far they stand below those savages we disdain because they trade gold and diamonds for glass beads and baubles!

Socrates, too, used to say that the sight of lovely youths gripped him with gentle emotions, unnameable feelings that drove him restlessly to do everything within his powers to make them virtuous and happy. Yet he showed through his speech as well as his actions how little external beauty without real virtue mattered to him.

If then love, as one ancient wise man**[10] taught, is the drive to ascribe goodness to what the eye sees as beautiful, so let us call friendship that higher union of two souls that does not require the medium of sensual beauty, of agreeable forms, to be mutually recognized, respected, and enjoyed. In this sense the following applies:

Stellest du Kypris auf in des Herzens Tempel, sie herrschet
Einsam, Tyrannen gleich, über der Freyheit Gebieth;
Aber zum Pantheon weihet das Herz die edlere Freundschaft,
Jedem Göttlichen flammt reiner ihr Bundesaltar.

*1 Samuel 20:17.

**Chrysippus in Diogenes Laërtius.

If you raise up Kypris[11] in the temple of your heart,
  she will reign
Alone, like a tyrant, over the realm of freedom;
But if the heart consecrates more noble friendship to
  the Pantheon,
Its united altar will burn more purely for everything divine.

I know some who are my age or somewhat older, said the young Theages* to his father, who before they had interaction with this man (Socrates) were good for nothing; but within a very short time after they came into his company they had become much better than all those who were otherwise better than they. And Aristides, who felt powerfully the decline of his intellectual and moral power with his separation from Socrates, said to Socrates: "As you yourself know, I have never really learned anything from you, but I grew whenever I was with you, even when I only lived in the same house with you, even when not in the same room of the house; and it seemed to me that I benefited even more when I beheld you in the same room of the house, when you spoke, much more than when I looked somewhere else. I grew most of all, though, and to the highest degree, whenever I myself sat next to you, and we touched one another closely. Now, however, all that power and skill is gone from me."[12]

It will be difficult for many who have never experienced something similar to convince themselves of the truth of this feeling, this wonderful healing power of higher friendship. But happy are they who have been kept in the Good by it, or led back to the right path, and blessed are those who led them.

We cannot always do everything by ourselves, under our own powers. Even with the clearest knowledge of the Good and the Beautiful, and all love for them, we must often grapple with deficiencies whose deep roots have been established in us by example and habit, and that we cannot uproot completely even with the most painful exertion. If for years we have been weak or bad, or have gone in the wrong direction through the corrupting influence of others, it is not within us to stop in an instant—to be strong where previously we were sensual and self-serving; even if earlier it might have been within our power not to make a habit of this or that faulty inclination.

How unhappy, then, is the person who recognizes with equal vividness his faults and the impotence of his resistance; who, as often as he grasps

*In Plato.

the intention of bettering himself, again and again relapses; who is now no longer free, no longer stands at the crossroad where the path to the Good, like that to Evil, stretches before him. Let no one pronounce a damning judgment on such weakness, more or less in greater or lesser matters. Are not most people in this situation?

How can such a person be improved or saved? Only if, incapable of governing himself and fulfilling the commands of his better knowledge, he throws himself into the arms of a friend and reveals to him his innermost self.

He will then no longer feel himself abandoned in battle, he will feel himself supported where he threatened to fall; the friend will pull him forcefully from the abyss toward which his momentary craving pressed him—and the pure, beautiful joys of love and goodwill, like a refreshing balm, will soothe the pains of struggle and inner reproof.

And now, when we begin to increase in goodness, to achieve ever greater proficiency in it with the assistance of a friend who comes to the aid of our goodwill—and then we are suddenly torn away from our support—could not what Aristides described about himself and his teacher indeed befall us?

Beyond this, a person can come to true knowledge of himself only through friendship; without it, his life will fade away in ignoble dullness, like a dream.

If an eye wanted to see itself, it would have to look into a mirror or something similar.*[13] Now, when someone looks into the eye of another, his own image is represented in the eye that faces him, as in a mirror, and indeed in its principal part, the power of which it sees—the real seat of the power of sight, which makes an eye an eye. Just so must the soul that wants to see and recognize itself look into the soul of a friend, and indeed into that part of the soul that is the seat of its most excellent powers. Now, there is surely no more divine portion of the soul than that through which it thinks and deals in accordance with reason; therefore this part is also the one similar to the divine, and whoever sees into it will best recognize both all that is divine, namely divinity and wisdom, as well as himself. Therefore let us be open in friendship, and full of trust, so that the Good may speak and through its pure fire purge our entire being ever more of all corruption.

But virtue, too, leads to friendship, for that is the nature of the Good, that the more we are occupied with its contemplation the more it instills

*Plato in the First Alcibiades.

in us love to the point of ecstasy [*Begeisterung*]. Now, where can we more clearly recognize, behold, and effectively love all good and beauty than in humans? And when we perceive virtue, love, innocence, and power in noble, childlike spirits—should we not then love, share, reach out our hands, and rise up together to the lofty goal of our destiny [*Bestimmung*], in feelings of immortality, above the dark earth ruled by death and decay?

Can friendship exist with many? We are delighted by the quiet shade of the grove and by the rock-strewn canyon and the mountain stream that rushes through it; by the cheerful meadow and the calm, clear mirror of the lake; by the splendor of the rising sun and the milder clarity of the moon—and with this ability to sense the beauty of nature in its most varied guises, should the soul be found wanting when it comes to recognizing the divinity of humanity in different forms?

The essence of friendship is not monotony, but rather harmonic consonance.* Therefore the statement that friendship can never exist among several as it can between two, since it is impossible to know several people so intimately, seems less correct to me than the words of that master of the art of loving: "Just as it is impossible for the Evil to be friends, so is it impossible for the Good not to be friends."[14]

Raphael
(vol. 2, 298–309)

The final selection from the Beyträge *translated here differs from Anton von Spaun's reflection on friendship in both origin and tone, although it deals with many of the same themes. "Raphael," from the second volume, is cast as a dialogue between one "Willibald" and "Friedrich." This selection has long been described as an excerpt because of the reference in the opening title footnote to* Das Leben Raphaels, *a short book published the year before in Munich. The initial "M." that concludes the piece has been taken as an indication that the book was excerpted by Johann Mayrhofer.*[15] *But an examination of the cited life of the painter, which offered a translation of an anonymous sixteenth-century biography, makes clear that* Das Leben Raphaels *was only a source of information and, to some extent, a perspective on the painter's life.*[16] *Mayrhofer, then, should be considered the dialogue's author.*

On the face of it, "Raphael" is a somewhat heavy-handed set piece that imagines the example of an older friend commenting on an exemplary life and what could be learned from it to an eagerly receptive, affectionate young friend. In that way, it

*Montaigne, "De l'amitié."

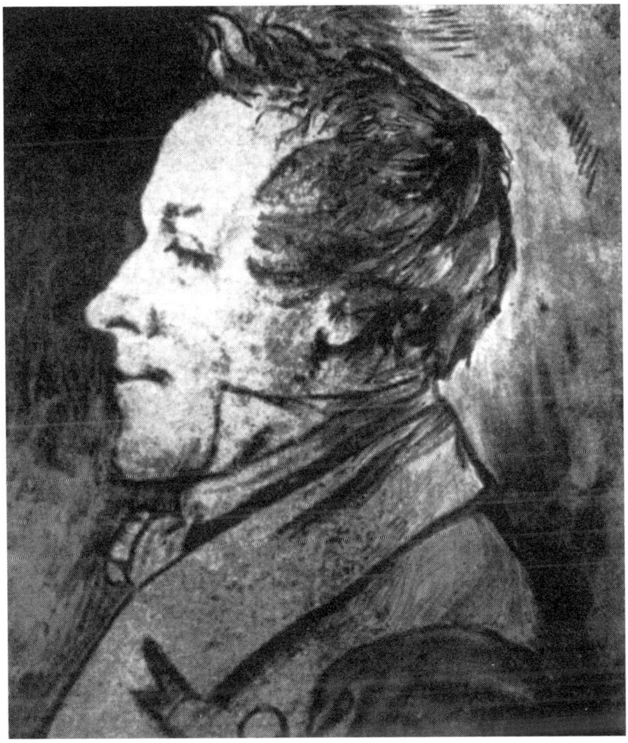

Figure 1. Portrait of Johann Mayrhofer by Moritz von Schwind.

again illustrates the activities integral both to self-cultivation and to transmitting that practice among friends. Beyond that, however, and despite the stilted dialogue, "Raphael" considers issues of art in relation to the friends' ideals in a way that gives the piece unusual interest. But there is more here, if we acknowledge our unavoidable hindsight as later readers. From its discussion of a precociously talented youth to the contrast it draws between crude and well-rounded musicians, and beyond that to its conclusion with the tragically early death of an artist, Schubert seems to hover uncannily around this text written not about him, but by one of his closest acquaintances during the early years of their friendship.

By setting the dialogue after its two characters have visited the art collections of Vienna's Belvedere Palace, Mayrhofer not only provides local color but also takes advantage of one more opportunity to express loyalty and gratitude to the Austrian throne—in addition to the concerns of state, the authorities are also interested in sharing great art with their subjects. The idyllic setting, as the friends watch the sun set over the city, also provides the opportunity to turn the reader's attention to both the sensual and the creative: the curious Willibald's evocation of the colorful scene is answered by Friedrich's hope to "speak well—so that nature, which spreads itself before us, weaving and creating, does not put me too much to shame!" With that preamble, the tone is set to consider an exemplary and specifically creative life.

The facts of Raphael's life are presented straightforwardly; Willibald's periodic interjections function largely to emphasize various points about the painter's virtues. By this means, Mayrhofer draws attention to his subject's dedication to learning, to his humility, and, of course, to the benefits he drew from the society of distinguished literary and artistic friends. At this point, Willibald interrupts with an apparent non sequitur, an expression of frustration with technically accomplished but crude musicians. Friedrich's reply moves from crudity to one-sidedness, using the opportunity to argue for broadly based rather than single-minded cultivation. But the choice of musicians to exemplify unfeeling, superficial artistry resonates with Josef von Spaun's much later assertion, cited above, that Schubert benefited from having literary and artistic friends rather than professional musical ones. It is tempting to imagine that Mayrhofer had Schubert in mind as a beneficiary of broad cultivation when writing these lines, but regardless, they attest to awareness of a gap between bourgeois literary cultivation and traditional musical training that would long play into Schubert's life and reputation.

The dialogue then lurches immediately from (male) friendship to the prospect of a heterosexual relationship. This turn is particularly noteworthy because it does not stem from the dialogue's source text, which separates the discussion of friendship from the painter's relationship to women, and because Friedrich himself dismisses it for the moment. The turn and deflection, though, provide another indication of the powerful affective charge of the homosocial relationships of the Beyträge*'s authors.*

Next, the dialogue departs from the biographical as Friedrich notes that Raphael turned to Greek models while studying the nude. This provides, first, an opportunity to dismiss as misguided medieval Christian art (and even more, its modern imitators), and to uphold the classical as the true and appropriate model—a reminder of a fundamental artistic and literary orientation from which Schubert would depart only later. But it also allows a brief return to the political, for the aberrant turn that characterizes medieval art ("Romantic" in the world-historical sense then current) can only be explained by "Germans' pain at the shameful position of their Fatherland and its political impotence, and by their longing for a time when they stood more honorably and powerfully."

The remainder of Raphael's career is dispensed with in a single brief paragraph, allowing Friedrich to return to the topic of Raphael's engagement with women, and to expand on the final, negative example that Raphael's life afforded—"his unfortunate passion." Ever since Giorgio Vasari, the painter's death at thirty-seven had been attributed to his excessive sexual activity, and the dialogue's source, Das Leben Raphaels, *followed this tradition.*[17] *For Friedrich, Raphael's giving in to "the enchantment of sensuality" becomes the basis for a reflection on the human duty to recognize the beautiful along with the good, to transcend base desires, and to ennoble beauty rather than seek to possess it. In the end Raphael, for all his virtues, provides a tragic negative example. Although Willibald briefly attempts to excuse him, Friedrich insists on the highest of standards, both for the gifted artist and, ultimately, for the observer: "Let us guard ourselves and preserve unspoiled the flame of a higher love in our breast." A brief return to the immediate scene, now suitably muted into twilight, precedes Raphael's epitaph, which brings the meditation to a close.*

Raphael: A Dialogue.*

Friedrich: So, dear friend, tell me, what do you think of the Belvedere?[18]

Willibald: I am dazed by all the splendors that we've seen this afternoon.

F: I believe you; we only did it to give you an overview of the treasures of art, and to establish in you the conviction that our princes also thought of *that*.

W: Both succeeded as you wished, and I have thereby been freed of yet another prejudice against our Fatherland, a prejudice that, as usual, had ignorance as its mother.

F: Of the paintings that we saw, which delighted you the most?

W: The two Madonnas by Raphael of Urbino.[19]

F: You're right, my friend, to take joy in them; they are excellent, no matter how many a piece we have that equals them, or even exceeds them. In any case, in mentioning Raphael you've given me the stimulus to chat with you about various things concerning this immortal artist.

W: Do that, Friedrich, and let's sit on this bench. There we'll look over the garden with its greening trees, the city with its towers bathed in evening gold, and sections of vine-covered land bordered with blue mountains. There! And now tell me all about Raphael.

F: May I speak well—so that nature, which spreads itself gloriously before us, weaving and creating, does not put me too much to shame! You know

*From: "Das Leben Raphaels." By a contemporary. Munich 1817.

in general about his short yet productive life, but I think that I will single out individual parts of it that are either unfamiliar, or to which you haven't yet, as it happens, paid attention. For believe me, my young friend, it is rewarding to inspect and examine the life of a man who brought forth immortal works—whether as a painter or a composer, an architect or a poet, a philosopher or a lawgiver. From one who has done much, much is to be learned. Our Raphael, too, whom nature adorned with the richest predisposition for art, was for a long, long time an apprentice; indeed he continued his apprenticeship until his death, convinced to the core of his being that simple genius would not suffice when it came to bringing something into being that future times would continue to recognize as beautiful, harmonious, and completely successful.

W: He received his first instruction from his father, Johann Sanctio,[20] if I'm not mistaken?

F: Whom he also soon surpassed, and who sent him on to the school of the celebrated Peter of Perugia.[21] Now, he studied Peter's works diligently, and the *Ascension of Mary* shows with what success. The student outstripped the master, yet the latter, free of petty jealousy, thanked Johann for honoring his school with his exceptional son and loved Raphael as he had before.

W: Behavior that must be deemed as rare as it is noble.

F: Thousands in Raphael's position, having achieved a reputation at sixteen that others would not at sixty, would have remained there, admired and acclaimed, for the influence of laurels achieved early is numbing to the human brain and usually an impediment to the more beautiful manly development of our disposition.

W: And it is true that only a rare person resists this influence out of humility, or in the fiery premonition that there are still higher prizes to be won.

F: From Perugia, Raphael moved to Siena, in order to adorn the library there with his brush. Pinturicchio commended him, but soon, lured by the call of Leonardo and Buonarotti, he moved to splendid Florence, in order to perfect himself in his art. Florence he found uncommonly enjoyable, in part because he came upon more excellent models to emulate, in part because the beauty of the city and the amicable environment were good for his open senses. The death of his father called him back to *Urbino*, and later we find him in *Perugia*;[22] in both cities he left behind immortal monuments. His heart, however, drove him constantly to Florence. How greatly he advanced through continuing study there he documented with his painting for the *Baglioni* chapel in *Perugia*.[23] The virtues of *Leonardo*, *Fra Bartolomeo,* and others seemed concentrated in him, and Rome strived to possess him. His *School of the Philosophers* won him the favor of *Julius II*,* who ordered that all older and newer paintings be taken away, so that Raphael could paint all of the halls.[24] The death of *Julius*, and the elevation of the Medici *Leo* to the papal throne didn't disturb him in his creations, each of which surpassed the other in perfection. Among them is his *Burning of the Burgo*. The ceiling of the hall in which he prepared this painting was painted by Master *Peter*, so Raphael opposed its destruction.

W: A tender trait of his appreciative nature—another of many such traits of our Raphael.

F: They are not lacking in his character; he was constantly surrounded by his students, who possessed a friend, indeed a father, in him.

W: Such a good man certainly had numerous friends.

F: To be sure, and very ingenious men at that. I need only mention *Ariosto*, *Aretino*, *Pietro Bembo*, *Paolo Giovio*, and *Andrea Fulvio*—a society that exercised the most fundamental influence on his production.

W: Dear friend, I have so often been annoyed by musicians who, though they delight others, seem to feel nothing, or when they put their instrument aside are insignificant, indeed sometimes crude and repulsive people.

F: If crudity or one-sidedness is already disagreeable in those who realize the thoughts of others, how much more so is it in those who think them. The Muses, after all, are sisters who love one another, and whoever offends one puts himself in danger of being abandoned by all of them

---

*In his Foreword to Plato, Stolberg says that in this splendid painting by Raphael, which is so famous under the name *The School of Athens*, Plato and Aristotle are represented as standing next to each other. Plato looks toward heaven with wise drunkenness; Aristotle looks to the ground with a penetrating gaze, as if all nature, and with it mankind in all its earthly as well as sociable relations, lay at his feet.

at the crucial moment. Permeated by this idea, Raphael occupied himself with the study of poetry and history and left out of consideration no branch of knowledge that was related to his art.

W: Certainly he was also fortunate to find a feminine being who joined herself to him, loving and beloved.

F: More about that later, Willibald; let us consider the course of his further education. In Florence he had already convinced himself of the inadequacy and aridity of the manner of *Peter of Perugia* and adopted a more accomplished style. But in Rome, in part because he saw there *Michelangelo*'s brilliant works come into being, it became clear to him that he would again need to become a student if he were to approximate the ideal that he envisioned for himself as an artist.

W: He and Michelangelo became rivals, then.

F: Yet in such a way that Raphael often thanked heaven that he had had the good fortune to be a contemporary of Michelangelo, who had taught him a better style than *Perugino*.

W: His student? Remarkable—yet in the two paintings in the Belvedere there is a grace and tenderness uncharacteristic of Michelangelo.

F: To judge correctly the extent to which Raphael imitated him, we would need to have before us all the paintings that originated in this period. More than that, don't forget that Raphael was an original mind, and thus could never sink to "imitatorum pecus."[25] Whatever he received or adopted he assimilated in his own way and stamped with his heavenly individuality.

Acquaintance with *Michelangelo* prompted him to study the *nude*, in part following anatomy and in part following ancient models; with this intent he occupied himself as a draftsman in all regions, as far even as Greece, and he drew diligently after Greek models.

W: But my God, what did he fail to take on? I would have thought he might have limited himself to the field offered him by Christianity and the Romantic; it is splendid and broad enough to satisfy many Raphaels.[26] Besides, to my mind those sensual forms are scarcely compatible with our ideas of chastity and dignity, much less his Madonnas.

F: On the contrary, note that he was an architect. Florence and Rome attest to it, as do the designs he prepared for St. Peter's. Beyond that, he was a sculptor. This double talent led him necessarily to the study of the Ancients, who created the greatest works of architecture and sculpture. As a painter he could do even less without them. Can you imagine that the thoroughly noble body and enchanting drapery of the seated Madonna we saw today could have come about if he had not been intimately acquainted with nature and the creations of the Ancients? Just think about the distortions and aberrations of the German school. Our countrymen set about drawing and painting diligently, with an effort and good nature that deserve admiration—what with the fall of the Roman Empire, the great migrations, feudalism, and the monastic spirit, the canon of the beautiful and the truthful, in a word, the classical, was hidden from them. Finally, Constantinople illuminated Italy, and Italy the rest of Europe. If these men were to be resurrected now that the sources of Hellenistic art have been opened, they would certainly create in a different spirit.

W: Now I understand your sour expressions at some of the paintings in the art exhibition. Nonetheless, you don't believe the old-fashioned manner will take root?

F: As little as Gothic poetry or Chinese architecture, which sometimes seem to be becoming the order of the day. They are aberrations and nothing more—time will vindicate me.

W: But how do you explain them?

F: By the Germans' pain at the shameful position of their Fatherland and its political impotence, and by their longing for a time when they filled a more honorable and powerful position. Their ancestors became enviable, and everything about them, even the vulgar and misguided, became respectable and worthy of imitation. The resurgence of our people will change this tendency.

W: Now, my dear friend, more about Raphael.

F: It was in his third style that we perceive the highest perfection of line, of color, of unity and expression. *St. Cecilia of Bologna* falls within this period, for many his most accomplished painting. He celebrated the triumph of his art, however, with his *Transfiguration*. Leo had made him supervisor of all works under construction in the Vatican. If everything else from Raphael's hand were to be lost, this palace alone would secure his immortality.

W: In what amount of time did he create these immortal things?

F: In thirteen years, during which he also completed numerous exquisite works for private patrons.

W: Unbelievable!

F: And now, concerning his unfortunate passion and his end. Each of us, my good Willibald, is born with a sense not only for what is good, but for what is beautiful—only it must be appropriately developed, regulated, and worthily directed toward worthy objects. The bestial person wants nothing more than to enjoy that which appears beautiful to him, and cares neither for the perfection nor the destruction of the object that attracts him. The one who has wrested himself freer of bestiality through science, art, or some other nobler occupation, though without heightening his reason enough to master his instincts, is naturally more refined in his enjoyment, which nonetheless remains his principal goal; around it he braids all the blossoms of his fantasy and art, much like the Ancients did with the animals they were preparing to sacrifice. But those in whom rational nature rules feel beauty deeply, but *purely*, and thus strive not so much to possess and enjoy, but rather to ennoble. Think of *Socrates*, think of *Petrarch*. This feeling, expressed through a life not profaned by low desire, is truly one of the most honorable for humans, but it can be achieved only through struggle and self-conquest. Indeed, our Raphael often said that he was carried away by the charm, not of the gender, but of its beauty, and his art was nourished by the splendid visages of feminine beings. But he did not resist the enchantment of sensuality, which entrapped him and brought about his death in his thirty-seventh year.

W: Friedrich! Let us mourn his early and, for art, irreplaceable loss, and its cause; beyond that, let us be fair, and remember that he lived in a depraved time, that he was a painter who blazed a trail, and that he always conducted himself so amiably, benevolently, and kindly.

F: These considerations indeed moderate his errors, without annulling them. He whose temple was kissed by Venus Urania already at birth may more justly than others be expected to dedicate himself to serving her purely. But let us guard ourselves and preserve unspoiled the flame of a higher love in our breast.

W: God grant that it flourish. Look—a gossamer mist settles over the garden and the city, and the evening star floats on the darker backdrop of the sky. Let us go.

F: Just a few more words. His body was solemnly displayed in a hall and the *Transfiguration* placed at his head. Leo mourned the artist's death more than others, and at his behest Pietro Bembo prepared the epitaph:

> *Ille hic est Raphael, timuit quo sospite vinci*
> *Rerum magna parens et moriente mori.*
>
> Here lies Raphael, from whom nature feared defeat
> while he lived and her own death when he died.

And now come!

—M.

NOTES

1. As Ilija Dürhammer notes, Josef Kenner and Josef Kreil, members of the same circle of friends, participated in the publication, though in a far less active way. See Dürhammer, *Schuberts literarische Heimat: Dichtung und Literaturrezeption der Schubert-Freunde* (Vienna, 1999), 64.

2. See Helga Prosl, "Der Freundeskreis um Anton von Spaun: Ein Beitrag zur Geistesgeschichte von Linz in der Biedermeierzeit (1811–1827)" (PhD diss., Innsbruck, 1951); Dieter Lyon, "Anton von Spaun: Ein Beitrag zur Geistesgeschichte des Vormärz" (PhD diss., Graz, 1964); Walther Dürr, "Der Linzer Schubert-Kreis und seine 'Beiträge zur Bildung für Jünglinge,'" *Historisches Jahrbuch der Stadt Linz* (1985), 51–59; David Gramit, "The Intellectual and Aesthetic Tenets of Franz Schubert's Circle" (PhD diss., Duke University, 1987); and Dürhammer, *Schuberts literarische Heimat.*

3. See Dürhammer, *Schuberts literarische Heimat,* as well as his *Geheime Botschaften: Homoerotische Subkulturen im Schubert-Kreis, bei Hugo von Hofmannsthal und Thomas Bernhard* (Vienna, 2006).

4. Josef von Spaun, "Some Observations on the Life of Schubert by Herr Ritter von Kreissle-Hellborn (1864)," in *Schubert: Memoirs by His Friends*, ed. Otto Erich Deutsch, trans. Rosamond Ley and John Nowell (London, 1958), 364. Spaun's immediate reference is the slightly later group of friends around Franz von Schober, but Schober came to know Schubert through his activity in this earlier circle.

5. Dürhammer, in *Schuberts literarische Heimat*, cites reviews from Vienna and Jena, 56.

6. The letter is preserved in the Wienbibliothek, Inv. no. 36627. For a discussion and an extended excerpt, see Gramit, "Intellectual and Aesthetic Tenets," 147–49 and 389–90.

7. Dürhammer, *Schuberts literarische Heimat*, 178–83.

8. For a more detailed consideration of the sources of Spaun's essay, as well as the challenges he faced in dealing with the physical and erotic aspects of relationships in those sources, see Dürhammer, *Schuberts literarische Heimat*, 148–55.

9. The passage to which Spaun refers is actually 2 Samuel 1:26; the earlier verse describes Jonathan's love for David as equal to his love for himself.

10. Chrysippus is discussed along with other Stoic philosophers in Book 7 of *The Lives and Opinions of Eminent Philosophers* by Diogenes Laertius.

11. Aphrodite.

12. Both speeches in this paragraph are found in the *Theages*, now not generally ascribed to Plato himself. The text is a translation of Spaun's German. For a standard English translation, see *Plato: With an English Translation*, vol. 8, trans. W. R. M. Lamb, Loeb Classical Library (London and New York, 1927). "For I know of some of my equals in age, and some a little older, who were of no account before they learnt from him, but after beginning to learn from him have in a very short time proved themselves superior to all whose inferiors they were before" (373). "'For I never yet learned anything from you, as you know yourself: but I made progress, whenever I was with you, if I was merely in the same house, without being in the same room, but more progress, when I was in the same room. And it seemed to me to be much more when I was in the same room and looked at you as you were speaking, than when I turned my eyes elsewhere: but my progress was far the greatest and most marked whenever I sat beside you and held and touched you. Now, however,' he said, 'that condition has all oozed away'" (381).

13. *The First Alcibiades,* another work whose authorship is uncertain, is available in a translation by Bernadotte Perrin at http://www.perseus.tufts.edu/hopper/text?doc=Perseus:text:2008.01.0006. For a close discussion of the passage in question, see Victoria Wohl, "The Eye of the Beloved: *Opsis* and *Eros* in Socratic Pedagogy," in *Alcibiades and the Socratic Lover-Educator*, ed. Marguerite Johnson and Harold Tarrant (London, 2012), 45–60.

14. Spaun's conclusion seems to be drawn from Plato's *Lysis*, which includes an extended discussion of good and evil in friendship, although it does not appear to be a literal quotation.

15. This interpretation originated with Moritz Bauer, "Johann Mayrhofer," *Zeitschrift für Musikwissenschaft* 5 (1922–23): 82. Dürhammer, in *Schuberts literarische Heimat*, includes the piece among the collection's excerpts without considering Mayrhofer's involvement (58).

16. *Das Leben Raphaels von einem unbekannten Gleichzeitigen* (Munich, 1817) is held by libraries including the Bayerische Staatsbibliothek in Munich and the Library of the Getty Research Institute, Los Angeles. The Munich copy is now also viewable on Google Books. As I suggested in "Intellectual and Aesthetic Tenets," the dialogue's numerous local references make clear that it was a newly written work (71n62).

17. *Das Leben Raphaels*, 25–27.

18. The Belvedere Palace, originally built for Prince Eugen of Savoy, hero of the Siege of Vienna, housed the Imperial art collection and was open to the public for viewing. The view from the upper palace toward the center of Vienna was (and remains) perhaps the best known of the old city.

19. Raphael's *Madonna im Grünen* (*Madonna and Child with the Infant John the Baptist*) came into the possession of the Habsburgs in 1662 and is still in the collection of the Kunsthistorisches Museum in Vienna, as is the *Heilige Familie mit Johannesknaben* (*Holy Family with Infant John the Baptist*), acquired in 1779 and now ascribed to Raphael and his workshop, which may be the other painting referred to here. See the Bilddatenbank of the Kunsthistorisches Museum, http://bilddatenbank.khm.at/viewArtefact?id=1502; and http://bilddatenbank.khm.at/viewArtefact?id=1503, respectively.

20. Giovanni Santi, active 1469–1494.

21. Pietro Vannucci, or Perugino, ca. 1446–1523.

22. Emphases for these geographical terms, and all other terms given in italics, are in the original text.

23. The Baglioni Altarpiece, 1507.

24. Cited here in Mayrhofer's footnote is Friedrich Leopold zu Stolberg-Stolberg (1750–1819), a poet and scholar who prepared numerous translations of classical literature into German, including Plato's Dialogues.

25. A reference to Horace's *Epistles*, 1.19.19: "O imitatores, servum pecus" (O imitators, you servile herd).

26. Here "Romantic" has the sense of a world-historical period associated with medieval Christianity.

"Those of us who found our life in art": The Second-Generation Romanticism of the Schubert-Schober Circle, 1820–1825

JOHN M. GINGERICH

Mention of the "Schubert circle" and its members' quintessential activity, the "Schubertiade," conjures up an irresistibly appealing image: the intimacy of chamber music, a presiding genius, convivial high spirits, the companionship of gifted friends, and the unlimited promise of youth. The romance of the Schubert circle is perhaps most memorably captured in two well-known depictions: a sepia drawing by Moritz von Schwind, *A Schubert Evening at Josef von Spaun's* (see Figure 1), and a watercolor by Leopold Kupelwieser, *Party Game of the Schubertians* (see Figure 2). Together they seem to illustrate several complementary aspects of the circle: playful and serious, fun-loving exuberance and a solemn devotion to art. And both show Schubert presiding from his accustomed position at the piano: in the Schwind drawing he is in the center, accompanying the singer Johann Michael Vogl, with the host at his left, in a position to turn pages, surrounded by some forty listeners; in the Kupelwieser painting Schubert is shown off to the left side, watching a group of five central figures who are acting out a charade or a tableau vivant, his left hand resting on the keyboard—giving a musical clue?—with Kupelwieser's dog Drago seated under the piano, both in an attitude of rapt attention to the tableau. Of these two representations, the Schwind drawing is the most iconic, and it also unwittingly illustrates, just beneath its appealing, romantic surface, problems that persist in the historiography of the Schubert circle.

Schwind's drawing is quite deliberately a retrospective composite. He worked on it in the immediate aftermath of the sensational discovery of the "Unfinished" Symphony in 1865, by which time Schubert had gained a fame he had never enjoyed during his lifetime, and Schubertiades had become enveloped in nostalgia. In revisiting an event that had taken place

Figure 1. *A Schubert Evening at Josef von Spaun's.* Drawing by Moritz von Schwind.

sometime between 1826 and 1828, he seems to have combined a wish to commemorate personal recollections of such evenings with a desire to provide an honor roll of Schubertians.[1] The listeners are grouped according to artistic field, with the painters Ludwig Kraißl, Ludwig Ferdinand Schnorr von Carolsfeld, Schwind himself, August Wilhelm Rieder, and Leopold Kupelwieser standing centrally behind the seated ladies, and the dramatists and poets Ernst von Feuchtersleben, Franz Grillparzer, Eduard von Bauernfeld, Johann Senn, Johann Mayrhofer, and Ignaz Castelli grouped on the far right. Schwind included in the crowded collection of faces several who could not possibly have been there: Senn, for example, had been exiled to Tyrol several years before Spaun began hosting Schubertiades, and Eleonore Stohl, who became a well-known Schubert singer during Schwind's lifetime, was not born until 1832.[2]

A Schubert Circle with Schubert at Its Center

As a representation of the Schubert circle, Schwind's drawing illustrates only too well the problematic nature of that term. Over the years the Schubert circle has been invoked time and again without defining its membership or delimiting chronological boundaries: Otto Erich Deutsch's venerable commentaries on the documents,[3] the standard biographies, and the more recent writings on Schubert's sexuality all assume that the

Figure 2. *Party Game of the Schubertians.* Watercolor by Leopold Kupelwieser.

Schubert circle is a self-explanatory entity. Anyone who drank *Schmollis* with Schubert,[4] anyone who shared a *Stammtisch* with him,[5] anyone who attended Schubertiades or reading parties, anyone who was a classmate at the Stadtkonvikt (City Seminary)[6] and stayed in touch, has become an undifferentiated member of the Schubert circle.

Rita Steblin, David Gramit, and before them Moriz Enzinger have expanded our knowledge of some of the subsidiary circles delimited by the Schubert circle. Although their discoveries about these circles tell us many fascinating things about Schubert's milieu, Schubert did not play a central role, nor was he a central member of most of them. In chronological order, "circles" of which Schubert was a peripheral member, or perhaps a member, or on the brink of becoming a member, are the Linzer Bildungskreis (Educational Circle in Linz, 1811–18), sometimes called the Linzer Tugendbund (League of Virtue), to which his connections were almost always at one remove, through friends;[7] the Unsinnsgesellschaft (Nonsense Society, April 1817 until no later than May 1819), of which he was likely a member, although his absence from the only membership list that survives is perhaps an indicator of his less than central status;[8] the Senn circle (most of 1819 until 20 January 1820), of which, as the name indicates, he was not the central member;[9] and the Ludlamshöhle (Ludlam's Cave, 1817–26), which he was on the verge of joining when it was disbanded by the authorities.[10] Of these, he was probably most active in the Unsinnsgesellschaft, but even there he does not seem to have been at its hub; its life and organization seems to have depended on the three Anschütz brothers, especially Eduard, and on Leopold Kupelwieser.[11] None of these subsidiary circles was a Schubert circle, although all involved some close friends of his. They add up to a Schubert circle only in the aggregate, and even the aggregate has no core that would justify naming it after Schubert. The only sense in which any of these were "Schubert" circles is *ex post facto*: he later became the most famous name associated with them.

Schubert did, however, form the core of one circle, along with his friend Franz von Schober. From 1820 through 1825 a small group of close friends revolved around Schubert and Schober. The Schubertiade is a practice and a term they invented: an evening devoted exclusively to Schubert's music, whether songs, four-hand piano music, or dances, with the first Schubertiade taking place on 26 January 1821(*SDB*, 162).[12] That one of their defining activities is named after Schubert is only the most obvious sign of his centrality. Schubert provided in many ways the living embodiment of the circle's ideals, while Schober was its mouthpiece, even as his example fell short.

The Schubert-Schober circle—or for the sake of euphony, the Schobert circle, a conflation which Schubert himself could not resist—is the hub in the vast wheel known as the Schubert circle.[13] Of all these circles, the Schobert circle is the only one to which Schubert was essential rather than incidental. Except as seen in the retrospective light of Schubert's fame, the Schubert circle without the Schobert circle would have been a composite like Schwind's drawing, but it would be Schwind's drawing with Schubert half-obscured by shadows somewhere in the last row, instead of front and center at the piano.

Several other factors also lend the Schobert circle a unique significance. The core members shared friendships of great intensity, and their fellowship together formed for a time the center of their creative as well as their social lives. At the peak of their organized activities during the winter of 1822–23 they met once a week for a Schubertiade at the Schober residence, and three times a week to read and discuss dramas and other literature.[14] In addition they frequently met less formally in the afternoon at coffee houses, and in the evening in a designated pub (*Stammlokal*). In the summers they gathered for festivals (*Feste*) at Atzenbrugg, a country estate made available for several weeks each year through Schober family connections (*SDB*, 184). All of these activities revolved around the core members but included others as well.

In addition to the tremendous amount of time committed to these regular meetings, there were other get-togethers that were more intensely personal. The atmosphere is captured in a letter Schubert later wrote to Schober (21 September 1824):

> If only we were together, you, Swind, Kuppel, and I, every mishap would seem but a trivial matter; but here we are, separated, each in a different corner, and that is truly my misfortune. I might exclaim with Goethe: "Who will bring back just one hour of that happy time!" That time when we sat together confidingly, and each exposed his artistic children to the others with motherly shyness, expecting, not without some trepidation, the judgment that love and truth were to pronounce; that time when each inspired the other, and thus a united striving for the highest beauty animated us all.[15]

This intense interaction between the friends occurred during crucial years when several members of the group were first exploring their vocations, while for Schubert those same years bridged his transition from obscurity to first fame. The circle became a crucible for testing its members' fledgling talents, but it was also, as Schubert's letter indicates, a place where they forged together a deeper sense of purpose for their art. For Schubert the fateful winter of 1822–23 was particularly poignant, since amid the most intense flurry of the circle's activities he also irrevocably lost his health when he became infected with syphilis.

As might be expected, this hothouse of creative ferment could not last. The circle began to dissolve in 1823 for the most pedestrian of reasons, when several core members, including Schober, left Vienna for extended stays abroad, while Schubert's syphilitic symptoms made him unfit for social gatherings for extended periods of time. The circle exploded in the fall of 1824 when a personal dispute between Schober and another member, Franz von Bruchmann, forced nearly everyone to take sides. But behind the personal acrimony lurked deeper divisions: the dispute soon enough revealed a break in the consensus the group had shared—a larger framework of political, social, and religious convictions that gave the arts an indispensable role in society. The fracture of the circle creates a unique prism not provided by any of the other circles for gauging Schubert's own values, because Schubert unhesitatingly and unwaveringly took Schober's side in the dispute with Bruchmann.

The Schobert circle, then, in addition to forming the hub of the Schubert circle due to its membership, was also central to the lives of its core members in ways that none of the other groups were. During this key transition in their lives each was struggling to find the work to which to dedicate himself and with it a happy meeting of inclination, talent, and a deeper sense of purpose. The importance they attached to the Schobert circle, the golden time they associated with it, is revealed in letter after letter they wrote to each other once it had dissolved.

After its dissolution Schubert never formed nor joined another similar circle, and although he looked back upon it with nostalgia, in many ways he had outgrown it. Not all, but many of the friendships endured, even while the circle did not. Painful as it was for Schubert, the end of the circle also freed him from their shared literary-musical-artistic preoccupations, so that beginning in 1824 he could concentrate on more purely musical matters with new compositions in Beethoven's instrumental genres.[16]

The Membership and Identity of the Circle

While the winter of 1822–23 was the high point in the life of the Schobert circle, a symmetrical extension of the time frame, from 1820 to 1825, provides the necessary context for understanding the buildup to that central winter and its aftermath. The core members during those five years were Schubert (b. 1797), Franz von Schober (b. 1796), Franz von Bruchmann (b. 1798), Leopold Kupelwieser (b. 1796), and Moritz von Schwind (b. 1804), with the significant additions of Johann Mayrhofer (b. 1787) during the first year, of Eduard von Bauernfeld (b. 1802) during the last year, and of Josef von Spaun (b. 1788) always in the background.

The mutual loyalty and admiration of Schubert and Schober formed the unassailable bedrock of their circle. Josef Kenner (b. 1794), who had extensive discussions and debates with Schober in the Linzer Bildungskreis, but rarely had personal contact after 1816 with either Schober or Schubert,[17] has given us the most extensive (and harshest) assessment of Schober's character:

> Schubert's genius subsequently attracted, among other friends, the heart of a seductively amiable and brilliant young man, endowed with the noblest talents, whose extraordinary gifts would have been so worthy of a moral foundation and would have richly repaid stricter schooling than the one he unfor-

> tunately had. But shunning so much effort as unworthy of genius and summarily rejecting such fetters as a form of prejudice and restriction, while at the same time arguing with brilliant and ingratiatingly persuasive power, this scintillating individuality, as I was told later, won a lasting and pernicious influence over Schubert's honest susceptibility. Anyone who knew Schubert knows how he was made of two natures, foreign to each other, how powerfully the craving for pleasure dragged his soul down to the slough of moral degradation, and how highly he valued the utterances of friends he respected, and so will find his surrender to the false prophet, who embellished sensuality in such a flattering manner, all the more understandable. . . . There reigned in this whole family a deep moral depravity, so that it was not to be wondered at that Franz von Schober went the same way. Only he devised a philosophical system for his own reassurance and to justify himself in the eyes of the world, as well as to provide a basis for his aesthetic oracle, about which he was probably as hazy as any of his disciples. . . . The need for love and friendship emerged with such egotism and jealousy that to his adherents he alone was all, not only prophet, but God himself. . . . Anyone who did not worship him exclusively and follow him blindly was unfit to be elevated to his intellectual heights and anyone who eventually turned away from him . . . , he allowed to fall away as being unworthy. These idiosyncrasies also effaced his respect for Mine and Thine, as regards marriage as well as in respect of the property of his followers. Just as he himself gave away what he did not happen to want, he had no hesitation in reclaiming it if he wanted it again . . . ; as regards women he was completely unscrupulous, for he had learned to recognize only two kinds: those with whom he was successful and were therefore worthy of him, and those with whom this was not the case and who were therefore not worthy of him (*SMF,* 85–87).

Kenner's testimony needs to be taken with a grain of salt; nevertheless, he helps us understand Schober's attractions and the direction of his influence.[18] Membership in the circle required at least a qualified endorsement of Schober's philosophy, but as we will see, the circle's appropriation of it did not always wear the unattractive face portrayed by Kenner.

The most revealing character sketch of Schober from within the circle is the 1825 *Sylvesternacht* (New Year's Eve) satire written by Eduard von Bauernfeld (*SDB*, 489–94). In this farcical drama Schober is Pantalon von Przelavtsch. After giving a thorough critique of Columbine's (Anna Hönig's) smallness of bust and shortness of thigh, Pantalon shares the distilled wisdom of his wide experience and study by holding forth at great and flowery length on the virtues of rest and sex (Scene 8). According to Pantalon, the essence of life is rest, embodied superlatively by the plant. The plant does not strive, nor gather; it only lets itself be viewed. But it is not therefore without movement and inner life. It lavishes clouds of scent; that is its movement. And it even allows itself an act, but only one, since there is only one essential act: permitting its manly seed to mix with the female, and so to propagate its noble, godly race. This is the highest vocation, and Pantalon is willing to show the way altruistically, sacrificing class, employment, and profession (*Stand, Beschäftigung, Gewerbe*). Two and a half years later Bauernfeld was still expressing satisfaction at the aptness of this characterization of Schober.[19]

Josef von Spaun (his nickname was "Pepi") played a kind of elder-brother role in the circle. He had been encouraging Schubert's musical talents ever since Schubert first came to the Stadtkonvikt in 1808, where Spaun was running the student orchestra and playing the violin while he pursued his law studies. In those early years Spaun kept Schubert supplied with music paper, gave him his first experiences of opera, and introduced him to an extensive circle of potentially useful social contacts. Spaun got to know Schober through the Linzer Bildungskreis, with which both he and Schober engaged in extensive discussions and correspondence about aesthetic and moral issues, and of which his brother Anton von Spaun (b. 1790) was a central member; when Schober moved to Vienna in 1815 to study law it was likely Spaun who first introduced him to Schubert (*SDB*, 49).

Over the years Spaun continued to be interested and supportive, but receded further into the background when he moved to Linz in the fall of 1821 to become a tax assessor, and then to Lemberg in distant Polish Galicia, where he received his next bureaucratic post. He did not return to live in Vienna until the spring of 1826, and in the meantime participated in the circle chiefly through his letters.[20]

In the years prior to their most intensive time together, the winter of 1822–23, the core members who gathered around Schubert and Schober tended to be young men they knew from preexisting circles. The circle around the poet Johann Chrysostomus Senn (b. 1795), who had been a fellow student of Schubert's in the Stadtkonvikt, contributed at least two important members to the Schobert circle.[21] The student of philosophy Franz von Bruchmann and Schubert had both been part of the Senn circle when it came to an abrupt and traumatic end after the police raided one of its gatherings in March 1820 on the suspicion that it was a nationalist student fraternity in the German mold.[22] The subsequent investigation led to Senn's arrest and internal exile to Tyrol in March 1821; Schubert never saw him again. Schubert first got to know Bruchmann well through Senn, and although Bruchmann had a falling out with Schober shortly after Senn's arrest, he rejoined the group around Schubert and Schober in the summer of 1822.[23] For a short time he became one of the circle's most important members, but by the fall of 1823 he had "lost his halo" (discussed below), and a year later (in the fall of 1824) he precipitated a crisis of loyalty and irrevocably parted ways with his erstwhile friends.

The poet Johann Mayrhofer participated in the Bildungskreis as well as in the Senn circle, although he was not present during the raid that led to Senn's arrest.[24] Schubert had known him since 1814 when he first set one of Mayrhofer's poems (*Am See*, D124) and Spaun then introduced them, but during the years of the Senn circle Mayrhofer was one of Schubert's most constant companions since they also lived together. After the dispersal of the Senn circle Mayrhofer, like Bruchmann, transferred his loyalties to the Schobert circle, but for Mayrhofer his living arrangements with Schubert and his participation in the new circle both ended before the year 1820 was out.

The job Mayrhofer had in the imperial bureaucracy as "dritter Bücherrevisor" (a post in the extensive censorship bureaucracy) conflicted with the ideals of the Senn circle, with those of the Schobert circle, as well as with his own, and even if the other members excused his job as an existential necessity, his attendance would have furnished a constant reminder of the disharmony in which he was living.[25] As Anton Holzapfel later remembered (1858): "Certainly the cleavage between Mayrhofer's inclination and his position in life, for he was compelled to act as a respectable Imperial book censor whereas he was an enthusiastic admirer of intellectual freedom, gave rise to the malady in his extremely sensitive soul and to the difficulty of [Schubert's] living with such a character."[26] Schubert moved out of their apartment toward the end of 1820, perhaps because he and Mayrhofer became estranged, or perhaps because they just found it difficult to live together (*SDB*, 163). He continued to set Mayrhofer's poems to music, and in June 1823 he dedicated his settings of three Mayrhofer poems, Op. 21, to the poet. In all Schubert set nearly fifty of Mayrhofer's poems, second only to the number of poems he set by Goethe.[27] On the other hand, Schubert set no Mayrhofer poems after 1824 (*SDB,* 332).[28] In addition, after 1820 there are only two documented occasions when Mayrhofer participated in an activity at which either Schober or Schubert were present: the 11 November 1823 Schubertiade at Bruchmann's, and the 15 December 1826 Schubertiade at Spaun's.[29] Mayrhofer's distance from the circle after 1820 and from Schubert after 1824 were probably due less to any clash over principles than to Mayrhofer's pessimistic intellectual outlook, at odds with the youthful optimism and idealism of the other members who were about ten years younger, coupled with Mayrhofer's increasingly melancholy, hypochondriac, and misanthropic disposition. Schubert's death was a further blow that nearly put a stop to Mayrhofer's writing.[30] He made an unsuccessful attempt at suicide in 1831, and succeeded in 1836.

Even before Mayrhofer had faded from the picture, the circle gained a new and vital member. During the summer of 1820, the second year Schubert participated in the Atzenbrugg festivals, a new "triumvirate" emerged, consisting of Schubert, Schober, and the painter Leopold Kupelwieser.[31] Schubert probably first met Kupelwieser in 1816 at Professor Heinrich Watteroth's house, where Spaun was then living, but his main point of contact with Kupelwieser may well have been the Unsinnsgesellschaft.[32] Though other members of the circle had some facility at sketching scenes and faces—Schober, for example, who had facility at everything—with Kupelwieser the circle had gained its first serious painter. It soon gained another.

In 1822 Moritz von Schwind began to spend more and more time with the circle, and by the fall of 1823 had become one of its most important members, the younger-brother counterpart to Spaun's elder-brother role in the circle. A later member of the inner circle, Eduard von Bauernfeld, who had known Schwind since school days, wrote the most vivid depiction of him during these years. Bauernfeld's retrospective essay (1869) gives us a glimpse of Schwind's moody temperament, his aesthetic predilections, and his hero worship of Schubert:

> Schwind, an artist through and through, was scarcely less cut out for music than he was for painting. The Romantic element that was in him was now awakened for the first time by the musical creations of his older friend [Schubert]—this was the music for which his soul longed! And so, with all the fervor and tenderness of his youth, he drew close to the master; he was utterly devoted to him and in the same way Schubert, who jokingly called him his beloved, took him

> completely to heart. . . . "The way he composes is the way I should like to paint!" was the cry in his heart. . . .
>
> Although the young artist's nature harbored much that was tender, soft, almost feminine, he often brooded and imagined the worst, was perpetually restless, and suffered self-inflicted doubts about his doings and leavings. . . . He was easily excited, and among friends, when he had hardly sipped wine or punch, he would suddenly cross from darkest brooding to the most frolicsome merriment.[33]

By late 1823 the circle's glory years were over, at least for Schubert. He himself was sick, and Schober and Kupelwieser had embarked on extensive travels abroad, to Breslau (Wrocław) in Silesia, where Schober had gone to escape unwelcome attention while he tried his hand at the socially unacceptable profession of actor, and to Rome, where Kupelwieser had accompanied the Russian nobleman Alexis Beresin as an artistic chronicler.[34] The letters they sent to each other during the course of the following year provide us the best insight as to the nature of the bonds among the friends, and as to how they themselves viewed the significance of the circle.

Schubert to Schober (in Breslau), 30 November 1823:

> Our circle, as indeed I had expected, has lost its central focus without you. Bruchmann, who has returned from his trip, is no longer the same. He seems to conform to the conventions of the world, and already thereby loses his halo, which in my opinion was due only to his determined disregard of all worldly affairs. . . . True, as a substitute for you and Kupelwieser we received four individuals, namely: the Hungarian Mayer, Hönig, Smetana and Steiger, but the majority of such individuals make the circle only more insignificant instead of better. What is the good of a lot of quite ordinary students and officials to us? If Bruchmann is not there, or even ill, we go on for hours under the supreme direction of Mohn hearing nothing but eternal talk about riding, fencing, horses, and hounds. If it continues like this, I don't suppose I'll stand it for long among them. . . . For the rest, I hope to regain my health, and this recovered treasure will let me forget many a sorrow; only you, dear Schober, I shall never forget, for unfortunately, what you meant to me no one else can mean. (*SDB*, 300)

Schwind to Schober (in Breslau), 20 January 1824:

> The greatest things known to me on earth are love, beauty, and wisdom. You have yourself ranked me with you and Schubert, and I could not bear the delight of it. Pain has cleansed me, so that to be third among you means everything to me. (*SDB*, 324)

Schubert to Kupelwieser (in Rome), 31 March 1824:

> At last I can once again wholly pour out my soul to someone. For you are so good and worthy, you will be sure to forgive many things that others would hold very much against me.— In a word, I feel myself to be the most unhappy and wretched creature in the world. . . . Thus, joyless and friendless, would I pass my days, if Schwind didn't visit me sometimes and turn on me a ray from those sweet days of yore.— Our circle (reading circle), as you probably know already, has done itself to death owing to a reinforcement of that rough chorus of beer-drinkers and sausage-eaters, and its dissolution is due in a couple of days—though I have hardly visited it myself since your departure. (*SDB*, 338–39)

Schwind to Kupelwieser (in Rome), 9 June 1824:

> [When I think about] how I long sought you, Schubert, Bruchmann, and was almost ashamed of this seeking, and trembled at the thought of finding you, how I came among you and found myself loved, while I dared wish for nothing more than to see you—how then could I have been different than I was? Now that all are gone, love sinks into the ground, and as vital fellowship has vanished, I am holding fast to appreciation and the essence of things, which is eternal and unshakable. (*SDB*, 351)

Schubert (from Zseliz) to Schwind, August 1824:

> I am still in good health, thank God, and would feel quite comfortable here if only I had you, Schober, and Kupelwieser with me. (*SDB*, 370)

Schober (in Breslau) to Schubert, 2 December 1824:

> You, my good, ever faithful friend, you continue to value my love, you have loved me for my own sake, as my Schwind and Kupelwieser also will remain faithful. And are we not

> precisely those who found our life in art, while the others merely entertained themselves with it, are we not those who solely and certainly understood our inmost natures, as only a German can? (*SDB*, 385)

In these letters and others the special relationship between Schubert, Schober, Kupelwieser, and Schwind is touched on again and again. Even before the open break with Schober, Bruchmann had "lost his halo" (Schubert's letter of 30 November 1823), and the only letter we have that places him within the charmed circle is Schwind's of 9 June 1824, where he names Bruchmann instead of Schober. With that single exception, no other names are poured into the crucible of passionate friendship, although Senn's name continues to be invoked as a distant inspiration.[35]

Whatever else may have comprised what Kenner called Schober's "philosophical system" and his "hazy aesthetic oracle," these letters reveal a commitment to the importance of art as the defining characteristic of the circle. What united them was a vocational commitment to art, of a sort that Schober (born in Sweden) considered possible only for "a German" (letter of 2 December 1824). The friends inspired, shaped, and criticized each other's work (Schubert's letter of 21 September 1824, quoted above). Schober made a distinction between the four friends who "found our life in art" and the others, who found only entertainment, while Schubert emphasized a fellowship of artistic creativity; those unable to produce "children" of their own had no place in it. This is consistent with other evidence: the friends sometimes called themselves the "Canewas" circle, because when a person was under consideration for possible membership, Schubert would invariably ask "Kann er was?" (Can he produce something?).[36] Bruchmann, too, confirmed the supremacy of art and the artist in the circle, although by 1827 when he wrote his lines, he was looking back with a jaundiced eye rather than with nostalgia. As he later recounted, he entered the winter of 1822–23, a winter whose "sparkling life, elevated with music and poetry, stupefied me," with the following credo:

> Only art has value, everything else is worthless. The productive artist is = creator = God. All others are but shades, are empty frumpery, useful only as means serving the ends of the artist. Human liberty is a delusion, an iron fate governs all, and even the gods are not excepted. Life after death is a phantom without proof, and only heroes and artists are immortal, because their fame lives on in the memory of humanity.[37]

If the overriding importance of art and of the creative artist was the creed of the Schobert circle, the Schubertiade was their holy communion at the altar of art. They did not object to fun; the Schubertiade was a party and it was a house concert, but it was also serious. The rapt absorption with which the Schubertians observed their rituals is captured by Schwind's commemoration of the Schubertiade, and Schubert's familiar setting of Schober's poem, *An die Musik* (D547), a hymn to the redemptive power of music, expresses well the religious fervor of their shared commitment.[38]

The intensity and passion of the circle's years from 1819 to 1823 would never return, but for several months in the spring of 1825 an important new friendship compensated partly for the loss of the earlier close-knit circle. Eduard von Bauernfeld drank *Schmollis* with Schubert in February 1825; he, Schubert, and Schwind were soon inseparable.[39] Bauernfeld was a talented author of *Lustspiele* (theatrical comedies); he had a lively mind, a caustic wit, and diligent work habits. The new friendship was soon interrupted, however, for in May Schubert left on a six-month tour of upper Austria with the singer Johann Michael Vogl (b. 1768).

In the summer of 1825 the old friends began to trickle back to Vienna. Schober returned in July, and Kupelwieser in early August (*SDB*, 428, 450); after nearly two years' separation there was at long last a great reunion among the friends when Schubert rejoined them in October (*SDB*, 469). And finally, in late April of 1826, Josef von Spaun returned to Vienna (*SDB*, 522). The old friends, without Bruchmann but joined by Bauernfeld, were all back together again, the circle reconstituted. At least superficially a gradual efflorescence of all its former activities began: it still functioned as a forum for a lively exchange of ideas and opinions; Schubertiades began again in early 1825;[40] the friends resumed their custom of meeting every second day or so at a *Stammlokal* by November 1826 at the latest;[41] and in early 1828 weekly readings of new literary and dramatic works, suspended since 1824, began afresh (*SDB*, 706).

But the circle never quite regained its former importance in the lives of its principal members. They had changed. For one thing they had grown older. No longer were they an idealistic and impressionable group of young men, discovering and inventing a new world together. Not only Schubert and Kupelwieser, but now also Schwind and Bauernfeld had established a record of promising success in his chosen field, and each was extremely involved in his own work.[42] Schober's idleness and lack of focus made for a glaring contrast, and though his friends (especially Schubert) remained loyal to him, his personality and his opinions began to be treated less reverently.[43] Immediately after returning from Rome,

Kupelwieser had lived with Schober for three months (August–October 1825), but soon distanced himself from the circle; by November, Schubert and Schwind were complaining that they hardly ever saw him. Anton Ottenwalt's letter to his brother-in-law Josef von Spaun leaves no doubt that the health of the old circle had not been restored:

> There is *no* circle around him [Schober]; Schwind follows him with slavish devotion, and Schubert too still likes his company, and a certain Bauernfeld is his roommate. . . . He [Kupelwieser] is . . . keeping to himself, so that Schubert and Schwind complain about their faithful old companion, and indeed about the decay of the old fraternity.[44]

The meetings of the reading group (*Lesegesellschaft*) were held every Saturday at Schober's house, with a few new, eager young disciples in attendance; presumably Schubert participated, since he once again lived with Schober.[45] Schober also presided with dependable regularity over the gatherings at the *Stammlokal*, but Schwind and Bauernfeld now frequently found these occasions of insufficient importance to keep them from their work.[46] Consequently a full quorum of friends was rarely present: usually it was just Schober, Schubert, Spaun, and two new drinking companions, Fritz and Franz von Hartmann.

During the early months of 1825 regular weekly Schubertiades had been revived, but on a new basis. They were now held in the home of Josef Witteczek (b. 1787) and his wife, which they shared for a time with Karl Ritter von Enderes (b. 1787). These men had both been introduced to Schubert by Spaun, were both Spaun's age (approximately ten years older than Schubert and Schober), and like Spaun they were art-loving career civil-service bureaucrats.[47] For the rest of Schubert's life either Enderes, Witteczek, or Spaun hosted the Schubertiades in Vienna.[48] They and the colleagues from the civil service they invited, along with wives and other family members, now set the tone on these occasions.[49] The musical evenings were no longer just another activity of the Schobert circle, but became a salon for an older group of bureaucrats and their wives, albeit a salon for which Schubert, Vogl, and the pianist Josef von Gahy (b. 1793) provided the entertainment.

The diffuse group of participants in the Schubertiades, *Stammlokale*, and the *Lesegesellschaft* after the fall of 1825 can be called a revived Schubert circle, but for the most important members of the erstwhile circle this loose agglomeration of activities and personalities was a pale continuation, honoring the vivid memories they cherished of the constitutive role the circle had once played in their lives, without replacing it. The friendships formed between Schubert, Schober, Bruchmann, Kupelwieser, and Schwind from 1820 to 1823, and between Schubert, Schwind, and Bauernfeld in the spring of 1825, had been more passionate, and remained more important, than any subsequent attachments to new members of the circle. Moreover, the ideology and practices of the circle during those years had formed a cohesive whole, had given a meaning and a direction to their lives to which all except Bruchmann remained dedicated. And so it is the friendships among these six men that we must investigate if we wish to understand the significance of the Schobert circle.

Egalitarianism and a Communitarian Ethic

The letters between Schubert, Schober, Kupelwieser, and Schwind, as well as Schubert's "Kann er was?" testify to a fellowship based to a large extent on artistic compatibility and achievement. Implicit in such a (qualified) meritocracy is a refusal to observe the class divisions that governed social relations in the larger society.

Schubert came from a family of schoolteachers, a profession that was respectable but did not pay well.[50] The first summer Schubert spent as a music tutor with the Esterházy family in Zseliz, for example, he earned almost as much each month as he had earned during the whole previous year of teaching for his father (75 florins CM/month as opposed to 80 florins CM/year).[51] Whatever its dignified pretensions to culture and learning, in its economic standard Schubert's family ranked near the bottom of that small minority of Viennese who earned their living through mental instead of physical labor. And, unlike Beethoven, Schubert never made a splash as a virtuoso in the salons of the high nobility, never secured highly aristocratic patrons willing to guarantee him a handsome yearly stipend merely to remain in Vienna, never taught the Archduke, and never cultivated the friendship of the wealthiest nobles in the land.

Schubert's humble background has often been invoked to explain his comparative dearth of hobnobbing with the high nobility. In fact, from his schooldays at the Stadtkonvikt, Schubert was used to socializing with the sons of the nobility, and as an adult many, if not most, of Schubert's friends belonged to the minor nobility. In the inner circle were Ritter von Bruchmann, Ritter von Schober, von Schwind, Edler von Spaun, and later von Bauernfeld; only Schubert, Mayrhofer, and Kupelwieser did not sport the telltale "von."[52] In the circle of next proximate circumference were Baron von Schönstein, Freiherr von Doblhoff, and Freiherr von Grünbühel (Ferdinand Mayerhofer) from the higher aristocracy; Ritter von Uysdael (Walcher), Ritter von Enderes, Edler von Sonnleithner (father and son got their titles in 1828), von Gahy, von Bocklet, von Streinsberg, von Smetana, and the various members of the von Hartmann family. Schubert was used to being treated as an equal by all these people.

In Schubert's fellowship with members of his circle (of whatever circumference), there seems to have reigned a social egalitarianism. This was a prerequisite for the straightforward candor and complete lack of pretense that by all accounts were central to Schubert's character, and that he treasured in his friends. Bauernfeld later wrote about the kind of socializing Schubert disliked:

> His favorite companions were artists and people with artistic affinities. On the other hand he suffered from a genuine dread of commonplace and boring people, of philistines, whether from the upper or middle classes, of the people, that is, who are usually known as "educated"; and Goethe's outcry: "I would rather become worse than be bored," was and remained his motto, as it did ours. Among commonplace people he felt lonely and depressed, was generally silent and apt to become ill-humored as well, no matter how much attention was paid to this man of rising fame.[53]

Just as Schubert did not hold aristocratic titles in awe, neither did formal education in the absence of artistic talent or achievement make someone a desirable companion. Everyone in the group except for Schubert had a background of studies in the Gymnasium, and all except Schubert had at least some university education. Spaun, Mayrhofer, Bruchmann, Bauernfeld, and Schober had all at least begun law studies, and Mayrhofer studied theology as well.[54] Schwind and Kupelwieser studied art at the university, and both later became professors. Schubert knew that his relative lack of formal education was a difference of choice rather than ability; when his voice changed in 1812 he could have chosen to continue his studies at state expense, after which one more year of humanities studies, and two more years of studies in philosophy would have prepared him for university.[55] The Schubert circle certainly did not lack for intellectual acumen or confidence, yet Schubert, despite his lack of formal education, held his own at its center. From the letter Anton Ottenwalt sent to Spaun (27 July 1825) we see that his friends deferred to Schubert not only because of his musical achievements, but also because of the force and persuasiveness with which he could articulate his convictions when he felt at ease:

> We sat together until not far from midnight, and I have never seen him like this, nor heard: serious, profound, and as though inspired. How he talked of art, of poetry, of his youth, of friends and other people who matter, of the relationship of ideals to life, etc.! I was more and more amazed at such a mind, of which it has been said that its artistic achievement is so unconscious, hardly revealed to and understood by himself, and so on. Yet how simple all this was!— I cannot tell you of the extent and unity of his convictions—but there were glimpses of a worldview that is not merely acquired, and the share that worthy friends may have in it by no means detracts from the individuality shown by all this. (*SDB*, 442)

Schubert's egalitarianism was much more than a mere character trait. It formed an explicit part of his ideology, part of what he had in mind when he harshly criticized Bruchmann for "conforming to worldly conventions."

Some of Schubert's friends—Bruchmann, Schober, Spaun—came from relatively well-off families whose money would always provide a cushion if a particular need arose. But other friends—especially Kupelwieser, Schwind, and Bauernfeld—depended like Schubert on their own resources from an early age, and earned their money more or less as freelancers. Kupelwieser began to earn more money at an earlier age than Schubert; by 1815 he was already in a position to support himself largely through the commissions he received.[56] But for all four of these self-supporting artists, what income they had arrived in unpredictable and irregular installments, incompatible with any notions of budgeting. They negotiated the vicissitudes of their precarious economic situation by practicing an informal community of goods. When Schubert was flush, they shared in his good fortune for a while; naturally, with such an arrangement, the money never lasted long.[57] Bauernfeld later gave a vivid description of the sort of life he, Schwind, and Schubert led together in the spring of 1825 (while Kupelwieser was in Rome):

> In the matter of property the communistic viewpoint prevailed; hats, boots, neckerchiefs, even coats and certain other articles of clothing too, if they but chanced to fit, were common property; but gradually, through manifold use, as a result of which a certain partiality for the object always

> ensues, they passed into undisputed private possession. Whoever was flush at the moment paid for the other, or for the others. Now it happened, from time to time, that two had no money and the third—not a penny! Naturally, among the three of us, it was Schubert who played the part of a Croesus and who, off and on, used to be swimming in money, if he happened to dispose of a few songs or even of a whole cycle, as in the case of the Walter Scott songs for which Artaria or Diabelli paid him f500 WW [fl. 200 CM]—a fee with which he was highly satisfied and which he wanted to use sparingly, though this, as always hitherto, remained merely a good intention. To begin with there would be high living and entertaining, with money being spent right and left—then we were short on commons again! In short, we alternated between want and plenty. To one such time of plenty I am indebted for having heard Paganini.[58]

The penurious members also relied on the generosity of the families of the well-to-do members of their circle when necessary, in particular the Schober and Bruchmann families. Schubert repeatedly depended on the Schobers, in their successive residences, to put a roof over his head: they enabled him to leave his parental home when they took him in as a guest from the fall of 1816 until August 1817; he also lived with the family for most of 1822 and 1823, and from March 1827 until August 1828, when they made three rooms available to him, the most living space he ever had to himself. Between 1816 and 1828 Schubert lived with the Schobers approximately four years. Although Schubert had the most occasion to take advantage of it, the Schobers' hospitality also extended to the other members of the inner circle. When Leopold Kupelwieser returned to Vienna in August 1825 from his long trip to Italy, he lived with Schober until he could find other quarters.[59] As soon as Kupelwieser moved out, Bauernfeld moved in, and stayed with Schober from October 1825 until February of the next year (*SDB*, 462). During the spring of 1826, both Schwind and Schubert stayed temporarily with Schober (*SDB*, 931). And in November of 1828, when Schober was near bankruptcy, he nevertheless sent money to Schwind in Munich, so that he could continue his studies there (*SDB*, 828, 899). Schober seems to have squandered most of his family's fortune, assisted by his indulgent mother, but his generosity could always be counted on to help one of his more diligent friends from the inner circle during a cash crisis (*SDB*, 230–31).

In addition to running a boarding house for destitute friends in Vienna, the Schobers made their summer retreat, Atzenbrugg, available to the Schobert circle. Apparently the Bruchmanns did the same with their summer house, Mutwille, from 1819 to 1823 (*SDB,* 278–79). Outside of Vienna, during his long trips of 1819, 1823, and 1825, Schubert was able to depend on Vogl's deep pockets and on the hospitality of the Spaun family and their friends in Linz; his old friend Anton Ottenwalt married Josef von Spaun's sister Marie in 1819, and Josef introduced Schubert to the Hartmann family in July of 1823 (*SDB* 284–85). In Graz Schubert could rely on Karl and Marie Pachler and the brothers Anselm and Josef Hüttenbrenner.

The Sexual Mores of the Circle

Twenty-five years after Maynard Solomon first posed the question, Schubert's homosexuality remains a matter of speculation, unproven and likely unprovable.[60] The strongest evidence that Schubert had sex with men is two references to his need for "peacocks," the first a letter to him from Schwind, the second an entry in Bauernfeld's diary.[61] Bauernfeld explicitly mentions Benvenuto Cellini in this context, while Schwind makes the point that the satisfaction of Schubert's fleshly needs requires money, which his friends do not have. But even these comments are equivocal, since Benvenuto Cellini was not only one of history's most flamboyant homosexuals, but also one of history's best-known syphilitics—and we know that Schubert had syphilis, so the two mentions of Benvenuto Cellini could refer to syphilis without necessarily indicating homosexuality.

As to the other men in the Schobert circle: no one over the last twenty-five years has provided grounds for speculation about the homosexuality of Spaun, Kupelwieser, and Bruchmann. The sexual orientation of the singer Johann Michael Vogl, and of Mayrhofer, Schober, Schwind, and Bauernfeld has been the object of some discussion, but a case for homosexuality for any of the latter three remains flimsy, based on nothing more than the hoariest stereotypes: Kenner's description of Schober as "depraved,"[62] Bauernfeld's description of Schwind as "tender, soft, almost feminine," and Bauernfeld's bachelorhood.

The evidence we do have concerning the sexual lives of Schober, Schwind, and Bauernfeld is unanimously heterosexual. Schober's continual involvement with a series of women, including Spaun's and Bruchmann's sisters, and references to his unscrupulous sexual behavior with women are well documented.[63] Schwind's stormy courtship of Anna "Netti" Hönig has left a pervasive trail in the Schubert documents from 1824 until after Schubert's death, and his involvement with other women both before and after Hönig is also documented.[64] As for Bauernfeld, when he joined the circle in early 1825 he was in love with "Clotilde," and had been so for at least four years.[65] He eventually decided not to marry her (the affair lasted from 1821 to 1826) "because he could not remain true to one woman alone."[66]

Other observations also testify to heterosexual practices: Schwind's jealousy on Netti's account could be easily aroused, as for example on one occasion when Bauernfeld walked her home at night.[67] On another occasion Schubert wrote to Ferdinand von Mayerhofer, who was on a surveying trip in Carinthia, to advise him to be more aggressive in his courtship of Jeanette von Mitis, because Schwind was "comforting" her.[68] Another example: Schober, Schwind, and Bauernfeld "worshipped" a particularly beautiful woman (no matter that she was married), provocatively named Kurzrock.[69] And one last example is Schober writing to Bauernfeld in June 1826: "Schwind's mawkishness also makes him so thankless toward fate that he doesn't even recognize his good fortune. For example, yesterday I met five young women at his place who were with him half the day, one of whom was gorgeous, yes, alluring, and would rather go to Grinzing [than] into the ruins of Windsor, but he is a painter, and will no doubt be looking for antiquities."[70]

Similar examples could fill many pages. They contradict the notion that the friends were united by secret homosexual affinities, and that homosexuality gave the circle its identity and sense of purpose. For though it makes good sense that the friends would use code to describe Schubert's sex life, given the political situation and the possibility that letters would be opened, one cannot reasonably suppose that, if homosexuality (or homoeroticism) was the affinity that gave their circle its identity, they would pepper their correspondence and their private diaries with references to the physical attractiveness of various women, flirtations with women, minute details of the progress of various courtships of women, and petty jealousies and teasings among themselves concerning all of these. That this was an elaborate design to frustrate prying eyes is not only wholly unbelievable, it would have also debased the very currency of their discourse among themselves, which is everywhere revealed as frank and intimate.

In summary, there is plenty of evidence that the primary sexual orientation of Schober, Bruchmann, Spaun, Schwind, Bauernfeld, and Kupelwieser was heterosexual, and no convincing evidence that any of them was bisexual, much less that the primary sexual orientation of the Schobert circle was a homosexual one, and still less that the cohesion and identity of the group depended on its status as a secret homosexual fraternity.

At the same time there is no doubt that a certain tension existed between the identity of the group, the loyalties of its members to one another, and the loyalties exacted by serious courtship and marriage. The break and subsequent feud between Schober and Bruchmann concerned Schober's courtship of Bruchmann's sister, and was the greatest conflagration experienced by the circle, but lesser flare-ups were also due to courtships that called into question the primacy of group loyalties. Sometime between the middle of April and the beginning of July 1825, for example, Schubert took a dislike to Anna Hönig, or at least Schwind felt this to be the case; Schwind remained upset for a time because Schubert seemed to be avoiding his company, and sent him a series of letters, assuring him that Netti had only the highest regard for him and would never have intentionally slighted him.[71]

The men of the circle whose courtships concluded successfully with marriage soon dropped out of the circle. Kupelwieser carried on a long courtship with Johanna Lutz, who participated in the circle's formal activities and kept him well apprised of his friends' doings while he was away in Italy. For the first several years of his courtship it does not seem to have affected at all his relationships within the circle, but by the time Kupelwieser and Johanna married in September of 1826, both confined their participation in the circle's activities to occasional attendance at Schubertiades.

Spaun returned to Vienna in the spring of 1826, after an absence of five years, during which he had served his professional apprenticeship in the provinces. As we have seen, over the next two years he frequently hosted Schubertiades and was one of the most regular participants at the evening *Stammtisch*. On 6 January 1828 he became secretly engaged to Franziska Roner von Ehrenwert; his friends discovered the plans a week later (*SDB*, 713). In his memoirs Spaun wrote about Schubert's reaction: "I was at that time engaged to be married. He said to me, 'While it makes me very sad that we are going to lose you, you are right and have chosen well, and although I ought to be angry with your fiancée I should like to do something to please her. Invite her and I will bring Bocklet, Schuppanzigh, and Linke and we will have some music as well'; and that is what happened" (*SMF*, 138). That was the last Schubertiade hosted by Spaun in Schubert's lifetime, and after his marriage on 14 April 1828, he and his new wife seem to have dropped out of the circle's activities completely.

Marriage seems to have presented more of a problem for the circle than paying for sex or promiscuity. Nowhere do we see any sign that the other members of the circle considered such sexual behavior grounds for reproof or shame, and their tolerant and somewhat casual attitude toward a variety of sexual behaviors would seem to have been privately shared by many Viennese of the time. However, the members of the Schobert circle differed from most Viennese in their attitude toward official, public prudery. This they considered hypocritical, and they were impatient with it.

Two episodes illustrate both the circle's private attitude toward sexual mores, and their desire to view those mores as publicly presentable ideals: their friendship with Katharina von Lacsny, and Bauernfeld's and Schubert's collaboration on the opera *Der Graf von Gleichen* (The Count of Equals—no pun in German).

Katharina von Lacsny (b. 1789) had been a singer at the court opera, was twice married, and rumored to have had many lovers, including several counts simultaneously during the Congress of Vienna. Two letters from Schwind to Schober give us our most revealing glimpse of how he and his friends regarded her. Schwind wrote the letters at a time when he was "ruled completely" by Anna Hönig. But upon first meeting Mme Lacsny, he confided to Schober:

> What a woman! If she were not nearly twice as old as I [thirty-six and twenty-one] and unhappily always ill, I should have to leave Vienna, for it would be more than I can stand. Schubert has known her a long time, but I met her only recently. She takes joy in my things and in me, more than anybody else except you; I had quite a shock the first time, the way she spoke to me and obliged me, as though there were nothing about me she didn't know. Immediately afterward she was taken ill again and spat blood, so that I have not seen her for a long time; but we are to eat there tomorrow. So now I know what a person looks like who is in ill repute all over the city, and what she does.[72]

And two months later:

> She is the only one about whom I care to talk to you, for she is a decisive and mighty figure, who in the greatest welter of temptation and licentiousness remained true to herself and who knows what she must honor. . . . God keep you for me, [and keep] the excellent Schubert and my pious girlfriend.[73]

Schwind's attraction to Mme Lacsny was tempered only by her age and her interruption of their interviews by spitting up blood. He admired her integrity, not in spite of her promiscuity, but rather because of it; she knew herself, and acted upon that knowledge rather than according to convention. And presumably Schwind's admiration was in some measure shared by Schubert, who had known her for a long time, and introduced her to his friend.[74]

Der Graf von Gleichen was the great opera project of Schubert's last years, even though in early 1824 he had given up ambitions of an opera career, at least unless and until conditions at Vienna's opera houses became more favorable to German opera. But in March of 1825, Eduard von Bauernfeld shared with him an idea that forged their friendship (it became the immediate occasion for addressing each other familiarly with "Du"), and brought Bauernfeld quickly into the inner circle (*SDB,* 410). Bauernfeld's proposed opera, *Der Graf von Gleichen*, had as its central conceit the glorification of a bigamous marriage. Bauernfeld eventually wrote the libretto in eight days in May of 1826 while on vacation in Carinthia; Schubert impatiently awaited the results (*SDB,* 530). It features a crusader who returns from the Orient with a second wife. The resulting triangle is so blissful that it inspires the pope to give his blessing. For its backdrop the story contains attractive possibilities for dramatic contrasts between, in Bauernfeld's words, "Orient-Occident, Janissaries-Crusaders, romantic courtship-spousal love, etc., in short a Turkish-Christian stew" (*SDB,* 24). Predictably, the censor forbade the libretto, despite the friends' appeal to the precedent of Goethe's novel about mate-swapping, *Die Wahlverwandschaften* (*Elective Affinities*).[75] The opera had no realistic chance of ever winning approval for performance, nor were the dismal prospects for German opera in Vienna likely to change in the foreseeable future. Nevertheless, Schubert maintained his enthusiasm for *Der Graf von Gleichen*. During the summer of 1827, while he was composing other works that faced no censorship barriers and held at least a promise of furthering his career, he worked on sketches for the opera;[76] deprived of other incentives, his belief in the importance of the opera and its subject can have been his only conceivable motivation for doing so.

Enthusiasm for the *Graf von Gleichen* was not limited to Schubert and Bauernfeld; Schwind also caught the *Gleichen* fever. Approximately a third of his thirty pen-and-ink illustrations for *The Marriage of Figaro* (completed by April 1825) were devoted to portrayals of imaginary guests at the wedding, from the Act 3 Finale of Mozart's opera (*SDB,* 412). For these imaginary guests he chose characters, among others, from *Der Graf von Gleichen*, and from Friedrich Schlegel's novel *Lucinde*, about which we will hear more later.

Der Graf von Gleichen did not necessarily represent in straightforward fashion the sexual ideology of the Schobert circle. After all, Schubert was an artist, not a propagandist. However, *Der Graf von Gleichen* and Schwind's idealization of Frau von Lacsny have in common a skepticism of monogamy, which is seen in both cases as a hypocritical worldly convention. In the Vienna of their day, with its flourishing trade in prostitution (toward which the authorities turned a blind eye, implicitly giving it official sanction and encouragement), it would not have been hard to feel that the traditional official and church-sanctioned monogamous form of marriage represented a pious hypocrisy. Much better to stop pretending. But the idealistic young men of the circle were not ready to concede a disillusioned loss of principle. A higher ideal had to be found, one that could be honestly embraced. Promiscuity, especially of the publicly indiscreet variety, seemed admirable if it had a suitably romantic coloration. Then it became principled promiscuity. The higher ideal was a sexual practice that follows the vicissitudes of the heart.

Religious Nonconformity

Discussions of religious attitudes and convictions within the Schobert circle during the years 1820–25 have left hardly a trace in the available documents; religious beliefs would seem to have been either unimportant to the shared identity of the circle or the circle shared a consensus on religious matters that was so unproblematic as to barely warrant discussion. Those two possibilities are not mutually exclusive, and they may both have been true for a time, but in the years after the circle dissolved, drastic changes in their religious convictions marked those who became alienated from the group—especially Bruchmann—from those whose loyalties remained with Schubert and Schober. Even if religion did not itself become a subject of controversy during the life of the group, it remained a potent indicator of important group-defining beliefs just below the surface.

By the standards of the age the Schobert circle was as a whole not devout. Schober could debate theological points—on at least one occasion he argued against immortality and personal life after death—and his only published work, *Palingenesien* (1826), was a book of sonnets on Old Testament themes (Jean Paul had written a book in 1798 with the same title), but Spaun's mother ended a growing attachment between Schober and her daughter Marie because Schober's behavior and conversation led her to believe he was "not religious."[77] Schwind too, after a lengthy engagement, was eventually rejected by Anna Hönig for his lack of piety; he once told her to "go fall in love with the pope," and later said, "Generally I can tolerate a pretty [*hübsch*] amount of Catholicism, but too much is too much" (*SDB*, 539, 901). Bauernfeld undertook a study of the New Testament in the original Greek with his two roommates in 1823–24, but soon confessed, "I don't possess the talent for faith."[78] But it was Schubert more than any other member of the group who engaged publicly with religious matters, and it is Schubert's views we know the most about.

In Schubert's childhood home religious matters formed a constant source of friction between his free-thinking brother Ignaz (twelve years older than Franz) and his dogmatically orthodox father; Ignaz and Franz formed a furtive alliance in their free-thinking rebellion against their dictatorial father (*SDB*, 105). Schubert's schooling by the Piarist order, and his later friendships with prominent churchmen provided him with further spurs to test and refine his unorthodox convictions. A letter from Ferdinand Walcher saying that he knew full well that Schubert did not "credo in unum Deum" shows that Schubert's unorthodox religious views were both well-enough known, and uncontroversial enough to be brought up in a lighthearted context.[79] Walcher's quotation of the opening of the Credo of the Latin Mass also locates the most public source of Schubert's departure from the norm: the text he used for his six Mass settings.

Schubert's unusual Mass texts were a result of his own conscious, informed choices, as I showed in an article published in 2002.[80] The pattern of excisions in the texts of the Glorias and Credos of Schubert's Latin Masses, combined with dovetailing patterns of telescoping—folding successive phrases together—permits no other conclusion. Contrary to a reception history that remained impressively monolithic right through the celebrations of Schubert's bicentennial, none of the changes Schubert made to the texts can be attributed to ignorance of Latin, ignorance of the orthodox version of the texts, carelessness, forgetfulness, or any other mental shortcoming, or to the existence of a yet-to-be discovered master text that Schubert unwittingly copied.[81]

The dovetailing patterns of excision and telescoping show not only that Schubert meant the words he set, but also that they were important to him. He cared enough about the Mass and the Church to keep composing Masses even though he dissented on key points. He began his life in music as a choirboy, his first great public triumph was the performance of the Mass in F in 1814, and a part of him always remained a church musician. His six Masses and other liturgical compositions kept him involved with churches throughout his life: the Lichtental parish church, St. Augustine's Court church, St. Ulrich's, Alt-Lerchenfelder, and the Dreifaltigkeitskirche. He maintained warm relations all his life with church music directors who included his brother Ferdinand, his first teacher and the dedicatee of his Mass in C, Michael Holzer, and his boyhood friend Michael Leitermayer. Unlike Beethoven's *Missa solemnis*, which, in spite of its complete, orthodox text, has always found a more comfortable home in the concert hall than in the church, Schubert's two late solemn Masses, in spite of their spacious amplitudes, were conceived for the church and are still appropriate there. In those two Masses, in A-flat (1819–22, revised 1826–27) and in E-flat (June 1828), Schubert needed to express something that could only be said in a Mass; he needed to speak to the church.

Certainly he also had professional incentives for writing the last two Masses: he consistently had greater success in gaining a public hearing for his Masses than for his symphonies, and he had some hopes of a Kapellmeister post for which the revised Mass in A-flat could have proved useful. But the time he lavished on the first version of the Mass in A-flat, a letter to Schott in which he listed it as a testament to his "striving after the highest in art,"[82] and the priority he gave to writing his Mass in E-flat after hope of a Kapellmeister post had vanished—all indicate that the Mass meant more to Schubert than a career opportunity. When Schubert decided to write these last two Masses instead of composing more songs, symphonies, or string quartets, it was surely because the Mass allowed him to say something offered by no other genre. And that something could only have concerned his faith and his church, expressed through his music and his text.

Schubert's Mass texts, even when examined with their musical settings, do not directly represent his beliefs but rather an intersection of his beliefs with the affirmations that he believed the words of the Mass expressed. In setting the Mass so that it did not violate his conscience, he would have had to struggle for clarity in his own convictions, avoid affirmations that violated those convictions, and make the most of the affirmations most important to him. Most difficult, he had to decide what to do about those affirmations to which he was relatively indifferent.

The one passage omitted in all of Schubert's Masses is "Et unam sanctam catholicam et apostolicam Ecclesiam" from the Credo; the next most consistently omitted passage, absent in all except the first Mass, is "Et exspecto resurrectionem," also from the Credo. Both of these excisions seem to be instances of Schubert cutting statements that violated his beliefs. Evidently he interpreted "one holy catholic and apostolic church" to mean "one holy (Roman) Catholic church" rather than "one holy universal church," and rejected claims to universal authority by the institutional church. Equally, he felt unable to embrace the statement of belief in the resurrection of the dead.

Schubert also cut passages in order to strengthen a point he wished to make. Beginning with his first Mass he gave a conspicuous treatment to the plea for mercy, "miserere nobis," in the Gloria. From this idea he gradually moved toward strengthening the connection between "miserere nobis" at the center of the Gloria, and the plea for peace, "dona nobis pacem," in the Agnus Dei, first by telescoping some of the text that did not contribute to his conception of the central section of the Gloria, and eventually by cutting that text.

Walther Dürr has traced Schubert's use in his last two Masses of a time-honored musical symbol for the cross, which further strengthens Schubert's textual parallels between the pleas for mercy and for peace.[83] Dürr links the appearances of the musical cross figure to a letter Schubert wrote in 1825 after viewing the site of a massacre of Bavarians by Tyroleans in the Lueg Pass, a letter that comes as close to any testimony we have in Schubert's own words to describing his theology, as well as his attitude toward what he considered hypocritical conventions of piety:

> This . . . they sought, with a chapel on the Bavarian side and a rough cross in the rock on the Tyrolean side, partly to commemorate, and partly, through the use of such holy signs, to expiate. You, glorious Christ, to how many shameful deeds must you lend your image. You yourself, the most gruesome memorial of human abomination, there they set up your image, as if to say: Behold! the consummate creation of the great God we have trampled with impudent feet, would it trouble us to destroy with a light heart the remaining vermin, known as humans? (*SDB*, 467)

Dürr endeavors to show not only how Schubert formally unified his two late Masses but how the themes of Christ's suffering, the suffering of humanity, the futile plea for peace, and the hope of expiation especially permeate and unify the Mass in E-flat.

Another excision, the first one in the Credo, also seems to belong to the category of text cut, not because Schubert objected to it but to strengthen a point made by the remaining text. In his last two Masses the first line of the Credo reads "Credo in unum Deum, factorem caeli et terrae," instead of "Credo in unum Deum, Patrem omnipotentem, factorem caeli et terrae." By cutting "patrem omnipotentem," Schubert gave the opening of the Credo a pantheist emphasis, consistent with more personal statements of faith he set outside the Latin Mass, such as *Die Allmacht* (D852, August 1825) to a poem by the Patriarch (Archbishop) of Venice, Johann Ladislaus Pyrker von Felsö-Eör, and Johann Philip Neumann's *Deutsche Messe* (D872, September 1827).[84]

Pantheism had emerged as the preferred theological emphasis of the so-called Josephinian Enlightenment (from Emperor Joseph II's reign, 1765–90), which had stressed rationalism and the church as a servant of the state, and Neumann and Pyrker were both Josephinian rationalists.[85] Pantheism stresses the all-embracing inclusiveness of God, conceived as divine immanence (the indwelling presence of God), as compared with the emphasis in traditional theism on God's transcendence, or separateness from the world; in practice pantheism emphasized the revelation of God in nature. Schubert's cut of "patrem omnipotentem" thus deemphasized God's transcendence while emphasizing God as the creator of nature. Pantheism was especially congenial to early Romanticism, since it could be interpreted as more critical and rational than traditional Christianity, and at the same time allow the infinite mystery of God to infuse the concrete mundane reality of the natural world. Because of its rational intellectual pedigree, pantheism also appealed widely to the Josephinian church bureaucracy, many of whom retained influential posts until 1848.[86] The mystical and rational strains did not necessarily clash, since they tended to play out in different spheres of activity, the mystical in poetry and the rational in metaphysics.

For the early Romantics, as for the Schobert circle, pantheism also provided a congenial theological counterpoint to their philo-Hellenism. The myths and gods of classical Greek antiquity furnish the imagery that animates most of Johann Mayrhofer's poetry, while the singer Johann Michael Vogl was sometimes called "der griechische Vogel" because of his passion for classical antiquity.[87] But beyond these two worshipers of antiquity, knowledge of Greek myths and even of the Greek language (by Mayrhofer, Bruchmann, and Bauernfeld, at a minimum) was widespread within the group.[88]

The combination of pantheism and a reverence for Greek antiquity was probably most pronounced in Bruchmann's thinking. He later described the shared convictions of the Senn circle (early 1819 to early 1820) thus: "Morality is replaced by a philosophy of totality, Christianity by a new paganism! A great pantheism again becomes the world religion, the circle of blessed gods gathers again!"[89] After two years of relatively solitary study and withdrawal Bruchmann rejoined his friends in the summer of 1822, and later described their shared religion: "There is no evil, there is only the beautiful and the ugly in the world. Consequently everything beautiful is good, and everything ugly is evil. Morality and philosophy are accordingly chimeras, as is religion—especially, as one can easily imagine, the Christian religion. Only the faith of the Greeks is true, because it is beautiful, and it is they alone whom we must imitate."[90] During his most intense time with the Schobert circle, from the summer of 1822 until the spring of 1823, Bruchmann prepared a draft of a grandiose manifesto in the mold of Johann Gottlieb Fichte's "Reden an die deutsche Nation" in which he argued that in order to rebuild the nation Germans should abandon Christianity and follow instead Homeric models, with the goal of remaking "the Germans into perfected Greeks."[91]

By his own account Bruchmann tended to push whatever philosophy or religion he found attractive to its logical extreme. Both in 1820–23, when he embraced pantheism and philo-Hellenism, and in 1827, when he (re)converted to Catholicism, he found pantheism incompatible with Christianity. His descriptions of both the Senn circle and the Schobert circles as pantheistic and anti-Christian were made retrospectively, with all the zeal of the newly converted, so that he deemed almost everything he had believed and done prior to his conversion un-Christian. In the early nineteenth century many Christians who called themselves pantheists, including many churchmen, saw no contradiction. That was probably true of most of the members of the Schobert circle as well, and undoubtedly true of Schubert. Of Schubert we know that the churchmen he most admired and whose words he set were pantheists, and that some of the textual changes he made to the Latin Mass made it more pantheistic. And while the religious feelings of the other members of the circle may have been distinguished primarily for their lack of fervor, we know that Schubert cared about the church—enough to write six Masses and to make his unorthodox convictions a matter of public record.

The Case of Bruchmann

The story of Bruchmann's exit from the circle brings into sharp relief many of the themes I have sketched above, especially the largely submerged but important role of religion. Already as a teenager Bruchmann led a life of great independence, and broke with Catholicism, the faith of his parents.[92] His personal quest led to several years of intensive solitary study of philosophy, particularly Fichte and the more philosophical of the Romantics, Friedrich Schelling, Friedrich Schlegel, and Friedrich Schleiermacher—an inclination toward Idealism and Romanticism that

Senn shared with him. During the time of the Senn circle his admiration for Goethe and Schelling knew no bounds, and he called Schelling the "greatest man our earth has ever borne."[93] After Senn's arrest in early 1820 Bruchmann again withdrew to a life of solitary reflection and study, including a perusal of the journal *Concordia*, which Friedrich von Schlegel (he received the "von" in 1815) had just begun publishing, and whose program included the regeneration of German spiritual and intellectual life by bringing Catholic Christianity to bear on the fields of history, philosophy, and literature. In *Concordia* Schlegel argued for a political and social order with the family as its fundament, the Catholic Church as its crown, and the state in between, in a form similar to the Holy Roman Empire as it had existed up until the Protestant Reformation.[94]

In early 1821 Schelling, who had been silent since 1806, began giving a series of lectures in Erlangen, Bavaria. Bruchmann traveled to Erlangen, and enrolled for the spring semester to hear him lecture in person, although study outside the Habsburg Empire was forbidden to university students.[95] Schelling was lecturing on mythology, part of a larger attempt to address the problem of theodicy, a project that also subsumed his earlier "positive" philosophy, which had been an attempt to convey the complete history of religion through philosophical thought by understanding the world in terms of a history of God. That winter (1821–22) Bruchmann had frequent meetings with Friedrich von Schlegel in Vienna, both alone and in company.[96]

The following summer, when Bruchmann joined the Schobert circle he wrote some poetry in accordance with his and their valuation of the artist above all other creatures.[97] Schubert even set some of Bruchmann's poems, but poetry did not engage Bruchmann's best talents nor could it satisfy his ambitions, and during the months when his involvement with the circle was most intense, during the year "elevated with music and poetry," he found time to sketch out his grandiose Fichtean scheme to remake Germans as perfect Homeric Greeks.

In August 1823 Bruchmann once again journeyed to Erlangen to partake of Schelling, but soon found that what had seemed of world-historical importance two years earlier no longer compelled him. After only two weeks he began his return trip to Vienna. Not only did the gospel of Schelling no longer appeal, but this time the Austrian authorities had been tipped off about Bruchmann's illegal studies abroad, so that he now had a black mark against him that would permanently sabotage a potential career in the vast Austrian civil service.[98]

That November Schubert wrote his letter to Schober complaining that Bruchmann was "no longer the same," that he now seemed "to conform

Figure 3. Franz von Bruchmann. Drawing by Leopold Kupelwieser.

to the conventions of the world."[99] Very likely Bruchmann's changed attitude toward philosophy and Schelling, and Schubert's observation that Bruchmann had become more conformist and conventional had a common source. The previous April Bruchmann had begun courting Julie von Weyrother, a young woman of the high aristocracy who was very pious, who "looked like asceticism personified,"[100] and whose family had held the office of Master of the Horse (*Oberbereiter*) in Austria for more than a hundred years.[101] As he put it later, he began "for the first time since he was a little boy" to think of duty (*Pflicht*) and morality (*Sittlichkeit*).[102] While in Erlangen he was obsessed with thoughts of the "holy institution of the family" (*Heiligthum der Familie*), and could not bring himself to care about Schelling instead.[103] In accordance with his new aspirations (and his father's long-standing wishes), Bruchmann rededicated himself to his law studies, even though his future prospects in Austria now looked bleak (*SDB,* 342).

Bruchmann was soon to give further evidence of changed attitudes and values that put him at odds with Schober and Schubert. His sister Justina had been carrying on a secret courtship with Schober—secret since the Bruchmann parents and especially father Bruchmann disapproved of Schober. Schwind often acted as secret courier, and his vicarious involvement in their affair was sometimes alarmingly intense,[104] but Bruchmann himself also occasionally passed on messages from Justina informing Schober how to time his visits to take advantage of the absence of his father.[105] Sometime in the summer of 1824 Bruchmann changed from collaborator to whistle-blower, and revealed all to his parents.[106] His betrayal of Schober caused a great rift: Schubert and Schwind refused to speak to, or even acknowledge any of the Bruchmann family, while many of the more peripheral members of the circle seemed gleeful that Schober had gotten his comeuppance.[107] This breach in the circle was never healed; Bruchmann and his family remained estranged from Schober, Schubert, and Schwind for the rest of their lives—although not from Kupelwieser, as we shall see.

Bruchmann's beliefs and life soon moved even further from those of Schubert and Schober. At the end of August 1826 he converted to "positive Christianity,"[108] a conversion in which he was following his brother-in-law Josef von Streinsberg's lead. Streinsberg had also been part of the Senn circle, and was present when Senn was arrested, so his change of direction was nearly as radical as Bruchmann's. The next step was to go to confession and resume communion as a Catholic, the faith he had grown up in, which he did on 27 and 28 February 1827.[109] Then came marriage, in which he again followed Streinsberg, who had married Isabella von Bruchmann in January 1826; Franz Bruchmann married Juliane von Weyrother in June 1827.[110] Friedrich von Schlegel and the bride's father were the official witnesses (*Trauzeugen*) on the occasion (*SDB*, 652).

The last of the *Bruchkinder*, as Schubert called them, followed the path of the first two when Justina married Rudolph Ritter von Smetana on 19 November 1828. Justina von Bruchmann's affair with Schober had furnished the proximate cause for her brother's break with Schober, and yet when she married Smetana on Schubert's death day, a member of the triumvirate, Kupelwieser, was one of the official witnesses. Thus, unlike Schubert and Schwind, Kupelwieser was not carrying on a feud with the Bruchmann family on behalf of Schober, nor was he put off by the new piety of the Bruchmann family salon.[111] Not only did he remain on good terms with Bruchmann, but in his religious and private life he had been moving steadily in the same direction as Bruchmann.

During Kupelwieser's stay in Rome in 1824–25 he associated with the Nazarenes, a colony of German artists there who sought national renewal through religious art that took its models not from antiquity, but from the late Middle Ages and Renaissance in Germany and Italy—from artists such as Dürer, Fra Angelico, Giotto, and Raphael. For a time they led a semi-monastic life together inspired by Fra Angelico, but their aesthetic ideals were shaped by the writings of the Romantics, especially Friedrich von Schlegel's *Ansichten und Ideen von der christlichen Kunst* (1802–23).[112] (The Nazarenes also had personal connections to Friedrich Schlegel through his wife, Dorothea, who had two sons from her previous marriage who were both painters and Nazarenes.)[113] Kupelwieser's association with the Nazarenes marked a turn in his creative and professional life; after his return from Rome he dedicated himself almost exclusively to religious art, particularly altar paintings.[114] As with the Bruchmann siblings, Kupelwieser's turn to greater religious fervor was soon followed by his marriage to Johanna Lutz. At the wedding Schubert played dances at the piano and would not cede to anyone else (*SDB*, 554). It is a testament to Kupelwieser's tact and temperate disposition that after the split he managed to remain on good terms with Schubert, Schober, and Schwind, as well as with Bruchmann and his family.

The influence of the Nazarenes on the members and former members of the Schobert circle was not limited to Bruchmann and Kupelwieser. Schwind's teacher in Vienna after 1821 was Ludwig Ferdinand Schnorr von Carolsfeld, whose younger brother Julius was one of the leaders of the Nazarenes.[115] Ludwig Ferdinand did not himself become a Nazarene, but he was profoundly influenced by their ideas, not least by their Catholic piety. He was also a close friend of Schlegel and of the dramatist, mystic, and preacher Zacharias Werner, and like them both he converted to Catholicism (in 1821). L. F. Schnorr von Carolsfeld participated in at least some of the readings and Schubertiades of the Schobert circle in 1821–22, just before his student, Schwind, began spending a lot of time with the circle. Schwind moved from Vienna to Munich in 1828 in part for the chance to work with Peter Cornelius, another important leader of the Nazarenes.[116] In Munich he also worked with Julius Schnorr von Carolsfeld. Both of the painters in the circle, Kupelwieser and Schwind, were thus very closely involved with the Nazarenes, although Schwind followed their painterly ideas, particularly the ideal of Raphael's beautiful line and clear shapes, rather than their religious ones.

The final steps in Franz von Bruchmann's journey away from Greek paganism and the gospel of art and away from Schubert and Schober took him a step beyond even Kupelwieser and the Nazarenes to monasticism. Like his first step toward religion, this ultimate step involved his family. First, his sister Justina died from complications of childbirth (25 August 1829), and her widower husband, Smetana, joined the Redemptorist order (12 November 1829). Next, his wife, Juliane, also died from complications of childbirth (26 October 1830). After a year of self-imposed preparation in Rome with the Nazarenes, Franz von Bruchmann followed his brother-in-law into the Redemptorist order (3 July 1831). Smetana rose to the position of General-Vikar, and Bruchmann became head of the German province of the order, serving in that capacity until two years before his death in 1867 (*SDB*, 950, 959).

The Redemptorists were a missionary order, founded in 1732, whose major work was the preaching of parish missions, retreats, and novenas, especially to the poor.[117] Its members took vows of poverty, chastity, and lifelong obedience.[118] In the first two decades of the nineteenth century their leader Clemens Maria Hofbauer worked tirelessly to promote the restoration of papal influence in Habsburg lands, seeking to undo both the inroads that Enlightenment rationalism had made in the Church and the control the state had seized over the Church under the Josephinian Reforms.[119] Because of "the prevalent spirit of Josephinism," the Redemptorists were not able to establish their first canonical house in Vienna until 1820, several months after Hofbauer had died.[120]

If Clemens Maria Hofbauer was the "heart and soul of the Roman Catholic revival," the "intellectual leader of the Roman Catholic restoration movement" was Friedrich von Schlegel.[121] In the years before his death Hofbauer was an "almost daily guest" in the home of Schlegel and his wife, Dorothea.[122] As we have seen, Schlegel was also important to the Nazarenes, a close personal friend of Schwind's teacher, Ludwig Ferdinand Schnorr von Carolsfeld, and since the winter of 1821–22 a frequent advisor and interlocutor to Bruchmann.

Bruchmann's religious journey had taken him from aesthetic paganism to Catholicism, to the Nazarenes, and to the ultramontane Redemptorists. His intellectual journey had taken him from being an ardent disciple of Schelling to being a follower of Friedrich von Schlegel—or at least a follower of the person Schlegel had become since his conversion to Catholicism and move to Vienna in 1808: the religious mystic, the apologist for Habsburg absolutism to the German people, and the spokesman for papal absolutism to German speaking lands.[123] By 1820 Friedrich von Schlegel had become the very embodiment of reactionary Romanticism, which Heinrich Heine was to skewer in *Die romantische Schule* (1835). But the publisher of *Concordia* had also once published *Athenäum*, and the author of "Ansichten und Ideen von der christlichen Kunst" had once written *Lucinde*. The split between Schubert and Schober on the one hand and Bruchmann on the other was also in many ways a split between the values espoused by the Friedrich Schlegel who helped found the Romantic movement in the last years of the eighteenth century and the Friedrich von Schlegel who lived and worked in Vienna during the 1820s.

“Some half-understood phrases from *Lucinde*”

The members of the Schobert circle believed first and foremost in the value of art and were artists, not critics and philosophers. Although Josef Kenner disparaged Schober's “philosophical system,” it is possible that they never felt it necessary to articulate a unifying rationale for the disparate traits of their community: artistic freedom, religious freedom, social egalitarianism, a loose community of goods, and an ideal of sexual freedom according to which sex should be at liberty to follow the pathways of sentiment. But the ideals and practices of the Schobert circle in the early 1820s are strikingly reminiscent of the ideals first propounded by the founders of the Romantic movement in Berlin and Jena twenty-five years earlier, and that congruence did not arise by chance. A work that the Schobert circle embraced as particularly relevant to their fellowship was also one of the seminal texts of early Romanticism: Friedrich Schlegel's semi-autobiographical novel *Lucinde* (1799).

Within the Schobert circle the lovers and chief characters of the novel, Julius and Lucinde, were closely identified with Schober and Justina von Bruchmann. In Bauernfeld's 1825 *Sylvesternacht* satire, the speech that he wrote for Schober's character, Pantalon von Przelavtsch, is a parody of *Lucinde*, combining much of the language of a famous passage in the novel with the sexual theme of the rest of the novel.[124] The passage comes from a section titled “Idylle über den Müßiggang” (Idyll on Idleness), in which Schlegel, speaking through his semi-autobiographical character Julius, questioned the work ethic of modern civil society:

> What is the point of all this striving and progress without interruption and focal point? Can this storm and stress give nourishing sap or a pleasing shape to the infinite plant of humanity, which grows by itself and shapes itself in silence? This empty, restless striving is nothing but a Nordic perversity, and produces nothing but boredom. . . . Industriousness and utility are the angels of death with the fiery sword, who bar to humans the return to paradise. Only with calm acceptance and meekness, in the holy silence of true passivity, can one remember one's whole self, and contemplate the world and life. . . . To sum it all up: the more godly a person or a person's work, the more they will resemble a plant, which is among all the forms of life the most moral, and the most beautiful. And thus the most perfectly consummated life would be nothing but a pure vegetating.[125]

Figure 4. *Friedrich von Schlegel.* Charcoal drawing by Philipp Veit, ca. 1810.

In other sections of *Lucinde,* Schlegel celebrated sensuality, lust, and sexual fantasy. When the novel was first published many considered it scandalous partly because Julius and Lucinde seemed to represent in undecently unveiled fashion Friedrich Schlegel and Dorothea Veit, Moses Mendelssohn's oldest daughter, who at the time was still married to Simon Veit. A generation later the novel was still controversial, hailed by the like-minded as the "proclamation of the emancipation of the flesh," and condemned by critics as "an expression of naked sensuality."[126] Schlegel had begun the Romantic campaign in a similar vein, with some aphorisms (*Fragmente*) in the first issue of his journal *Athenäum* (1798) designed to *épater les bourgeois*. Nothing could be more hypocritical, Schlegel argued, than the prevailing prudery, "the affectation of innocence without innocence." Most modern marriages were in his view little better than concubinage; in enforcing them the state prevents true marriage, which is a unity of souls. Then Schlegel added a few lines designed to shock: "It is difficult to see what one could reasonably object to in a marriage *à quatre*."[127]

Lucinde consistently celebrates those vices that Schober cultivated most egregiously, idleness and lasciviousness, and no doubt one of the reasons Schober was not offended by Bauernfeld's playlet was that he was flattered by the implied analogy between himself and the young Schlegel. Justina von Bruchmann, for her part, was identified with *Lucinde* to such an extent that after the Bruchmann-Schober rift Schwind hurried to hide his drawings of some characters out of *Lucinde* when Schubert and Bauernfeld unexpectedly came calling.[128]

Bruchmann corroborated the importance of *Lucinde* to the Schobert circle. After his conversion he described it, along with Schleiermacher's *Reden über die Religion* (*On Religion: Speeches to Its Cultured Despisers*) and Schelling's early works, as putting the final touches on what he had already arrived at through studying Fichte, namely a nihilism that denied good and evil.[129] This was the "wisdom" with which Bruchmann entered the Senn circle, and when after Senn's arrest that circle dissolved into two groups, the group he later rejoined, the Schobert group, was characterized by "dedicating their whole lives to pleasure, and a fairly material pleasure at that, and they propped up this shabby bit of wisdom with some half-understood phrases from *Lucinde*, while the other group was too honest and conscientious to let these kinds of principles guide life, art, and science."[130] Remarkably, even after his conversion, when he was ready to damn almost all he had held dear prior to it, Bruchmann remained reluctant to categorically condemn *Lucinde*; he implies that his erstwhile friends' wisdom would have been less shabby had they understood *Lucinde* better! Indeed, in a letter Schwind wrote to Schober, he complained about the difficulty of understanding *Lucinde*: "I'm reading *Lucinde*, but can't make any progress. Those things I understand I'd like to memorize right away; those I don't I read three or four times to convince myself that hastiness is not the cause."[131]

Bauernfeld's New Year's Eve satire, the work of literature most closely identified with Justina von Bruchmann, and Franz von Bruchmann's post-conversion condemnation of the Senn circle and the Schobert circle had in common Schlegel's *Lucinde*. Whether parodied, celebrated, or condemned, the friends seemed to agree on *Lucinde* as a defining text of the Schobert circle, and as a kind of representation of the circle itself, particularly of the constitutive part Schober played in it.

Lucinde had been one of the most radical of the early Romantic critiques of bourgeois society and the emerging industrial economy in Germany. The "Idylle über den Müßiggang" was part of a broader challenge to a new kind of consumer, someone the Romantics called a philistine. For the philistine nothing had intrinsic worth, value could be reduced to price, and in general, life was reduced to its economic side. For the sake of comfort and security the philistine was willing to spend his time in mindless repetitive routines and conform to the moral, religious, and political status quo. Worst of all, the philistine reduced social relationships to means of achieving mutual economic benefit. To oppose the new materialism the Romantics sought to create a true community of love, which they felt could only be achieved through an open exchange between individuals freed of the pressure to conform. Art would play a crucial role in such a community, awakening all the powers of human empathy and imagination needed to participate in the education of the whole personality, in *Bildung*. Art could inspire to action where reason alone would fail, and art would restore the magic, beauty, and mystery of the natural and social world, so that the individual could again feel at one with it.[132]

Lucinde as embraced by the Schobert circle displayed the reciprocal relationship between criticism, art, love, sex, and community as the young Romantics had conceived of it. In Schlegel's allegorical exposition of his philosophy in *Lucinde* the same work both disrupted old habits of thought and then healed. The healing function, the spirit of love that is the bond of the true community, and must according to Schlegel be "invisibly visible" everywhere in the work, is present in *Lucinde* both as prose about sex and more abstractly in the purpose of the novel as a whole.[133] *Lucinde* helps us understand not only the sexual attitudes of the members of the Schobert circle, but also how and why they construed those attitudes as criticism, and why Schubert cared so much about preparing *Der Graf von Gleichen* for the public, against all odds. The reciprocal functions of *Lucinde* also help us understand why Schubert and Schwind seemed to feel that Bruchmann's betrayal of Schober was more than personal, why it was also a betrayal of the core beliefs of the Schobert circle.

Schlegel's quest for community was the constant that guided his political shift from liberal reformer to supporter of Clemens von Metternich,[134] but his vision of the utopian community held together by love and mutual obligation between free and equal persons came to focus more and more on an ahistorical, idealized model of German feudalism in the Middle Ages, supported by a resurgent Roman Catholic Church. The members of the Schobert circle, with their much less grandiose vision for changing the world, probably realized as closely as possible within their small countercultural circle Schlegel's original vision for a community of love; and their modest and fragile version of the utopian community allowed them—unlike Schlegel—to retain Schlegel's original political views. On an ideological level, Bruchmann's estrangement from his friends in the circle can be seen as a rift between early and late Romanticism; or, more accurately, a rift between a second-generation Romanticism that kept the ideals of early Romanticism but scaled down its political ambitions and a second-generation Romanticism that kept its grand political ambitions but changed its ideals to accommodate them. But it was also a rift between those, as Schober put it, "who found our life in art," and those like Friedrich Schlegel and Bruchmann who were more philosophers than artists, who were inspired by the much grander vision of a community shaped by the German nation and Christianity.

NOTES

1. Otto Erich Deutsch, ed., *Schubert: A Documentary Biography*, trans. Eric Blom (London, 1946), 784 (hereafter *SDB*), contains a partial key to Schwind's drawing, which is reproduced on the facing page. Maurice J. E. Brown, "Schwind's 'Schubert-Abend bei Josef von Spaun,'" in his *Essays on Schubert* (London, New York, 1966), 155–68, gives a history of the Schwind drawing. The Kupelwieser painting is reproduced on the page facing, *SDB,* 484.

2. Otto Erich Deutsch, ed., *Schubert: Memoirs by His Friends*, trans. Rosamond Ley and John Nowell (London, 1958), 370 (hereafter *SMF*).

3. The documents Deutsch collected and annotated are still the starting point for any Schubert scholar. He first published these in German in 1913, then in a revised English version as *SDB*; then a U.S. version, *The Schubert Reader: A Life of Franz Schubert in Letters and Documents* (New York, 1947); and finally again in German, Otto Erich Deutsch, ed. *Schubert: Die Dokumente seines Lebens* (Kassel, 1964) (hereafter *DsL*). Although in this article quotations from these documents cite *SDB*, I have often amended the somewhat Macaulayesque translations.

4. That is, anyone with whom Schubert drank brotherhood and with whom he was therefore on a familiar "Du" basis. See the explanation of "drinking brotherhood," *SDB,* 296.

5. A regular gathering in a pub.

6. The school run by the Piarists at which Schubert was a scholarship student. See *SDB,* 7–8, for more on the term and the variety of students in the Stadtkonvikt.

7. David Edward Gramit, "The Intellectual and Aesthetic Tenets of Franz Schubert's Circle: Their Development and Their Influence on His Music" (PhD diss., Duke University, 1987). For the dates of the circle's formation, see 32; see Appendix 1, 376–91, for correspondence with or about Schober, including letters written by Anton Spaun, Anton Ottenwalt, Josef Kenner, and Josef Spaun.

8. Rita Steblin, *Die Unsinnsgesellschaft: Franz Schubert, Leopold Kupelwieser und ihr Freundeskreis* (Vienna, 1998); see 11, 44, for the membership list.

9. Moriz Enzinger, introduction and ed., *Franz v. Bruchmann, der Freund J. Chr. Senns und des Grafen Aug. v. Platen: Eine Selbstbiographie aus dem Wiener Schubertkreise nebst Briefen* (Innsbruck, 1930), 128–29; all translations are mine.

10. Steblin, *Unsinnsgesellschaft*, 2–5.

11. See Rita Steblin's essay on the Nonsense Society in this volume.

12. Hans Joachim Kreuzer, "Freundschaftsbünde–Künstlerfreunde: Das Erbe von Aufklärung und Empfindsamkeit im Schubert-Kreis und seine Verwandlung im romantischen Geist," in *Schubert und Brahms: Kunst und Gesellschaft im frühen und späten 19. Jahrhundert. Dokumentation der Veranstaltungsreihe der Hochschule für Musik und Theater Hannover 3.–25. November 1997,* ed. Arnfried Edler (Augsburg, 2001), 80–81. Kreuzer postulates that in the Schubert circle starting in 1820–21 a new culture of sociability (*Geselligkeitskultur*) in which music was central replaced the old understanding of (male) friendship that was centered on language and literature.

13. For Schubert's use of "Schobert," see *SDB,* 98. Another conflation would be that used by Friedrich von Schlegel writing to Schwind's teacher, Ludwig Ferdinand Schnorr von Carolsfeld, who spoke of "Dein Schober- u. Schuber-Dienstag" (*SDB,* 254).

14. Schubert to Spaun, 7 December 1822 (*SDB,* 248). The Schubertiades were held most regularly (once a week at Schober's on Tuesdays) from about December 1822 to about April 1823.

15. Sent from Zseliz to Breslau, *SDB,* 374. Swind was Schubert's nickname for Schwind, while the whole group called Kupelwieser Kuppel.

16. See John M. Gingerich, *Schubert's Beethoven Project* (Cambridge, 2014).

17. *SMF,* 85, 89.

18. On the love-hate relationship that leading members of the Linzer Bildungskreis, especially Kenner and Anton Ottenwalt, had with Schober, see Ilija Dürhammer, "'Affectionen einer lebhaft begehrenden Sinnlichkeit': Der 'Schobert'-Kreis zwischen 'neuer Schule' und Weltschmerz," in *Schuberts Lieder nach Gedichten aus seinem literarischen Freundeskreis: Auf der Suche nach dem Ton der Dichtung in der Musik. Kongressbericht Ettlingen 1997*, ed. Walther Dürr, Siegfried Schmalzriedt, and Thomas Seyboldt (Frankfurt, 1999), 39–58.

19. Bauernfeld to Ferdinand von Mayerhofer, 27 August 1827, in *Neue Dokumente zum Schubert-Kreis: Aus Briefen und Tagebüchern seiner Freunde*, ed. Walburga Litschauer (Vienna, 1986), 67; all translations are mine.

20. *SDB,* 418. After April 1826 Spaun returned to Vienna to take up the office of Third Assessor for the state lottery commission (*SDB,* 522).

21. Senn himself described this circle retrospectively (1849) as arising spontaneously from the spirit left behind by the "wars of liberation" (*Befreiungskriege*) of 1813–15 and specifically mentioned Mayrhofer and Schubert as contributors. See Werner Aderhold, "Johann Chrisostomus Senn," in *Schuberts Lieder nach Gedichten aus seinem literarischen Freundeskreis*, 99, 107, citing Hugo Klein (1921).

22. After August von Kotzebue, a dramatist of absolutist political views, was assassinated in 1819 by a student, the authorities regarded all student fraternities as extremely suspicious (*SDB,* 129). See Enzinger, *Franz v. Bruchmann,* 129–31, for details on Senn's arrest.

23. See the letter Senn wrote to Bruchmann, 28 April 1820, in which he says that since he is being forced to choose between Bruchmann and Schober he will choose Schober (Enzinger, *Franz v. Bruchmann,* 287–88). In an undated letter, estimated by Enzinger as written in February 1822 (291–93, 360), Senn agrees to resume friendship. Bruchmann gives the summer of 1822 as the time when he "once again entered into closer relations with that portion of our earlier group of which I spoke earlier, which had anchored the ἐν και παν [*en kai pan* or "one and all"] 'of its wisdom in the enjoyment of life'" (216, my translation).

24. Ibid., 128–29. See also Ruth Melkis-Bihler, "Politische Aspekte der Schubertzeit," in *Schuberts Lieder nach Gedichten aus seinem literarischen Freundeskreis*, 92, where Senn and Mayrhofer were two of twelve persons listed, presumably by the police, as belonging to a "burschenschaftlicher Kreis" (fraternity).

25. *SDB,* 44. Josef Spaun said that Mayrhofer was "extraordinarily liberal-minded, yes even democratic," and when Spaun kidded him about his reputation as a strict censor, Mayrhofer said his duty and his opinion differed. Spaun, "Aus den Lebenserinnerungen des Joseph Freiherrn von Spaun," ed. Carl Glossy, *Jahrbuch der Grillparzer Gesellschaft* 8 (1898), 295. Mayrhofer was appointed as "dritter Revisor" in November 1814, about the same time he first got to know Schubert. Michael Lorenz, "Dokumente zur Biographie Johann Mayrhofers," *Schubert durch die Brille* 25 (June 2000): 29-30.

26. *SMF,* 63.

27. However, there are more Schubert settings to poems by Schiller, more than sixty settings to more than thirty poems, than settings to poems by Mayrhofer, since Schubert often set and reset the same Schiller poem in several versions.

28. Mayrhofer's poems were published in Vienna in October 1824 while Schubert was in Zseliz (Lorenz, "Dokumente zur Biographie Johann Mayrhofers," 47), which would explain the absence of Schubert's name from the list of subscribers if the poems were subscribed after the end of May when he left for Zseliz. Now in Slovakia, Zseliz was then part of the Habsburgs' Hungarian lands.

29. *SDB*, 302, 571.

30. Adam Haller quoting Feuchtersleben: "Mayrhofer's genius is wasting away, since with Schubert's death his life has lost its harmonization" (*SMF*, 56; my translation).

31. In a letter to Schober (5 March 1822), Josef von Spaun refers to Schober, Schubert, and Kupelwieser as the "poetisch-musikalisch-malerische Triumvirat" (*SDB*, 212–13).

32. Steblin, *Unsinnsgesellschaft*, 109; *SDB*, 58–59.

33. In *SMF*, 239, from a lengthier passage in Eduard von Bauernfeld, "Jugendfreunde—Schwind und Schubert" (hereafter "Jugendfreunde"), chap. 4 in "Aus Alt- und Neu-Wien," *Gesammelte Schriften von Bauernfeld*, vol. 12 (Vienna, 1873), 63–66.

34. Schober left Vienna in August 1823 for Breslau and returned in July 1825 (*SDB*, 287, 428); Kupelwieser left Vienna on 7 November 1823 and returned in August 1825 (*SDB*, 295–96).

35. Otto Stoessl, *Moritz von Schwind: Briefe* (Leipzig, n.d. [1924?]), 21, 27, 31; *DsL*, 203.

36. *SDB*, 178. The name "Canewas" is said to date from the time when Wasserburgers Café was the *Stammlokal* of the Schobert circle, that is, 1822. Schober later couched his rejection of Ferdinand Sauter (Dinand) in similar terms: "He doesn't contribute anything to the society" (*SDB*, 564).

37. Enzinger, *Franz v. Bruchmann*, 218.

38. Walther Dürr, in "'Tatenfluten' und 'bessere Welt': Zu Schuberts Freundeskreisen," in *Schubert und Brahms: Kunst und Gesellschaft im frühen und späten 19. Jahrhundert*, 92, discusses *An die Musik* as the "Motto" for what he calls "the Schober circle" and traces the poem's connections to Friedrich Schlegel's understanding of "Universalpoesie" and "Universalkunst" from *Athenäum* Fragment 116 (1798).

39. *SDB*, 403; "Jugendfreunde," 76; *SMF*, 227.

40. After a year's hiatus, a Schubertiade was hosted on 29 January 1825 by Enderes and Witteczek (*SDB*, 397). They continued to be held on a weekly basis for four months until April 1825 (*SDB*, 401) and then were not resumed with regularity until December 1826 (*SDB*, 571). But Schwind did not find the new Schubertiades entirely satisfying: "a mix of faces that are all the same," he reported to Schober (*SDB*, 401).

41. Records of these meetings survive mostly in the diaries of the Hartmann brothers, whom Schubert knew from visiting their family in Linz. Fritz and Franz had both been students in Vienna for several years, but only started socializing with the Schobert circle in November 1826 (*SDB*, 564).

42. At the end of August 1825, Bauernfeld was preparing to translate *The Comedy of Errors* (Litschauer, *Neue Dokumente*, 30), for the Sollinger (Trentsensky) edition of Shakespeare. During the next three years he also translated Shakespeare's sonnets and poems (*SDB*, 548) and *The Rape of Lucrece* (Litschauer, 60) and wrote three comedies of his own, *Der Zweifler*, *Leichtsinn und Liebe*, and *Der Brautwerber (SDB*, 663).

Schwind worked on etchings for Weber's *Freischütz* in September 1824 (*SDB*, 373); he had also finished thirty pen and ink drawings, *Der Hochzeitszug des Figaro*, by March of 1825 (*SDB*, 412). He then began producing *Mandelbogen* (single sheets with cutout figures) for Trentsensky, as well as slipcovers and two large vignettes for the volumes of the Viennese Shakespeare edition (*SDB*, 462, 471); he also illustrated various poems (*SDB*, 676–77).

43. See, for example, the New Year's Eve 1825 satire by Bauernfeld (*SDB*, 486–501); a difference of opinion between Schober and Spaun over Schubert's piano sonatas, Opp. 42 and 53, which Schober disliked (*SDB*, 589); an argument between Schober and Spaun over duels (*SDB*, 704); Bauernfeld's diary, end of March 1826, "Schubert and

I hold together against many a Schobertian foolishness; Moriz sways back and forth" (Litschauer, *Neue Dokumente*, 38); an argument between Bauernfeld and Schober about "nationality," September 1826 (Litschauer, 52), which led to a lengthy exchange of letters between them before they were reconciled. Bauernfeld and Schober had another quarrel, 6 March 1827, because Bauernfeld satirized Schober's habit of spending evenings at the tavern, which Schober "bore about as well as the lion does the crowing of the rooster" (Litschauer, 59). In March 1827 Bauernfeld wrote in his diary, "Schwind and Schober ever more in conflict. Schober's total lack of occupation and his relationship with a woman of our circle are the chief sources" (Litschauer, 60).

44. Ottenwalt to Spaun, 27 November 1825, my translation and emphasis (see also *SDB*, 476). Kupelwieser married on 17 September 1826 (*SDB*, 554), and thereafter he and his wife made only one (recorded) appearance at a function of the Schobert circle, namely on 15 December 1826, at Spaun's first festive Schubertiade (*SDB*, 573–74).

45. At the very least the *Lesegesellschaft* met on 5, 12, 19, 26 January 1828; 2, 9, 15 February 1828, with Karl Enk von der Burg, Franz von Hartmann, Ferdinand Sauter, and Hieronymus von Kleimayrn in attendance; 23 February 1828; 1, 8, 15, 22, 29 March 1828; 5, 23, 26 April 1828, 21 June 1828; 12, 19 July 1828; 2 August 1828 with Enk, Josef Bayer, and Franz von Hartmann.

46. See *SDB*, 662. In 1827, for example, Schwind did not attend a tavern (*Beisel*) with his friends in January, attended only three times in February, three times in March, once in April, and once in June, not again until he left for Munich in August, and not again after he got back in October. By comparison, Schubert, Schober, and Spaun frequented a *Beisel* together between two and three times a week whenever they were in town. Bauernfeld attended these gatherings even less frequently than Schwind. His diary entry of 21 February 1826: "This week I receive the last of the Shakespeare money from Trentsenski. — Now what? Unde vivam? — Otherwise I spend a lot of time alone working hard. The friends have nicknamed me "Caveman" [*Spelunk*] since I seldom creep out of my cave in Landstraße [a suburb of Vienna]" (Litschauer, *Neue Dokumente*, 38).

47. Witteczek married Wilhelmine Watteroth (b. 1800) in 1819; she was the daughter of law professor Heinrich Josef Watteroth, who had taught Spaun (*SDB*, 302). Witteczek was a Hof- und Staatskanzleikonzipist (*SDB*, 573–74). In 1825 Enderes was Konzipist in the Finanzministerium (*SDB*. 397), a Konzipist being someone with an academic education waiting for an appointment to a civil service post with life tenure (a *Beamte*) (*SDB*, 569).

48. The one exception was a Schubertiade hosted by Karl Hönig on 16 December 1826 (*SDB*, 573). Outside of Vienna there was a Schubertiade at Retz near the Moravian border, hosted by Prof. Vincentius Weintridt and Schwind, and several in Graz, hosted by the Pachlers.

49. For many of these Schubertiades we have a fairly complete guest list. The evening at Spaun's on 15 December 1826 is representative (*SDB*, 571–72).

50. See Herwig Knaus, *Vom Vorstadtkind zum Compositeur* (Vienna, 1997).

51. *DsL*, 64–65, 592–93. CM refers to Conventionsmünze; four florins CM were worth ten florins WW (Wiener Währung).

52. The titles are not redundant: "Freiherr" was better than "Ritter," which was better than "Edler," which was better than plain "von."

53. *SMF* 230; "Jugendfreunde," 81.

54. On Mayrhofer, see Lorenz, "Dokumente zur Biographie Johann Mayrhofers,"and Spaun, "Aus den Lebenserinnerungen des Joseph Freiherrn von Spaun," 294.

55. Both a week before and two days after the great victory over Napoleon at Leipzig in October 1813, the "Völkerschlacht," Emperor Franz found the time personally to approve papers granting a continued scholarship to Schubert, on the condition of raising his mathematics grade from a "2" to a "1" (*SDB*, 34–37).

56. Constant von Wurzbach, *Biographisches Lexikon des Kaiserthums Oesterreich*, 60 vols. (Vienna, 1856–91), 13:292–96. Kupelwieser needed to start earning his own money at the

age of seventeen when his father died on 27 May 1813. See Rupert Feuchtmüller, *Leopold Kupelwieser und die Kunst der österreichischen Spätromantik* (Vienna, 1970), 12.

57. Bauernfeld's diary, August 1826: "Schubert without money, as are all of us" (*SDB,* 548). See also *SDB,* 451, 805–6; and Litschauer, *Neue Dokumente*, 56.

58. *SMF,* 228–29; "Jugendfreunde," 77.

59. Kupelwieser wanted to get married as soon as possible upon his return, and initially seems to have planned to stay with Schober until the wedding (*SDB,* 451), but plans must have changed, since he did not get married until September 1826 (*SDB,* 554), although he had moved out of Schober's apartment almost a year earlier (*SDB,* 462).

60. See Maynard Solomon, "Franz Schubert and the Peacocks of Benvenuto Cellini," *19th-Century Music* 12 (1989): 193–206; and a special issue of that journal entitled *Schubert: Music, Sexuality, Culture*, edited by Lawrence Kramer, and including Rita Steblin's response, "The Peacock's Tale: Schubert's Sexuality Reconsidered," *19th-Century Music* 17(1993): 5–33; as well as Kristina Muxfeldt, "Political Crimes and Liberty, or Why Would Schubert Eat a Peacock?" *19th-Century Music* 17(1993): 47–64; and Maynard Solomon, "Schubert: Some Consequences of Nostalgia," *19th-Century Music* 17 (1993): 34–46; and Charles Rosen, *New York Review of Books*, 20 October 1994.

61. Schwind to Schubert, 14 August 1825 (*SDB,* 451), and Bauernfeld's diary entry, August 1827 (*SDB,* 548).

62. *SMF,* 85–87. Note that Kenner considered Schober's whole family "depraved," including his mother.

63. From Schober's courtship of Marie von Spaun prior to 1819 (*SMF,* 350), to Bauernfeld's diary in March 1827 when he reported spats between Schwind and Schober over Schober's relationship with a "woman from our circle" (Litschauer, *Neue Dokumente*, 60).

64. Schwind first became interested in Hönig on 22 February 1824 (Stoessl, *Schwind Briefe*, 27–28), in part because she had the same name as his earlier infatuation, Netti Prunner (*SDB,* 196; Stoessl, *Schwind Briefe*, 22, 24, 25); the earliest indication of a relationship between Schwind and Hönig in the Deutsch documents is April 1825 (*SDB,* 411–12). They announced their engagement in March 1828 (*SDB,* 754); in October 1828 Schwind moved to Munich to study at the Academy there "for Netti's sake" (*SDB,* 817); the affair ended in October 1829 due to religious differences and Schwind's impecuniousness (*SDB,* 539). See also Litschauer, *Neue Dokumente*, 38.

65. We do not know Clotilde's full name or identity. Most of Bauernfeld's diary entries concerning Clotilde were edited out by Glossy. In the foreword to his edition, Josef Bindtner, in *Erinnerungen aus Alt-Wien: Mit 28 Bildern* (Vienna, 1923), ix–xi, published the diary entries for 7 February 1821, when Bauernfeld first mentioned Clotilde and his infatuation with her; May 1822, a physical description of Clotilde; December 1823, 4 January 1824, and April 1825, the only entry concerning Clotilde that made it into *SDB,* 413. Further diary entries mentioned by Bindtner concern 17 April 1826, when Bauernfeld embraced Clotilde for the last time, and 25 April 1827, when she married someone else. My thanks to Kristina Muxfeldt for bringing the Bindtner foreword to my attention and making it available to me.

66. Steblin, "The Peacock's Tale," 31n69.

67. See ibid., 16; and Bauernfeld's diary entries for 14 May 1825 and June 1825 (Litschauer, *Neue Dokumente*, 30).

68. Steblin, "The Peacock's Tale," 16; and Litschauer, *Neue Dokumente*, 45.

69. *SDB,* 573–74 (17 December 1826).

70. Litschauer, *Neue Dokumente*, 46.

71. See Schwind to Schubert, 2 July 1825 (*SDB,* 424–25), 1 and 6 August 1825 (*SDB* 443–44), and 1 September 1825 (*SDB* 451–52).

72. *SDB,* 401–2, 14 February 1825.

73. *SDB,* 414, 18 April 1825 (rev. trans.).

74. Schubert and Schwind continued to visit Mme Lacsny when her health permitted. Schubert met Hiller and Hummel at her house in March of 1827 (*SDB*, 619). He possibly also met Luigi Lablache at her house (*SDB*, 667). She died before Schubert, on 3 July 1828 (*SDB*, 789).

75. *SDB*, 561; and Litschauer, *Neue Dokumente*, 57. Kristina Muxfeldt's chapter on the opera, "The Matrimonial Anomaly (Schubert's Opera for Posterity)," in *Vanishing Sensibilities: Schubert, Beethoven, Schumann* (Oxford, 2012), 41–83, attempts, as nearly as possible given the available sources, to understand why the censor forbade the opera, given that the story had been around since the thirteenth century and had been treated many times in German literature, most recently (1824) in a libretto for Carl Eberwein.

76. Richard Kramer, "Posthumous Schubert," *19th-Century Music* 14 (1990): 197–216 traces connections between the opera and *Winterreise* (*Nebensonnen*) and Schubert's 1815 setting of Goethe's poem "Wonnen der Wehmut"; he also discerns the influence of *Fidelio* and *Figaro* at crucial points in the music.

77. In his diary, June 1828, Bauernfeld noted a debate between Schober and Ferdinand von Mayerhofer, who later married the pious Anna Hönig (Litschauer, *Neue Dokumente*, 69). On Schober's courtship of Marie von Spaun, see *SMF*, 350.

78. "Jugendfreunde," 30.

79. *SDB*, 597, 25 January 1827.

80. John M. Gingerich, "'To how many shameful deeds must you lend your image': Schubert's Pattern of Telescoping and Excision in the Texts of His Latin Masses," *Current Musicology* 70 (Spring 2002): 61–99. The discussion here of Schubert's Mass text quotes freely from this article.

81. The notion that Schubert copied an unorthodox master text was supported by Otto Wissig, *Franz Schuberts Messen* (Leipzig, 1909), 34; Alfred Einstein, *Schubert*, trans. David Ascoli (London, 1951), 61; and Paul Badura-Skoda, "Schuberts korrumpierte Meßtexte—Absicht oder Versehen? Gedanken zum Buch von Hans Jaskulsky *Die Lateinischen Messen Franz Schuberts*," *Das Orchester* 38 (1990): 132.

82. *SDB*, 740, 21 February 1828.

83. Walther Dürr, "Dona nobis pacem: Gedanken zu Schuberts späten Messen," in *Bachiana et Alia Musicologica: Festschrift Alfred Dürr zum 65. Geburtstag am 3. März 1983*, ed. Wolfgang Rehm (Kassel, 1983), 62–73.

84. For an interpretation of the particular kind of pantheism present in *Die Allmacht*, see Walther Dürr, "Die Allmacht (D852): Schubert, Schelling und der Pantheismus," in *"Laudato si, mi Signore, per sora nostra matre terra": Zur Ästhetik und Spiritualität des 'Sonnengesangs' in Musik, Kunst, Religion, Naturwissenschaften, Literatur, Film und Fotografie*, ed. Ute Jung-Kaiser (Bern, 2002), 103–16.

85. See Susan Youens, *Schubert's Late Lieder: Beyond the Song Cycles* (Cambridge, 2002), 93–144, for a description of Pyrker as a champion egotist, self-promoter, and opportunist. By the early 1830s he had already become much more conservative than when Schubert knew him, and after Emperor Franz's death Pyrker completed his transition from emperor-worship to pope-worship, and from having been a pantheist and Josephinian he became a staunch advocate of supreme papal authority—an Ultramontanist.

86. Adam Bunnell, *Before Infallibility: Liberal Catholicism in Biedermeier Vienna* (Rutherford, 1990), 42; Robin Okey, *The Habsburg Monarchy: From Enlightenment to Eclipse* (New York, 2001), 43–44, 58, 66, 100.

87. On Mayrhofer, see Spaun, "Aus den Lebenserinnerungen des Joseph Freiherrn von Spaun," 296; on Vogl, *SDB*, 99.

88. Philo-Hellenism seems to have generated surprisingly little enthusiasm of the Byronic sort in the Schubert circle for the modern Greek war of independence (1821–29), or at least generated surprisingly few records of such enthusiasm.

89. Enzinger, *Franz v. Bruchmann*, 193. Dürr, "Schubert, Schelling und der Pantheismus," 108, speculates that Bruchmann's "Totalitäts-Philosophie" refers to Schelling.

90. Enzinger, *Franz v. Bruchmann*, 218–19.

91. "Die Deutschen als vollendete Griechen." Ibid., 220.

92. Ibid., 128.

93. In a letter to his sister Sybille, 23 July 1819, Bruchmann called Schelling "den grösten [*sic*] Menschen, *den unsere Erde je trug*." Ibid., 284, emphasis Bruchmann's.

94. See Friedrich Schlegel's "Vorrede," *Concordia* 1 (1820): 1; and "Signatur des Zeitalters," *Concordia* 1 (1820): 59-62.

95. *SDB*, 187–88; Enzinger, *Franz v. Bruchmann*, 135. After the Carlsbad decrees of 1819 university students were not permitted to study abroad for much the same reason Senn had been arrested, because the Austrian head of police Sedlnitzky was leery of the contagion of German nationalist university fraternities (see *SDB*, 129–30).

96. *SDB*, 254. In a letter to his father, 7 May 1822, Bruchmann explained that as much as he admired Schlegel and his friends, he personally still found it impossible to convert to Catholicism (Enzinger, *Franz v. Bruchmann*, 297).

97. All five of Bruchmann's poems set by Schubert (D737, 738, 746, 762, 785) are dated to sometime in 1822 or 1823 by Otto Erich Deutsch, *Franz Schubert: Thematisches Verzeichnis seiner Werke in chronologischer Folge* (Kassel, 1978).

98. *SDB*, 287; Enzinger, *Franz v. Bruchmann*, 146.

99. Schubert to Schober, 30 November 1823, *SDB*, 300.

100. "Wie die Askese in Person": this according to Rudolph von Smetana, who became her brother-in-law (Enzinger, *Franz v. Bruchmann*, 158).

101. *SDB*, 303; and Wurzbach, *Biographisches Lexikon*, 55:208ff.

102. Enzinger, *Franz v. Bruchmann*, 158, 222.

103. Ibid., 223.

104. See especially Stoessl, *Schwind Briefe*, 31–32, for Schwind reading and reacting to their letters to each other. Ibid., 35–36.

105. See *SDB*, 342, 314–15, 330–31 for letters from Schwind to Schober and Justina; see Enzinger, *Franz v. Bruchmann*, 315, for a letter from Bruchmann to Schober.

106. A long letter from Schwind to Kupelwieser in Rome, sent on 9 June 1824, indicates that by that time Justina had ended the affair with Schober, but that Schwind as yet had no inkling of Franz von Bruchmann's role in Justina's change of mind. Feuchtmüller, *Leopold Kupelwieser*, 31.

107. *SDB*, 384, 405–6.

108. The term "positive Christianity" is from Enzinger (*Franz v. Bruchmann*, 155) and Deutsch (*SDB*, 569) and probably refers to ideas put forward by Friedrich von Schlegel in his journal *Concordia* (1820–23), rather than to Schelling's "positive" philosophy.

109. Enzinger, *Franz v. Bruchmann*, 155–56.

110. Ibid., 158–59.

111. Ibid., 157. Also worth noting is that Bruchmann addressed his father, Senn, and Schober with "Sie," and Kupelwieser with "Du." (See the letters at the end of Enzinger's volume, 283–358.)

112. Rudolf Bachleitner, *Die Nazarener* (Munich, 1976), 19.

113. Jonas Veit (b. 1790) and Philipp Veit (b. 1793).

114. Bachleitner, *Die Nazarener*, 161: "In Rom wurde Kupelwieser Nazarener—er blieb es bis zu seinem Ende." Feuchtmüller, in *Leopold Kupelwieser*, emphasizes Kupelwieser's differences from other Nazarenes (113–21), and his individual working out of influences both German and Italian, in which, for example, Raphael's predecessors play a larger role than do Raphael's followers (116). Unlike the religious works, the commissioned portraits Kupelwieser painted in the first years after his return from Rome were done not out of inclination but for the money (118).

115. Although Schwind "probably" had regular lessons with L. F. Schnorr von Carolsfeld, he definitely learned how to paint in oils from Kupelwieser, who was thus both friend and teacher, and whose absence in Rome in 1824–25 left Schwind at loose ends. See Andrea Gottdang, "'Ich bin unsern Ideen nicht untreu geworden': Moritz von Schwind und der Schubert-Freundeskreis," *Schubert: Perspektiven* 4 (2004): 3.

116. In a letter to Schober, 3 September 1827, Schwind described his first conversation with Cornelius in Munich, in which Cornelius was critical of Friedrich von Schlegel, and critical of the direction in which Schlegel had taken L. F. Schnorr (Stoessl, *Schwind Briefe*, 53).

117. Bunnell, *Before Infallibility*, 95.

118. Eduard Hosp, "Hofbauer, Clemens Johannes Maria," *Lexikon für Theologie und Kirche*, 2nd ed. (Freiburg, 1960), 5:413–14.

119. Bunnell, *Before Infallibility*, 47.

120. *Catholic Encyclopedia*, "Redemptorists (Congregation of the Most Holy Redeemer)," http://www.catholic.org/encyclopedia/view.php?id=9891.

121. Bunnell, *Before Infallibility*, 47.

122. Ibid., 47–48.

123. *SDB*, 254.

124. However, the names of the characters in Bauernfeld's skit, Pantalon, Columbine, and Harlequin, had a long history in the traditions of the Viennese "Hanswurst-Komödie." Eduard Bauernfeld, "Intermezzo—Die Wiener-Volks-Komödie," in chap. 3 of "Aus Alt- und Neu-Wien," in *Gesammelte Schriften*, vol. 12, 34.

125. Friedrich Schlegel, *Lucinde* (Stuttgart: Reclam, 1963), 34–35 (translation mine). This passage should be compared with Scene 8 of Bauernfeld's *Sylvesternacht* (1825) satire, *SDB*, 493–94.

126. Praised by the "Jungdeutscher" Karl Gutzkow in 1835, and condemned by Søren Kierkegaard in 1841. Karl Konrad Pohlheim, Postscript to *Lucinde*, 116.

127. Frederick C. Beiser, *Enlightenment, Revolution, and Romanticism: The Genesis of Modern German Political Thought, 1790–1800* (Cambridge, MA, 1992), 260, from *Fragmente* nos. 31, 34.

128. *SDB*, 411–12, 2 April 1825. Schwind had managed to work characters from *Lucinde* and from *Der Graf von Gleichen* into sketches illustrating *The Marriage of Figaro*.

129. Enzinger, *Franz v. Bruchmann*, 188.

130. Ibid., 198.

131. Schwind to Schober, 6 January 1824, in Stoessl, *Schwind Briefe*, 26, my translation.

132. Beiser, *Enlightenment, Revolution, and Romanticism*, 231–34.

133. Ibid., 229–34.

134. Ibid., 261. Beiser dates the shift back to 1799. It was a shift for the Romantics in guiding texts from Schiller's *Aesthetische Briefe* to Schleiermacher's *Reden über die Religion* (239–40).

Schubert's Kosegarten Settings of 1815: A Forgotten *Liederspiel*

MORTEN SOLVIK

In 1815 Franz Schubert composed twenty vocal works to poems by Gotthard Ludwig Kosegarten. This in itself is not a remarkable observation about a time period in which the composer produced an enormous number of Lieder, at least 138 in that year alone. But there is something unique about these works that has, until recently, been overlooked by music historians: collectively they share both a clearly constructed plot and musical devices that connect them into a coherent whole, suggesting the rather surprising conclusion that the songs belong together as a unified set, even as a type of cycle. Although some of the research presented here is known to specialists, the major points of evidence that support such an argument have yet to reach a wider audience.[1] The following is an account of that discovery, a summary of the pieces of the puzzle as they came to light and how they fit together.

Manuscripts and Statistical Anomalies

The first indication that Schubert's Kosegarten settings might form a unique collection of songs emerged quite by accident. In the course of conducting a broad survey of Schubert's song manuscripts and working methods I decided to put together a statistical overview of the sources to all of Schubert's surviving Lieder, some 625 in all. The method of cataloging relied on the three fundamental types of song manuscripts widely used in Schubert studies: sketches, rough drafts, and fair copies. Sketches (*Entwürfe*) are incomplete renderings of songs, either in the extent of melodic material or accompaniment that Schubert put to paper or, though they appear to be fully scored songs, only a portion survives. This latter type is more properly called a "torso"; approximately 8 percent of Schubert's songs have a manuscript in this category. Rough drafts (*erste Niederschriften*) are completely rendered songs that are performable but have a hasty appearance and often contain corrections; this is by far the largest group, with about 54 percent of his songs represented. Fair copies (*Reinschriften*) are carefully prepared presentation copies of songs that Schubert wrote out in a clean, careful hand; this is a much smaller group, about 23 percent. There is also a fourth category that is often overlooked: songs for which we have no manuscripts in Schubert's hand; this accounts for a surprisingly large number of works, 142 in all, or 23 percent of his songs.[2]

I was specifically looking for groupings within these three main types of manuscript, especially among the fair copies, relationships that might reflect unknown larger-scale organizations of songs. The documentation of Schubert's life is so incomplete that it did not seem implausible to speculate that even today some of his musical projects may have been left unnoticed in the historical record. The information at first seemed haphazard, but the survey started suggesting some patterns when I began matching the percentages given above with poets whose works Schubert had set. During the course of his short life the composer turned to texts by 98 authors. The vast majority of these writers (83) were set fewer than ten times, and only seven were set twenty or more times, as can be seen in Table 1. The large number of works set to Goethe, Mayrhofer, and Schiller reflects an ongoing engagement with these poets' works throughout Schubert's composing career, as can be seen in the dates of composition. For Müller the concentration centered on his last years; Matthisson, Hölty, and Kosegarten held Schubert's interest only in his highly productive early period.

Table 1. Schubert's Most Frequently Set Authors of Lied Texts

Author	**Total settings**	**Dates of composition (yrs)**	**Fair copies**	
			Number	As % of total for author
Goethe	70	1814–1826 (13)	32	46%
Mayrhofer	47	1814–1824 (11)	10	21%
Schiller	45	1811–1823 (13)	8	18%
Müller	44	1823–1828 (6)	15	34%
Matthisson	29	1812–1817 (6)	5	17%
Hölty	26	1813–1816 (4)	3	12%
Kosegarten	20	1815–1817 (3)	19	95%

These numbers speak for Schubert's sometimes shifting literary taste, but—as already intimated—there is yet another way to measure their importance in his output: by examining the number of fair copies he produced for each. Fair copies required more time to prepare than rough drafts and were usually put together for a particular reason. These were the patterns I was looking for, and I could largely explain the results. In 1816 Schubert planned to bring out a series of volumes of German songs for distribution and publication. The first two volumes contained a total of 24 songs by Goethe but was met with rejection by the great poet and the project was called off.[3] Fair copies of Mayrhofer settings over the years make sense, as he was a close friend of the composer. The Müller fair copies were compiled in the preparation of *Winterreise*.[4] But what was the motivation for the abundance of Kosegarten in fair copy, second only to Goethe? This anomaly was even more glaring considering that Schubert copied out virtually every Kosegarten setting he ever wrote (95 percent, last column). No poet—not even Goethe—came close to this type of treatment. A glance at the numbers, then, suggests a short but intense engagement with this writer that may have led to the production of a collection of fair copies. An odd conclusion, given that the research on Schubert's Kosegarten songs suggested no such large-scale project.

Piqued by this observation, my thoughts eventually moved from statistics to a consideration of what might explain the anomaly. Curious, but with no expectations, I started examining the evidence. The more I looked, the more I found, and as one clue led to the next it became increasingly obvious that something important was emerging from the data, a conclusion that seemed too significant to have remained hidden all this time: that the Kosegarten songs constituted a cycle. In the months that followed it was necessary to test the veracity of such a possibility, but the more I shook the foundations of this notion, the more the pieces fell into place.

The logical place to begin an investigation was with the actual autograph scores. This in itself presented some difficulties, since making sense of the fair copies also required understanding the rough drafts on which they were based. This doubled the number of manuscripts that had to be considered from 11 to 22. A further complication was that, of these 22 documents, 14 were held in public archives in Austria, Germany, the UK, and the United States, 6 were in private collections in unknown locations, and 2 had disappeared entirely.[5] It would be no small task simply gathering the information. Nevertheless, work progressed and a number of important observations came to light. The first concerned the dating of the manuscripts. If the fair copies had been compiled as a set, it would make most sense if this process had been undertaken for all of the songs at about the same time and after all of the rough drafts were finished. The dating of the rough drafts was largely unproblematic, as in most cases Schubert himself provided this information in marginal annotations. A look at the dates of these drafts (Table 2) reveals the remarkable intensity of the output of these songs, most produced in conjunction with other Kosegarten settings over only a day or two. After producing thirteen such songs over the course of roughly the month of July (including five

Table 2. The Rough Drafts to Schubert's 1815 Kosegarten Settings, by Date

Dates are noted by Schubert on the manuscript except for those given in brackets or parentheses; those in square brackets are taken from the Witteczek-Spaun Collection (A-Wgm) as given in the Deutsch Catalogue, and the date in parentheses is inferred from a dated composition on the same leaf. The sigla shown in the Rough Draft column stem from RISM, the international index for music sources.

<table>
<tr><th>Date</th><th>D</th><th>Title</th><th>Rough Draft</th></tr>
<tr><td>25 June</td><td>219</td><td>Das Finden</td><td>A-Wn Mus.Hs. 40.992</td></tr>
<tr><td>[7 July]</td><td>228</td><td>Von Ida</td><td rowspan="2">[private]</td></tr>
<tr><td>7 July</td><td>229</td><td>Die Erscheinung</td></tr>
<tr><td>7 July</td><td>227</td><td>Idens Nachtgesang</td><td>GB-Lbm Add. 29999</td></tr>
<tr><td>7 July</td><td>230</td><td>Die Täuschung</td><td rowspan="2">[private]</td></tr>
<tr><td>8 July</td><td>231</td><td>Das Sehnen</td></tr>
<tr><td>[15 July]</td><td>221</td><td>Der Abend</td><td rowspan="2">[lost]</td></tr>
<tr><td>[15 July]</td><td>233</td><td>Geist der Liebe</td></tr>
<tr><td>25 July</td><td>236</td><td>Das Abendrot [SSB]</td><td rowspan="3">A-Wn Mus.Hs. 41.628</td></tr>
<tr><td>25 July</td><td>237</td><td>Abends unter der Linde</td></tr>
<tr><td>(25 July)</td><td>238</td><td>Die Mondnacht</td></tr>
<tr><td>27 July</td><td>240</td><td>Huldigung</td><td>D-Bds Schu 36</td></tr>
<tr><td>27 July</td><td>241</td><td>Alles um Liebe</td><td>D-Bds Schu 48</td></tr>
<tr><td>19 October</td><td>313</td><td>Die Sterne</td><td>[private]</td></tr>
<tr><td>19 October</td><td>314</td><td>Nachtgesang</td><td rowspan="4">US-Wc Moldenhauer</td></tr>
<tr><td>19 October</td><td>315</td><td>An Rosa I</td></tr>
<tr><td>19 October</td><td>316</td><td>An Rosa II</td></tr>
<tr><td>19 October</td><td>317</td><td>Idens Schwanenlied</td></tr>
<tr><td>19 October</td><td>318</td><td>Schwangesang</td><td rowspan="2">A-Wst 2030</td></tr>
<tr><td>19 October</td><td>319</td><td>Luisens Antwort</td></tr>
</table>

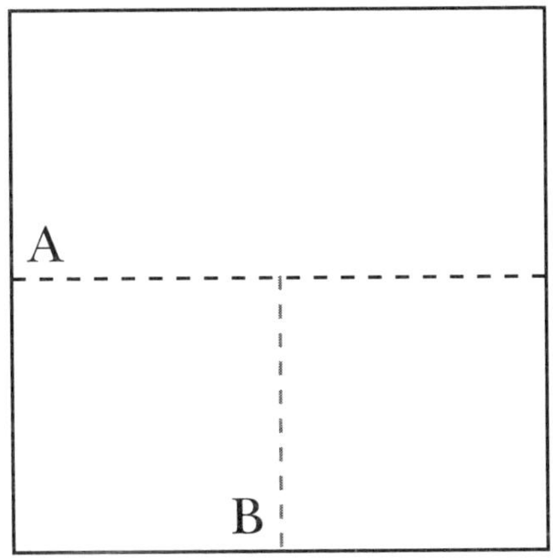

Figure 1. Cutting and folding of paper into a bifolio.

Kosegarten songs on 7–8 July and five on 25–27 July), Schubert stopped until three months later, when, on a single day, 19 October, he wrote the remaining seven.

Establishing the dates of the fair copies proved far more elusive. Schubert merely indicated the work's title on these documents. Solving this dilemma required turning to an arcane branch of musical research: paper types. Understanding this method of dating requires some knowledge of paper manufacturing in Schubert's day. The process involved dissolving cotton fiber in a chemical mixture that broke down the bonds between the strands of the material into a gooey broth. The papermaker then needed a large porous screen made of metal wire arranged in a crisscross pattern and held in place by a wooden frame around the perimeter. The screen was first dipped into the mixture and then, while being held flat, carefully lifted out of the vat. As the liquid ran through the screen and over the edges, the cotton would immediately start to re-bond in a flat layer on top of the screen. The screen with the material forming on it would be pressed to free up excess water, the wet paper lifted out and laid on racks to dry. The large sheets were eventually cut, often along one axis, A, and then folded along another axis, B. The result was a "bifolio," consisting of a folded sheet forming two pages and four sides (see Figure 1). If the paper was to be used for music notation, a device called a rastrum was employed to create the lines of the staves across the width of the page.

Fortunately for historians, paper production was a process that led to slight variations in the finished product. Paper mills commonly left their imprint on the paper by hand-weaving letters or symbols with copper wire into the dip screen; when the paper was pressed, water would form along the edges of these shapes and leave behind a gray shadow inside the paper that would become permanent. This "watermark" functioned as a type of stamp of origin that could be traced back to the manufacturer. What is more, as screens had to be replaced after extended use, the watermark wiring would usually differ ever so slightly from its predecessors, a natural consequence of the manual process involved. These slight discrepancies can be very important in isolating unique batches of paper. Other differences can be noted as well. The process of cutting the paper rendered the bifolios (and single leaves) oblong or upright in orientation. Different formats could be used for adding staff lines (usually 12 or 16 to a page), which in turn determined the dimensions on the page—a measurement known as the "total span," from the top of the top staff to the bottom of the bottom staff. Thus Schubert's manuscripts can be examined and categorized according to their physical characteristics. Since the composer tended to use up piles of paper in sequence, we can plausibly group works with the same traits to the same period of notation; and if several of these manuscripts are dated within a specific time frame, it is reasonable to assign undated works on the same paper type to the same period. Even if exact dates are not possible, these groupings at least allow us with certainty to exclude the possibility of manuscripts being written before their respective types appeared.[6]

Applying this method to the Kosegarten manuscripts revealed three distinct types of paper (see Table 3). Type 1 appears in the Kosegarten

Table 3. Kosegarten Settings, Paper Types, June 1815-April 1816

Four leaves of rough drafts, D221/233, 227, 230/231 and 313, have not been examined; the watermark to D236/237/238 is illegible; and D241 is notated on older paper. Fair copy leaves not examined: D236/237, 238, and 315/316. "Kiesling" and "Weilhartiz" refer to two paper manufacturers whose names appear on the respective watermarks. "Type" is used for illustrative purposes. For a more detailed treatment, see the critical edition of Franz Schubert's works that uses a different classification: Types 1 and 2 listed here would be included in "Type II" and Type 3 in "Type I."

Paper Type	Staves	Total Span	Orientation	Watermark	Dates	Manuscript Type
1	16	19.6 cm	oblong	Kiesling	June–July 1815	Rough draft
2	12	18.5 cm	oblong	Kiesling	October 1815	Rough draft
3	12	18.5 cm	oblong	Weilhartiz	April 1816	Fair copy

songs set in June and July, Type 2 in the October songs, and Type 3 for all of the fair copies. By identifying dated manuscripts from each of these types, we can isolate the time period in which they were notated. For the dated rough drafts this is clear; for the undated fair copies, related documents suggest a time frame around April 1816.[7] In other words, Schubert returned to all of the Kosegarten songs a number of months after the last of them had been composed in order to copy them out again in a clean hand. He did so on the same paper and likely within a short period of time.

It was beginning to look like the fair copies constituted a set of some sort, but the next question loomed even larger: Why were they compiled? The historical record provides no indication of a special occasion or a dedication that would explain such a major project or singular event. My investigation might have ended there, were it not for a curious development. In collating what I could of the fair copies, I noticed numbers in the lower left-hand corner on all of them, numbers that suggested a sequence from 1 to 20 that had nothing to do with the order of composition. Perhaps this could explain the existence of the fair copies. If so, the questions had shifted: Who had numbered them and for what purpose?

Cracking the Code

To answer these questions I needed to return to the manuscripts and take a closer look. In doing so, I found that, for my purposes, the most important information regarding the documents lay not in the composer's own notations but rather in the markings left behind by others. Figure 2 shows the autograph of the rough draft of *Schwangesang* and divides the inscriptions found on the page into eleven elements: 1–6 stemming from Schubert and 7–11 attributable to later hands.

Schubert's inscriptions:

1. The score is quite legible and represents a complete rendering of the work. The noteheads are mostly round and clearly positioned; the text underlay of the first verse is complete; dynamic markings, phrasings, and accents are also inserted. Corrections are infrequent, though revealing. In measure 4 the voice line half note on the third beat is changed to a fermata quarter to allow for the anacrusis to the next measure. Note that the piano right hand shows no such correction (quarter note fermata following long quarter rest), implying that the voice line was notated first. A similar change in the

vocal line in measure 14 (last measure in system 3) demonstrates the same characteristic. A cross-out in measure 15 shows the composer simply finding a better voice-leading solution for the descending seventh in the piano left hand.

2. Schubert carefully wrote out and underlined the title toward the center of the page.
3. Schubert notes the exact day, month, and year of the manuscript, a common procedure during this period for this type of autograph, though it was a habit he would later largely abandon. Schubert wrote out eight Lieder that day, seven of them set to texts by Kosegarten.[8]

4, 5. Instrumentation ("S[ingstimme]" and "P[iano]F[orte]") and clefs, tempo marking, time signature, and key signature are all provided at the beginning of the work with the key signature and clef repeated in each system. This is hardly an unusual procedure in a musical composition, yet not always the case in Schubert's less polished song scores.

6. Schubert identifies the author of the text, "Koseg[arten]," at the end of the score and makes a note of how many additional verses not written out here should be appended to the strophic song ("6 Str[ophen]").

Later inscriptions (not in Schubert's hand):

7. A reference to a copy of the song "in Franz Schubert's hand" listed as "[Number] 17" of Series "Abth[eilung]" IV.
8. A listing of songs from the "Repertorium" with similar titles, giving text, author, publishing information, publisher or plate number ("3523") and location or catalogue number of these related manuscripts. *Idens Schwanenlied*, for instance, is listed as "No. 32, Series II."
9. A number in the lower-left-hand corner in black ink ("24").
10. A temporary plate number ("16755"), though not yet engraved ("noch nicht gest[ochen]").
11. Various markings in various colors to the left of the title.

Though these marginalia at first seemed like little more than cryptic scribblings, curiosity drove me to wonder what they meant and who had gone to the trouble of adding this information. The references to plate numbers in items 8 and 10 indicated the work of someone in the publishing industry in the nineteenth century, but item 9 turned out to be far more puzzling. This number in the lower-left-hand corner turned up in dozens of manuscripts, yet clearly did not indicate plate numbers. Intriguing connections seemed to emerge between the seven Kosegarten

Figure 2. Inscriptions on rough draft of *Schwangesang* (D318).

rough drafts written on 19 October, with 23, 24, 26, 29, 30, 31, and 32 appearing in this position, whereas only two of the five songs from 7–8 July were even numbered (8 and 9), and the numbers from 25–27 July read 12, 13, 14, 1, and 2.

The key to understanding the mysterious numberings turned out to be not the numbers themselves but the references to them provided in item 7. In the case of this manuscript of *Schwangesang*, the annotator provides the following information, as mentioned above: "A copy (or fair copy [*Reinschrift*]) in Franz Schubert's hand see 17 Series IV." There is in fact a fair copy of this song, *Schwangesang*, in Schubert's hand; see Figure 3. Fair copies such as this resemble the rough drafts, but a few differing features stand out. The musical notation is more carefully prepared, with rounder note heads; there are more musical performance indications, and usually no corrections. At the top of the page, Schubert merely indicated the title of the song; the author attribution ("Kosegarten") and date ("comp[osed] 19/10 [1]815") were added by the annotator mentioned above, as was most of the rest of the marginalia.

Figure 3. Fair copy of *Schwangesang* (D318).

The connection between the marginalia numberings on the rough draft and the fair copy of the same song now became obvious. In the lower-left corner of the fair copy stood the number "17," as indicated in the annotation on the rough draft. What is more, this fair copy provided a cross-reference to the rough draft in a perfectly complementary fashion; it referred back to the other manuscript as follows: "Das ursprüngliche Manuscript vide Nr 24 Schubert's Lieder mit Namensfertigung und Datum Abth. I" (The original manuscript see No. 24 of Schubert's Lieder with signature and date Series I). Compare the numbers in the lower-left corners of both manuscripts along with the references in the marginalia along the bottom edge in Figures 2 and 3. Whoever made these markings was concerned about pointing out manuscripts of the same song. Oddly, the rough drafts and fair copies were assigned not the same but separate "series" designations. What is more, the number in the lower-left corner, though associated with a specific series, never appeared with its Roman numeral designation; this could only be derived from the autograph that referred to it. Thus the "17" on the fair copy appears with no Roman numeral next to it; the assignation of the fair copy to "Series IV" could only be determined by consulting its rough draft, where it states: "A copy (or fair copy [*Reinschrift*]) in Franz Schubert's hand see 17 Series IV." Likewise, the fair copy explains the "24" in the lower-left-hand corner of the rough draft: "The original manuscript see No. 24 of Schubert's Lieder with signature and date Series I."[9]

Having unlocked the secret of the numbers in the lower-left corner, it was now possible to organize the manuscripts by what looked like someone's attempt to put the songs in order. The sequence that emerged on the rough drafts of the Kosegarten songs led to no significant patterns, but the case with the fair copies proved highly suggestive (see Table 4). By

Table 4. Kosegarten Fair Copies Arranged by Series IV

Note that the lower-left-hand corner of A-Wst 6429 verso is water damaged, precisely where the number "10" might otherwise be found; the recto leaf is clearly numbered "9."

Series IV/. . .	**D**	**Title**	**Fair Copy Manuscripts**
1	240	*Huldigung*	A-Wn Mus. Hs. 40.990
2	241	*Alles um Liebe*	
3	228	*Von Ida*	US-AUS Lake Collection
4	229	*Die Erscheinung*	
5	219	*Das Finden*	A-Wn Mus. Hs. 40.993
6	227	*Idens Nachtgesang*	
7	313	*Die Sterne*	US-C Houghton b MS 108 (21)
8	314	*Nachtgesang*	
9	230	*Die Täuschung*	A-Wst 6429
[10]	231	*Das Sehnen*	
11	238	*Die Mondnacht*	GB-Cfm 616
12	237	*Abends unter der Linde*	[lost]
13	236	*Das Abendrot* [SSB]	
14	233	*Geist der Liebe*	A-Wn Mus. Hs. 43.946
15	221	*Der Abend*	
16	317	*Idens Schwanenlied*	US-NH Jackson Lib
17	318	*Schwangesang*	
18	319	*Luisens Antwort*	A-Wst 16.400
19	315	*An Rosa I*	[private]
20	316	*An Rosa II*	

referring to the rough drafts of the 1815 Kosegarten settings, it was possible to determine that all twenty of the fair copies of these songs belonged to Series IV. In fact, Series IV would turn out to include only these twenty works. What is more, the twenty formed a set numbered consecutively from 1 to 20 that did not reflect the order of composition or sequences in any other series. But what criteria had determined these markings? Were these numberings arbitrary or did they reveal the sequence of songs as they had been grouped together as a set? It was necessary to identify who had entered these marginalia and the purpose for doing so.

Johann Wolf and the Sources

The most striking feature about these inscriptions is that nearly all of them were written in the same hand (type 7–9 and sometimes type 10).[10] Fortunately, the writer left an important clue to his identity in another Schubert manuscript, where we find his signature: "Johann Wolf."[11] Aside from a note in an index by Alexander Weinmann, there is virtually nothing in the secondary literature about this person,[12] yet in the manuscript collection at the Wienbibliothek we find two items that help shed some light on his murky biography.[13] One is a letter from "Johann Wolf" written on 13 May 1848 to Adolf Bäuerle, editor of the *Allgemeine Theaterzeitung*.[14] Wolf writes to correct a detail in a notice he had written for the paper concerning publications soon to appear at the publisher H. F. Müller, including several of his own works.[15] The letter also contains a request to withhold certain information in lieu of the settlement of a dispute with Anton Diabelli over rights to a text. Thus the writer of the letter was obviously involved in the publishing business and also a composer. This aligns convincingly with the references to plate numbers and publishing firms in the marginalia of the Schubert song manuscripts. Significantly, the signature on this document matches exactly that found in the Schubert manuscript.

The second item at the Wienbibliothek is an album put together in honor of the publisher and music patron Karl Haslinger (1816–1868).[16] This sumptuously bound volume compiled in 1862 contains dedications from over 120 friends and acquaintances, many of whom were leading figures of the music scene in Vienna in the mid-nineteenth century. Each contributor—including the likes of Simon Sechter, Carl Goldmark, Joachim Raff, and Johann Strauss—wrote a simple greeting, a short musical work or an incipit, signed his name, and provided a photograph of himself. On folio 65 we find a contribution by Johann Wolf with two short musical compositions, a signature, and a photo. Again, the signature (see Figure 4) exactly matches that found in the Schubert

Figure 4. Johann Wolf (1862).

manuscript. The accompanying compositions confirm Wolf's activities as a composer, but also reveal something more significant. The first of these two pieces provides indirect evidence that Wolf may have had privileged access to Schubert manuscripts. The work is a short vocal trio for men's voices, titled *Punschlied* and set to a text by Schiller. Schubert also wrote a short vocal trio for men's voices to the very same text (D277), a work that, significantly, was not published until 1892, thirty years after Wolf's contribution to the Haslinger album.[17] The publisher of the first edition of the Schubert part song, as well as many of Wolf's compositions, was C. A. Spina. A Viennese publisher who took over the firm established by Anton Diabelli in 1852,[18] Spina brought out numerous first editions of Schubert Lieder in the 1860s. Wolf's connection to this publisher is probably no coincidence: in all likelihood Spina hired Wolf to organize and annotate the Schubert manuscripts in question.[19]

Table 5a. An Overview of Wolf's Manuscript Categories (Original German)

Abt. I:	[Autograph] mit eigenhändiger Namensfertigung und Datum
Abt. II:	[Autograph] ohne Namensfertigung, jedoch mit Datum
[Abt. III]	[None]
Abt. IV:	Eine Copie (respect. Reinschrift) von Fr. Schubert's Hand . . . aus der Sam[m]lung dessen Bruder Ferdinand herrührend
Abt. V:	Eine andere Bearbeitung
Abt. VI:	Copien von annäherungsweise Schubert's Handschrift oder eines Verwandtens
Abt. VII:	Copie (von Ferdinand Schubert) . . . der Copien F. Schubert'scher Lieder
Abt. VIII:	Copien von verschiedenen Handschriften

Several types of information provided in the margins of the Schubert manuscripts support this conclusion. In writing out his marginal comments, Wolf relied substantially on a catalogue known as the "Repertorium." This catalogue must have contained detailed information about Schubert manuscripts such as titles, authors, dates of composition, and location, all of which Wolf dutifully notates. Several extant documents devoted to Schubert are labeled "Repertorium,"[20] yet none provide the depth of information evident in the Wolf inscriptions. Instead, it seems likely that our scribe relied on a catalogue compiled by Anton Diabelli that is now lost, a probable scenario given Diabelli's activities as a publisher and his unequaled access to Schubert manuscripts after the composer's death.[21] This suggestion is supported by yet another telling characteristic of the Wolf marginalia. Although publishers' names (Leidesdorf, A.O. Witzendorf, etc.) often appear as part of information on publication, Wolf usually provides only the plate number if Diabelli or Spina published the song in question—a perfectly understandable procedure if Wolf was conducting an internal survey for the publishing house.

Comparing plate numbers and publication dates made it possible to determine with virtual certainty that Wolf added the inscriptions in the 1860s. Still, it was necessary to untangle the rationale behind the various designations, and particularly the numberings added to these pages as Wolf went about cataloguing the Schubert manuscripts. This, in turn, required reconstructing the problem he set out to solve. Wolf had the unenviable task of sifting through dozens if not hundreds of songs in manuscript, some published, some not, some dated, some signed, and so on. To make sense of this chaos, he had to design a system that provided him with the most important information in the most efficient manner. After culling through marginal inscriptions by Wolf on dozens of Schubert manuscripts it was possible to isolate seven categories that Wolf used repeatedly in dividing up the documents at his disposal (Table 5).[22]

Table 5b. Overview of Wolf's Manuscript Categories (Translation)

Series I:	[Manuscript] with autograph signature and date
Series II:	[Manuscript] without autograph signature, but with date
[Series III]	[None]
Series IV:	A copy (or fair copy) in Franz Schubert's hand . . . from the collection stemming from his brother Ferdinand
Series V:	Another version
Series VI:	Copies in a hand similar to Schubert or one related
Series VII:	Copies (by Ferdinand Schubert) . . . of the copies of Lieder by Franz Schubert
Series VIII:	Copies in various hands

The scheme shows a clear progression from those manuscripts easiest to identify to those not even attributable to Schubert's hand. Series I and II are ranked highest for being dated and sometimes also signed by the composer. This suggests that Wolf attempted as far as possible to order the manuscripts according to date of composition.[23] Series III receives no mention in any of the manuscripts I have examined.[24] As explained below, Series IV would turn out to be an exceptional group. Series V refers to reworkings of a previously existing Lied or Lied text. This category would make sense for someone trying to identify discrete Schubert songs, deciding to group later settings of the same text in a separate class.[25] Series VI–VIII all refer to "copies": VI in a hand closely resembling Schubert's; VII apparently set aside for copies by his older brother Ferdinand; VIII copies by any other copyists obviously not Franz Schubert or his brother. Thus Wolf's classification scheme was laid out according to chronological and orthographical considerations that allowed him to construct a rough overview of Schubert's Lied compositions and, more important, file them in a fashion that made for easy retrieval. Since the marginalia frequently referred to published songs and songs of similar title, Wolf's mission no doubt included identifying works that had not yet been printed. When publication decisions were made or when a particular song manuscript was needed, a quick glance at a catalogue would immediately provide its location. This would also explain the missing series numbers on the manuscripts themselves, since they would have been filed as physically separate groups. Once collated and archived the individual manuscripts could be found by going to the series, then searching ordinally for the number in the lower-left corner.

Series IV, the Kosegarten group, seems to have been compiled according to a rather different criterion, namely as "fair copies stemming from the collection (*Sammlung*) of Franz Schubert's brother, Ferdinand." The designation raises a puzzling question, for nearly all of the manuscripts

Wolf surveyed had come from Ferdinand after the composer's death. Many were published by Diabelli and Spina directly from Schubert's "Nachlaß" (estate). The term "Sammlung," then, refers to something rather more specific, a matter that emerges from the locution more clearly on second reading: not from Ferdinand Schubert's collection, but rather from a collection in Ferdinand Schubert's possession. This reading not only strongly supported other evidence that was coming into focus around the Kosegarten songs, but also suggested another dimension in interpreting Wolf's numberings. If these manuscripts truly represented a self-contained collection, it would explain not only their isolated occurrence in Series IV but also the sequence Wolf assigned to them. Since all of these fair copy manuscripts lacked both date and signature, the reasonable assumption would be that Wolf numbered them as he found them gathered in the set.

It was all the more important, then, to determine if the Kosegarten fair copies had at one time physically belonged together. The opaque formulation "collection" in the descriptions of Series IV and establishing that all the fair copies consisted of the same paper type supported this conclusion, but not definitively. The problem in attempting such a reconstruction lay in the fact that the surviving manuscripts were literally scattered around the world among numerous institutions and private collectors. Ironically, it was in tracing how the manuscripts came to be so dispersed that I found evidence for their common origin. In May 1952, the auction house Faber in Munich put five items on the block from the "Cranz Sammlung" (lot nos. 1114–1118). These consisted solely of fair copies of Schubert's settings of Kosegarten. Fifteen of the twenty settings—all but three leaves—were included in the sale (see Table 6).

The identity of the seller of these manuscripts corroborates the connections already made with Wolf and the publisher Spina, for it was the Cranz family that finally took over Spina after it had been acquired by Friedrich Schreiber.[26] The fact that so many pages of an earlier "collection" had remained together so long in the hands of the caretakers of materials handled by Wolf is itself suggestive, but the sale revealed even more important information. Lots 1117, 1115, and 1118 consisted of bifolios. Today these double leaves are separate manuscripts, but the auction in 1952 shows much of the original pagination of the set. Most striking is the alignment of the Wolf numbers with the leaves in the foliation, proof that Wolf's sequence 1/2 (on two sides of the same leaf) was indeed followed by 3/4 on the leaf that was originally literally joined to it (the same applies, of course, to 12/13–14/15 and 16/17–18). Just why the pagination was destroyed is not difficult to determine. The

Table 6. Kosegarten Fair Copy Manuscripts and Lots Sold at Karl & Faber, 1952

The lot numbers in the first column come from the Karl & Faber catalogue *Handschriften Bücher + Autographen, 19–21 Mai 1952* (Munich, 1952), 148–49.

Lot	Song	D	Wolf No.	Leaf No.	Original Foliation
1117	*Huldigung*	240	1	1	bifolio
	Alles um Liebe	241	2		
	Von Ida	228	3	2	
	Die Erscheinung	229	4		
1114	*Das Finden*	219	5	3	bifolio?
	Idens Nachtgesang	227	6		
Not sold at Faber, 1952	*Die Sterne*	313	7	4	
	Nachtgesang	314	8		
	Die Täuschung	230	9	5	bifolio?
	Das Sehnen	231	10		
	Die Mondnacht	238	11	6	
1115	*Abends unter der Linde*	237	12	7	bifolio
	Das Abendrot	236	13		
	Geist der Liebe	233	14	8	
	Der Abend	221	15		
1118	*Idens Schwanenlied*	317	16	9	bifolio
	Schwangesang	318	17		
	Luisens Antwort	319	18	10	
1116	*An Rosa I*	315	19	11	single leaf/bifolio?
	An Rosa II	316	20		

reservation price for Lot 1115, a bifolio consisting of D237, 236, 233, and 221, was DM 2,400; five years later, that figure for a single leaf (D237, 236) came in at DM 2,500.[27] It seems the owners more than doubled their money by literally cutting the bifolio in half.

Wolf, we must remember, catalogued manuscripts in a state far more representative of the manner in which Schubert produced them, thus his work points to continuities now lost. Bifolios were still intact, sequences could be more readily reconstructed. To be sure, by the 1860s not all manuscripts were still in their original foliation; damage had already been done. For instance, Ferdinand Schubert gave away and sold manuscripts after his brother's death, and publishers undoubtedly separated songs out of their original order. But Wolf was closer chronologically to the act of creation and very concerned about making sense of these documents. Since none of these manuscripts bear a date nor an author attribution,

Wolf would have had no motive to intervene in the original foliation. As the paper type and auction sale of the fair copies strongly suggest, his numberings reliably reflect a group of manuscripts as he found them.[28]

Poet, Poems, and Plot

Although physical evidence suggested that Schubert may well have left behind a specially prepared collection of Kosegarten Lieder in fair copy, the manuscripts alone could not tell me what the composer intended with the set. To attribute this gathering of songs to Schubert's artistic intention I had to probe much further into the collection and ask if its constituent parts likewise pointed to a large-scale construction. It made sense to begin with the text to see what may have attracted Schubert to these poems, where he found them, and how he integrated them into his song settings.

Gotthard Ludwig Kosegarten (1758–1818)[29] was born in Mecklenburg but spent most of his life in Swedish Pomerania, a region in northern Germany that had come under the control of Gustav II in the 1630s. Educated in theology and classical philology, Kosegarten started his professional life as a private tutor for the well-to-do of Rügen, an island off the Pomeranian coast in the Baltic Sea, and became a preacher and eventually a professor in Greifswald, the commercial and administrative center of the region. He mingled with the educated classes and even taught such influential artists of the period as Philipp Otto Runge and Caspar David Friedrich.[30] Kosegarten's activities as a poet covered a wide range of lyric genres; his style was characterized by dramatic landscapes, Romantic longing, and occasional allusions to political struggle—themes typical of his generation. The turmoil of the Napoleonic Wars inspired in him a curious mixture of German nationalism and reverence for the French conqueror. Whereas many young nationalists initially saw an ally in Kosegarten, his subservience as an administrative official to the Napoleonic state and especially his speech in honor of Napoleon's birthday in 1809 put him out of favor with progressive circles.[31]

Although he enjoyed a modest reputation in his own day, Kosegarten's qualities as a writer were even then called into question. Friedrich Schiller, in a letter to Goethe from August 1797, writes:

> I once told you that I had given Kosegarten my opinion [of him] and that I was eager to hear his response. He has now written to me and was very thankful for my

Figure 5. Portrait of Kosegarten.

> frankness. Nevertheless, I can see there is no helping him, for accompanying the same letter was a publication announcement of his poems that only a lunatic [*Verrückter*] could have written. Some people are beyond help and God took this particular specimen and forged an iron plate around his brow.[32]

Schubert nevertheless felt drawn to his work. Part of the reason for this no doubt lies in the tone of the texts Schubert chose. Kosegarten's style shares a clear thematic and stylistic affinity with the works of Ossian, Klopstock, and Matthisson, all poets Schubert set during the same period.[33]

A look at Kosegarten's publications reveals that the twenty poems Schubert set in 1815 were not printed as a separate set or isolated story. In all likelihood, Schubert found these texts in *L. T. Kosegarten's Poesieen. Neueste Auflage*, a three-volume work dated "Berlin, 1803" (no publisher is given).[34] The edition (Figure 6) demonstrates that Schubert was very selective, since the three-volume work contains a total of 144 poems.[35]

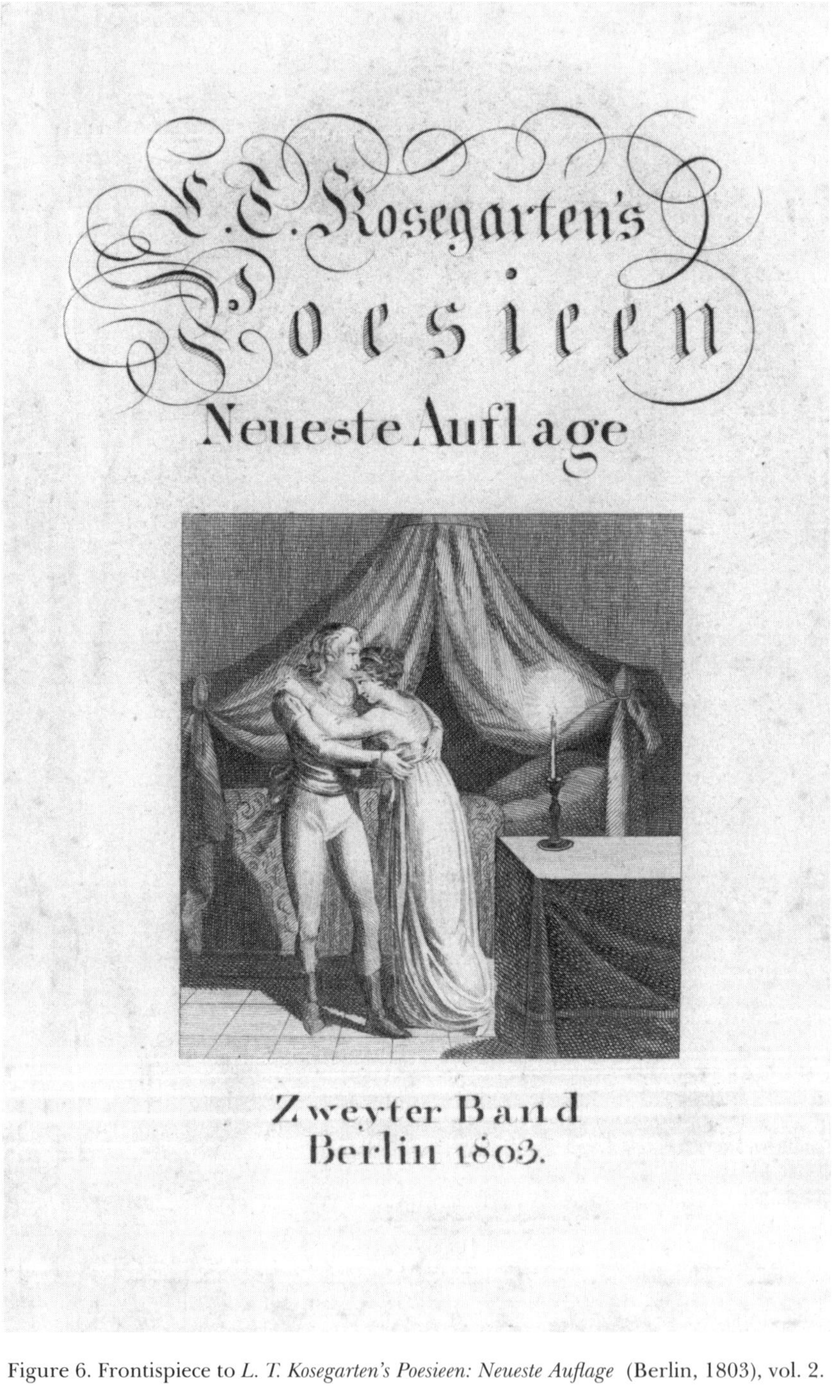

Figure 6. Frontispiece to *L. T. Kosegarten's Poesieen: Neueste Auflage* (Berlin, 1803), vol. 2.

The verses show no strong pattern of coherence in the books, although, as is the case with the twenty Schubert selected, most tend to share a lyrical vein, strophic structure, clear scansion and rhyme schemes, and are almost all topically related to the idea of love lost and found followed by tragic demise.[36] The texts also sometimes relate to one another through references to common names or events. This loosely structured, uncomplicated poetic source, though not profound in content, served Schubert with materials sufficiently pliable to craft together a larger structure.

A look at the arrangement of the poems in the printed collection compared to the Schubert settings demonstrates the point (see Table 7). In terms of continuity, the table shows numerous isolated settings as well as Schubert's tendency to set consecutive poems (column 1), a tendency that also surfaces in the order in which they were written in rough draft (column 2). However, in the order suggested by Wolf's fair copy numbering (column 3), the relationship to the original published source is reduced to a few paired texts. Far from the haphazard result one might expect from such a rearrangement, this departure from the Kosegarten publication demonstrates remarkable logic. In fact, the fair copy ordering strongly suggests an aesthetic intention operating independently of the poetic source. Through at times drastic intervention, it seems Schubert, perhaps working with his friends, re-formed the textual material into a sequence with clearly narrative tendencies.[37]

Not only do the texts collectively tell a story, they do so through the voices of three separate protagonists. Though only a few of the songs are definitively associated with a specific character—for instance, those with "Ida" in the title—it is not difficult to assign the roles as implied by the drama. The resulting story centers on a male suitor whose amorous attentions flit from one woman to the next (see Table 8). The feelings of the adventurer, Wilhelm, and two of his broken-hearted mistresses, Ida and Luisa, are presented in short strophic songs set within the typical Romantic conceits of longing and bliss. The first episode of the cycle opens with Wilhelm, who is infatuated with Elwina (song 1) but, it seems, is more enamored of love itself (2). Ida enters, despondent over a lover who has abandoned her (3). As she wanders through a grove of alderwood trees she appears to Wilhelm as if in a vision (4). The two meet; Wilhelm (5) then Ida (6) proclaim their happiness. The tryst continues as Wilhelm urges Ida to look to the stars where a far greater power resides (7). The liaison is short-lived as Wilhelm hears Luisa consoling herself under the night sky (8) and is lured away (second episode) (9). Ida succumbs to the longing that seems deemed to be her fate (10), while Wilhelm

Table 7. Schubert's Arrangement of the Kosegarten Texts

Songs by Text Source		**Songs by Date of Rough Draft**			**Songs by Order of Fair Copy**		
Title	Kose-garten	Date day/mo./yr.	Title	Kose-garten	W#	Title	Kose-garten
Die Sterne	II 6–9	25/06/1815	*Das Finden*	II 52–54	1	*Huldigung*	III 15–18
Nachtgesang	10–11	07/07/1815	*Idens Nachtgesang*	II 112–113	2	*Alles um Liebe*	19–21
Das Finden	II 52–54	07/07/1815	*Von Ida*	II 120–121	3	*Von Ida*	II 120–121
An Rosa I	II 84–85	07/07/1815	*Die Erscheinung*	II 196–198	4	*Die Erscheinung*	II 196–198
An Rosa II	86–87	07/07/1815	*Die Täuschung*	199–200	5	*Das Finden*	II 52–54
Idens Nachtgesang	II 112–113	08/07/1815	*Das Sehnen*	III 12–14	6	*Idens Nachtgesang*	II 112–113
Von Ida	II 120–121	15/07/1815	*Geist der Liebe*	III 10–11	7	*Die Sterne*	II 6–9
Idens Schwanenlied	II 126–129	15/07/1815	*Der Abend*	III 41–43	8	*Nachtgesang*	10–11
Schwangesang	II 152–154	20/07/1815	*Das Abendrot* [SSB]	44–46	9	*Die Täuschung*	II 199–200
Die Erscheinung	II 196–198	25/07/1815	*Die Mondnacht*	47–48	[10]	*Das Sehnen*	III 12–14
Die Täuschung	199–200	25/07/1815	*Abends unter der Linde*	III 201–202	11	*Die Mondnacht*	III 47–48
Luisens Antwort	II 216–222	27/07/1815	*Huldigung*	III 15–18	12	*Abends unter der Linde*	III 201–202
Geist der Liebe	III 10–11	27/07/1815	*Alles um Liebe*	19–21	13	*Das Abendrot* [SSB]	III 44–46
Das Sehnen	12–14	19/10/1815	*Die Sterne*	II 6–9	14	*Geist der Liebe*	III 10–11
Huldigung	15–18	19/10/1815	*Nachtgesang*	10–11	15	*Der Abend*	III 41–43
Alles um Liebe	19–21	19/10/1815	*An Rosa I*	II 84–85	16	*Idens Schwanenlied*	II 126–129
Der Abend	III 41–43	19/10/1815	*An Rosa II*	86–87	17	*Schwangesang*	II 152–154
Das Abendrot [SSB]	44–46	19/10/1815	*Idens Schwanenlied*	II 126–129	18	*Luisens Antwort*	II 216–222
Die Mondnacht	47–48	19/10/1815	*Schwangesang*	II 152–154	19	*An Rosa I*	II 84–85
Abends unter der Linde	III 201–202	19/10/1815	*Luisens Antwort*	II 216–222	20	*An Rosa II*	86–87

continues his escapades with a new mistress (11, 12). The cycle comes to a parenthetical caesura as all three characters sing a trio in praise of the evening (13). The third episode begins, once again, with Wilhelm praising love (14). At this point, Wilhelm's description of the evening takes on an unaccustomedly dark tone (15). This unease proves prophetic as events take a tragic turn. The ever-distraught Ida sings of her torment (16) and decides to take her own life (17), while Luisa, Wilhelm's beloved of the second episode, swears her fidelity even as Wilhelm betrays her (18). Wilhelm's final appearance finds him pining for yet another woman, Rosa (the vision in the trio at the outset of episode three), who is absent (19) and who has also most likely taken her life in the face of her lover's insincerity (20). Wilhelm is devastated, a victim of his own fickle heart.

The unfolding of a plot in Schubert's arrangement of the texts can hardly represent the product of happenstance, especially as the resulting story echoes an archetype of the time. There is, admittedly, interpretation in assigning the characters to specific songs, but where the poetic titles do not directly reveal the identity of a figure, the situation and the content of the verses usually provide ample suggestion, such as the tryst between Wilhelm and Ida. Overall, there are three major episodes in this tale: the first focused on Wilhelm and Ida, the second introducing Luisa, and the third implying another lover, Rosa, while the women take their desperate leave.

Schubert's Musical Setting

As surprising as it was to find a Romantic tale emerging from the sequence of songs arranged according to Wolf's numbering of the documents supposedly in their original order, it was still necessary to determine whether any of this found expression in Schubert's music. Only proof of the composer's response to the structure of the story and an attempt to unify its disparate elements with conscious artistic devices could eliminate the chance of a possible, if highly unlikely accidental alignment of independent factors. A close reading of the Lieder does, in fact, reveal musical constructions that support the narrative outline and lend the twenty settings a strong sense of coherence.

The first of these techniques involves motivic and other resemblances between songs identified with specific characters and moments in the unfolding of the drama. Schubert emphasizes the three-episode scheme in his composition by linking songs positioned just after the beginnings of each of these sections: *Alles um Liebe* (No. 2), *Die Täuschung* (No. 9), and *Geist der Liebe* (No. 14). All are homages to love in E major sung

Table 8. Overview of the Kosegarten Lieder
Voice: W=Wilhelm, I=Ida, L=Luisa; names provided directly in texts to songs 3, 6, 7, 16, and 18.

W#	D	Title	Key	Text and Topic	Kose-garten	Voice
1	240	*Huldigung*	E major	(Episode 1) *Ganz verloren, ganz versunken* / In praise of Elwina, united in eternity	III 15–18	W
2	241	*Alles um Liebe*	E major	*Was ist es, das die Seele füllt?* / In praise of love, everything for her	III 19–21	W
3	228	*Von Ida*	F minor	*Der Morgen blüht, der Osten glüht* / He has left, oh please return	II 120–121	I
4	229	*Die Erscheinung*	E major	*Ich lag auf grünen Matten* / Sees a girl, she disappears	II 196-198	W
5	219	*Das Finden*	B♭ major	*Ich hab' ein Mädchen funden* / Description of her	II 52–54	W
6	227	*Idens Nachtgesang*	B♭ major	*Vernimm es, Nacht, was Ida dir vertrauet* / Description of him	II 112-113	I
7	313	*Die Sterne*	B♭ major	*Wie wohl ist mir im Dunkeln!* / O Ida, if we ever part look to the eternal stars where we shall meet again	II 6–9	W
8	314	*Nachtgesang*	E♭ major	(Episode 2) *Tiefe Feier schauert um die Welt* / Sorrow leave me as I fall asleep	II 10–11	L
9	230	*Die Täuschung*	E major	*Im Erlenbusch, im Tannenhain* / Apparition appears again, decides to follow	II 199–200	W
[10]	231	*Das Sehnen*	A minor	*Wehmuth, die mich hüllt* / For what do I long so, oh moon? Pain, fear, and tears	III 12–14	I
11	238	*Die Mondnacht*	F♯ major	*Siehe wie die Mondesstrahlen* / Relieving torment, being united with you	III 47–48	W
12	237	*Abends unter der Linde*	F major	*Woher o namenloses Sehnen ... Mir schmeichelt...linde des grauen Abends lauer Hauch* / The heavenly spirits at night	III 201–202	W

Table 8. Continued

W#	D	Title	Key	Text and Topic	Kose-garten	Voice
13	236	*Das Abendrot* [SSB]	A major	(Episode 3) *Der Abend blüht, der Westen glüht* / Sea, valley, rosy warmth, Hesperus sends his greetings	III 44–46	W, I, L
14	233	*Geist der Liebe*	E major	*Wer bist du, Geist der Liebe* / Love's mysterious powers, holy origins	III 10–11	W
15	221	*Der Abend*	B major	*Der Abend blüht, Temora glüht* / Nature: pay tribute to her name	III 41–43	W
16	317	*Idens Schwanenlied*	F minor	*Wie schaust du aus dem Nebelflor, o Sonne* / Nature sad, goodbye world, beloved	II 126–129	I
17	318	*Schwangesang*	F minor	*Endlich steh'n die Pforten offen* / Goodbye world	II 152–154	I
18	319	*Luisens Antwort*	B♭ minor	*Wohl weinen Gottes Engel* / How can I live without you, Wilhelm, never forget your Luisa who will always love you	II 216–222	L
19	315	*An Rosa I*	A♭ major	*Warum bist du nicht hier* / Missing Rosa	II 84–85	W
20	316	*An Rosa II*	A♭ major	*...Ihre Urne nie blumenleer!* / Rosa is dead	II 86–87	W

by the effusive protagonist, Wilhelm. Though composed over the span of several weeks, these three songs share obvious similarities. As can be seen in Example 1, all three of these songs open with virtually the same head motive, focusing on the E-major triad and finishing with an upward gesture in a dotted rhythm spanning a third. The subsequent melodic structure of these pivotal songs of the cycle displays the same close relationship (see Example 2). Note the persistence of dotted rhythms and the ascent that delineates first the third C♯–E then D♯–F♯ (see also mm. 9–13 of *Huldigung*). The relationship between *Geist der Liebe* and *Alles um Liebe* is even more profound (see Example 3). Here the melody (a1) and even the inner voices (b and c) are modeled on one another. The completion of the opening phrase in the piano (B–D♯–E) can be found at

Example 1. Head motive in *Alles um Liebe, Die Täuschung,* and *Geist der Liebe.*

Example 2. Melodic affinities between *Alles um Liebe, Die Täuschung,* and *Geist der Liebe.*

the end of the vocal line in *Geist der Liebe*: the last three notes (a2) spell out precisely this sequence, both answering *Alles um Liebe* and citing a motto ($\hat{5}$–$\hat{7}$–$\hat{1}$) that occurs in many of the Lieder throughout the cycle.

Ida's songs, too, are linked by strong motivic affinities. Her first song, *Von Ida*, contains two gestures that will recur later. The first (Example 4) is a chromatic ascent from C to F (mm. 9–10) that both recalls the chromatic motion from $\hat{5}$ to $\hat{1}$ in Wilhelm's *Alles um Liebe* (and following settings) and points to *Idens Nachtgesang* (mm. 7–9). Likewise, the descending thirds at the end of the song (measure 11) anticipate the opening of *Idens Schwanenlied* (measure 1); see Example 5. Note also that the idea of thirds spanning a melodic third (mm. 1–2) had already been introduced in Wilhelm's *Huldigung* (measure 16) and will occur later in *Die Erscheinung* (measure 14).[38]

Consecutive songs linked by musical devices are common in the cycle as well. Wilhelm's first two songs are tied together by voice leading at

Example 3. Motivic references between *Geist der Liebe* and *Alles um Liebe*.

Example 4. Chromatic ascent in Ida's songs.

Example 5. Descending thirds in Ida's songs.

the end of the first (*Huldigung*, measure 20) that refers directly to the voice leading at the opening of the second (*Alles um Liebe*, mm. 1–2).[39] Another example links *Die Erscheinung* and the following *Das Finden* with statements of "horn fifths," a hunting sonority highly appropriate for Wilhelm's successful pursuit of Ida (Example 6).

Example 6. Hunt motive in Wilhelm's songs.

Similar, too, is the persistence of a dotted melody in *Abends unter der Linde* on C♯ at the word "Abendroth" (measure 9) heralding the opening of the following song, *Das Abendrot* (measure 1), with precisely the same gesture. In the case of *Idens Schwanenlied* and the following *Schwangesang* we find strong resemblances in the piano texture and voice line. After the opening gestures in the voice that both trace the F-minor triad, the voice line of *Idens Schwanenlied* (measure 1) can be found in the lowest line of the right hand in the piano accompaniment to *Schwangesang* (measure 1), whereas the lowest line of the piano accompaniment in *Idens Schwanenlied* is echoed by the left hand in *Schwangesang*. There are other similarities lurking here, but note especially the adherence to the same rhythmic patterns in both songs.

Portraying individual characters and linking consecutive songs lend a sense of sequential logic to the set as a whole, but Schubert goes further. Within the set we find subtle musical references to moments in the unfolding of the drama between the main protagonists. The tryst between Wilhelm and Ida, for instance, is depicted in three consecutive songs in B-flat major,[40] the tonal midpoint between the respective realms of E major and F minor, the keys associated with Wilhelm and Ida, respectively (see Table 8).[41] Soon thereafter, Wilhelm and Ida go their separate ways, or, to be more precise, Ida suffers (*Das Sehnen*) as Wilhelm finds himself in the throes of another romance (*Die Mondnacht*). In setting Ida's complaint to a prominent descending tritone (*Das Sehnen*, mm. 7–8), Schubert anticipates the tragic demise of *Idens Schwanenlied* (tritone, measure 5) and an echo in Wilhelm's *Die Mondnacht* (mm. 7, 11, 12, and 21).[42] The text of the latter example is especially noteworthy in its use of an ingenious reversal of meaning. Ida's lament of yearning (verse 1: "Fliesset, fliesset, Thränen!") takes place not only at night, but also under the moon (verse 2). Wilhelm's night song, on the other hand, forms a pendant to this song in a series of oppositions: he, too, sings to the moon, but does so out of joy; what is more, his adulation of the night quickly reveals itself as an homage to a distinctly earthly passion that expressly fulfills his longing: "Eines in andre gar versunken . . . Solches . . . kühlte das Sehnen, / Löschte die Wehmuth mit köstlichen Thränen" ("One sinking into the other . . . This . . . cooled the longing / Extinguished the sorrow with precious tears," verse 3; see also "labende Thränen," verse 2). Such blatantly sexual imagery leaves no doubt of the act being described, yet it accomplishes much more. The "precious tears" of Wilhelm's fulfillment play ironically upon the "flowing tears" of Ida's longing, a dialogue, as it were, over the distance that separates desire and consummation.

Schubert strikingly invokes motivic quotation in another section of the drama as well: toward the end of the set when Wilhelm's forsaken mistresses take their leave. We literally hear the presence of the frivolous lover in the laments by Ida and Luisa as Schubert inserts Wilhelm's signature head motive into their melodies (Example 7). Hearing echoes of Wilhelm's enthusiasm as Ida openly greets death and as Luisa swears her faithfulness acts as a twist of the knife, an acerbic musical representation of fidelity in the face of betrayal and its tragic consequences.

Example 7. Remembering Wilhelm.

Figure 7. Rough draft of *Alles um Liebe* (D241).

That Schubert was aware of the significance of the head motive emerges in another context as well—in a telling alteration made during the composition of one of the Wilhelm songs. In the rough draft to *Alles um Liebe* (Figure 7) Schubert changed the vocal line in precisely the opening phrase, thus manipulating the musical idea in order to make patent its link with the other songs. As is clear from Example 8, had Schubert retained his first idea, the head motive would not have emerged. Instead, he crossed out the opening notes and reshaped the line into a descending triad followed by the upward dotted motion of a third, thus explicitly applying the head motive to the song.

In all, motivic references, voice leading, rhythmic constructions, textual continuities, an overall plot, a systematic use of key areas, and alterations in the musical scores lend the Kosegarten Lieder in the sequence suggested by Wolf's numbering a compelling sense of unity and common intention. Such a preponderance of musical devices linking twenty songs together both in character depiction and dramatic interaction along with the manuscript evidence points to the conclusion that Schubert was constructing a set of Lieder intended as an integrated whole. But are we

original version

revised version

Example 8. Alterations to the head motive in *Alles um Liebe*.

to understand this as a cycle? How were these twenty settings performed? And how does the set reflect the musical practice of the day?

Songs, Cycles, and Society: The *Liederspiel* in Schubert's World

The starting point for most considerations of Schubert's song cycles is a set of twenty songs composed in 1823, *Die schöne Müllerin*. A look at Wilhelm Müller's poems reveals that the plot of the cycle bears a striking similarity to the Kosegarten set but with the gender roles reversed: the story of a miller apprentice who falls in love with the daughter of the master miller, only to have his heart broken as she chooses another suitor; in the end he takes his life by drowning himself in a brook. In 1827, Schubert composed *Winterreise* to yet another set of poems by Müller, this time a more abstract tale: wandering through a winter landscape, the fraught character passes the places associated with a bygone love, seeking solace in an unforgiving world. Despite the common tragic tinge of love gone wrong, these later collections share a notable feature absent in the 1815 Kosegarten settings: the presentation of a highly personal telling of a story through the sole perspective of the protagonist, a solo voice with piano charting an inward journey. The performative and psychological framework in the late sets thus departs radically from the multi-character, essentially dramatic quality of the Kosegarten songs.

The Müller settings have made such a powerful impact on the notion of song cycle that we take for granted the overall features of both as a standard for the genre, though this does not reflect assumptions about collections of songs at the time. Schubert's contemporaries were perplexed by *Die schöne Müllerin*. The set was not published as a single work but appeared in five volumes over the course of 1824. There is no known performance of the cycle during Schubert's lifetime, and the premiere, sung by Julius

Stockhausen, did not take place until 1856, twenty-eight years after the composer's death.[43] Perhaps not surprisingly, German Lied production of the 1820s and earlier demonstrates a very different approach from that of Schubert's mature cycles. Songs could be published individually or, more commonly, in small groups. These songs often had little in common, but at times they were united by a theme or mood or even suggested a loosely narrative structure. The vast majority of Schubert's Lieder appeared in print in precisely this fashion, and it is notable that publishers played a large role in determining how these works were released.

This is not to say that Schubert did not experiment with groupings of songs early in his career. Although not widely known, musical and codicological investigations of Schubert's Lieder over the last few decades have turned up new evidence tying together what were once thought to be disparate musical compositions. Walther Dürr, for instance, has pointed to groupings of manuscripts in Schubert's output such as the *Selam Musenalmanach* songs of 1815 that reveal an aesthetic affinity spanning seven songs.[44] David Gramit has brought our attention to a "cluster of songs" centered on the Johann Mayrhofer settings from *Heliopolis*,[45] and Richard Kramer has focused on "distant" connections between various songs spanning most of Schubert's career.[46] Nor should we forget such sets as the *Don Gayseros* songs (probably of 1816) or the Novalis *Hymnen* of 1819. Schubert's 1815 settings of Kosegarten have been considered in this light as well, at least some of them. Already in 1928, Alfred Heuß found compelling similarities between *Die Erscheinung*, *Die Täuschung*, and *Die Mondnacht* and suggested that they be performed together.[47] Kramer isolates a "modest Trilogy to the Night" in *Die Mondnacht*, *Das Abendrot*, and *Abends unter der Linde*.[48] Walther Dürr refers to a "type of cycle" in the seven Kosegarten settings of October 1815; his arguments in favor of grouping these works are partly based on manuscript evidence, partly poetic mood, partly stylistic likeness.[49]

Truly narrative collections, with at least one clearly defined protagonist and the unfolding of dramatic content, can also be found in the song literature of other composers of the time. The most famous of these is certainly Beethoven's *An die ferne Geliebte* (1816), in which a pensive lover tells the story of his longing for a distant beloved in an uninterrupted sequence of six Lieder. Beethoven makes the unusual decision to tie together the whole by means of musical links between the songs, thereby solidifying the set into a type of through-composed composition. Though this approach is virtually unique, the idea of consecutive songs organized into the telling of a story is not. In 1799 Josef Woelfl published a set titled *Die Geister des Sees* that relates another tale of longing, this time of a woman who finally encounters her lost mate in the form of a ghost. Friedrich Methfessel's *Des Sängers Liebe, ein kleiner Roman in Liedern* (1806?) comes to a similarly tragic end as the blooming of a romance is cut short by the death of the girl. And in *Alexis und Ida* (ca. 1814) Friedrich Heinrich Himmel assembled forty-six songs "for one, two and several voices" relating the sentiments of a pastoral romance between a shepherd and a maiden.

The twenty Kosegarten settings of 1815 have all the trappings of these types of collections and demonstrate that Schubert was engaged in a similar project of compiling a sequence of songs sung by several characters meant to be performed together—eight years before his radical reconception of song cycle in *Die schöne Müllerin*. The works are all strophic in construction, short, quite approachable for the amateur singer, and no doubt intended for presentation in a Biedermeier salon. As we have seen, the story of Wilhelm and ill-fated love is a familiar one, echoing those sketched above and countless others from the period. In all, the plot, the musical simplicity, and even the grouping of songs to act out such a story reflect the conceits and cultural practices of its day.

The most common term associated with such groups of songs that collectively told a story and involved multiple characters from this time period was "Liederspiel." Literally a "song play," the genre involved the dramatic interaction of several characters, usually spoken dialogue, and Lieder performed at key moments of the story to present the sentiments of the individual figures. The songs demanded little vocal ability, were nearly always strophic, and focused on a single mood or thought. The composer usually credited with inventing the art form is Johann Friedrich Reichardt (1752–1814). Writing in the *Allgemeine musikalische Zeitung* in 1801, Reichardt tells of his abhorrence of vocal exaggeration in the theater, a fashion simply meant to rouse audiences by elevating the aria with effective but empty histrionics: "That inspired in me the thought of trying it with a short, songlike piece whose whole character was set on awakening but a single, pleasant impression and whether the theater public could be made interested in the simple and simply pleasant."[50] Reichardt launched a successful series of theatrical works such as *Lieb und Treue* that drew their texts largely from well-known poems and highly approachable, sometimes familiar tunes accompanied with a minimum of orchestration. The technique of borrowing implied here drew its inspiration in part from the French tradition of vaudeville, though the dramatic emphasis focused less on raucous parody and more on sentimental, sometimes patriotic topics. Other examples of the form include works by Friedrich Heinrich Himmel (*Fanchon oder das Leyermädel*, 1804) and Franz Carl Adelbert Eberwein (*Lenore*, 1829).

Often forgotten in discussions of the Liederspiel are the domestic origins of the genre. In the very next sentence of the passage quoted above, Reichardt continues: "I looked around for something and thought I had found it in a little piece that I had prepared several years previous for a completely different purpose: a domestic party for my own family."[51] The "little piece" that Reichardt transformed into a stage work for the theater reflected a practice of music making in the home that would continue for decades. Although intended for a private audience, such works shared many features with their theatrical namesake: stories told by text and verse involving several characters and the presentation of amateur songs. When produced at home the Liederspiel became something of a parlor game in which the literary sources, song texts, tunes selected, and stories told were chosen and arranged mainly by those attending. This was entirely in keeping with the Biedermeier practice of combining high culture and entertainment: poetry recitations, readings, charades, word games, dramatic sketches, dances, singing, and instrumental performance were all combined, presented, and received for the edification and pleasure of a gathering of friends. This is reflected compellingly in the following contemporaneous review of Hans Georg Nägeli's *Liederkranz auf das Jahr 1816*:

> The general purpose, which always remains foremost as regards the *whole* audience, is here, too, to offer these *solo* songs as a way to promote *sociability*. The texts are chosen so that they can be sung not *by* the group but nevertheless *in* the group by alternating singers. They are especially well suited for small circles where several people capable of singing come together, even though in terms of number and the character of their voices they do not constitute a choir. Such [people] can, in this manner, entertain themselves in a kind of *Liederspiel*, whose charm will be all the more elevated by the contrast in individuality and voice types, etc.[52]

This entertainment for friends to be played at home clearly enjoyed a fair share of popularity. The most famous example of this practice is described by Ludwig Rellstab in his biography of the composer Ludwig Berger:

> A circle of talented young people had formed in the house of the privy state councilor Stägemann which gave each other poetic assignments . . . . They posed a type of dramatic puzzle by the name of "Rose, the miller maiden" that one

> could only solve by linking together Lieder. Rose, the pretty miller-maid is loved by the miller, the garden boy, and the hunter; carefree and a little careless, she gives her heart to the latter, though not without earlier having favored and raised the hopes of the miller. The roles were divided between the members of the circle. The bright daughter of the house [Hedwig Stägemann], endowed with an unusually fine talent for poetry, took the role of the miller maid; Wilhelm Müller became the miller; the painter [Wilhelm] Hensel, later the husband of Fanny Mendelssohn, played the hunter. Each had to express themselves in Lieder in which the relationships to one another were more clearly stated. The game grew to enjoy great popularity.[53]

As described above, Wilhelm Müller and numerous friends met regularly in the Stägemann home in Berlin and, during the course of their soirees, hit upon the idea of producing a poetic-dramatic rendering of a literary idea that they had borrowed from a popular tale. It was here that Wilhelm Müller found the inspiration for his own cycle of poems, *Die schöne Müllerin*, written and published years later. Each of the participants was responsible for producing poetry suitable to his or her part at various points in the story. The result was a simply staged play in which the feelings and thoughts of the protagonists and the unfolding of the plot were presented in a sequence of short poetic recitations. When Berger joined their circle some time later, he was employed to set the poems to music so that the roles could be sung. The result was a Liederspiel in which sociability and individual creativity were blended together into a consummate Biedermeier art form. The Berlin friends took their work seriously enough to have it published in 1818 (Figure 8). As Rellstab relates:

> There were in all seven suitors around Rose, the pretty miller maiden. Berger initially composed ten purely strophic songs with simple accompaniment titled: "Songs from a Societal Liederspiel: The Pretty Miller Maid" that originally ended with the death of the repentant maiden and the hunter grieving at her grave (as in Goethe).[54]

Schubert's Kosegarten settings of 1815 show every indication of having been precisely such a work. The selection of texts to tell a popular story of a fickle heart, infatuation, and tragic despair, the short, strophic songs to be sung by amateurs portraying multiple characters—all point to a Liederspiel.

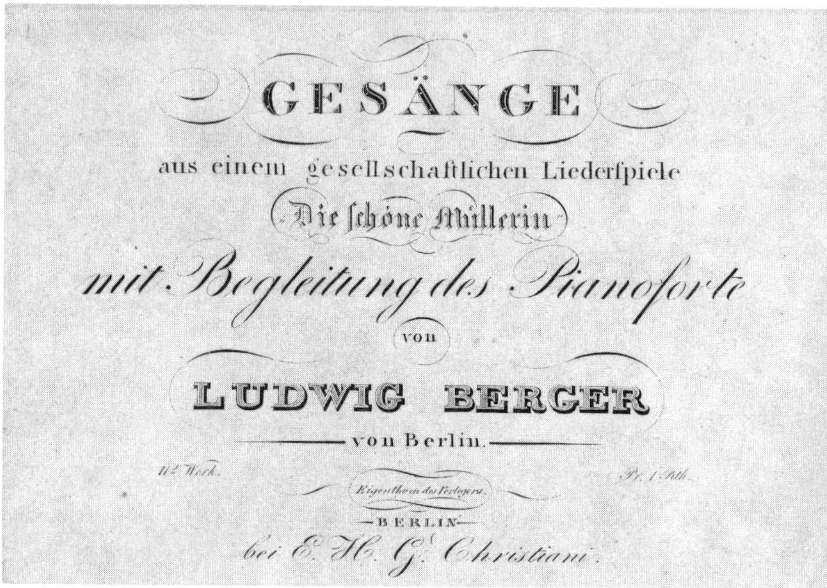
GESÄNGE

aus einem gesellschaftlichen Liederspiele

Die schöne Müllerin

mit Begleitung des Pianoforte

von

LUDWIG BERGER

von Berlin.

Eigenthum des Verlegers.

BERLIN

bei E. H. G. Christiani.

Figure 8. Title page, Ludwig Berger's *Die schöne Müllerin* (1818).

Even the notion of game-playing can be found here, for the song *Luisens Antwort* reveals Schubert at work in presenting his friends with a type of double parody: Kosegarten's text constitutes an answer to a very popular poem of the time, "Das Lied der Trennung" by Klamer Eberhard Karl Schmidt. Schmidt's poem depicts Wilhelm wondering whether his beloved Luisa will remember him now that they are apart; Kosegarten's *Antwort* (answer) portrays Luisa confirming how deeply committed she remains to Wilhelm, and even now, "never will Luisa forget you." Schubert was clearly cognizant of the relationship between these two poems and he chose an ingenious way of acknowledging the connection. Not long after its initial publication, "Das Lied der Trennung" was set to music by Mozart. In turning to Kosegarten's echo of Schmidt, Schubert likewise invokes Mozart in both the accompaniment pattern and the rhythm of the melody (see Example 9).[55] The clever paraphrase was almost certainly not lost on Schubert's companions.

Yet another feature of the Kosegarten songs points to its unusual construction. The thirteenth piece in the set, *Das Abendrot*, is, properly speaking, not a Lied at all but a vocal trio. Though Schubert set numerous texts in arrangements for two tenors and bass during his life, the voice parts here imply two female singers and one male singer. This interpretation is supported by the texture of the piano accompaniment,

Mozart, *Das Lied der Trennumg* (K519), mm. 1–4

Schubert, *Luisens Antwort* (D319), mm. 1–10

Example 9. Schubert's parody of Mozart.

but such a constellation is most unusual. In fact, it is the only vocal trio in Schubert's output that calls for this combination of voices.[56] Positioned as it is within the Kosegarten set, however, the part-song makes a great deal of sense. The singing characters of the Liederspiel are joined together in a parenthetic moment of reflection before the last segment of the work turns to its denouement and sorrowful conclusion.

Conclusion

Much of Schubert's life has gone missing in the two hundred years that have transpired since 1815, the year he composed these songs. We have no additional documents that corroborate the existence of this Liederspiel, but we know very little of the details from that year at all. If such material had been preserved, it would no doubt mention the type of music making and socializing that cultivated the domestic Liederspiel in the homes of the culturally inclined of Schubert's world. Indeed, it would be odd if this highly productive and supremely talented song composer had not attempted to write such a set for his friends given the artistic setting described in what later became known as Schubertiades. Schubert was too aware of the artistic tastes and social practices of his day not to try his hand at this increasingly popular musical innovation. The private nature of such an entertainment combined with its dating to early in Schubert's career could explain why no effort was made to publish this as a collection.

Eight years would pass before Schubert compiled a cycle he deemed worthy to print. In completing *Die schöne Müllerin* he unwittingly followed the path of its author Wilhelm Müller, who had taken the Liederspiel that he and his friends had written in 1816 and transformed it into his own poetic project. In so doing, the author radically altered the telling of the story. Rather than having individual figures reflect on their thoughts in a presentational style, Müller interiorized the entire sequence of events into the mind of the miller apprentice. The multi-character play was now an interior monologue, told by a participant in the story whose emotional involvement renders his narrative increasingly unreliable and whose voice is ultimately surrendered to the brook. The cyclical depiction of the sole protagonist caught in a reality that undoes him must have gripped Schubert as it inspired him to set a new a standard for Romantic song. Yet even in reaching for new forms of expression he must have recognized in the plot the outlines of a story or even a "song play" echoing a more innocent perspective from somewhere in his past. By 1823 that time was over, but the Kosegarten settings may well have proved an important early attempt at large-scale organization of songs, an art form that Schubert would come to master as no other. These songs, then, provide us with a previously unobserved perspective on the development of his genius.

NOTES

The initial research for this work was made possible by the Jubiläumsfond of the Austrian National Bank. The author wishes to express his gratitude for this support and to thank especially Otto Brusatti, the project coordinator.

1. This is the first publication that treats the details of this discovery in English; a monograph on the subject is planned. Aspects of this research are discussed in Morten Solvik, "Lieder im geselligen Spiel—Schuberts neu entdeckter Kosegarten-Zyklus von

1815," *Österreichische Musikzeitschrift* 53/1 (1997): 31–39; "Finding a Context for Schubert's Kosegarten Cycle," in *Schubert und seine Freunde*, ed. Eva Badura-Skoda, Gerold Gruber, Walburga Litschauer, and Carmen Ottner (Vienna, 1999), 169–82; and "Of Songs and Cycles: A Franz Schubert Bifolio," in *Music History from Primary Sources: A Guide to the Moldenhauer Archives*, ed. Jon Newsom and Alfred Mann (Washington, D.C., 2000), 392–99. See also Elizabeth Norman McKay, "Zu Schuberts Vertonungen von Kosegarten-Texten aus dem Jahr 1815," *Schubert durch die Brille* 24 (2000): 141–46; Jörg Büchler, "Zur Diskussion über die zyklische Zusammengehörigkeit von Schuberts Kosegarten-Vertonungen aus dem Jahre 1815," *Schubert: Perspektiven* 10/2 (2010): 139–55; and *Schubert Liedlexikon*, ed. Walther Dürr, Michael Kube, Uwe Schweikert, and Stefanie Steiner with Michael Kohlhäufl (Kassel, 2012), 158.

2. Since some songs have survived in more than one type of source, the percentages do not add up to 100 percent. This data is culled from Otto Erich Deutsch, *Franz Schubert: Thematisches Verzeichnis seiner Werke in chronologischer Folge*, rev. ed. (Kassel, 1978). "Lied" is defined as a song in German for solo voice and piano. These figures include compositionally separate settings of the same text (*Bearbeitungen*=versions) but not variants (*Fassungen*) of a single song. For a discussion of this distinction, see Maurice J. E. Brown, *Essays on Schubert* (London, 1966), 268.

3. For more on the Schubert Liederheft project, see Christopher H. Gibbs, *The Life of Schubert* (Cambridge, 2000), 79–80. This project was also to include Matthisson and Hölty settings.

4. None of the original fair copies of *Die schöne Müllerin* have survived, and original manuscripts for only four of the songs are known; see Deutsch, *Verzeichnis*, 488–89.

5. Two of the manuscripts held in private hands have since been acquired by public collections: A-Wn Mus. Hs. 43.946 and A-Wst 16.400, both fair copies (sigla here and elsewhere stem from RISM, the international index for music sources).

6. See Robert Winter, "Paper Studies and the Future of Schubert Research," in *Schubert Studies: Problems of Style and Chronology*, ed. Eva Badura-Skoda and Peter Branscombe (Cambridge, 1982), 209–75.

7. This is confirmed by Walther Dürr in *Franz Schubert: Neue Ausgabe sämtlicher Werke*, Series IV, vol. 8: *Lieder* (Kassel, 2009), xvii, passim.

8. The exception is *Hektors Abschied*, D312 (text by Schiller), today located in a separate manuscript at the Bibliothèque nationale in Paris.

9. It is thus all the more surprising that until now virtually no serious scholarly effort has sought to make sense of these marginalia. Ernst Hilmar, in "Die Schubert-Autographe der Sammlung Hans P. Wertitsch: Katalog," *Schubert durch die Brille* 13 (1994): 3–42, does note inscriptions of this type but provides no explanation for them.

10. Not all marginal markings were added by Johann Wolf. Additional numberings and annotations, especially regarding typesetting, can also be found on many of these pages. Walther Dürr raises this point about sequences of numbers in red crayon (Rötel) frequently situated in the upper-left corner of Schubert manuscripts (Dürr, IV/8, xviii); so far, no comprehensive documented explanation for this different set of numbers has been proposed.

11. On folio 2 recto of A-Wn L14 Münze 2.

12. In Alexander Weinmann, *Verlagsverzeichnis Giovanni Cappi bis A. O. Witzendorf. Beiträge zur Geschichte des Alt-Wiener Musikverlages*, series 2, no.11 (Vienna, 1967), 207, Johann Wolf is listed as a composer of piano vignettes and paraphrases of Lieder, published mostly from the 1840s through the 1860s.

13. My thanks to Rita Steblin for bringing these to my attention.

14. Handschriftensammlung, Wienbibliothek, I.N.3584.

15. The notice had appeared in the *Allgemeine Theaterzeitung* 108 (5 May 1848): 436.

16. "Herrn Karl Haslinger zur Erinnerung an den 25-jährigen Bestand seiner musikalischen Abende gewidmet 1862," Handschriftensammlung, Wienbibliothek, I.N.49883.

This item is no longer available for study. Haslinger's father was Tobias Haslinger (1787–1842).

17. Another work from Wolf's œuvre suggests the same conclusion. His "Etüden-Variationen über Franz Schuberts Lied Das Abendroth," was evidently based on D627 (or possibly the trio D236); D627 was published in 1867, D236 in 1892.

18. See Otto Erich Deutsch, *Musikverlags-Nummern,* 2nd ed. (Berlin, 1961), 11; and Alexander Weinmann and John Warren, "Diabelli, Anton," in *The New Grove Dictionary of Music and Musicians,* 2nd ed. (London, 2001), 7:279–80.

19. That Wolf worked for Spina and not Diabelli can also be seen in other marginal notes. On the verso of A-Wn 43.946 (*Geist der Liebe,* D233), we find a Wolf reference to a song in the "Verlags Cat. Spina" that is not yet engraved, a sure sign that Wolf had access to an internal listing at C. A. Spina; see *Autographen aus verschiedenem Besitz: Auktion am 17 Mai 1960 in Marburg,* J. A. Stargardt Catalogue 548 (Marburg, 1960), item 537 after page 126. Walther Dürr, in "Franz Schubert: Das Finden. Von der ersten Niederschrift zur Reinschrift," in *Beiträge zur musikalischen Quellenkunde,* 346, also concludes that Johann Wolf worked for Spina, but does not explain the marginalia.

20. The Witteczek-Spaun collection contains two indices of Schubert's songs titled "Repertorium"; see *Franz Schubert: Neue Ausgabe sämtlicher Werke,* Series VIII: Supplement Band 8, Quellen 2: *Franz Schuberts Werke in Abschriften: Liederalben und Sammlungen* by Walther Dürr (Kassel, 1975), 108.

21. This listing might be the "Aufstellung Schubertscher Lieder von Anton Diabelli" last seen at an auction in Vienna around 1922; see Deutsch, *Verzeichnis,* 87 ("Anmerkung" to D122).

22. Examples of numberings for each of the categories (except III) can be found in the following manuscripts: I—US-AUS Lake Collection (D228, 229), v; II—A-Wn Mus. Hs. 40.990, r; IV—A-Wn Mus. Hs. 41.628; V—US-Wc Moldenhauer (*Das Mädchen aus der Fremde,* D117), 1r; VI—US-CA bMS Mus 108(21), r; VII—A-Wn 40.993, r ("~~von verschiedenen Handschriften~~"); VIII—US-AUS Lake Collection (D228, 229), v.

23. A look at the songs in these two groups confirms this: the Lieder of Group I and Group II that I have thus far identified are clearly ordered in this fashion. There are only two exceptions among the 41 Lieder that I have been able to assign to these two categories: "I, 57" seems to refer to D645, which we only have in sketch form and might be dated early 1819; it may well have been written before "I, 49" (D923, 1827); "II, 45" seems to refer to D252, written 12 August 1815, long before "II, 43," D867 (January 1826).

24. It might refer to a generic designation for manuscripts bearing neither signature nor date or signature and no date. Such a determination is at this point not possible.

25. See the discussion of different song versions above.

26. In 1876 Alwin Cranz (1834–1923), proprietor of the music publishing house of August Cranz, bought the firm of C. A. Spina from Friedrich Schreiber. Albert Cranz, a descendant, in the 1950s helped run a part of the firm in Brussels. See *Riemann Musik Lexikon* (Mainz, 1959), "Personenteil A–K," 349.

27. Stargardt, September 1957, lot 421.

28. This conclusion may be confirmed by a marginal note in A-Wn Mus. Hs. 41.628, folio 1 verso (early version of *Die Mondnacht*): in pencil to the right of Wolf's reference to Group IV is written what appears to be "20 Gesänge." "Gesänge" is difficult to decipher, but the number is indisputable, which itself seems suggestive.

29. Kosegarten, it seems, used variants of his name throughout his life. The name given here appears on his certificate of baptism; in 1777 he substituted "Theobul" for "Gotthard" and from 1815 went by "Ludwig Gotthard." See H. Franck, *Gotthard Ludwig Kosegarten. Ein Lebensbild* (Halle, 1887), 2–3 and 402n1. See also the biography by Kosegarten's son: Johann Gottfried Ludwig Kosegarten, *Kosegartens Leben: Dichtungen*

von Ludwig Gotthard Kosegarten, vol. 12 (5th ed., Greifswald, 1827); and Lewis M. Holmes, *Kosegarten: The Turbulent Life and Times of a Northern German Poet* (Berne, 2004).

30. For more on Kosegarten's connection to German Romanticism, see Lewis M. Holmes, *Kosegarten's Cultural Legacy: Aesthetics, Religion, Literature, Art, and Music* (Berne, 2005); and Albert Boime, *Art in an Age of Bonapartism: 1800–1815*, vol. 2 of *A Social History of Modern Art* (Chicago and London, 1990), 315–635, esp. 377–79, 411–16, and 587–602.

31. For more on this speech, see Kosegarten, *Kosegartens Leben*, 235–39.

32. Franck, *Kosegarten*, 240–41 (here and elsewhere all translations mine). The publication announcement to which Schiller refers is probably the same as that which appeared at the back of the Göttingen *Musen Almanach* of 1798.

33. See the commentary of nineteenth-century literary historians on Kosegarten in Franck, *Kosegarten*, 161; see also Holmes, *Kosegarten* and *Kosegarten's Cultural Legacy*.

34. Maximilian and Lilly Schochow in their *Franz Schubert: Die Texte seiner einstimmig komponierten Lieder und ihre Dichter*, 2 vols. (New York, 1974), 1:243–72, propose a volume of *Gedichte* published in 1788 as well as the complete edition of Kosegarten's works of 1824 as possible text sources, but admit that neither could have been used by Schubert. Walther Dürr suggests two possibilities in *Franz Schubert: Neue Ausgabe sämtlicher Werke* (Kassel), Series IV. In vol. 3b (1982), 265. Dürr identifies Kosegarten's *Poesieen* (Leipzig, 1802) as the text source for all but the last of Schubert's Kosegarten settings but revises his proposal in vol. 5b (1985), 284, to *Kosegarten's Dichtungen. Siebenter Band. Lyrischer Gedichte. Siebentes, achtes, neuntes Buch* (Greifswald, 1813) or some related source; in vols. 8 (2009) and 9 (2011) he returns to the 1802 edition as the likely text source. The 1803 source I suggest here, like the 1802 edition, departs very little from Schubert's text, preserves all titles as they appear in Schubert's manuscripts, and includes all the Kosegarten settings Schubert ever set (including *An die untergehende Sonne*, D457). The 1803 edition nevertheless comes closer to the texts in Schubert's manuscripts; see, for instance, in *Abends unter der Linde,* (D237), "Mondenblitz" in Schubert's text underlay and the 1803 edition, not "Morgenblitz" as in the 1802 edition (see vol. 8, 251).

35. The 1815 settings were all taken from vols. 2 and 3. Vol. 1 contains 41 poems, including *An die untergehende Sonne*, first set by Schubert in 1816, though apparently not completed until 1817 (see Deutsch, *Verzeichnis*, 271).

36. Marie-Agnes Dittrich contends that not all of these poems are particularly suited to a musically strophic treatment; see Marie-Agnes Dittrich, *Harmonik und Sprachvertonung in Schuberts Liedern*, Hamburger Beiträge zur Musikwissenschaft, vol. 38 (Hamburg, 1991), 58.

37. Walther Dürr (Series IV, vol. 9, xxvi) and Jörg Büchler ("Schuberts Kosegarten-Vertonungen," 144–46) take issue with the contention that these songs form a narrative structure. Though the resulting story seems incontestable, just when the whole plot was pieced together from disparate poems remains a valid question. A detailed treatment of the topic would explode the bounds of this essay, but a good argument can be made for a story operating within the thirteen settings already completed by the end of July 1815.

38. Büchler, "Schuberts Kosegarten-Vertonungen," 146–51, points to further examples of third textures throughout the set and some additional unifying melodic and rhythmic motives not mentioned here.

39. Richard Kramer, *Distant Cycles: Schubert and the Conceiving of Song* (Chicago and London, 1994), 19 and 21, makes this point as well.

40. Wilhelm proclaims "Ich hab' ein Mädchen funden" at the very outset of *Das Finden*, while Ida reveals her discovery ("Ich habe ihn gefunden") in verse 2 of *Idens Nachtgesang*. In the following song, *Die Sterne*, Wilhelm mentions Ida by name in verses 1, 4, and 6. Note that these are widely scattered poems in the text source (see Table 7).

41. Technically speaking, there is no chromatic center between two pitches a major seventh apart; either B♭ or B could serve this purpose. The implications of key characteristics in the Kosegarten songs are discussed in Solvik, "Schubert's Kosegarten

Settings of 1815: A Newly Discovered Song Cycle, Final Report from the *Schubert Liedskizzen* Project," 55–58 (unpublished); and Büchler, "Schuberts Kosegarten-Vertonungen," 153.

42. Schubert's use of the tritone points to an obvious awareness of the negative associations of this interval in a long tradition of musical rhetoric. For a discussion of such examples, see Hartmut Krones, "'Ein Accumulat aller musikalischen Modulationen und Ausweichungen ohne Sinn, Ordnung und Zweck': Zu Schuberts 'schauerlichen' Werken der Jahre 1817–28," in *Franz Schubert zum 200 Geburtstag*, special edition of *Österreichische Musikzeitschrift* (January 1997): 32–40.

43. *Winterreise*, it seems, suffered a similar fate in terms of publication and performance. Schubert's posthumously published sets of Ludwig Rellstab and Heinrich Heine, often collectively titled *Schwanengesang*, may represent similar though shorter projects at the end of his life.

44. Walther Dürr, "Lieder aus dem 'Selam': Ein Schubertsches Liederheft," in *Beiträge zur musikalischen Quellenkunde: Katalog der Sammlung Hans P. Wertitsch in der Musiksammlung der Österreichischen Nationalbibliothek*, ed. Günter Brosche (Tutzing, 1989), 353–61. See also Dietrich Berke, "Zu einigen anonymen Texten Schubertscher Lieder," *Die Musikforschung* 22 (1969): 485–89.

45. David Gramit, "Schubert and the Biedermeier: The Aesthetics of Johann Mayrhofer's 'Helipolis,'" *Music and Letters* 74 (1993): 355–82.

46. Kramer, *Distant Cycles*.

47. Alfred Heuß, "Ein trunkenes Jünglingslied von Franz Schubert," *Zeitschrift für Musik* 95 (1928): 619–24, 679–82.

48. Kramer, *Distant Cycles*, 19. Though he finds affinities between other songs as well, Kramer concludes that "to seek authenticity in some larger reconstruction of the Kosegarten settings is an exercise in futility" (20).

49. Walther Dürr and Arnold Feil with Walburga Litschauer, *Reclams Musikführer: Franz Schubert* (Stuttgart, 1991), 50–51. Dürr also refers to the Kosegarten settings as a "closed group," in "Franz Schubert: Das Finden," 345–51, here 350.

50. Friedrich Reichardt in "Etwas über das Liederspiel," *Allgemeine musikalische Zeitung* 3/43 (1801): 709–17, here 711.

51. Ibid.

52. *Allgemeine musikalische Zeitung* 18/47 (20 November 1816): 810–11 (original emphasis). The quotation is taken from a review of Hans Georg Nägeli's *Liederkranz auf das Jahr 1816*, 809–16, a collection of 24 Lieder to texts by "Körner, Wagner, Usteri, Hottinger, Müchler, Arndt, Kosegarten, Matthisson, C. Schreiber, Wessenberg, Voss, Herder, Jacobi, Gries, Hill, Vogel" and one anonymous poem.

53. Otto Erich Deutsch, "Schuberts schöne Müllerin," in *Wiener Musikgeschichten* (Vienna, 1993), 89–104, here 99, from Ludwig Rellstab's 1846 biography of Ludwig Berger.

54. Ibid., 100.

55. This likeness also pointed out in Walther Dürr and Arnold Feil with Walburga Litschauer, *Reclams Musikführer: Franz Schubert*, 51.

56. *Franz Schubert: Neue Ausgabe sämtlicher Werke* (Kassel), Series III: "Mehrstimmige Gesänge für gemischte Stimmen," vol. 2a (1996), ed. Dietrich Berke, makes special note of D236 having no voice designations in the manuscript score, speculating that it might be sung by three male voices, as in other examples of trios notated by Schubert without voice parts (ix). This seems highly unlikely, given that Schubert provides a piano part exactly doubling the SSB vocal parts. For a similar doubling of an SATB texture, see D439, *An die Sonne*, where the parts are provided in Schubert's hand. This is also no doubt the reason *Das Abendrot* appears in this volume of the critical edition.

The Queen of Golconda, the Ashman, and the Shepherd on a Rock: Schubert and the Vienna Volkstheater

LISA FEURZEIG

Popular theater of Schubert's time, generally known as the Volkstheater tradition, was a vivid and expressive component of Viennese culture.[1] Performed in suburban theaters outside the city walls, Volkstheater plays attracted a broad audience ranging from prostitutes to royalty. The plays held a special position as one of the only outlets, despite censorship, for the social and political concerns of the public. The famous actors and the latest plays and songs—for there was much music in Volkstheater plays—were familiar throughout the city.

In his 1924 introduction to the music for works by playwright Ferdinand Raimund (1790–1836), musicologist Alfred Orel made the claim that the Viennese Classical style was rooted in folk music, observing that "through the deficient knowledge of Viennese folklike music, a great chasm yawns, preventing the rightful understanding of Haydn's and Beethoven's works . . . not to mention Franz Schubert, that most Viennese of all the great masters, who sprang up entirely from the ground of folklike music and raised it to the highest power."[2] Orel does not clearly separate folk and folklike (*volkstümliche*) music in this comment—which is quite understandable in discussing music of the early nineteenth century, when such concepts were vaguely defined. The important aspect of his observation is that he recognized a pathway leading from the music practiced and enjoyed by ordinary Viennese people to the elevated music of Viennese Classicism—a pathway that even now remains largely unexplored.

"High" and "low" artistic realms in Viennese musical life frequently intersected. As a young man in the early 1750s, Haydn played for the theatrical producer Joseph Kurz and wrote the music for his play *Der krumme Teufel* (The Crooked Devil); there is a marvelous anecdote of how Kurz histrionically imitated a shipwreck to inspire Haydn's improvisation at the keyboard.[3] Beethoven too was well aware of the Volkstheater, as can be seen in his conversation books: his nephew Karl avidly passed along the theater gossip of the day, and his friend and assistant Anton Schindler was concertmaster of the orchestra in the Josefstadt Theater, founded in 1788—one of three principal venues that presented Volkstheater.

Theatricality was an important part of social life for Schubert and his friends, and their interest in theater took various forms. At the most casual and amateur level were such activities as the game of charades that Schubert, Franz von Schober, and others played at the castle of Atzenbrugg in July 1821.[4] At the most ambitious were the plays and operas that Schubert and several librettist friends created in the hopes of having them professionally performed at theaters.

The theatrical activities of the Unsinnsgesellschaft, or Nonsense Society, a group discussed by Rita Steblin in this volume, might be considered as falling somewhere between the improvised and the composed. The handwritten journal *Archiv des menschlichen Unsinns* (Archive of Human Nonsense) issued by this society in 1817–18 parodied contemporaneous journal publishing by including assorted materials, from reports on politics and science to literary works. Among the latter were several plays that mocked the literary conventions of the time. One example is a play titled *Der Feuergeist* (The Fire Spirit) that Steblin believes to have been performed in April 1818. Although the journal issues that would have contained the text of the play are lost, a picture representing a scene from it survives, and Steblin argues that this play may have been a source for Schubert's 1820 melodrama *Die Zauberharfe* (The Magic Harp), which was performed at the Theater an der Wien, one of the venues presenting a mixed repertoire, including Volkstheater.[5]

Schubert's circle of friends both loved and practiced the arts; thus it is only to be expected that they were aware of theatrical news and events throughout Vienna. The writings of Franz von Hartmann, who arrived as a law student from Linz in 1825, suggest the atmosphere. He wrote to his sister Anna von Revertera of the high level of artistic quality in Vienna, "especially galleries and art collections, which all far exceeded my imaginings. As does the theater, the Burg as well as the Leopoldstadt, totally opposed as they are to each other."[6] It is significant that Hartmann mentions both these theaters. The first functioned as the center for classical drama, whereas the Leopoldstadt, founded in 1781 just across the Danube Canal from the inner city, was the central venue for Volkstheater.

Hartmann's comment shows that a sophisticated member of the upper middle class was drawn to both repertoires.

Given this cultural context, it is reasonable to assume that the two documented occasions when Schubert attended specific Volkstheater plays represent just the tip of the iceberg—he and his friends were no doubt immersed in this theatrical tradition.[7] Furthermore, they were linked to the most important Volkstheater playwright of the 1820s, Ferdinand Raimund, who began his career as a comic actor and was well known to Schubert's good friend Eduard von Bauernfeld, who may have introduced the composer and the dramatist.[8] Both Raimund and Schubert were torchbearers at Beethoven's funeral in March 1827. As it happens, Schubert also knew Johann Nestroy (1801–1862), whose more cynical plays would take over the Viennese stage in the 1830s. Nestroy had been a fellow student at the Stadtkonvikt (City Seminary). Schubert attended some of Nestroy's performances as an opera singer, and Nestroy, who was a fine bass, participated in public performances of some of Schubert's vocal quartets both in Vienna and in Amsterdam.[9]

The purpose of this essay is to explore several instances in which Schubert's music is notably similar to that of extremely well-known Volkstheater songs—similar enough to suggest that Schubert may have intended deliberate references to Volkstheater music.[10] In one such example the play involved was a classic of the genre, dating from the 1790s, and in the other three cases Schubert composed his work soon after the premiere of the relevant play. Taken together, these situations suggest that he was familiar with both the enduring Volkstheater tradition and the latest important works. The first two cases are based on observations already made by others; the second pair is presented here for the first time. In all instances the examples depend on a combination of musical and textual resemblances between the works compared. The musical similarities are not conclusive on their own, but when combined with shared textual elements—ranging from a single syllable to plot similarities to an overarching idea—they carry much more weight.

Such complex forms of reference offer a remarkable window into Schubert's creative mind. It is widely recognized that as a song composer he unified music and text in extraordinary ways. The theatrical situations—in which textual relationships and musical connections to an outside source go hand in hand—provide further examples of how his mind operated. They may suggest models for similar readings of other works, helping us to identify larger meanings for Schubert's music.

Schubert does not directly quote his musical sources from the Volkstheater; rather he reshapes certain elements in ways that suggest another piece of music was a partial source for his own. This was a shrewd strategy given the Austrian political situation in Clemens von Metternich's Vienna. Censorship and police surveillance were the norm—but within that context Volkstheater plays took some liberties, criticizing government and society in ways that were impossible elsewhere—and deniability was advantageous.[11]

Ich hört' ein Bächlein rauschen and *Wer niemals einen Rausch hat g'habt*

In an article about Schubert written some forty years after his death, Eduard von Bauernfeld recalled some discussions with the composer in which he criticized various aspects of his friend's compositional style:

> With Schubert, so much about form, musical declamation, and the fresh melodies can be reproached. [The melodies] sometimes sound too national [*vaterländisch*], too Austrian; they recall folk tunes whose rather low tones and unbeautiful rhythms do not have full rights to push their way into the poetic art song. On this topic, it sometimes came to little discussions with Master Franz. Thus when we tried to prove to him that certain passages in *Die schöne Müllerin* recalled an old Austrian grenadiers' march or Wenzel Müller's *Wer niemals einen Rausch hat g'habt.* — He grew seriously angry about such petty, carping criticism, or else he laughed at us and said, "What do you understand? That's the way it is, and it has to be that way!"[12]

Evidently, the link between Classical and folk traditions that Orel posited in 1924 would have troubled some young intellectuals a century earlier. Bauernfeld's account makes it clear that Schubert did not share that perspective. When his friends made class distinctions between folk music and art song, he either grew angry or simply laughed at the notion that to mix these genres was inappropriate.

The song in which Schubert's friends heard a link to Wenzel Müller's *Wer niemals einen Rausch hat g'habt* must be the second song of *Die schöne Müllerin*, namely *Ich hört' ein Bächlein rauschen*. The passages quoted in Examples 1 and 2 show the openings of both.

Example 1. Wenzel Müller, *Wer niemals einen Rausch g'habt*, vocal line, mm. 16–22.

Example 2. Franz Schubert, *Ich hört' ein Bächlein rauschen*, vocal line, mm. 2–6.

Each melody moves up to the fifth scale degree, hovers on or around it, and then moves downward a full octave before coming to rest on the tonic note. In the process of descent, both melodies use the figure $\hat{5}$–$\hat{3}$–$\hat{1}$ followed by other arpeggiations. These musical relationships are quite noticeable on their own, and they are strengthened by the texts, because the syllable *rausch* appears at the same moment in each phrase.

This textual parallelism creates a kind of pun, because the words *rauschen* and *Rausch* have entirely different meanings. The verb *rauschen* means to rustle or murmur and describes the sound that the miller hears as he approaches the brook. The noun *Rausch* means the state of being intoxicated. The character who sings *Wer niemals* in the play *Das Neusonntagskind* (Fifth Sunday's Child) is quite the opposite of the protagonist in *Die schöne Müllerin*. While the miller is young, innocent, and hopeful as he sets out to seek his fortune, the play's Hausmeister (Caretaker) is jaded and grumpy (though basically goodhearted), fond of the pleasures of alcohol, and prone to become deaf whenever someone needs him to open the door—unless the jingle of coins is added to the soundscape. The play by Joachim Perinet premiered in 1793, and the character of the Hausmeister became a Viennese classic.[13] Indeed, the Hausmeister's song praising drunkenness soon moved into the category of a folksong.[14] There is specific evidence that friends of Schubert were familiar with the song, as it is mentioned in an 1817 document of the Nonsense Society. The motto at the top of the society's newsletter of 4 December is the opening of the Hausmeister's song, "Wer niemals einen

Rausch hat g'habt der ist kein braver Mann!" (Anyone who has never been drunk is not a good man!)—which is then labeled as being from Act 7, scene 36 of *Don Carlos*.[15] Thus Perinet is implicitly and satirically equated with Friedrich Schiller. Both the implication that Schiller is long-winded and the idea of linking such a revered writer of Weimar classicism with an icon of the popular theater are very much in the spirit of Viennese comedy of this period. One common literary practice in the Volkstheater tradition was the *Verwienerung* (or "Viennacization") of well-known stories including Bluebeard, Othello, and various Greek myths. In musical quodlibets within their Volkstheater plays, composers delighted in mixing operatic and symphonic selections from composers such as Haydn, Mozart, Rossini, and Spontini with folksongs and songs from other popular plays.[16] By allowing a folklike tune into his elevated song cycle, Schubert showed more affinity with these musical practices of the Volkstheater than with the taste of his friends.

The connection between the two songs goes beyond the play on the words *Rausch* and *rauschen*. It also suggests a deeper foreshadowing: the miller's encounter with the brook will lead to intoxication, and the apparently innocent *rauschen* will culminate in a deadly *Rausch*.

Aline and the "Wanderer" Fantasy

We move next to a more elaborate connection, this one between a theater song and an instrumental work based on one of Schubert's Lieder. On 19 October 1822, Schubert went to the Leopoldstadt Theater and saw *Aline, oder Wien in einem andern Welttheile* (Aline, or Vienna on Another Continent), a play by Adolf Bäuerle with music by Wenzel Müller. The author of the play was important not only because he was one of the three central playwrights of his day, but because as editor of the *Theaterzeitung* he had a huge influence on theatrical matters in Vienna.[17] A month after attending this performance, Schubert composed his Fantasy in C Major (D760), generally known as the "Wanderer" Fantasy because of its quotation from Schubert's song *Der Wanderer* (D489) on a text by Schmidt von Lübeck. Hans Költzsch, in his seminal study of Schubert's piano music, pointed out similarities between the waltz theme in the scherzo section of that piece and a duet from *Aline* that begins "Was macht denn der Prater, sag blüht er recht schön?"[18] See Examples 3 and 4.

As in the previous case discussed, we find definite similarity without direct quotation. The dotted rhythms are a strong link, and the melodies are quite similar. At the end of the fourth bar of each passage, the melodies diverge,

Example 3. Wenzel Müller, duet from *Aline*, vocal lines, mm. 32–40.

Example 4. Franz Schubert, "Wanderer" Fantasy, right hand, waltz theme, mm. 405–20.

with Müller's ending on the third scale degree, while Schubert's ends on the fourth. At the openings of their second phrases, however, each tune immediately moves to the scale degree that was emphasized by the other one, creating a kind of virtual cross-relation.

Költzsch pointed out the relationship between these two passages, but provided no interpretation, leaving it an open question why Schubert might have linked his piano fantasy with a recent Volkstheater song. To suggest an answer, it is once again important to know some particulars about the play and the song. The "Wanderer" Fantasy has no sung text that we can turn to for answers, but its association with Schubert's earlier song links it to the Romantic archetype of the wanderer.[19] How might this be related to Bäuerle's play and the duet?

The play's ancestry goes back to the French novella *Aline, reine de Golconde* (1761), written by the Chevalier Stanislas de Boufflers (1738–1815). The heroine is a milkmaid who is seduced by a fashionably decadent young nobleman, as in many eighteenth-century French "philosophical" novels.[20] Instead of falling into ruin, she rises through the demimonde until she becomes the enlightened monarch of Golconda, a prosperous state in India. Many years later, when her former lover shows up there, she wins him back by using the resources at her command to stage a re-creation of the scene of her initial seduction, with herself costumed as the milkmaid she once was, convincing him of the value of what he had thrown away when he was too young to appreciate it.

This story captured the European theatrical imagination, inspiring numerous ballets and operas across Europe from the 1760s until well into the nineteenth century.[21] The most widely known version was a French opera composed in 1803 by Henri Berton (text by J. B. C. Vial and E. G. F. de Favières) that in 1804 reached Vienna, where it was performed twenty times in the court theaters in German translation. Johann Michael Vogl, later the preeminent champion of Schubert's songs, performed the important role of Osmin, and he also composed the duet *Ich widme dir mein ganzes Leben* to be substituted in the Vienna version for a duet by Berton. Vogl's duet was sufficiently familiar to Viennese audiences to be included together with many well-established favorites from both Volkstheater and opera sources in the smash hit quodlibet play performed at the Theater an der Wien for the 1809 carnival season: *Rochus Pumpernickel*.[22] Schubert himself had encountered the Aline story before the performance of Bäuerle's play at the Leopoldstadt. The first play with music by Schubert to be performed in a major theater, *Die Zwillingsbrüder*, had six performances at the Kärntnertor Theater, each time as the first half of a double bill, and on 21 July 1820 it was paired with a ballet version of *Aline*.[23]

The story of Aline evokes the conflicting emotions of Romantic wanderers, who typically feel the urge to leave their homes but are then tormented by longing (*Sehnsucht*) for what they have lost. Aline—an example of the rare female wanderer in this period—travels a great distance to another continent, but then paradoxically wins her former lover back through nostalgic memories of her humble childhood home. (In Bäuerle's Vienna-centered version, the specific location she conjures up is the Brühl, a forest area outside the Vienna suburb of Mödling.)

Schubert's waltz theme echoes the Bäuerle-Müller duet mentioned earlier, which is sung by the play's secondary couple of Zilly—Aline's confidante, also from Austria—and Bims, the ship's barber. Zilly, posing as the queen and pretending to know nothing about Vienna, nevertheless asks very pointed questions that show her specific knowledge of the city, and Bims fills her in on the latest developments in the Imperial capital. (This duet provides clear evidence of the improvisatory element in the Volkstheater, as variants are seen in several sources. Rommel's reprint of the play and two piano-vocal scores all differ in textual details.)[24]

The duet text alternates between praise and satire. An example of praise:

Nur noch ein Wört'l, was g'fällt denn in Wien?	One more word: What do people like in Vienna?
Ehrliche Leut' und ein fröhlicher Sinn.	Honest people and a merry spirit.

On the ironic side, the disastrous finances of the empire are skewered in other passages:

Nun, und der Kalteberg[25] [sic] *ist noch in Wien?*	So, is the Kahlenberg still in Vienna?
Den habn's jetzt verschrieben, er geht nach Berlin.	They've signed it over, it's going to Berlin.
Ist noch die Schwimmanstalt, schwimmt man noch dort?	Is there still a public pool, do people still swim there?
Mit Schulden da schwimmen s' ohne Wasser oft fort.	They're swimming away in debt, even without water.

In most versions, the duet ends with a lovely self-referential twist:

Was jetzt im Leopoldstädter Theater vorgeht?	And what's happening now in the Leopoldstadt Theater?
Da singt just die Zilly mit dem Bims ein Duett.	Zilly is singing a duet with Bims.[26]

This multivalent message leaves the question open of just how the refrain is intended. "Ja nur ein Kaiserstadt, ja nur ein Wien" (Yes, only one Imperial city, yes, only one Vienna) seems to express praise, but if said in the proper ironic tone, it could be meant cynically instead, as in "Yeah, it's only Vienna." The cynical reading is supported by Bäuerle's next play, *Wien, Paris, London, Constantinopel*, which premiered five months after *Aline* in March 1823: the main characters receive a set of magical objects as they set out on their journeys, one of which is a purse that fills up with money whenever they think nice thoughts about Vienna.

By obliquely referencing the *Aline* duet, Schubert may have meant to evoke in his audience a sophisticated mixture of emotions: the tragic Romantic yearning of the poem "Der Wanderer" and of Schubert's setting is intermingled with Bäuerle's down-to-earth language and ironic rhetorical strategy that critiques Vienna in the very process of praising it. Perhaps this emotional mix reflects the ambivalence of the intelligent artist who in 1822 might both want to leave home and at the same time feel the need to stay.[27]

Winterreise and *Der Bauer als Millionär*

On 10 November 1826, a new play, Raimund's *Das Mädchen aus der Feenwelt, oder der Bauer als Millionär* (The Maiden from the Fairy World, or The Peasant as Millionaire) had its premiere at the Leopoldstadt Theater. It was an enormous success, first in Vienna and then in several German cities. Raimund played the title role of Fortunatus Wurzel, a simple peasant who is used as a pawn by magical forces so that he becomes fabulously rich and then loses his money and his youth overnight. The music was composed by Joseph Drechsler (1782–1852), and two songs instantly became favorites, probably because they went beyond the particulars of the plot to become emblems of a widespread and general state of mind. There is significant evidence to support the belief that Raimund himself wrote the melodies of these songs; Orel includes facsimiles of both, written in music notation in Raimund's handwriting, along with quotations from Raimund documents commenting on his compositional work.[28]

No documentation exists to prove that Schubert attended this play, but we know that his friends the Spauns did, on 21 December 1826, and that Schubert was with them later that evening, so it is likely that the play was discussed.[29] I argue that both of these songs have parallels in Schubert's *Winterreise* that are identifiable through musical and textual relationships.

Commentary from the time reveals how deeply the play—and in particular Fortunatus Wurzel, the central figure played by Raimund himself—moved the audience. For example, renowned German actor Ludwig Devrient "under [Raimund's] spell, exclaimed, 'The man is so true that a miserable person like myself freezes and suffers along with him.' . . . 'The whole house rejoiced, laughed, and cried, and I rejoiced and laughed and cried with them,' reported an eyewitness.'"[30]

In order to grasp the play's connection with Schubert's music, we must examine Wurzel's key scenes. Before the play begins, he is a simple peasant who is raising a foster daughter, little realizing that her mother, Lakrimosa, is a once-powerful fairy undergoing a punishment for her vainglory. For Lakrimosa to be redeemed, her daughter must grow up simply and marry an ordinary person by her eighteenth birthday—but two years before the play begins, the allegorical Envy, enraged after being rejected by Lakrimosa, has taken revenge on her by making Wurzel a wealthy man. He now lives in a great city, surrounded by flattering admirers; he indulges his appetites to excess; and he insists that his daughter must marry a rich man rather than the fisherman she loves. As Lottchen's eighteenth birthday approaches, a grand battle of supernatural beings rages around the unknowing Wurzel. Angry at Lottchen for defying his wishes, he throws her out of the house, and he then receives a visit from an unknown person who claims to be an old friend: Jugend, or Youth. This role was played by Therese Krones, a beloved actress of the time, and Zentner observes that she "fascinated all Vienna. She too had found a task perfectly suited to her nature, and her legacy in theater history lives mostly through this role."[31]

Jugend has come to say good-bye to Wurzel, who does not recognize this "old friend" or understand what is happening. In the first famous song, *Brüderlein fein*, Jugend begs Wurzel to forgive him and not hold a grudge when he departs. Wurzel first tries to bribe Jugend to stay, then grows angry—but finally the two sing an affectionate farewell. This song reached folksong status in Vienna, apparently because it captured a sorrowful, nostalgic mood that suited the 1820s, when the exciting years of the Congress of Vienna and the defeat of Napoleon were giving way to the frustrations of Metternich's Restoration.

After Jugend goes offstage, Wurzel receives another visit, this time from Old Age (*das hohe Alter*). He is instantly transformed into an old man, his mansion disappears, and he finds himself back in the countryside. When he next appears in the play, he has just begun his new job as an Aschenmann, a collector of ashes. He expresses his newfound humility in the *Aschenlied*, whose text contrasts the vanity of wealth and ambition with the true values of love and faithfulness. In its original form, the song had three stanzas; here, to give a sense of its style and meaning, are the first and third:

So mancher steigt herum,	Many a man rises up,
Der Hochmut bringt ihn um,	Arrogance brings him down,
Trägt einen schönen Rock,	Wears a nice coat,
Ist dumm als wie ein Stock.	Is dumb as a stick.
Von Stolz ganz aufgebläht,	All swollen with pride,
O Freundchen, das ist öd,	O my friend, that is empty,
Wie lang stehts denn noch an,	However long you put it off,
Bist auch ein Aschenmann!	You're also an ashman!
Ein Aschen, ein Aschen!	Ashes! Ashes!

Figure 1. Therese Krones as Jugend.

Doch vieles in der Welt,	Yet much in the world,
Ich mein nicht etwa's Geld,	And I don't mean money,
Ist doch der Mühe wert,	Is really worth the trouble
Daß man es hoch verehrt.	That we should honor it highly.
Vor alle braven Leut,	To all good people,
Vor Lieb und Dankbarkeit	To love and gratitude,
Vor treuer Mädchen Glut,	To the ardor of faithful maidens,
Da zieh ich meinen Hut.	I take off my hat.
Kein Aschen! Kein Aschen![32]	Not ashes! Not ashes!

Like the *Aline* duet, this song was a perfect candidate for added stanzas caricaturing various types of people, and recent performances continue to feature such additions, frequently commenting on current events or scandals.[33] Just a month after Raimund's death in 1836, two newly written stanzas in tribute to him were sung on the stage of the Leopoldstadt. The use of this song as a vehicle for such homage reflects how closely the Viennese public identified Raimund with the poignant figure of the Aschenmann.[34]

Two songs from the second half of Schubert's *Winterreise* can be linked to *Der Bauer als Millionär*: *Der greise Kopf* and *Die Krähe*. In *Der greise Kopf*, the winter wanderer notices that his head has been sprinkled with snow, giving him the appearance of an old man—but alas, this is only an illusion. The lines

Vom Abendrot zum Morgenlicht	From sunset to morning light
Ward mancher Kopf zum Greise	Many a head has turned gray

were probably intended metaphorically by Wilhelm Müller—but in *Der Bauer als Millionär* this literally happens to Wurzel. The link to the song cycle is strengthened by the circumstance that Wurzel's transformation is accompanied by the sudden magical onset of winter.

The song *Brüderlein fein* is a reflection on friendship at the moment that the allegorical friendship between Wurzel and Jugend is ending, in the sense that his youth is saying farewell to him. In *Die Krähe*, the wanderer questions the faithfulness of a crow who is following him:

Krähe, wunderliches Tier,	Crow, marvelous animal,
Willst mich nicht verlassen?	Wilt thou not abandon me?

The crow, he realizes, is expecting his death and hopes to eat his corpse, but he ironically compares its steadfastness with the fickleness of his beloved:

Krähe, laß mich endlich sehen	Crow, let me finally see
Treue bis zum Grabe.	Faithfulness unto the grave.

What is noteworthy here is that the situations are inverted. Jugend is leaving Wurzel, but still wishes him well and begs for forgiveness. The crow stays beside the wanderer like a faithful lover or friend, but its behavior results from its selfish needs rather than true concern for another. This inversion makes the comparison between the two situations all the more interesting.

Let us presume that Schubert deliberately incorporated references to the two famous songs from *Der Bauer als Millionär* into *Winterreise.* To do so while still preserving the musical style and expressive goals of his song cycle must have been a challenge. As a result, the resemblances between the two pairs of songs are fleeting and subtle, particularly in *Die Krähe*.

Example 5 shows the first half of the *Aschenlied*, omitting the introduction. Example 6 shows the key phrase of *Der greise Kopf*, which is heard three times in the song: as the piano introduction, the first vocal phrase, and then again near the end of the song; the final occurrence is shown here. The Schubert phrase first ascends, in a slightly winding arpeggiated melody, then arrives at an accented tritone (B–F) before descending in a more direct manner. Susan Youens interprets this phrase as a summary of the emotional trajectory of the song, with the ascent representing the wanderer's joy when he believes himself to be old and the descent representing his disillusionment that this is not the case.[35] The two-bar phrase at the end of the *Aschenlied* example shares the ascent-descent contour and also features a central accented tritone (C–F♯). Youens points out that the prosody of the Schubert phrase is very unnatural the first time it is sung, on the words "Der Reif hatt' einen weißen Schein mir übers Haar gestreuet" (The frost had sprinkled white over my hair), with strong beats falling on the unaccented syllables "ei(nen)" and "ü(bers)"—yet when the phrase is heard later, "the prosodic accents more accurately and expressively emphasize the last light of dusk and the first light of morning, the nocturnal span in which others grow old but not the unfortunate wanderer."[36] This shift from awkward to appropriate prosody suggests that Schubert was thinking of the later phrase—the one that matches Wurzel's story—when he first composed the melody.[37]

Example 5. Joseph Drechsler, *Aschenlied*, mm. 1–8.

Example 6. Franz Schubert, *Der greise Kopf*, mm. 30–33.

Example 7. Joseph Drechsler, *Brüderlein fein*, mm. 1–5.

The musical connection between the other two songs is principally in their opening motives. The plaintive melody that opens *Brüderlein fein*—which occurs twice in a row and is sung repeatedly by both Jugend and Wurzel—served as a symbol for the whole song and its significance (Example 7). *Die Krähe* opens with the same three-note neighbor motive, but then drops a fourth instead of a third (Example 8). This could be a chance similarity—but the prominence of Raimund's play and its particularly famous songs at the precise time when Schubert was composing *Winterreise*, along with the other connection to *Der greise Kopf*, bolster the argument for seeing it as more than that.

Another network of connections between *Winterreise* and the songs of *Der Bauer als Millionär* deserves brief mention. Just as the first four notes of *Brüderlein fein* became that song's signature, so the last notes of the *Aschenlied* came to represent that song as well. On the words "Ein Aschen" or "Kein Aschen," the singer first drops a sixth, then moves up a half step: C–E–F. Though this musical gesture is not uncommon, its recognizability as the melody for the *Aschenlied*'s refrain marked it as significant. Schubert uses this same set of intervals, on the same exact pitches, at the ends of several phrases in *Das Wirtshaus*, the twenty-first song of the cycle. And this recalls yet another song in *Der Bauer als Millionär*, *Die Menschheit sitzt um bill'gen Preis* (Mankind Sits for a Low Price), in which Wurzel compares

Example 8. Franz Schubert, *Die Krähe*, mm. 6–9.

the stages of a human life to a meal at a *Wirtshaus*—and the phrase "so endigt sich der Lebensschmaus" (so ends the feast of life) ends with this same motive of a falling sixth followed by a half step.

Der Hirt auf dem Felsen and Fantasy's Aria

The final case to be presented concerns another Raimund play, *Die gefesselte Phantasie* (Fantasy Bound), whose premiere took place at the Leopoldstadt Theater on 8 January 1828.[38] In this play, Raimund—who, according to Bauernfeld, was always convinced that he was meant to be a tragedian—reflects somewhat satirically on the relation between high and low art. Queen Hermione is in love with Amphio, a shepherd who is also a good poet, so she proposes to marry whoever wins a poetry contest. Some evil spirits, determined to thwart the queen's desires, tie up Fantasy, the muse, so that none of the poets are able to create anything at all. She is finally released only when she desperately begins to sing a quodlibet, which persuades Jupiter to smash her chains with a thunderbolt. Reunited with Fantasy, Amphio is able to write a winning poem and all ends happily. Ironically, it turns out he is actually a prince in disguise, but in the meantime Raimund has made various points about the relative merits of high and low art.

Act 1, scene 12 of *Die gefesselte Phantasie* features Amphio alone. The opening stage direction reads "Amphio sits on a stone and plays a soft song on his flute." This scenario recalls Schubert's scena or extended song, *Der Hirt auf dem Felsen* (*The Shepherd on the Rock*, D965), which was composed in October of that same year. The shepherd in that work, also sitting on a rock, thinks longingly of his beloved while looking into the valley below, and he too is accompanied by a woodwind instrument (though it is a clarinet rather than a flute). These connections suggest the possibility that music from *Die gefesselte Phantasie* may be associated with Schubert's piece.[39] Another, more subtle relationship arises when we realize that although the shepherd in *Der Hirt auf dem Felsen* is a male character, the work was composed for soprano Anna Milder-Hauptmann. Similarly, Therese Krones, who sang the soprano role of Fantasy, was best known for playing the male character Jugend in *Der Bauer als Millionär*.

As with two of the Volkstheater works discussed earlier, the music for this play was written by Wenzel Müller, close to the end of his long career. When Fantasy first appears she introduces herself with a delicate song, suitable to the words that describe Fantasy's whimsicality and her many guises. The opening stanza begins as follows:

Ich bin ein Wesen leichter Art,	I am a being of a light kind,
Ein Kind mit tausend Launen,	A child with a thousand whims,
Das Nied'res mit dem Höchsten paart,	Who pairs the low with the highest,
'S ist wirklich zum Erstaunen.	'Tis truly astonishing.

Müller writes a substantial introduction before Fantasy begins to sing (the beginning is shown in Example 9). The opening motive tellingly pairs low and high, beginning with an elaboration of the note F in bass clef and ending much higher, with parallel sixths descending a third in the soprano range. The first mini-phrase (mm. 1–2) outlines an interval of a sixth (F–D), and its altered repetition in mm. 5–6 extends the span to a seventh (F–E♭). The opening vocal melody (Example 10) composes out the two versions of the introductory motive by filling in that seventh.

Like this piece, *Der Hirt auf dem Felsen* opens in 3/4 time and in the key of B-flat major. The opening gesture, though, seems to hover on D minor, hinting at a G minor that does not arrive here but will later be heard as

Example 9. Wenzel Müller, Fantasy's aria, mm. 1–8.

Example 10. Wenzel Müller, Fantasy's aria, vocal line, mm. 17–20.

the key of the middle section. Where Müller's opening elaborates on the pitch F and leaps up a sixth to D before dropping a third, Schubert begins on D, elaborates on this pitch, and then drops a fourth (see Example 11). The third and fourth bars of Schubert's version are reminiscent, in an indirect way, of Müller's first two bars. At the same time, this melancholy, yearning opening meets Schubert's own expressive needs.

Müller's opening gesture finds another echo much later in the Schubert piece, at the start of the final section. As noted above, Fantasy's aria expands from a leap of a sixth to that of a seventh, and the seventh is then filled in as a scale in the vocal melody. (The presence of a grace-note F in the vocal line does two things. On the one hand, it fills out the whole octave; on the other, by putting a little interruption between scale degrees 6 and 7, it reinforces both the sixth and the seventh that existed as leaps in the introduction.)

Schubert completes the process in his final section, in which the melody ascends a sixth, leaps back down, and then ascends a seventh—thus far imitating Müller's opening. Schubert's vocal line then rises through the full octave, taking a different path from that point on.

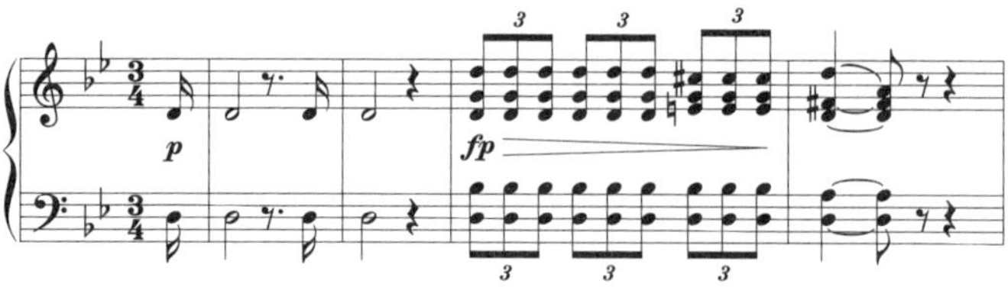

Example 11. Franz Schubert, *Der Hirt auf dem Felsen*, mm. 1–4.

Example 12. Franz Schubert, *Der Hirt auf dem Felsen*, clarinet part, mm. 1–3 of Allegretto.

Final Reflections

Taken together, these four case studies link pieces by Schubert to famous Volkstheater works of his day—or, in the first example, to a piece from an earlier generation that had endured in the collective Viennese memory. They vary in the degree of musical and textual similarity, and perhaps also in the purpose and meaning of any intended correspondence. The first two cases present stronger musical resemblances than the later pair. Yet the striking plot relationships between the Schubert works and the two Raimund plays—in which we encounter a person whose hair turns white overnight, and there really is a shepherd on a rock thinking of his beloved—give meaning to the musical ties, though they are fleeting and subtle.

There is no way to prove that these references are deliberate. If Schubert was aware of what he was doing, he was not trying to draw attention to the connections, for had he wanted to, he could have quoted much more directly. If these were conscious references, I believe they were intended for his own understanding and that of anyone else who would both recognize the links and take them in the proper spirit. As Bauernfeld remembered, Schubert responded angrily when his friends appeared to criticize connections of this kind.

While some composers, such as Alban Berg, devised hidden musical references that concealed information about their personal lives,[40] Schubert's associations of his music with Volkstheater works do not veil secrets of that kind. Rather, they first signal his interest in those works and then draw connections between them and his own music. By associating his music with the popular tradition, Schubert was allying himself with the comprehensive Viennese approach to the arts that Alfred Orel acknowledges when he attributes the strengths of the Viennese Classical tradition in part to its roots in folk music. Schubert was repudiating the purist approach exemplified by some of his friends when they argued that he should not use such common sources as folk tunes and marches in elevated genres such as the Lied. He was accepting the exuberant, irreverent side of Viennese culture that delighted in quodlibets, juxtapositions of "high" and "low" art, clever intertextual references, and surreptitious critiques of the authoritarian government. He was absorbing, developing, and commenting on the thoughts and perspectives of Volkstheater writers—Bäuerle's satiric praise of the Imperial capital, Raimund's poignant tribute to honesty and goodness in a world of corruption and deception—while also paying tribute to the music of his Viennese theatrical colleagues, Wenzel Müller and Joseph Drechsler. He was avoiding the simple categories that divided music in his time (as in our own), and embracing the full complexity and diversity of his native city.

Recent writing on Schubert has revealed many aspects of his music that were unrecognized or unformulated in the past, broadening our understanding of his numerous complicated strategies as a composer. Some scholars have focused on musical elements, discovering new and elaborate musical structures and approaches to harmony.[41] Others have emphasized his approaches to poetry that include dramatic, psychological, and intellectual elements in various cases, depending on the text.[42] These connections between Volkstheater works and Schubert's compositions reveal another aspect of Schubert the interpreter: one who drew upon the vibrant popular tradition of his home city for his own expressive purposes.

NOTES

Although I am the author of this essay, all the work described here was done jointly with John Sienicki, who has explored the Volkstheater repertoire in depth. He was the first to notice and investigate some of the musical relationships discussed. I am grateful to Raymond Erickson and Walter Frisch, who offered very helpful feedback on an earlier version of this essay.

1. The Volkstheater tradition has not received much scholarly attention. The essential and magisterial history of the subject is Otto Rommel, *Die Alt-Wiener Volkskomödie: Ihre Geschichte vom barocken Welt-Theater bis zum Tode Nestroys* (Vienna, 1952). Rommel also published several important plays in reprint editions. More recent works include Jürgen Hein, *Das Wiener Volkstheater* (Darmstadt, 1997); and Beatrix Müller-Kampel, *Hanswurst, Bernardon, Kasperl: Spaßtheater im 18. Jahrhundert* (Paderborn, 2003). Hein has also published a set of reprints, *Parodien des Wiener Volkstheaters* (Stuttgart, 1986). All these writers are literary scholars, and they do not discuss the music beyond acknowledging that it was usually present. For an overview in English of the Vienna theaters during Schubert's lifetime, see Simon Williams, "The Viennese Theater" in *Schubert's Vienna*, ed. Raymond Erickson (New Haven, 1997), 214–45. Alfred Orel's introduction to the music volume of Raimund's complete works includes a brief but impressive discussion of Volkstheater music, with attention to general characteristics, various genres, and differences between composers. Peter Branscombe also wrote about Volkstheater music; see "Music in the Viennese Popular Theater of the Eighteenth and Nineteenth Centuries," *Proceedings of the Royal Musical Association* 98 (1971–72): 101–12.

2. Alfred Orel, *Ferdinand Raimund: Die Gesänge der Märchendramen in den ursprünglichen Vertonungen*, in *Sämtliche Werke*, vol. 6 (Vienna: Schroll, 1924), ix.

3. See Rommel, *Alt-Wiener Volkskomödie*, 364.

4. See Otto Erich Deutsch, *The Schubert Reader* (New York, 1947), 184–85.

5. See Rita Steblin, *Die Unsinnsgesellschaft: Franz Schubert, Leopold Kupelwieser und ihr Freundeskreis* (Vienna, 1998), 26–31, 196. The Theater an der Wien (1801) was first established as the Freihaus Theater in 1787.

6. See *Neue Dokumente zum Schubert-Kreis,* vol. 2: *Dokumente zum Leben der Anna von Revertera*, ed. Walburga Litschauer (Vienna, 1993), 34 and 56. The "Burg" or Burgtheater was another designation for the Kärntnerthor, or the court theater. Two years earlier, in October 1823, Anna's future husband had also visited Vienna, and he wrote to his fiancée about his visits to three theaters: the Josefstadt, Kärntnerthor, and Leopoldstadt. In 1826, Franz von Hartmann's diary refers to Schwind and Schober's attending Karl Meisl's play *Die beiden Spadifankerl* and the Spauns attending Ferdinand Raimund's play *Der Bauer als Millionär*. See Deutsch, *Schubert Reader*, 578, 580.

7. Peter Branscombe assembled a list of the twenty-two occasions when Schubert is reported to have attended various theatrical performances; see "Schubert and the Melodrama," in *Schubert Studies: Problems of Style and Chronology*, ed. Eva Badura-Skoda and Peter Branscombe (Cambridge, 1982), 110–11. The two Volkstheater plays on that list are Adolf Bäuerle's *Aline*, on 19 October 1822, and J. A. Gleich's *Herr Josef und Frau Baberl*—mentioned by Schubert, but with "Josef" misnamed as "Jacob" in a letter to Eduard von Bauernfeld—in May 1826. For both plays, the music was by Wenzel Müller. See also Deutsch, *Schubert Reader*, 236 and 528.

8. See Bauernfeld, *Bilder und Persönlichkeiten aus Alt-Wien: Erinnerungen an Moritz von Schwind, Franz Schubert, Franz Grillparzer, Ferdinand Raimund, Johann Nestroy, Anastasius Grün und Nikolaus Lenau*, ed. Wilhelm Zentner (Altötting, 1948), 50–55.

9. For details on Schubert's links to Nestroy and Raimund, see *Schubert-Enzyklopädie*, ed. Ernst Hilmar and Margret Jestremski (Tutzing, 2004), 2:513–14 and 581–82.

10. Schubert's own theatrical works do not seem to refer to the Volkstheater in similarly specific ways, though of course it is possible that connections will be identified in the future. My best guess as to why we do not find Volkstheater references in Schubert's operas is that he was less practiced in that genre and perhaps always anxious to follow stylistic models in order to achieve success.

11. Kristina Muxfeldt discusses Viennese censorship and hidden messages in theatrical works in *Vanishing Sensibilities: Schubert, Beethoven, Schumann* (New York, 2012), 12–17. She also considers possible expressions of rebellion in Schubert's opera on a text by Franz von Schober, *Alfonso und Estrella* (22–26). Her idea that the tyrant Mauregato may represent Metternich, as their names both begin with "M," suggests how cautious artists were in that milieu. An 1823 play by the important Volkstheater playwright J. A. Gleich, *Der Leopard und der Hund*, was much more direct and bold in referring to Metternich—but after the royal family attended a performance, the play disappeared from Vienna. See *Theaterzeitung*, 4 December 1823, supplement no. 145, between pp. 581 and 582, and 23 December 1823, 619. Another Volkstheater example that demonstrates how it was possible to challenge the authorities is the piece known as *Das beliebte Quodlibet* from Gleich's 1826 play *Der Eheteufel auf Reisen*. In this piece, the texts of selected musical snippets continually emphasize the need for silence because of the constant danger of police intervention. This work is reprinted with commentary in Lisa Feurzeig and John Sienicki, *Quodlibets of the Viennese Popular Theater* (Middleton, WI, 2008), xx–xxi and 275–84.

12. Otto Erich Deutsch, *Schubert: Die Erinnerungen seiner Freunde* (Leipzig, 1957), 199; my translation. Bauernfeld's article "Einiges über Franz Schubert" is supposed to be from 17 and 21 April 1869, but I was unable to find it in an online version of *Die Neue Freie Presse*, so those dates may be incorrect.

13. This was the first adaptation that Perinet and Müller made together during the 1790s of the plays of Philipp Hafner (1735–1764); it is a reworking of Hafner's play *Der Furchtsame*. They eventually turned all eight of Hafner's complex morality plays into musical comedies.

14. More specifically, it is frequently categorized as a student song, which implies that it found a willing public among university students. For example, it is found on a German recording of student songs performed by student groups, *Studentenlieder*, Sonia, 77198 (1993).

15. Steblin, *Die Unsinnsgesellschaft*, 263. Steblin presents evidence that Schubert was involved with the Nonsense Society at precisely the time when the 4 December 1817 issue of their journal, *Archiv des menschlichen Unsinns*, appeared (22–24).

16. See Feurzeig and Sienicki, *Quodlibets*.

17. The other two central playwrights of the day were Josef Alois Gleich and Carl Meisl.

18. *Franz Schubert in seinen Klaviersonaten* (Leipzig, 1927), 24–25. Költzsch uses the connection to *Aline* to argue against the then-accepted view that Schubert had written the fantasy in 1820. Interestingly, he also refers to this as "one of the few definitely demonstrable cases in which Schubert took melodies directly from the then inexhaustible Viennese ground of the people" (25). This comment suggests that Költzsch found it reasonable to believe that there were many other such cases that were less easily proven.

19. Maurice Brown argued against this link, pointing out that Schubert never labeled the fantasy with a name. Though he acknowledged the presence of a musical reference to *Der Wanderer* in the slow movement, he was uncomfortable with interpretations that then expanded this idea by associating the whole work with the sentiments in those poetic lines. See Brown, *Schubert: A Critical Biography* (London, 1958), 124–25. Nevertheless, others have continued to make this association, and Susan Wollenberg recently argued that this piece "shows Schubert creating a profound reflection on the song of that name in the variations at the work's centre" and even more broadly that "like the 'Wanderer' Fantasy, the chamber works featuring a variations movement based on a pre-existent Lied treat this not simply as an added element inserted into the movement cycle, but as a

generative force for the whole work." See *Schubert's Fingerprints: Studies in the Instrumental Works* (Aldershot, 2011), 213–14.

20. Robert Darnton comments on the links between philosophy and eroticism in literature of this period in *The Forbidden Best-Sellers of Pre-Revolutionary France* (New York, 1996). See in particular chapter 3, "Philosophical Pornography."

21. Aside from those discussed in the main text, other versions included a ballet at the Paris Opéra in 1766, adapted by Michel-Jean Sedaine; *Aline, reine de Golconde* by J. A. P. Schulz (Rheinsberg, 1787), later adapted and very popular in Denmark as *Aline Dronning i Golconda*; *Aline, reine de Golconde* by Boieldieu (St. Petersburg, 1804); *Alina, regina di Golconda* by Donizetti (Genoa, 1828); and Franz Berwald, *Drottningen av Golconda* (Stockholm, 1864–65).

22. The Viennese quodlibet took various forms. Most common was a single musical number, usually but not always within a Volkstheater play, in which several preexisting musical pieces were quoted in short snippets, with surprise and disjunction being important aspects of the genre. A quodlibet play was a whole play in which entire musical numbers from preexisting works were borrowed. In both types of quodlibet, the text of the original could be left as is or changed to suit the dramatic situation. John A. Rice discusses some interesting examples that were performed at the Imperial court, including a quodlibet commissioned for Emperor Franz's name day in 1805 by his wife. See *Empress Marie Therese and Music at the Viennese Court, 1792–1807* (Cambridge, 2003), 132–40. The humor of quodlibets clearly depended on the audience's recognition of the quoted material to be effective, so these works inform us about what music was known by their intended audiences. The very existence of the quodlibet also shows how significant the practice of quotation was in Viennese cultural life, supporting the broader points of this essay. For the Vogl duet, see the edition of *Rochus Pumpernickel* in Feurzeig and Sienicki, *Quodlibets*, 90–97 and 288–89.

23. Deutsch, *Schubert Reader*, 141–42.

24. Otto Rommel reprinted the play in his *Alt-Wiener Volkstheater*, 7 vols. (Vienna, Teschen, Leipzig, 1917), 5:81–165; in this version, the duet has five stanzas. In one publication of sheet music—*Sammlung komischer Theater-Gesänge* no. 21 (Vienna, ca. 1822)—there are three stanzas, two almost identical to the reprint and another that includes lines from two other stanzas in the reprint. In another sheet music version, clearly printed several years later as there is a note by Bäuerle referring to his 1826 edition, there are three stanzas, once again with words reordered and stanzas recombined. I have also found reference to a version of the duet printed by C. G. Förster in Breslau in 1822, in which the text opens "Wie gehts denn bei Liebichs," referring to a famous Breslau landmark; presumably the text of the play was altered so that Aline comes from Breslau rather than Vienna.

25. The misspelling of Kahlenberg, a mountain just north of Vienna, could reflect dialect pronunciation or could be evidence that this version was printed outside Vienna.

26. This is from the post-1826 printing.

27. There is much to be said about the keen awareness of the Volkstheater shown by both Hugo von Hofmannsthal and Richard Strauss in *Der Rosenkavalier.* For example, they deliberately quoted the *Aline* duet. In Act 1, rehearsal number 219, at the moment when various merchants are showing their wares to the Marschallin, the Marchande de Modes announces that she has "Le chapeau Paméla, La poudre à la reine de Golconde." (The Pamela hat, Queen of Golconda powder). The upper line in the orchestra at this moment plays the pitches B–E–D♯–F♯–A, forming exactly the same intervals as the beginning of the refrain to Müller's *Aline* duet, while omitting repeated notes. The vocal melody is not identical, but it opens with B–E–E, adding the element of repetition that the orchestra has omitted. Strauss's quotation creates an interesting anachronism, as the opera is set "in the early years of the reign of Maria Theresia"—that is, in the 1740s, even before the

original literary work had been written and about eighty years before the Müller-Bäuerle theatrical version. See Strauss, *Der Rosenkavalier*, piano-vocal score (London, 1985), 3, 98.

28. Orel, *Ferdinand Raimund*, xviii–xxi.

29. Deutsch, *Schubert Reader*, 580. Franz von Hartmann describes a gathering at the Anker, with a list of various people who were there. The list includes the Spauns (not identified any more clearly), who had just attended the play, and also Schubert.

30. Wilhelm Zentner, in the afterword to Raimund, *Der Bauer als Millionär* (Stuttgart, 1952), 83; my translation. Zentner also lists German cities where the play found acclaim: Munich, Leipzig, Berlin, and Hamburg.

31. Ibid.

32. Raimund, *Der Bauer als Millionär*, 67–68.

33. This is shown, for example, in a performance from the Salzburg Festival of 1988 that is available on DVD, Arthaus Musik, 101 836. As explained in the accompanying notes by Werner Thuswaldner, the added stanzas in this production had to do with controversies about fighter planes, sex education, and television programming (10).

34. The text of the added stanzas is given in Fritz Brukner, ed., *Ferdinand Raimund in der Dichtung seiner Zeitgenossen* (Vienna, 1905), 63–64. It ends as follows: "Wer solches hat erstrebt, / Hat nicht umsonst gelebt. / Kein Aschen!" (Whoever has striven for this / Has not lived in vain. / No ashes!) Brukner specifies that the verses were sung by "Hrn. Weiß" (v), and I assume this was Eduard Weiß, who played some of Raimund's roles when he was performing elsewhere.

35. Specifically, Susan Youens writes of "a broadly arching, symmetrical phrase that seems a musical metaphor for awakening, ascending to heights of joy, and then descending to disillusionment." *Retracing a Winter's Journey: Schubert's "Winterreise"* (Ithaca, NY, 1991), 237.

36. Ibid., 237–38.

37. Such arguments are sometimes employed regarding Schubert's compositional process for strophic songs; if the melody fits one stanza particularly well, then Schubert was probably composing it with that stanza in mind. For example, in the song *Des Fischers Liebesglück* (D933), the octave leaps are particularly well suited to the text of the final stanza.

38. We have no specific reference to this play in the Schubert documents. However, both Bauernfeld and J. (presumably Josef) Kupelwieser wrote poems about Raimund. Kupelwieser's was published in the *Theaterzeitung* on 18 March 1834 after the performance of Raimund's *Der Verschwender*, and Bauernfeld wrote his in response to Raimund's death in 1836. Bauernfeld's poem appears to refer to *Die gefesselte Phantasie* along with the myth of Prometheus in the final stanza: "Angeschmiedet war der Dichter / An den Fels Melancholie, / Und ein Geier fraß das Herz ihm, / Riesen-Geier: Phantasie." (Fettered was the poet / To the rock Melancholy, / And a vulture ate his heart, / The giant vulture Fantasy." These are reprinted in Brukner, *Ferdinand Raimund in der Dichtung seiner Zeitgenossen*, 32–33 and 69–70.

39. For other recent writings on this piece, see Frank Samarotto, "Intimate Immensity in Schubert's *The Shepherd on the Rock*," in *Structure and Meaning in Tonal Music: Festschrift in Honor of Carl Schachter* (Hillsdale, NY, 2006), 203–23; and Till Gerrit Waidelich, "'Der letzte Hauch im Lied entflieht, im Lied das Herz entweicht!' Varnhagens *Nächtlicher Schall* als letzter Baustein zum *Hirt auf dem Felsen*," *Schubert: Perspektiven* 8 (2008): 237–43.

40. Musical aspects of several of Berg's works, including the *Lyric Suite*, the Violin Concerto, and *Wozzeck*, have been linked to the composer's close friendships and secret love affairs. See Douglas Jarman, "Alban Berg, Wilhelm Fliess, and the Secret Program of the Violin Concerto," in *The Berg Companion*, ed. Douglas Jarman (Boston, 1989), 181–94 and Douglas Jarman, "Secret Programmes," in *The Cambridge Companion to Berg*, ed. Anthony Pople (Cambridge, 1997), 167–79.

41. See, among many examples, Susan Wollenberg, *Schubert's Fingerprints*; Richard L. Cohn, "As Wonderful as Star Clusters: Instruments for Gazing at Tonality in Schubert," *19th-Century Music* 22/3 (Spring 1999): 213–32; and Su Yin Mak, "'Et in Arcadia Ego': The Elegiac Structure of Schubert's *Quartettsatz* in C minor (D703)," in *The Unknown Schubert*, ed. Barbara M. Reul and Lorraine Byrne Bodley (Aldershot, 2008), 145–53.

42. See, among many examples, Susan Youens, *Schubert's Poets and the Making of Lieder* (Cambridge, 1996); Marjorie Wing Hirsch, "Mayrhofer, Schubert, and the Myth of 'Vocal Memnon,'" in Reul and Bodley, *The Unknown Schubert*, 3–23; and Xavier Hascher, "'In dunklen Träumen': Schubert's Heine-Lieder through the Psychoanalytical Prism," *Nineteenth-Century Music Review* 5/2 (2008): 43–70.

Liszt on Schubert's *Alfonso und Estrella*

INTRODUCED AND TRANSLATED BY ALLAN KEILER

During the winter and summer months and into the fall of 1854, Liszt published a series of articles on twelve dramatic works, all but two of them operas, connected with performances he conducted in Weimar. The pieces, in the order they were performed, were Gluck's *Orfeo ed Eurydice,* Beethoven's *Fidelio*, Auber's *La muette de Portici*, Weber's *Euryanthe*, Beethoven's music for *Egmont,* Mendelssohn's music for *A Midsummer Night's Dream*, Bellini's *I Capuleti e i Montecchi*, Meyerbeer's *Robert le diable*, Wagner's *Der fliegende Holländer*, Boieldieu's *La dame blanche*, Donizetti's *La favorita*, and Schubert's *Alfonso und Estrella*. Liszt's first six articles, as well as the one on Wagner's *Der fliegende Holländer,* were initially published in the *Weimarer Zeitung* within a week or two after the performance, many in several installments. Throughout the year, all of them, in their final form and definitive order, appeared in the *Neue Zeitschrift für Musik*.[1]

The premiere of *Alfonso und Estrella*, which Liszt gave in Weimar on 24 June 1854 to celebrate the birthday of the Grand Duke Karl Alexander, entails a journey with more than its share of false starts, mishaps, and ironies. If we turn to the article, little of the difficulties and drama that led to its performance by Liszt are discernible. What we have is a deeply heartfelt appreciation of Schubert's gifts as a song composer as well as a more general rumination on the nature of talent and genius. When it comes to the work itself, Liszt in at least one regard is more practical than usual in comparison with the other essays of the series. Because neither the work nor the libretto was published, he provides his audience with a detailed summary of the plot and action, scene by scene and act by act.

In biographical matters, Liszt often resorts to uncritical generalities or guesswork, as in his biography of Chopin, for example, and in this essay too he is vague and inaccurate when he explains that "the work in question [is] a product of [Schubert's youth] . . . its weaknesses . . . understandable given the rapidity with which he went about his work." Schubert wrote *Alfonso und Estrella* between September 1821 and February 1822,

Anfang dieser Vorstellung halb 7 Uhr.

Hof-Theater.

Weimar, Sonnabend den 24. Juni 1854.

Bei festlich erleuchtetem Hause:

Zum Erstenmale:

Alfonso und Estrella.

Romantische Oper in drei Akten. Musik von Franz Schubert.

Mauregato, König von Leon, ... Hr. Höfer.
Estrella, seine Tochter, ... Fr. Milde.
Adolfo, sein Feldherr, ... Hr. Mayerhofer.
Froila, entthronter König von Leon, in dem Gebirge bei Oviedo lebend, unter dem Namen: Bermudo, ... Hr. Milde.
Alfonso, sein Sohn, ... Hr. Liebert.
Ein Anführer der königlichen Leibwache, ... Hr. Fuhrmann.
Guisto, ein Hirte, ... Hr. Knopp.
Krieger, Anführer derselben.
Landvolk. Jäger. Estrella's Frauen.
Hirten. Verschworne.

Zeit: 790.

Die Handlung spielt theils in der Residenz Oviedo, theils in den nahen Gebirgen.

Zu Anfang der Vorstellung:

Fest=Ouverture.

Componirt von A. Rubinstein.

Nach dem Schluß der Oper:

Fest=Marsch.

Nach zwei Melodien des Sängerstreites auf der Wartburg von Wolfram von Eschinbach und Heinrich von Ofterdingen, orchestrirt von W. Stade.

Zwölfte Vorstellung im Eilften Abonnement.

Die Preise der Plätze sind bekannt.

Anfang halb 7 Uhr. Ende nach halb 10 Uhr.

Das Theater wird halb 6 Uhr geöffnet.

Die freien Entréen sind erst halb 7 Uhr giltig.

Schluß der diesjährigen Theater=Saison.

Figure 1. Playbill of *Alfonso und Estrella,* Weimar 1854.

during a period of his creative life that was crucial for him compositionally as well as personally. During this time he acquired new ambitions, particularly in works for the stage, left many pieces unfinished, including the "Unfinished" Symphony and the single movement "Quartettsatz," but also completed, by the end of the period, such works as *Der Musensohn*, the Mass in A-flat, and the "Wanderer" Fantasy. It is a period of tremendous growth, new aspirations, and wildly fluctuating challenges. If anything, then, *Alfonso und Estrella* is a product of this first maturity.

Contrary to Liszt's view, composition of the opera proceeded with somewhat less haste and spontaneity than was often the case with Schubert, and for the most part in a more relaxed and concentrated manner. Schubert began the first act toward the end of September 1821. His librettist arranged for the two of them to work together without distraction at St. Pölten, where the bishop, a relative of the librettist, gave them accommodations. They returned to Vienna before the second act was finished. Encouraged again at the end of the year to resume work, composer and librettist completed the opera sometime in February.

The reader will notice that I have failed to mention the name of Franz von Schober, the librettist of *Alfonso und Estrella*, a somewhat disingenuous way of calling attention to the similar omission on the part of Liszt, who in his essay does not once identify him by name, although he does not hold back in criticizing the inadequacy of the libretto. Whether consciously or not, this omission could hardly have been inadvertent, as the reader will come to understand. Liszt's relationship to Schober, which lasted for more than a decade, is an integral part of the story that would eventually lead to the first performance of *Alfonso und Estrella* by Liszt, an "act of reverence," "the settlement of a debt of honor," he writes, but one that, as Maria Eckhardt has rightly argued, "probably precipitated the alienation of their friendship."[2]

Franz von Schober is well known as an intimate and influential member of Schubert's circle, and his close friendship with the composer is also well documented. His relationship to Liszt is less familiar and for the most part haphazardly documented, with inaccuracies and lacunae that await clarification. In the meantime, what interests us is the role he played in connection with Liszt's premiere of Schubert's opera. It is not clear when they first met, probably sometime during the late 1830s. In the documented record we encounter them together for the first time in Pest during Liszt's return to his native Hungary from December of 1839 to the end of January 1840—after his childhood one of the most famous and colorful episodes of his career. The central image amid the nationalistic fervor that accompanied Liszt during those weeks is the famous "sabre

Figure 2. Portrait of Franz von Schober by Leopold Kupelwieser.

of honor" presented to him at his concert at the Hungarian National Theater by a small group of noblemen and civic officials. The entire episode—idolatrous outpourings about Liszt by the Hungarian press, Liszt parading in the streets of Pest in Hungarian costume, attempts to remake him as a symbol of Magyar nationalism—became easy prey for the European press, especially French journalists, who ridiculed his posturing, the presentation of the sabre, and much else. Liszt, with the aid of his mistress Marie d'Agoult, made repeated attempts at damage control, but the whole affair made him keenly defensive over his seriousness of purpose as an artist, his pride in and his fervor over his homeland.[3]

It was at this point that Schober entered Liszt's life. He was an eyewitness to the presentation of the sabre and accompanied Liszt to other Hungarian cities, to Vienna, and then again to Hungary. Whatever conversations the two may have had at the time, Schober was sympathetic enough to Liszt's aims and ideals to write a series of articles in the German press about his experiences traveling with the Hungarian idol. For his part, Liszt was pleased enough with the series to propose that Schober publish the pieces, which resulted in the pamphlet *Briefe über F. Liszts Aufenthalt in Ungarn* (Letters About F. Liszt's Sojourn in Hungary). Schober's account takes its place, then, among a series of biographical sketches and reportages from the early 1840s—those of Johann Wilhelm Christern, Ludwig Rellstab, and J. Duverger (an alias for Marie d'Agoult)—that formed a part of Liszt's active attempts to create a biographical image in the French and German press that would reflect his ideas and objectives about art and society.[4]

Schober was a versatile talent, but he lacked perseverance. He gave up the study of law after only a single year; he then tried his hand at landscape painting, and for two years flirted with the profession of acting, and then changed course entirely when he assumed the directorship of the Viennese Lithographic Institute. What drew Liszt to Schober was not simply that he revealed himself to be a sympathetic ally in the midst of a highly troublesome and even embarrassing episode. Surely Liszt also admired his attractive and engaging personality. Schober was a brilliant conversationalist, well traveled, charismatic, a figure of cosmopolitan background with an enormous knowledge of German literature, the latter particularly appealing to Liszt. Just as important was his connection to Schubert, a composer Liszt held as much admiration for and drew at least as much influence from as he did Beethoven. Whether the subject of *Alfonso und Estrella* came up during these early years between Schober and Liszt, we do not know, but it would arise soon enough.

In the meantime, Schober was valuable to Liszt in various ways. He acted as translator, and provided Liszt with the poem "Titan," on whose setting Liszt worked for a number of years. When Liszt was appointed Kapellmeister in Weimar in 1843, Schober accompanied him as he arrived to take up his duties. Eventually Liszt used his influence with Grand Duke Alexander, recommending that he appoint Schober Legationsrat (legation counsellor). In the years following his appointment, Liszt continued to depend on Schober to help spread his ideas about his future plans in Weimar. When Liszt finally settled there, Schober provided other texts, for the cantata *Hungaria* and the dithyramb *Weimars Toten*, for which Liszt provided musical settings.[5] Liszt must have found Schober useful in discussing his plans for the musical and cultural revival he was contemplating for the years ahead, so it is not surprising that the idea emerged of a performance of *Alfonso und Estrella*: Schubert's lone through-composed opera and, along with *Fierabras*, his major dramatic work. It may have been Schober who raised the idea in the first place, for, in fact, he had striven for several years to have the opera performed.

The first evidence we have that Schober and Liszt reached some conviction that a performance of *Alfonso und Estrella* should be given in Weimar is a letter dated 7 February 1848 that Schober wrote to Schubert's brother Ferdinand, asking him to send the opera to Liszt. We learn about this request about a month later, in a letter that Ferdinand writes to Breitkopf & Härtel, with which he is in negotiations to publish the opera as well as other works of Schubert: "On 7 February I received a letter from the librettist of this final opera, who is at present Legationsrat in Weimar, in which I was asked in the friendliest terms to send this opera to Weimar, because Franz Liszt (who is now Hof-Kapellmeister there) wants one of Franz Schubert's operas to finally see the light of day."[6] Only a few weeks later, Liszt writes to Carolyne Sayn-Wittgenstein about his intention: "And perhaps there is still time to stage one of Schubert's unpublished operas, *Alphons und Estrella*, for which my friend Schober wrote the text."[7]

Of course, Ferdinand Schubert and Schober were attached to the future of *Alfonso und Estrella* in quite different ways. Ferdinand saw himself as the responsible custodian of his brother's works in a manner that looked to the future and the eventuality of other performances as a result of publication with Breitkopf. Schober, on the other hand, had his mind set on this specific performance of a piece that he helped create and worked tirelessly to hear performed. "For eight years, in alliance with your dear brother, I strove to bring it to the stage under such auspicious conditions as would never again return, applying in vain to theaters in Vienna, Dresden, Berlin, Prag, Pest, Graz, etc," wrote Schober in a blistering letter to Ferdinand, in response to the latter's unwillingness to act quickly to send the score of the opera to Liszt.[8] Schober saw the whole affair as an issue of ownership: "Does some kind of pronouncement, purchase, exchange, or contract give you the right to call the text of *Alfonso und Estrella*, which belongs to me, your own property and thereby dispose of it high-handedly, and without asking me?"[9] Liszt's interest in producing the opera had by then become something of an obsession with Schober—the answer to his prayers—and he tried to convince Ferdinand to cooperate. By the end of Schober's appeal, there was understandably more than a hint of desperation: "There is still time. Send the opera at once or I will hereby prohibit every one of your provisions concerning this work and will accordingly inform Breitkopf & Härtel and will publicly explain both of our courses of actions. . . . I will wait no longer than ten days for an answer."[10]

Ferdinand, perhaps out of pique, did not reply, but six months later he was ready to launch an agreement between Breitkopf & Härtel and the Weimar Hoftheater. A performance of the opera in Weimar under Liszt now seemed assured. But there was a hitch: Liszt had not yet seen the libretto or the score. Once he did it would be six years full of disappointments, aborted attempts at producing the opera, and even plans for a revision of the libretto, before the opera was finally staged.

The first such attempt occurred early in 1849. We learn the details from Eduard Genast, the Regisseur of the Hofoper, with whom Liszt had clearly discussed the viability of performing the opera. "Liszt had proposed Franz Schubert's *Alfonso und Estrella* for February 16. As Regisseur I was opposed to this, for as much as I admire and love Schubert as a Lieder composer, this work cannot be called an opera, for it offers nothing more than a sequence of beautiful melodies and Lieder, for which reason a monotony arises that cannot but become painful. Liszt has stood by his choice. A number of piano rehearsals have already taken place and as a result he himself has come to the fortunate idea to set the opera aside and to choose instead *Tannhäuser*."[11]

Liszt's next attempt to perform the opera came in the early months of 1850. We learn that again Liszt has held piano rehearsals for the opera, intending to begin full rehearsals at the end of February and perform the opera sometime during the beginning of April. But again the whole affair was aborted, this time because Liszt was now at least open about his dislike of the libretto. He wrote to Breitkopf in February: "As for the Schubert opera, a recent experience has confirmed me entirely in the view that I had already taken at the time of the first piano rehearsals we held last spring: the view that the delicate and interesting score of Schubert ends up as if crushed under the weight of the <u>libretto</u>! However, I do not give up hope to be able to present this work successfully—but this success appears to me possible under only one condition: that of adapting another libretto to Schubert's music."[12] From the end of the year until the first weeks of 1854, Liszt busied himself with what he considered a viable solution, one that was directed exclusively at the libretto. His idea was to have a new libretto prepared, this time in French, and have the opera given at the Opéra-Comique in Paris. With this scheme in mind he entered into negotiations not only with Breitkopf to obtain permission for this new arrangement but with music publisher Léon Escudier in Paris as well.

The first task in this new scheme was to have a piano-vocal score prepared to send to Escudier. Liszt appealed first to his colleague Joachim Raff as early as December 1850: "As soon as everything is in order concerning your *Alfred*, do not entirely forget Schubert's *Alfonso und Estrella*. Escudier is waiting for it. The piano arrangement must be comfortable and easy to play."[13] By March of the following year there seemed to be no progress, and Raff was urged again to prepare a version of the score, "to take up and bring to a conclusion the piano arrangement of the Schubert opera. If the arrangement bores you, entrust it to Reissmann or someone else."[14] In April Liszt told Sayn-Wittgenstein that he was still intending to have the piano score completed. A month later he told her merely that "I will still deliver to them [Escudier] Schubert's opera."[15] In June, the score was not yet complete, as we learn in a letter to Raff: "Reissmann should send me here as quickly as possible the other acts of the Schubert opera."[16] Several years went by. We hear nothing until the beginning of 1854, when Liszt informs Escudier that he is still thinking of adapting the opera, with a new libretto in French, for performance in Paris. It was never to be, and no trace of Raff's or Reissmann's endeavors has survived.

It seems that Liszt, in spite of his interest in an eventual performance of the work in Paris, was also still planning to perform the work in Weimar later that year. We know this from a letter to Louis Köhler: "I believe that for the last theater performance of this season (the end of June) we will still perform Franz Schubert's opera *Alfonso und Estrella*," a work he found "altogether interesting, fully endowed with inner, natural charm."[17] At the end of March, in a letter to Breitkopf, Liszt makes clear more of what he has been up to: "So far, we have held a half-dozen rehearsals, which have clearly resulted in a sufficiently large number of cuts, and which I have not hesitated to carry out, and if you should later have the intention to publish the piano reduction, I myself would see to it that you arrange your edition so that it corresponds to our performance—with the reservation that the deleted passages be added at the end as an appendix."[18]

On the evening of 24 June 1854, the Hoftheater was brilliantly lit to celebrate the birthday of the new Grand Duke Karl Alexander, whose father Karl Friedrich had died the previous July. Karl Friedrich had been a cautious administrator, inevitably more concerned with bolstering the city's flagging economy than in reviving Weimar's artistic past. "It was left to . . . Karl Alexander," as Alan Walker has written, "to dream of reawakening Weimar's past glories, and it was to his everlasting credit that when the twenty-three-year-old duke first set eyes on Liszt, he recognized a man of genius around whom Weimar's artistic regeneration might be accomplished."[19] This was to be the first of such birthday celebrations, which Liszt continued each year for the remainder of his tenure as Kapellmeister. The work Liszt chose for the occasion was *Alfonso und Estrella*, the culmination of his years of hopeful but troubled planning. To mark the musical occasion even more auspiciously, Liszt conducted before the opera a *Festival Overture* of Anton Rubinstein, and at the end of the opera, a *Festival March* on melodies by Eschinbach and Ofterdingen orchestrated by one von W. Stade. The cast of the opera could not have been more brilliant. Froila and Estrella were sung by Herr and Frau von Milde, the two most celebrated and beloved singers of the Hoftheater ensemble.

Liszt's letter to Breitkopf makes it clear that what the audience heard in the Weimar Hoftheater the evening of 24 June was not, strictly speaking, Schubert's *Alfonso und Estrella* but Liszt's revised version of the opera. The performance of the opera, given the program as a whole, could not have lasted for much longer than two hours—somewhere between thirty and forty minutes were thus cut from the score. A small number of arias or ensembles were removed entirely. Of Froila's two arias, each one placed at the beginning of the first two acts as part of the parallel dramatic whole of the first six numbers of the first two acts, Liszt cut entirely the second aria. In the second act, Liszt made cuts in all but one of the eleven numbers. What Liszt was after, apparently, was to create greater dramatic and musical concision and continuity. In the opening Introduction of the first act, with both choral and soloistic sections, Liszt cut the solo portions. In the fourth and fifth numbers—a duet for Alfonso and Froila, and a recitative and aria for Froila—he cut introductory passages. In the second of these two, he also cut the recitative material. Often his cuts included additional strophes or some identical recapitulatory passages. In keeping with the strict use of accompanied recitatives in the opera and the many long through-composed sections, he seized on these, sometimes eliminating recitative or closing and opening material and adding newly composed transitional material for the purpose. The result of these many cuts and revisions must be considered a new, rather radical performing edition of Schubert's opera.[20]

Liszt's efforts to bring *Alfonso und Estrella* to the stage of the Weimar Hoftheater were long and sustained. Perhaps the most interesting aspect of this journey is the psychological strain those efforts must have caused him. This was not simply a case of pure selfless musical admiration of an unknown or unpublished work that concerned Liszt deeply, in one way or another, during most of his active musical life. He made the decision to perform Schubert's *Alfonso und Estrella* without any foreknowledge of it musically or dramatically. Schober had of course played a decisive role in convincing Liszt to perform a work in which he himself had been so deeply engaged. The decision, through the agency of one of Schubert's closest associates and friends, created a musical link for Liszt to the actual figure of Schubert, for whose talents Liszt had unbounded admiration. Having made the decision to do honor to Schubert in this way—"an act of reverence" as he says in the essay that follows—he had to live with the consequences once the work came into his hands. Surely Liszt came to the same musical conclusions as Genast had in early 1849. But he had made a vow or promise to himself (and as he must have felt, to Schubert), and would not be deterred. The reader will notice that although Liszt was willing to criticize openly the libretto, even planning to replace it with a French text, he must have admitted the dramatic weaknesses of the work to himself, found excuses for them, and convinced himself one way or another that they could somehow be overcome in actual performance. Only after the act of performance was Liszt able to set aside these psychological maneuvers and detach himself enough from the opera to judge it according to his true musical convictions. And these are what we find in the essay that follows.

Schober's struggle during the years that led to the first performance of *Alfonso und Estrella* was more removed and private than Liszt's, one that no doubt included its share of resistance to criticism and eventually estrangement. In the end he himself confirmed what Liszt had written in his essay. In 1876, more than twenty years after the premiere of *Alfonso und Estrella*, Schober wrote these touchingly self-critical words to a friend: "Such a miserable, stillborn concoction of a libretto that even such a genius as Franz Schubert could not bring it to life."[21]

Schubert's *Alfonso und Estrella*

Franz Liszt

This work was written in 1818, ten years before the death of the composer, and given its first performance in 1854, that is, thirty-six years later.

We are well aware of the great mission Schubert fulfilled in the service of the art of music, of how he devoted virtually his entire life to the poetry of tones. Whereas the act of creation is for many artists no more than an episodic occupation of a life engrossed in every possible storm and stress and in personal distractions, and others ruminate tirelessly over works they have completed—the former devoting only a few hours a day to the act of creation, the latter only a few years—Schubert removed himself from the real world, from the urges of his private feelings, from his personal life, so to speak, so that he might aspire only to poetry, to breathe music. He breathed out his very soul in its fragrance; his vitality seemed to gush forth in the full torrent of his pen. In this way, time rushed forward for him, years crowded together into months, and although snatched from art while still young, he lived long enough to experience the maturity of his artistic genius, for in the last ten years of his life he exceeded three times over in the number and significance of his creations what someone else might accomplish in a lifetime. This last period of his life was for him the richest in the experiences that taught him to understand the nature and range of his genius.

We must, therefore, look upon the work before us as a product of his youth. Moreover, its weaknesses are understandable given the rapidity with which he went about his work, which did not give him enough time to think through the layout of his works, about how to refine them carefully as he was working or once they were completed, or to judge for himself how his creations would stand in relationship to the art of his time and to the past. Quickly following his inspiration, he gave immediate expression to the feelings ablaze in his soul. As if enflamed by the noblest of wines, he gave life to his enthusiasm for great poetry, finding pleasure only when he could pour forth in divine song the overabundance of his spiritual and poetic life.

One finds it difficult to accept the premise that a soul like Schubert, accustomed to substantial, refined, and poetic fare, should not have noticed the inadequacy of the libretto he had chosen. However, accustomed as he was to conveying impressions conjured ardently and vividly out of lyric poetry without examining the literary design of his subject beyond the feelings expressed in the verses, so too did he proceed with the composition of his opera without, in this case, subjecting the verses to criticism. Furthermore, seeing that Italian operas based on the most mediocre texts enjoyed great success day in and day out, he fell easily into the error of believing that the literary insignificance of an operatic text might be an unavoidable misfortune, and not rack his brains for long over the reasons for it. Because he did not live in close contact with the literary heroes of his time, he could not possibly expect any libretto from them; besides, it is doubtful whether even in the most fortunate instance they would have furnished him with a libretto that would have easily revealed to him its shortcomings in regard to a musical setting.

If one considers the poetic material that even a Goethe chose as the basis for operas or cantatas, one is easily persuaded how hastily highly gifted poets of this time dealt with material intended for music. Schubert lived in too modest and humble seclusion to reach the envied regions of composers whose music was regularly performed. *Alfonso und Estrella* was never performed nor published. If the opera had been performed, it could most likely have given pleasure and would probably have allowed him to achieve fame more quickly than his songs which, although more a token of his genius, were slow to be recognized. The demands placed on drama by the previous generation had not yet reached that stage of development where the poetic text would necessarily have appeared as inexcusably insipid as it does to our generation.

The literature of the French Empire had propagated a taste for idyllic situations, unexpected scenes of recognition, gradual achievement of universal happiness, for a mixture of military peripeteia and pastoral scenes. Overthrown kingdoms and tender love exercised a daily influence on their mutual fates, and the events portrayed blended with reality. Paris greatly admired *Les Battuécas* of Mademoiselle de Genlis and its portrayal of the native folk hidden away in the Spanish Sierras, very much like the native folk raised in pastoral happiness by the dethroned King Froila in Schubert's opera. In melodic quality, the opera outweighs those of Gyrowetz, Winter, or Weigl that were so popular at the time. But just as those operas have today nearly disappeared from the stage, so a performance of *Alfonso und Estrella* can only be seen as an act of reverence: the settlement of a debt of honor owed by unrelated heirs that could not be settled with the creditor during his lifetime. Had the work been performed successfully when it was written, it would have enjoyed a revival only with difficulty. Since it was made to suffer unjustly, however, it is the task of the artist to present it as an accepted fact of history, one that could lead to interesting observations.

In the first act we see Froila, the King of Léon, who, overthrown by a rival king, has taken refuge in a valley, where he brings happiness to its small number of isolated inhabitants. His son (Alfonso) has just carried off the prize in games and exercises that turns the victor into the leader of the valley's youth for one year. But this renown does not satisfy his burning desire for action. He would like to break through the boundaries set by his father's strict rules, which have held back his subjects for many years. He expresses to his father his distress over such a frustrating obstacle, though he keeps his impulsive drives at a distance. In turn his father makes him a promise that, as a sign of good will, the prohibition will be removed one day, and gives him a golden chain as a pledge in fulfillment of his promise. The scene changes to the palace of the usurper (Mauregato), whose Commanding General, returning victoriously from battle, asks for the hand of the King's daughter, Estrella, since the King promised to grant him any reward he might choose for his heroic deeds. Estrella, however, dislikes the General. Her father, though condemned for being a notorious tyrant, is unwilling to break her heart and explains that, by virtue of a holy dictum, the only one who will possess the hand of Estrella is he who wins back for him the holy chain of St. Eurich, missing from the treasure house since the overthrow of the previous King.

In the second act we see Estrella lose her way in Froila's hills during a hunt and come upon Alfonso by chance. Their young hearts become aflame with love as they stare at each other, captivated with each other's charms, and when they part Alfonso gives her, as a token of this moment, the golden chain his father had given him. Meanwhile the lovelorn General, having ravaged and plundered every nearby Moorish and Christian castle yet failing to discover the fateful chain anywhere, finds it easier to remove his King from the throne. He conspires toward this end with the leaders of the army, which happens at just the right moment, for his resolution gives rise to two of the best numbers in the opera: the chorus of conspirators, who have gathered together at night among the ruins; and the chorus of nobles, who remain loyal to Mauregato and promise to defend him. The latter receives news of the insurrection at the moment his daughter, having returned from the hunt, tells him about the charming stranger who had presented her with the chain—at once revealed as the treasure of St. Eurich, for which our *Orlando furioso ed innamorato* had been searching in vain.

In the third act the insurgents are victorious in battle in a region not far from the mountainous region where Froila dwells. The General encounters the fleeing Estrella and is just about to drag her away when, at her cry for help, Alfonso rushes to her side, frees her and takes the guilty General prisoner. When he learns that his heart's desire is the daughter of the defeated King, he calls his comrades to arms and rushes to assemble under his command the faithful soldiers who had been scattered by the defeat. The young Princess has for some time found asylum in this lonely valley, where fate has also guided Mauregato, pursued by the insurgents. Mauregato, suddenly catching sight of Froila, takes him now to be the vengeful spirit of the legitimate King and, seized with terror, begs for mercy and lays the stolen chain at his feet. Estrella arrives, followed by Alfonso, victorious over the rebellious troops. The two kings, after reaching an agreement, renounce their rights to the throne of Léon, and entrust it to the pair of lovers, thus uniting the parties and fulfilling the dictum.

The role of Froila was written for the Viennese singer Vogel [*sic*] and includes some of the most beautiful parts of the opera, in which virtually everything, from beginning to end, is nobly sustained. Much is graceful and charming and reveals the distinguished composer at every turn. Only one thing is lacking: the element of drama.

The opera must be considered in the fullest sense a Singspiel. It consists of a series of light and pretty vocal numbers sustained in a broadly melodic manner. Everything carries the stamp of Schubert's lyricism and much must be included with the best of his song collections. Often one comes across his favorite intervals, cadences, and turns of phrase. But the lack of theatrical experience and dramatic understanding is noticeable at every turn, and the symphonic virtues, for example, do not compensate for the work's defects, since the musical effect is nowhere strong enough. The instrumentation plays a very subordinate role; it is really only piano accompaniment arranged for orchestra. The frequently employed violin arpeggios, the so-called batteries, are especially tiresome, so too is the monotony with which chords, figures, and passages are doubled by different instruments without the others introducing the slightest episodic contrast or variety. Schubert allows the orchestral accompaniment to sink far below the significance that Gluck and Mozart, not to mention Beethoven, gave to it. In his songs, on the other hand, he allows the piano to play so important a role as to effectively unify the whole; his accompaniments create a kind of instrumental miniature, a scenic background and decoration for the vocal line. Duets and trios appear in this work like a sequence of romances which the characters sing, one after the other, until they join voices at the conclusion in a small ensemble. So naive and simple, yet so far from adequate.

Schubert, so masterful within smaller frameworks, suffers the loss of much of his natural genius in broader expanses. He fulfilled the important mission of raising the level of lyric composition, of endowing it with an unimagined artistic significance, of placing it on an equal footing alongside the most important artistic genres. But though he broadened the dimensions of the lyric, those of the stage exceeded his powers and might have actually crushed them. The rich, powerful flow of his melodies, diverted into too broad a channel, lacked depth. One has to say that the rays of his genius possessed more intensity than range, and reached the stage from too far a distance for the objects they encountered to cast enough of a shadow to emerge. And so I could compare his opera with *Peter Schlemihl,* which was also robbed of this property so necessary to give reality to his actual person. So too, as with *Peter Schlemihl,* do we find here melodic character in truth and reality, yet we are tempted to doubt its very existence since it does not cast the indispensable shadow.

If indeed the libretto promised little in the way of scenic development, then we must ask how much better Schubert would have fared if he had had a better subject. He poured out the whole of his gift for lyric song into this opera, but dramatic contour and declamatory expression are missing everywhere. Whoever wishes to do so can find evidence of how much the balance between the lyric and the dramatic fluctuates for composers, and how silly the generally held view is that anyone who possesses all of the special musical-technical skills also simutaneously possesses the necessary qualities to compose an opera. We have before us not only a significant musician, but an exceptionally gifted, brilliant tone poet who utterly misjudged the requirements of stagecraft, which entitles us to doubt whether he would ever have completely fulfilled these requirements, since his theatrical attempts—among which *Alfonso und Estrella*, if not the last, is certainly the most important—support such a view.

Certainly the last thing we want to do is deny richly endowed organizations the capability to present very different emotions and feelings in the most varied artistic genres, or even in different art forms. We have always argued on principle against the usual manner of ordering artists into particular categories and then treating prejudicially those works that belong to a different genre than those that were once successfully cultivated by them. One does not need to adduce the example of a Mozart or Michelangelo or anyone else in order to repudiate the notion of classifying artists like shops or cities that become well known because of certain foodstuffs or a choice morsel, some because of their wine, others by virtue of their cheese, some on account of their patés, others because of sweets. Still, it would be a mistake not to realize that a genius does not always have the ability to manage all the genres of an art form. Like the forms of nature and all forms adopted by our emotions, individual art forms have a legitimate essence of their own, and each will be brilliantly and fully developed through the powerful outpouring of a specially endowed genius. We admired in Chopin the example of an extraordinary ability to limit itself to that framework most congenial to it. Schubert warrants something similar. In his extraordinarily creative life, his attempts at dramatic and symphonic works can only be considered secondary. The theater in particular possessed too broad a scale for someone of his outlook. Moreover, the dramatic texture demanded by the stage was too complicated for his impulsive and direct inspiration.

How different it is to express emotions in limited or sharply distinctive contours, in pleasing yet brief formulations, in energetic yet concise expressions that one would like to call aphorisms of the heart—how different from giving life to the feelings of fictitious characters, allowing these characters to preserve a firmly logical character when actions conflict with one another, to confer on them forceful yet natural language in complicated situations, providing them with the true accent by which their emotions may come to light as they struggle. Schubert had the gift of dramatizing lyrical inspiration to the highest degree. He understood how to develop out of poems small in range the entire quintessence of feeling and the compelling power of the emotions, by bestowing on the often more apparent than actual pains, joys, and sentiments of a few verses a power of expression, dazzling brilliance, penetrating intensity, wonderful delicacy, and a glaze of color, so that we see them flare up before our eyes, take possession of our souls, and enjoy the delightful or bittersweet aftertaste of impressions he pours into our hearts like drops of magic elixir. In the short duration of a Lied he transforms us into observers of brusque but deadly conflicts, allows us to behold and perceive the broken sighs and overflowing tears of agony, or feel the fluttering pulsation of blessed love; he leads us through all the misery and sorrow of hopeless pain or lifts us into the regions of the ideal and eternal. Might he have reached the same goal within an expanded frame by intensifying the reach of his characters?

Moral constitutions, like physical ones, are diverse; intellectual qualities and preferences are just as manifold as corporeal ones. One moment the eye is sharper and more acute, another, less so, the ear more or less accurate and true; in some, the muscles are better developed, in others, the nerves. In one temperament, melancholy, dreaminess, and feeling prevail; in another, reflection, conjecture, calculation. In one case, liveliness and the momentary, in another, reserved and lasting ardor. Some are full of simplicity, like single-stringed instruments, others create a fully harmonious sonority. The latter are the rarest and only to these is it granted to encompass what appears to be mutually exclusive, to combine the most heterogeneous qualities, to be at the same time spontaneous and reflective, enthusiastic and erudite, forceful and gentle, vivacious and profound. And whoever wishes to choose the stage as his realm must belong to the ranks of the latter, for though the lyric is for the most part subjective by nature, dramatic works require the objectivity of character and action. Thus it is more likely that a dramatic poet will distinguish himself as a lyric poet than that a lyrical nature will fasten upon dramatic elements with lasting success. Or that one will encounter as rarely among us musicians as one will among writers talents who are endowed with the necessary profusion of intellectual virtues—especially since the musician who wishes to master the stage must demonstrate all the qualities of the tragic poet. Before one embarks on dramatic works, therefore, a serious testing of powers is of increasing and pressing necessity.

Schubert was destined to render an extraordinary service, albeit indirectly, to the dramatic Muse. He has exercised on operatic style perhaps a greater influence than has until now been recognized. By employing and bringing into relief harmonic declamation in a more highly intensified manner than Gluck, he has raised it to a power and energy not yet considered possible in the Lied, exalting poetic masterworks with its expression. In this way he disseminated and popularized declamation, facilitated its acceptance and understanding. By teaching us to value the joining together of noble poetry and profound music, he imbued the latter with the affecting accents of the pathos inherent in poetry; he made natural, as it were, poetic thought in the realm of music, uniting them like body and soul, and thereby instilling disgust and aversion toward the kind of vocal music that clings annoyingly to bad verse, verse without heart or soul.

It was Schubert's nature to sing out in the purest way, full of vitality and life; he was ablaze with divine fire and anointed with the chrism of the Holy Spirit, but his heavenly Muse, her glance lost in the clouds, liked above all to let the folds of her azure mantel stream over elysian fields, forests, and mountains, in which she wandered about in capricious strides, at first contemplatively, then jumping about, ignorant of the artificially winding path upon which the dramatic Muse carefully strolls between the wings and rows of lights, his winged strophe experiencing an uncanny fear of the clattering of gears and stage machinery. Schubert is to be compared more to a mountain stream that breaks free from the bosom of a snow-covered mountain peak, and in steep, frothy waterfalls inundates the rocky descent with a thousand colorfully sparkling drops, than to the majestic river that waters the plains and reflects the images of cathedrals on its mirror-like surface. In art he is and remains great because in art—as in nature—greatness, nobility, and grandeur are not measured in terms of material dimensions, because its creations are not measured in terms of the size and weight of commercial products, but according to those incorporeal laws whose secret the human spirit possesses yet is unable to reveal.

NOTES

1. A thirteenth essay, on Wagner's *Das Rheingold*, is now generally grouped with the others, though it has a somewhat different genesis because it was not associated with any performance. At the end of September Liszt received the completed score of the opera from Wagner, and, as he told the composer, permitted himself a slight indiscretion in bringing to the attention of the public without his consent the vast tetralogy Wagner intended: "I hope you will not be angry with me. I meant well by it, and it cannot do any harm to have made the public a bit more aware of the whole thing." (Unless otherwise specified, translations are those of the author of the present article.) The essay appeared in the *Neue Zeitschrift für Musik* at the beginning of the New Year 1855. For a careful chronological study of the publication history of all of the essays, see *Franz Liszt,*

Sämtliche Schriften, vol. 5: *Dramaturgische Blätter*, ed. Dorothea Redepenning and Britta Schilling (Wiesbaden,1989), 154–59.

2. For an important study of the relationship of Schober and Liszt, see Maria Eckardt, "Schubert's and Liszt's Friend and Poet: Franz von Schober," in *Liszt Saeculum I*, no. 56 (Budapest, 1996), 13–19.

3. On the Pest affair, see Alan Walker, *Franz Liszt, the Virtuoso Years, 1811–1847* (Ithaca, NY, 1988), 319–42. For a valuable corrective to Walker's uncritical defense of Liszt, see Dana Gooley, *The Virtuoso Liszt* (Cambridge, 2004), 117–56.

4. For more on these biographical sketches, see Allan Keiler, "Ludwig Rellstab's Biographical Sketch of Liszt," in *Franz Liszt and His World*, ed. Christopher H. Gibbs and Dana Gooley (Princeton, 2006).

5. Eckardt, "Schubert's and Liszt's Friend," 13–19, discusses these works in some detail.

6. Ferdinand Schubert to Breitkopf und Härtel, Vienna, 2 March 1848, in *Schubert: Die Erinnerungen seiner Freude*, ed. Otto Erich Deutsch (Leipzig, 1957), 482.

7. Franz Liszt, 28 February 1848, in *Franz Liszts Briefe*, ed. La Mara (Marie Lipsius) (Leipzig, 1899), 4: 24.

8. Franz von Schober to Ferdinand Schubert, Weimar, 18 March 1848, in Deutsch, *Schubert: Die Erinnerungen*, 485.

9. Ibid.

10. Ibid, 486.

11. Eduard Genast, *Aus Weimars klassischer und nachklassischer Zeit* (Stuttgart,1904), 316.

12. Liszt to Breitkopf und Härtel, 24 February 1850, in Deutsch, *Schubert: Die Erinnerungen*, 372.

13. Liszt to Raff, 30 December 1850, in Helene Raff-München, "Franz Liszt und Joachim Raff: Im Spiegel ihrer Briefe," *Die Musik* 1/10 (1902): 863.

14. Liszt to Raff, 19 March 1851, in Helene Raff-München, "Franz Liszt und Joachim Raff: Im Spiegel ihrer Briefe," *Die Musik* 1/13 (1902): 1162. August Friedrich Wilhelm Reissmann (1825–1903) was a music critic and composer. He resided for a few years, in the early 1850s, in Weimar.

15. Liszt to Princess Sayn-Wittgenstein, 13 May 1851, in La Mara, *Franz Liszts Briefe*, 4:119.

16. Liszt to Raff, Eilsen, 8 June 1851, in Helene Raff-München, "Franz Liszt und Joachim Raff": 1167.

17. Liszt to Louis Köhler, Weimar, 2 March 1854, in La Mara, *Franz Liszts Briefe*, 1:151.

18. Liszt to Breitkopf und Härtel, Weimar, 27 May 1854, in Deutsch, *Schubert: Die Erinnerungen*, 493.

19. Walker, *Franz Liszt: The Weimar Years 1848–1861* (Ithaca, NY, 1989), 92.

20. A fairly detailed summary of Liszt's revisions can be found in Till Gerrit Waidelich, *Franz Schubert: "Alfonso und Estrella"* (Tutzing, 1991), 41–46. Also see discussion of revisions in Keiler, "Liszt and the Weimar Hoftheater," *Studia Musicologica Academiae Scientiarum Hungaricae* 28 (1986), 431–50.

21. Franz von Schober to Heinrich Schubert, 2 November 1876, in *Schubert: Memoirs by His Friends*, ed. Otto Erich Deutsch, trans. Rosamond Ley and John Nowell (London, 1958), 208.

Schubert's Freedom of Song, if Not Speech

KRISTINA MUXFELDT

For Richard Kramer

In these pages I wish to probe the freedom imagery in a surprising number of Franz Schubert's songs, some written in the heady atmosphere of the so-called *Befreiungskriege*, the "wars of liberation" of 1813 to 1815, others composed only over the following decade, in the reactionary police state that Austria had become. Because the political dimension is more transparent in poetry from the earlier time I will first turn our attention to Schubert's settings of several poems by Theodor Körner (1791–1813), the poet of German patriotism who took up arms in the wars against Napoleon and died a martyr for that cause in August 1813 at the age of twenty-one. Then we will take a closer look at Schubert's continued preoccupation with similar imagery in songs set after the war to poems by Johann Mayrhofer and Johann Gabriel Seidl—this in the face of Austria's by-then firm stand against a constitutional *Vaterland* for its people.

Schubert produced his Körner settings toward the close of an era when dozens of other composers, most prominently Beethoven in Vienna, openly addressed current affairs of state in celebratory songs and occasional music—a striking contrast with opera, which frequently took a longer, and more critical, historical view.[1] Patriotic lyrics flooded the marketplace during those years, helping to drum up support for the war effort. This is not to say that opinion was uniform, though, since all publications were closely monitored—for civility of discourse as well as for political conformity. One surprisingly personal invective against the self-crowned emperor of the French with whom Austria earlier had tried to forge an alliance by political marriage (in 1810) was an ironic "Ode to Napoleon" attributed to the German poet, librettist, playwright—and diplomat—August von Kotzebue (1761–1819). It appeared anonymously in Moscow (not even the publisher was identified). As the "Genius of Freedom" weeps in slavery's chains, he laments elegiacally before building to a mocking tirade: "Let thousands go to ruin, suffocated by hunger, plague, and sword; Just so that Your flags wave victorious, and nothing disturbs Your plan. Inhuman tiger [*entmenschter Tyger*] all the world calls you! Defiling swindler of trust and belief! No matter, You alone are victor! That goal is worth any means."[2]

True, some people vacillated between admiration (perhaps rivalry) and disdain for Napoleon, yet whatever their thoughts on the intense German-national chauvinism that sprang up in reaction to French imperialism, or their loyalties or antipathy toward the old monarchies, everyone in Napoleon's path felt the military threat and economic burdens of foreign occupation; commodity and food shortages, troop quartering, plunder of artworks and other property, and heavy taxation were common complaints. During this chaotic period the restless Körner, a native of Dresden, bounced from university to university, first expelled for his involvement in political-gang skirmishes while a student of the law in Leipzig, next a student of history and philosophy in Berlin, until his record began to catch up with him.

In August 1811 Körner moved to Vienna, where he sought out the Prussian ambassador Alexander von Humboldt (brother of the linguist, Wilhelm) and Friedrich Schlegel, and swiftly gained a position as a court poet following a number of successes as a playwright and librettist. He received competing offers from Count Pálffy at the Theater an der Wien and Prince Lobkowitz at the Burgtheater. Josef von Spaun introduced him to Schubert at a performance of Gluck's *Iphigénie en Tauride*, after which the teenaged composer and the poet, six years older, bonded over their mutual admiration for the singers Johann Michael Vogl and Anna Milder. Körner seemed to be putting down roots in Vienna—he became engaged to the local actress Antonie Adamberger; yet in March 1813 he enthusiastically answered Friedrich Wilhelm of Prussia's call for volunteers to free his homeland from Napoleonic occupation.[3] (Austria, with its dynastic ties to the French Emperor, would enter the coalition against Napoleon only in August.) Körner joined the elite Lützow Freikorps also known as the Lützower Jäger (hunters), a specially skilled unit that drew into its ranks a number of academics and writers as well as workers, tradesmen, and even women. Among his cohorts was the soldier Eleonore Prochaska, who successfully maintained her disguise as a man until she fell in battle in early October, 1813. Her story, a variation on "don't ask don't tell," was celebrated in an 1815 play titled *Leonore Prohaska*, written by Friedrich Duncker, a Prussian delegate at the Congress of Vienna; Beethoven supplied incidental music for it. Hopes ran high among many of the young volunteers, *Kriegsfreiwillige*, that their patriotic sacrifices would bring about a genuine citizenry, the foundation for a German nation based on constitutional principles. So long as military enrollees were still needed, the authorities did little to dispel their enthusiasm, and martyrdom of writers such as Körner, who was killed in battle in mid-August, only aided in recruitment.

The war had galvanized the German nationalist movement and for a short time patriotic sentiment was directed against a common foe. This unity masked the dissatisfactions and widening political rifts within and between the German states and the Austrian Empire (its diverging emphases owing to the intricacy of the Empire's ties to Rome and, like the Catholic Rhineland, to France). At stake were the role of monarchy, demands for constitutionalism, and basic questions of national identity and unity: who was the "we" mobilizing against "them"?

Those cracks in Austro-German political unity were not about to close with Napoleon's defeat. And so, in the decade after 1815, authorities in the Austrian Empire, the kingdom of Prussia, and in other German monarchies broke the links to the nationalist movement that they had cultivated in the last years of the Napoleonic era.[4] Hopes of the German nationalists and of all in Europe who aspired to independent nationhood were betrayed when the Congress of Vienna met after Napoleon's defeat to reapportion Europe among the major powers—the old empires and monarchies. Under the auspices of Prince Clemens von Metternich the Restoration government ruled with an iron hand, aggressively suppressing all nation-oriented patriotic sentiment in central Europe: *Vaterland* was to mean only "land of the Father, the Habsburg emperor." This effort to turn back the hands of time to a pre-revolutionary—even pre-Josephinian—world order notably included "the reenactment of Jewish disabilities that had been somewhat relieved in Napoleonic times," as Jeffrey L. Sammons gingerly puts it, and a drastic tightening of the restrictions on free speech.[5] Joseph II had loosened these in the early 1780s and also promoted religious tolerance for practitioners of minority faiths and for the growing community of Freemasons. After the March 1819 murder in Mannheim of August von Kotzebue by the radicalized student Karl Ludwig Sand, who believed the former liberal, then emissary to Russia, was spying on nationalist groups, the Carlsbad Decrees were issued. Among the new measures were restrictions on student travel from or into Austria to stifle contact with the German, Bohemian—and soon after, Italian—nationhood movements that threatened absolutist Imperial rule; the 1821 Greek war of independence from the Ottoman Empire sparked similar fears.[6] Reactionary government officials were quick to label extremist any opposition whatsoever and sought to rehabilitate and oversee all those they could not expel (sometimes by enlisting them as censors).[7] In James J. Sheehan's spirited formulation, "Metternich saw Sand's murder of Kotzebue as a godsend. In July 1819 he rushed to Teplitz where Frederick William was on holiday and repeated his insistence that a representative constitution was merely the first step on the road to revolution."[8] The following year the Vienna *Schlussakte* would affirm the principle of Imperial autocracy. Spies infiltrated daily life, books were confiscated, and an army of bureaucratic censors, some reluctant, went to work crossing out whatever hints they could find of seditious sentiment. Within a few years' time Vienna's chief of police Josef Sedlnitzky could dismiss as fanatical *Hirngespinste*—"phantoms of the mind"—those dangerous visions of "citizenry and a system of representation"[9] promulgated by the poet Johann Senn (1795–1857), one of Schubert's friends from his Stadtkonvikt days. The police chief's language echoes the preamble to the 1810 censorship code, thought to have been written by Friedrich von Gentz (later Metternich's trusted advisor):

> No ray of light, from wherever it may emanate, shall in future remain unrecognized or unacknowledged in the Monarchy or shall be hindered from realizing its potential usefulness; but with a careful hand the hearts and minds of minors shall be protected from the corrupting misbirths of hideous fantasy, from the poisoned breath of self-serving seducers/corrupters [*Verführer*], and from the dangerous mental webs [*Hirngespinsten*] spun by twisted minds.[10]

The talent in all social classes was to be channeled to serve the interests of the state, and by the 1820s language crafted to denounce the sexual exploitation of youth was just as easily turned against anyone who opposed absolute monarchy. Metternich's government discovered dangerous new enemies of the state on the flip side of the Napoleonic coin and panicked that local nationhood supporters might follow Sand's lead. Instead of dying on the battlefield as Körner had, Senn would endure a different form of sacrifice, finding himself imprisoned without due process for fourteen months in the city he called home before being expelled permanently from Vienna in the spring of 1821.[11]

The political leanings of Schubert and his friends may be construed as an Austrian version of what Christian Jansen calls "oppositional nationalism": in the wake of the victory against Napoleon and the Congress of Vienna in 1814–15, European heads of state buttressed the monarchies and redrew the map of Europe, creating institutions of "the German nation," including the German Confederation and its bodies. "However, the liberal and democratic opposition perceived these organizations merely as a new foreign rule, which had its center in Vienna instead of Paris. Compared with the cases of western or northern Europe, oppositional nationalists in the German lands scarcely identified themselves with the institutions of the state, particularly after the Prussian Reforms and Carlsbad Decrees of 1819."[12] Jansen highlights three peaks in the "waves" of what he terms "organized nationalism" that rose to public (open) expression in Germany, spreading from the academic elite into the wider cultured bourgeoisie: 1812–19, 1830–32, and 1848–49.[13] The first two periods essentially bookend Schubert's compositional career. These peaks are bounded on one side by the crackdown on free speech, travel restrictions, and other measures enacted in Carlsbad, and on the other side by the 1830 July Revolution in France (which placed Louis-Philippe I on the throne, whose father, the Duke of Orléans, had actively supported the 1789 Revolution before he became a casualty of the Terror) and the 1832 Hambach Festival in the Rhineland. More localized energies form a counterpoint of smaller peaks and troughs. During the mid-1820s, for example, the Mühlviertel in Upper Austria was believed to be "on the eve of a revolution."[14] In Linz and Vienna during 1825 and 1826 the authorities also feared trouble.[15] Moreover, limitations on free speech were publicly tested with increasing frequency, even in the theaters, if only to shame the enforcers.[16]

From Teutomania to Songs of Sunrise

One eloquent witness deserves to be heard here, although the scenes Heinrich Heine recalls happened at some distance from Vienna. What emerges with such clarity in Heine's 1840 recollections is that a broad-spectrum shift in the trajectory of conversations around German nationhood took place precisely over the span of Schubert's compositional career. Heine opens book four of *Ludwig Börne: A Memorial* with some impressions contrasting the political temper that prevailed at the October 1817 Wartburg Festival in Thuringia—where several hundred fraternity students, *Burschenschafter*, commemorated the decisive 1813 Battle of Leipzig,[17] assembling at the castle where Martin Luther had translated the Bible—and the "fundamentally different spirit articulated in Hambach" fifteen years later. Whereas "the specter that spooked around on the Wartburg" was a "narrow Teutomania," at the Hambach celebrations in May 1832 "the modern age jubilated in songs of sunrise and drank the pledge of eternal friendship with all mankind. . . . French liberalism delivered its most intoxicated Sermons on the Mount, and even if many irrational things were said, still reason itself was recognized as the highest authority." A vivid memory of the earlier time follows: "In the beer cellar at Göttingen I used to have to admire the thoroughness with which my Old German friends created their proscription lists for the day when they would come to power. Whoever descended in the seventh generation from a Frenchman, Jew, or Slav was to be condemned to exile. Whoever had written the least thing against, say, Jahn or any Old German absurdities could prepare himself for death."[18] As disagreeable as the blinkered colluding of these "Old Germans" had been, Heine found it more disquieting that in the heat of the July Revolution "many of these Teutomaniacs, in order to take part in the general movement and the triumphs of the spirit of the times, forced themselves into our ranks, the ranks of the fighters for the principles of the revolution."[19]

Heine's reference to "the general movement and the triumphs of the spirit of the times" describes a majority, with the extremists safely bracketed. All the various factions opposing the state would have fought side by side for nationhood, this much Heine granted, but he brooded that the old opposition, fixated on German *Nazionalität* (national identity), still outnumbered the cosmopolitans in the new liberal opposition. The *Deutschthümler*—easy to identify in the aftermath of the wars of liberation because back then they paraded their Germanness in the cut and color of their clothes, their mannerisms and speech—underwent political conversions or, more troubling, merely masqueraded as liberal revolutionaries.[20] We can add to these considerations that because the Prussian regime had cultivated ties to nationalist groups during the war their rhetoric was able to spread throughout the coalition, exerting an influence on official forms of patriotism within the Austro-German confederation as well as on the opposition. After all, visitors affiliated with the Congress of Vienna had increased the city's population by nearly a third, and ideological arguments, reading matter, and local talk traveled with them (some 100,000 visitors flooded into the city for the Congress).

Heinrich Heine's is only one voice, yet the unsettling mutability of political allegiances he observed is something we can also expect to see signs of elsewhere. It certainly surprised him to find that in Berlin in 1822 the songs of Theodor Körner, once taken up by patriotic choral and gymnastic societies, still could be heard (many of the poems were designed to be sung to familiar chorale melodies). In the third of the *Letters from Berlin* he tells of an anniversary party at which Körner's "Schwertlied" was performed by twelve young women. "As you can see, Theodor Körner's poems are still sung here. Naturally, not in circles of good taste: in these it is already said openly how fortunate it was that in 1814 the French could not understand German, and so could not read these bland, shallow, flat verses devoid of poetry that made us good Germans wax so enthusiastic."[21] Regrettably, Heine left no dispatches from Vienna to help us gauge the rise and fall of political temperatures in the diverse strata of society there. He did, however, compose an estimation of Austrian official politics in a preface to the 1832 *Letters from Paris*:

> Austria was ever an open and honest enemy, which never denied, nor did it for a moment suspend its attack on Liberalism. Metternich never ogled with loving eyes the Goddess of Liberty; he never played the demagogue with troubled anxious heart; he never sang the songs of Arndt while drinking white beer; he never played at gymnastic exercises on the Hasenheide; he never played the pietist, nor did he ever weep with the prisoners of the fortresses while he kept them chained. . . . He acted magnanimously in the spirit of a system to which Austria had been true for three centuries.[22]

1815: The Lyre of a Patriot

Theodor Körner's poetry appeared in two significant collections in the years immediately following his death: *Leyer und Schwert* (Lyre and Sword) was published in 1814 and a two-volume *Nachlass* edition appeared in 1815. Schubert set over a dozen poems of Körner that year along with a one-act opera, *Der vierjährige Posten* (The Four-Year Sentry Duty), about a military deserter who escaped prosecution for treason by claiming it was he who had been abandoned four years earlier; he'd never left his post. Körner's poetry attracted many composers at this time, but Ilija Dürhammer speculates that Schubert was inspired to make his settings only after meeting Johann Mayrhofer (1787–1836), an ardent admirer of Körner.[23] This would be interesting, if true, because both Mayrhofer's and Senn's names appear on a watch list of a dozen *Burschenschafter* in Vienna, as Ruth Melkis-Bihler reports in her admirable overview of Schubert's political times. She notes that this was a very small cohort compared with fraternity membership lists from German university towns, suggesting that they were closely overseen. In fact, more of Schubert's friends and acquaintances appear on this list than Melkis-Bihler conveys.[24] Mayrhofer was a decade older than Senn or Schubert and by 1815 he had accepted the censor's post that would become a source of inner conflict for the rest of his life, which ended dramatically in 1836 when he leapt to his death from the censorship building. Notably, his position did not prevent his 1817 *Beyträge zur Bildung für Jünglinge* from being banned after two issues. (See the selections from this collection of poems, essays, and aphorisms devoted to the civic education of youths, introduced by David Gramit, in this volume.) From the fall of 1818 to the end of 1820 Mayrhofer and Schubert shared the same rooms on the Wipplingerstrasse formerly occupied by Körner.

Interspersed throughout the Körner collections are poems of youthful passion for a girl, and ones extolling battle and the yearning for an ideal. The ideal, like the girl, is named only indirectly: "Die Liebe"—words that can mean simply "love," the emotion, or can be treated as a name, pointing to a particular beloved "*die* Liebe," "*the* beloved one," or even to a personification of love. Telling apart the intended referents can be challenging because both kinds of poems speak of *Sehnsucht* (yearning), of "sweet lights," of hope, and elevated strivings. Sometimes the ideal *Liebe* is figured as a bright star in the heavens whose appearance signals a rosy dawn, the spring of a new age. If that symbolism seems an obvious political cipher, it is useful to consider the cognate in Goethe's memorable epithet "ein rosenfarbnes Frühlingswetter" (a rosy-colored spring weather) for the dewy flush that forms on the satisfied lover's face.[25] Far less skillfully than Goethe but striving for a similar tone of mystery, Körner worked images of glowing heavenly brides into both his political canvases and his poems forecasting domestic bliss. (Heine disliked his simple rhymes on technical as well as ideological grounds.) Indeed, the deeper we read into Körner's collection the harder it is to separate confidently the two categories of poems: a pervasive religiosity colors any sensual or political reading. Compare the opening lines of *Der Morgenstern* (D172, D203, in seven stanzas), a hymn to Venus, the morning star—

Stern der Liebe, Glanzgebilde, *Glühend wie die Himmelsbraut* *Wanderst durch die Lichtgefilde* *Kündend, daß der Morgen graut.*	Star of love, radiant image, glowing like the bride of heaven, you wander through the realm of lights heralding the morning gray.

—with the opening stanzas of *Sängers Morgenlied* (D163, D165, six stanzas), in which a sweet light breaks triumphantly through the night and love's gentle wafting in the breezes, as translated below, though it could just as well be the Beloved (Freedom) swaying in the breeze, swells the poet's heart as he greets the roseate splendor of the dawn. Speaking in either metaphor, the language is secretive, whether we hear private intimacies expressed or whisperings of political hope.

Süßes Licht! Aus goldnen Pforten	Sweet light! Through golden portals
Brichst du siegend durch die Nacht.	you break victoriously through the night.
Schöner Tag! Du bist erwacht.	Glorious day! You have awakened.
Mit geheimnisvollen Worten,	With mysterious words,
In melodischen Accorden	in melodious strains
Grüß' ich deine Rosenpracht!	I greet your roseate splendor!
Ach! Der Liebe sanftes Wehen	Ah, love's gentle breezes
Schwellt mir das bewegte Herz,	make my moved heart swell
Sanft wie ein geliebter Schmerz.	as softly as a beloved pain.
Dürft ich nur auf gold'nen Höhen	If only upon golden heights I might
Mich in Morgenduft ergehen!	bask in morning fragrance!
Sehnsucht zieht mich himmelwärts.	Yearning draws me heavenward.

In this excerpt, from a lengthy patriotic poem in *Leyer und Schwert* not set by Schubert, "Was uns bleibt" (All that remains for us), a star's identification with political freedom is made explicit:

Wenn auch jetzt in den bezwung'nen Hallen	Even though now in vanquished halls
Tyrannei der Freiheit Tempel bricht; —	tyranny breaks Freedom's temple; —
Deutsches Volk, du konntest fallen,	German people, you could fall,
Aber sinken kannst du nicht!	but sink under you cannot!
Und noch lebt der Hoffnung Himmelsfunken.	The heavenly spark of hope lives on.
Muthig vorwärts durch das falsche Glück!	Courageously onward through false fortune!
'S war ein Stern! Jetzt ist er zwar versunken,	'Twas a star! Though he has now faded
Doch der Morgen bringt ihn uns zurück.	the morning shall return him to us.
'S war ein Stern! —Die Sterne bleiben.	'Twas a star! —The stars remain.
'S war der Freiheit gold'ner Stern. [26]	'Twas Freedom's golden star.

Körner's poems about death in battle revel in wedding imagery, notably so in "Schwertlied," which draws out what today seems a ludicrous metaphor into a sixteen-stanza conversation between a soldier and his sword (its stanzas are in quotation marks). The dialogue promises young men an experience in battle as intense as the wedding night. The soldier's sword is his beloved bride and the performers in Schubert's setting for a unison chorus and solo voice are instructed to clink swords on those sixteen "hurrahs," just as Körner indicated in a footnote, making a communal racket as noisy as the traditional breaking of porcelain at a *Polterabend*, the festivities on the eve of a wedding. Did Schubert find this absurd or did he take it seriously?

Schwertlied (D170, stanzas 3, 4, and 12):

Ja, gutes Schwert, frey bin ich, *Und liebe dich herzinnig,* *Als wärst du mir getraut,* *Als eine liebe Braut—Hurrah!*	Yes, my good sword, I am free, and love you dearly as if you were my betrothed, as if my sweet bride—Hurrah!
Zur Brautnachts Morgenröthe *Ruft festlich die Trompete;* *Wenn die Kanonen schreyn,* *Hol' ich das Liebchen ein.—Hurrah!*	The festive trumpet heralds the bridal-night's rosy morn; when the cannons shriek, I shall catch up to my dearest.—Hurrah!
. . . .	. . . .
"Ach herrlich ist's im Freyen, *Im rüst'gen Hochzeitsreihen* *Wie glänzt im Sonnenstrahl* *So bräutlich hell der Stahl!"—* *Hurrah!*	"How glorious to be in open air, in a wedding round so hale, where the sunlit steel gleams like bridal white!"— Hurrah!

Even an apostrophe to the beloved so innocently pious as "Liebesrausch" (Love-Intoxicated) invites political reading when it is found amid these martial poems. The use of the diminutive *Mädchen* at first masks that this rapturous poem might sing of the ideal—for Susan Youens it is a love poem that "does not rise much above the level of platitude"[27]—but what eventually strikes our ears are the endings of each stanza and the narrowing of focus in the last verse: at the close of the first stanza, "your noble image shines for me"; at the end of the second, "and all my loveliest songs name only you"; and the third, with Körner's emphases, "Only *one* longing lives in me, only *one* thought here in my heart: the eternal quest for you." As with several Körner poems, Schubert attempted two settings (D164 and D179, in March and April 1815).

Here is the entire poem, "Liebesrausch":

Dir, Mädchen, schlägt mit leisem
Beben
Mein Herz voll Treu' und Liebe zu.
In dir, in dir versinkt mein Streben,
Mein schönstes Ziel bist du!
Dein Name nur in heil'gen Tönen
Hat meine kühne Brust gefüllt;
Im Glanz des Guten und des Schönen
Strahlt mir dein hohes Bild.

For you, maiden, my heart pounds,
a quiet trembling of devoted love.
In you, in you my striving ceases;
you are my life's fairest goal.
Your name alone, a sacred tone,
fills my bold breast.
In the radiance of all that's good
and beautiful
your noble image shines for me.

Die Liebe sproßt aus zarten Keimen,
Und ihre Blüthen welken nie!
Du, Mädchen, lebst in meinen
Träumen
Mit süßer Harmonie.
Begeist'rung rauscht auf mich
hernieder,
Kühn greif ich in die Saiten ein,
Und alle meine schönsten Lieder,
Sie nennen dich allein.

Love [the Beloved] sprouts from
tender seeds,
and its [her] blossoms never wither!
You, maiden, live in my dreams
in sweet harmony.
Rapturous inspiration comes over
me,
boldly I pluck the strings,
and all my loveliest songs,
they name only you.

Mein Himmel glüht in deinen Blicken
An deiner Brust mein Paradies.
Ach! Alle Reize, die dich schmücken,
Sie sind so hold, so süß.
Es wogt die Brust in Freud und
Schmerzen,
Nur eine *Sehnsucht lebt in mir,*
Nur ein *Gedanke hier im Herzen:*
Der ew'ge Drang nach dir.

My heaven glows in your glances;
my paradise upon your breast.
Ah! All the charms adorning you,
they are so noble, so sweet.
My breast undulates in joy and
pain;
only *one* desire dwells in me,
only *one* thought here in my heart:
eternal passion for you!

Finally, Körner himself spelled out the ambiguity, conflating Liberty and Venus, in a poem titled "Abschied vom Leben" (Departure from Life) written on the eve of a near-brush with death three months before he finally succumbed in battle. By the poem's end freedom and love can no longer be meaningfully distinguished:

Und was ich hier als Heiligthum erkannte,	And that which I knew to be sacred here,
Wofür ich rasch und jugendlich entbrannte,	for which quickly and youthfully I became enflamed,
Ob ich's nun Freiheit, ob ich's Liebe nannte:	whether I called it Freedom, or whether Love:
Als lichten Seraph seh' ich's vor mir stehen—	As luminous Seraph I see it standing before me now—
Und wie die Sinne langsam mir vergehen,	and as my senses slowly leave me,
Trägt mich ein Hauch zu morgenrothen Höhen.	a breath carries me to rosy-morning heights.

I do not wish to linger over Schubert's Körner settings here, I merely wish to observe that a vocabulary of images found in his (and not only his) poetry from this time resounds through many other poems that Schubert chose to set in later years. This was one way around the ever stricter censorship restrictions that came in the wake of the Congress of Vienna. Heard in isolation, faint echoes of revolutionary freedom imagery might be easily dismissed by readers, or, for that matter, could be deliberately masked by poets.

The Death of Actaeon

Especially complex examples of such concealment of freedom imagery are found in poems of Johann Mayrhofer, the conflicted censor who maintained his oppositional, at times markedly Germanic liberalism while dutifully serving the state for twenty years. Schubert's friend Josef von Spaun would later characterize him as "extraordinarily liberal, indeed democratic, in his views . . . passionate about freedom of the press."[28] Mayrhofer, in his own 1829 recollection of Schubert, hinted intriguingly at a deepening rift between the two intimate friends whose personalities had often clashed even while they lived together: "The cross-currents of circumstances and society, of illness and changed views of life kept us apart later, but what had once been was no more to be denied its rights."[29] Mayrhofer's poetic oeuvre is steeped in classical literature and Greek mythology, often presenting familiar episodes with surprising twists or omissions. We can see this in the following poem about Diana, the goddess who roams the forests freely with her handmaidens. (Her father

Zeus promised he would never force her to marry against her will.) Just when Mayrhofer wrote the poem "Der zürnenden Diana" is not known; Schubert's song dates from December 1820, the final month of his stay with Mayrhofer (by which time their mutual friend Senn had already languished in prison for nearly a year and his fate was still uncertain).

Ja, spanne nur den Bogen, mich zu tödten, *Du himmlisch Weib! im zürnenden Erröthen* *Noch reizender. Ich werd' es nie bereuen,* *Dass ich dich sah am blühenden Gestade* *Die Nymphen überragen in dem Bade,* *Der Schönheit Funken in die Wildniß streuen.*	Yes, draw your bow to slay me, you heavenly woman! in the flush of anger more enchanting still. I shall never regret that I saw you on the flowering bank, towering over the nymphs in the bath, spreading rays of beauty into the wilderness.
Den Sterbenden wird noch dein Bild erfreuen. *Er athmet reiner, er athmet freyer,* *Wem du gestrahlet ohne Schleyer.* *Dein Pfeil, er traf, doch linde rinnen* *Die warmen Wellen aus der Wunde;* *Noch zittert vor den matten Sinnen* *Des Schauens süße letzte Stunde.*	Your image will yet gladden the dying one. He who has beheld your unveiled radiance breathes more purely, more freely. Your arrow—it struck, yet warm waves spill gently from the wound. Still trembling before failing senses is the last sweet hour of sight.

Der zürnenden Diana (Of Diana Enraged; D707) tells the familiar story from book three of Ovid's *Metamorphoses* of the hunter Actaeon accidently stumbling upon the goddess bathing in a pool. Her virgin nymphs use their own bodies to shield her from Actaeon's gaze, "but the goddess stood head and shoulders over all the rest," as Ovid tells it "and red as the clouds which flush beneath the sun's slant rays, red as the rosy dawn, were the cheeks of Diana as she stood there in view without her robes." Diana, infuriated, gazes back at Actaeon, splashes him with water and robs him of his speech: "Now you are free to tell that you have seen me all unrobed—if you can tell," she taunts him (how could a censor-poet not have noted this challenge?) and she makes horns sprout from his

Figure 1. Titian, *The Death of Actaeon*.

forehead so that his hounds will mistake him for a stag, the very prey they have chased all day. Unable to command the dogs as before, Actaeon will be torn to shreds by them.[30]

In Ovid's telling Diana is unarmed when Actaeon happens upon her, her quiver and her unstrung bow resting with one of her handmaidens. Not so in Mayrhofer's poem, where Actaeon is struck by Diana's arrow—as he is in Titian's memorable portrayal of *The Death of Actaeon* (1559–75), which fixes forever the instant when an athletic, rosy-cheeked Diana, clad in a rose-colored tunic, has just let fly her arrow (see Figure 1). With her right arm still drawn back and her bow-arm outstretched one breast is exposed to the viewer, who inadvertently becomes a voyeur. We do not notice immediately that on the right, blended into the brownish thickets in the distance, a partly transformed Actaeon is being mauled by bloodthirsty hounds. The picture's time scale is complex, more like a photographic double exposure than a single moment in snapshot. (Titian's Diana, we might note, bears a striking resemblance to the equally unforgettable figure who strides across the battlefield in Eugene Delacroix's 1830 canvas *Liberty Leading the People*. As Liberty holds high the tricolor flag, her flushed cheek and exposed breasts are illuminated by the blazing heavens; only gradually do we notice the dying Revolutionary at her feet hoisting himself up to catch a last glimpse of her. Buried in plain view in both canvases is the doomed beholder of an awe-inspiring female figure.) I do not know if Mayrhofer knew Titian's work, either by reputation or in copy, but it is not unlikely. Until the early 1790s the Duke of Orléans owned Titian's painting. In an effort to ride out the storm of upheaval in the late 1780s he had engraved copies produced of all his paintings before he offered his magnificent collection for sale. This series was printed between 1786 and 1808, interrupted for a time by the chaos of the revolution. The Duke, or Philippe Égalité as he was known, did not live to see his Titians and other masterpieces on display in London during the early years of the nineteenth century, where they were enthusiastically viewed by many. As a member of the royal family, in line for the throne, he was guillotined. The Congress of Vienna held extensive deliberations about the fate of artworks that had changed hands during the French Revolution and the First Empire. With the rise of public museums across Europe came questions not only about stolen artworks but about the status of royal art collections as personal or national property.[31] Curiously, in the *Mort d'Acteon* found among the Orléans engravings Titian's graceful Diana is made to appear remarkably masculine (see Figure 2).

In Mayrhofer's "Der zürnenden Diana" all mention of the stag's antlers and the hounds is left out, except, perhaps, for his choice of the verb *zittert* (trembles) in the penultimate line—"noch zittert vor den matten Sinnen"—evoking the convulsive shivers of the wounded animal as it expires. Other features in the poem leap out: the words "du himmlisch Weib," because high esteem for any woman is a striking anomaly in this poet's output. More significantly, Mayrhofer tells the story from the perspective of a defiant Actaeon (though not once named in the poem) who welcomes the fatal arrow, refuses remorse, and insists that the forbidden vision was worth dying for even as warm blood gushes from his wounds and his senses leave him. This stands in stark contrast to those Renaissance accounts of Ovid's tale that present the wayward hunter as a hapless victim punished for his error by a tyrannical goddess who knows no mercy, at least not forgiveness. Man's fortune can spiral out of control in an instant: this was one lesson for early modern observers

Figure 2. Jacques Couché, engraving based on Titian's *Death of Actaeon* in the Gallery of the Palais Royal with historical commentary by the abbé de Fontenai.

of Parmigianino's Actaeon frescos, for example, and the warning is still there in Titian.[32]

Mayrhofer declares his radical remove from such traditional ecclesial and courtly interpretation in strophe 2, when the mythical hunter's singular experience is generalized: he who has glimpsed the towering beauty's rays scattered into the wilderness, who has seen her without her veils—*he* will breathe more purely, will breathe more freely. Rather than warning the viewer who gazes at a painted image of Diana's nakedness not to repeat Actaeon's error, the defiant hunter in this poetic fable invites emulation. "Er athmet reiner, er athmet freyer / Wem du gestrahlet ohne Schleyer": the second *er* appears to have been added by Schubert to intensify the meaning; it does not appear in the text Mayrhofer published in 1824.[33] About this stanza we might also speculate that the word *Schleyer* (veil), a rhyme for the adverb *freyer* (freely), could evoke a symbol—a *Sinnbild*—borrowed from a late eighteenth-century Masonic imaginary: the veils of Isis. The Egyptian nature goddess's veils concealed mysteries that only her initiates could fathom.[34]

Mayrhofer's stripped-down telling of Actaeon's story makes possible rosy-cheeked Diana's transferal from the realm of myth into the domain of *Sinnbild* (the German term, literally a "sense picture," a pictograph), allowing her image to lend concrete shape to an abstraction. Yet it is Schubert's absorbing music that actually lulls us into forgetting the mythic veil. Commentators on the song have remarked on the needless repetition of phrases in Schubert's setting: words conveyed clearly the first time through are repeated over and over again. When we pay heed to the rhetoric of those repetitions to see what is emphasized thereby, what is downplayed, and how local harmonies, modulations, and dynamics color our perception of the words, we can appreciate how much greater the freedom of song is for releasing those symbolic associations that the compact poem cloaks in myth.

In Schubert's ten-bar piano introduction to the poet's words in *Der zürnenden Diana* there is already a hint of a poetic image, as yet inchoate, in the repeating figuration used to make a crescendo from *piano* to *forte* then pulled back to *pianissimo* just before the singer's entry. From sharp *fp* attacks on the downbeats the quivering chordal triplets in the treble build to a climax in the accented middle of each bar. At the crescendo's high point in measure 5 a diminished seventh thwarts a move to the relative minor, making the *Feurig* tremors shake yet more forcefully before the harmony veers around to a tonic cadence in A-flat major by way of a passing German augmented sixth on F♭. The coordination of tonal surge and dynamic swell draws our attention to an emerging form.[35]

Making bold, the singer begins—"Ja, spanne nur den Bogen mich zu tödten"—and once again the harmony bends to F minor and an arresting E♮ "promissory note"[36] against the C♮ root of that key's dominant, "Du himmlisch Weib" (see Example 1). On repetition, those words are inflected by the wondrous glow of F-flat major, I–V (the earlier leading tone now a root, and the melodic contour twisted to put C♭ into the outer voices). At play in the architecture of the song is basically a tension between the tonic-major and parallel minor modes: simply put, the relative minor, F minor, is a minor-mode adjunct to A-flat major (because its dominant sits a major third above A♭); F-flat major is a poignant major mode adjunct to A-flat minor (its dominant sits a minor third above A♭.). Much else intervenes, it needs hardly be said, but the reach of these combined harmonic and dynamic inflections extends all the way to the end of the song. For his portrayal of the cherished vision still trembling before the *Sterbender*'s eyes Schubert summons the strongest dynamic contrast yet, reinforced by the indications *stark* and *leise* in the vocal part, and colors the final closure in the tonic-major with a dab of F♭ as if the singer had not the strength to reach a semitone higher.

That Schubert's song is addressed to Liberty, freedom personified—a multivalent image carrying political, sexual, even anarchic associations,

Example 1. *Der zürnenden Diana*, D707, mm. 14–30.

Example 1. continued

and fast vanishing from open public discourse due to censorship—may be suggested in the exquisite harmonies enveloping "du himmlisch Weib" and in the threefold repetition of "im zürnenden Erröthen" that lays stress on the rosy hew in this aural canvas. Next repeated is "Ich werd' es nie bereuen," made even more emphatic when Schubert later repeats the declaration in this rewording: "*Nie werd' ich es bereuen*, dass ich dich sah." The place where Diana is first seen by Actaeon is indicated in a whisper, a *pianissimo* stream of rising and falling eighth notes: "am blühenden Gestade die Nymphen überragen in dem Bade" (on the flowering bank overtowering the nymphs in the bath). These are practically the only words in the song not to be emphasized by local repetition and further bracketed by crescendi carrying the thought through to its radiant goal. Consider that if the *pianissimo* words were cut away altogether, the sentence would remain perfectly coherent: "Nie werd' ich es bereuen, dass ich dich sah, der Schönheit Funken in die Wildniß streuen" (Never shall I regret that I saw you, scattering Beauty's rays into the wilderness). Schubert lets us hear the latter clause twice in soaring cadential phrases (four times if we count the weaker cadences to C-flat major in measures 46 and 50), bringing the first half of the song to a close in B major (Example 2). A temporal caesura is made by transforming this last root into a leading tone: from an isolated B♮ a downward arpeggio through a G-major dominant-seventh takes us to faraway C major where the action is paused and a narrating voice in sympathy with the wounded man avows that he breathes more freely now that he has been illuminated by Diana's unveiled radiance. "Wem du gestrahlet ohne Schleyer" is heard four times, giving us ample chance to feel the scrim evaporate before our eyes. Twice the fatal arrow strikes its mark and the repetition in its wake creates something like a tableau vivant, an almost cinematic simulation of real-time dying: the narrating, now "autobiographical" voice clings to the radiant vision as his senses slowly leave him. The entire closing scene recalls Körner's vision of a Lützower Jäger's death on the battlefield: "Whether I called it Freedom, or whether Love: as luminous seraph I see it standing before me now; and as my senses slowly leave me a breath carries me to rosy-morning heights." It takes little effort to hear this song as an elegy for a fallen comrade.

Paired in one *Liederheft* (a gathering of songs) with *Der zürnenden Diana* is another song on a Mayrhofer text, *Nachtstück* (D672), which Schubert dedicated to the singer Katharina von Lacsny, née Buchwieser. In the February 1825 publication announcement in the *Wiener Zeitung* the publisher Cappi took credit for the selection of the two songs in Opus 36: prospective buyers were assured that both had been well received in

Example 2. *Der zürnenden Diana*, D707, mm. 50–73.

Example 2. continued

Johann Michael Vogl's performances for the most select private circles.[37] Surely Schubert approved the dedication and selection. The musicologist Clemens Höslinger has speculated that the song about Diana's nakedness must have called up not only the beautiful "Catinka" Buchwieser's many love affairs but also a scandalous naked orgy said to have been planned in November 1812 at Count Pálffy's palace in Hernals. The police got wind of it and punished all the associates of the "*Adamiten und Maurerloge*." (Since Vienna's Masonic chapters were shut down two decades earlier, mention of an active lodge surprises almost as much as the pairing of Adamites with Freemasons.) The noblemen paid hefty fines; the women, including Buchwieser, were given a flogging, and then the poor singer had to appear onstage the next day as the Princess Navarra in François Adrien Boieldieu's opera *Jean de Paris*.[38] Quite possibly the dedication did invite such associations "in the most select circles"—or, worse, prompted performances meant to embarrass the singer, who was respectably married by the time Schubert composed the song.

Höslinger wonders further whether the 1869 picture of Diana in the Schwind Foyer at the Vienna Court Opera might be an homage to the former singer. The trompe l'oeil statue of Diana in the fresco by the Viennese painter and Schubert friend Moritz von Schwind (Figure 3) has just released her arrow, and her right arm is still pulled back, her bow arm outstretched, rather like Titian's. A symbol of Luna, the crescent moon, often associated with Diana (as in Titian's earlier *Diana and Actaeon*, another picture in the Orléans collection), adorns her head, and a thin shawl is snaked around her naked body. Since Schwind was introduced to Frau Lacsny by Schubert in 1825, the same year Schubert published and dedicated his *Der zürnenden Diana* to her, it seems reasonable to imagine that she was on his mind when he designed the tryptych portraying Diana along with other themes from Schubert's works (also visible in Figure 3 is Goethe's "Der Fischer").

These suggestions are by no means mutually exclusive: to take the allusion to the former Catinka Buchwieser and the 1812 sex scandal at face value (not as a *Schleyer* for another political meaning) is only to acknowledge that sexual freedom, freedom from social convention, was an element in Schubert's political credo. How entwined Restoration political agendas were with the regulation of private behavior is revealed by a later event. The right to privacy would not gain legal recognition for decades. But in March 1848, the year censorship restrictions were briefly lifted, the *Wiener Zeitung* announced that not only was censorship gone but the police would cease spying. Henceforth, invasive police intrusion into the private lives of the city's residents was strictly forbidden.[39] Whatever else we may

Figure 3. Moritz von Schwind, *Diana*, Vienna Staatsoper.

imagine, the dedication to Lacsny extends to both songs in Opus 36, the Actaeon tale, Op. 36, No. 1, and the haunting *Nachtstück*, No. 2, composed in 1819. Both were published a half step lower than originally conceived, perhaps to accommodate a favorite singer. The subject matter of *Nachtstück*? When the fog descends and Luna does battle with dark clouds, "Der Alte," the old rhapsode, takes his lyre and sings this apocalyptic prophecy into the forest: "Du heil'ge Nacht: bald ist's vollbracht."[40] What shall be soon completed? "Soon I shall sleep the long slumber, and be released from all suffering." The old man seems already to have lived for far too long, like old Tithonus, lover of Eos (the dawn), who grew aged but could not die. Luna's name is the only overt hint, as in many Mayrhofer poems, of a mythological basis. The meaning of the song (and of the entire opus) changes depending on which *Alter* we imagine sings the prophecy "Holy Night: soon it shall be accomplished." Is he Endymion, destined eternally to slumber in youthful beauty so that Luna may penetrate him on nightly visits, siring their many daughters? Or is he Tithonus, likewise granted longevity by his beloved Eos, in his case, however, in the form of old age? Tithonus is traditionally represented as a bard carrying a lyre or harp. The troubled, Baroque, C-sharp-minor counterpoint with which Schubert's eerie tone-painting begins yields to blurred arpeggios created "with raised dampers" as the prophetic words are sung in a muted voice (*gedämpft*). Twice, novel deceptive cadences accentuate the words "old man," then on the last page otherworldly harmonies sink mysteriously (the old man listens for Death), transforming the atmosphere for the C-sharp-major close. Moments before, the narrating voice relates that many a dear bird (*mancher liebe Vogel*) calls out, "Oh let the old man rest in his grassy tomb." The fictional scene is punctured. No matter which old man came to contemporary listeners' minds, this exhortation must have sounded like a very personal message when sung by Johann Michael Vogl.

1826: Oppositional Politics in Sehnsucht

For another case of concealed political content, let us consider a song from 1826, a year when censorship restrictions came to be tested and enforced in particularly infuriating ways. That spring, the great comic playwright and actor (also former opera singer and performer of Schubert part-songs) Johann Nestroy was jailed in Brno for the improvised lines he introduced in performance, following which the police canceled his contract and he relocated to Graz. It mattered not whether his extemporary jokes criticized heads of state or offended sexual mores or moral and religious norms: to depart from an approved script—to bring down the house without prior permission—was against the law.[41] That year, too, the Parisian satirical weekly *Le Figaro* was founded: on its masthead appeared the words "Without the freedom to criticize, praise is empty" from Figaro's soliloquy in Beaumarchais's *Le mariage de Figaro*, the speech that had smashed through the barricades of Parisian censorship in 1784. The year 1826 also saw the formation of a secret society in Linz involving several of Schubert's acquaintances. They called themselves *Eos* (Dawn) or the Frühaufstehgesellschaft—The Early-to-Rise Society—perhaps after the morning societies that formed in the early days of the French Revolution. The members were known as "Memnonites." According to legend, a colossus associated with Memnon—son of Eos and Tithonus, he fell in battle defending Troy—gave out a lamenting cry at the hour of sunrise and then was mute for the rest of each day.[42] The Memnonites had written an elaborate constitution and statutes and held assemblies in which democratic protocol could be practiced on mundane, seemingly apolitical subjects, preparing them for a post-uprising world. A branch organization was started in Vienna after two of its members, the brothers Franz and Fritz Hartmann, both students of law, moved there; they also attended Schubertiades at Spaun's. The society's statutes, membership, and its journal *Morgenstern* (later *Lampe*) have attracted renewed attention of late from scholars doubting that all this was simply harmless Biedermeier entertainment.[43]

Nearly a decade after the Congress of Vienna, outrage over censored speech filled the air in that city. Now writers and artists could unite against this assault on their profession without needing to probe one another's political persuasions because the most basic prerequisite for any form of representative government was open discussion. In 1826 there was no "foreign" tyrant to oppose; democratic-nationalist opposition was directed against Metternich's Restoration government. This was the climate within which Schubert set the poem "Sehnsucht" by Johann Gabriel Seidl (1804–1875), a local Viennese poet who a dozen years later would himself take a position as a part-time censor. Schubert's delightfully catchy song invites scrutiny because it is difficult to get the words of the poem to mean quite what the music's character—its demeanor—and the rhetoric of its repetitions and phrase structure would imply; indeed, music plays an even greater role in shaping meaning here than in *Der zürnenden Diana*. Doubly alluring is that the poem also strikes an autobiographical pose; the fourth stanza depicts a poet struggling to overcome his writer's block to compose this very song, *Sehnsucht* (D879):

Die Scheibe friert, der Wind ist rauh, *Der nächt'ge Himmel rein und blau:* *Ich sitz' in meinem Kämmerlein,* *Und schau' ins reine Blau hinein!*	The pane frosts over, the wind is raw, the nighttime sky so clear and blue. I sit in my little room and gaze into pure blue!
Mir fehlt etwas, das fühl' ich gut, *Mir fehlt mein Lieb, das treue Blut:* *Und will ich in die Sterne seh'n,* *Muß stets das Aug' mir übergeh'n!*	Something is lacking, this I well feel; I miss my love, my true life's blood, and when I gaze into the stars my eye must brim over with tears!
Mein Lieb, wo weilst du nur so fern, *Mein schöner Stern, mein Augenstern?!* *Du weißt, dich lieb' und brauch' ich ja,—* *Die Träne tritt mir wieder nah.*	My love, where do you tarry so far away, my beautiful star, star of mine eye?! You know 'tis you I love and need,— Again my tears well up.

Da quält' ich mich so manchen Tag, *Weil mir kein Lied gelingen mag,—* *Weil's nimmer sich erzwingen läßt* *Und frei hinsäuselt wie der West!*	I've tormented myself many a day, because no song will come together,— for song never will be forced and murmurs forth freely like the west wind!
Wie mild mich's wieder g'rad' durchglüht! — *Sieh nur—das ist ja schon ein Lied!* *Wenn mich mein Loos vom Liebchen warf,* *Dann fühl' ich, daß ich singen darf.*	How the mild glow suffuses me again just now!— Ah, look—it is a song already! If my lot has cast me from my love, then I feel that I may sing.

Seidl's poem is in five stanzas. The scene is a small chamber late at night. From here the poet gazes out into the nighttime sky; a rough wind frosts the windowpane. The first three stanzas concern a beloved absent star, addressed as "mein Lieb" in stanza three: "My love, where do you tarry so far away, My beautiful star, star of mine eye?!" (*mein Augenstern*). Stanza four shifts to unexpectedly inward expression, revealing a poet suffering from writer's block: he has tormented himself for many a day but no song will come together because song will not be coerced but murmurs forth freely like the west wind: "Weil's nimmer sich erzwingen läßt und frei hinsäuselt wie der West." (To the west of Austria, we might reflect, lies France.) Suddenly the star's rays create a warm glow—passing right through the frozen window—and look, already here is a song!

As soon as the poet's muse appears his song comes together in a blink. Very charming. The next lines are puzzling, though. The final couplet is cast as a pithy summation whose "if-then" clause is meant to explain how the meditation on writer's block follows from the yearning for the absent beloved. But something is amiss—why does no meaning spring into place? "If my lot has cast me from my love, then I feel that I may sing." What does this intend? Why should the poet feel he *can* sing when his beloved is far away? We may be reminded of those famous lines from *Pause* in *Die schöne Müllerin*—"Ich kann nicht mehr singen, mein Herz ist zu voll" (I can sing no more, my heart is too full)—but that will not help us here because Seidl's poem has nothing to do with unrequited love. What then? We step closer to understanding when we note that the words in the final verse are not "daß ich singen kann" (that I can sing) or "singen muss" (must sing) but "daß ich singen *darf*" (*may* sing). It is not that I am obliged to sing; rather, I am not barred from doing so. Moreover, "daß ich singen darf" makes a conceptual rhyme with the previous stanza's "Weil's nimmer sich erzwingen läßt / Und frei hinsaüselt wie der West!" The verbs "dürfen" and "erzwingen" ever so gently suggest a commanding presence, someone or something able to grant or force things. "Darf" and "warf" are not run-of-the-mill Lieder rhymes; "darf" plainly was chosen to sustain the murmur of protest in the previous lines.

Hearing the song in performance our attention may snag (mine does) on a disjunction between the meaning, on its face, of those words "Wenn mich mein Loos vom Liebchen warf, dann fühl' ich, daß ich singen darf" (downcast at first, then cheery) and Schubert's crystal-clear rhetoric, which turns to the major mode at the start of the strophe and builds to emphatic, almost triumphant, cadencing for the repeated pronouncement "daß ich singen darf, daß ich singen darf." Nothing signals any ambivalence. Indeed, nothing suggests that these lines mean anything other than exactly what they say. By some mechanism, we must be able to hear what they say in a way that aligns with D-major song and dance, followed by the piano's wistful commentary on it. Schubert's setting makes us intuit a coherent meaning even if the words of the poem do not want to comply.

The song begins with a piano introduction in D minor with agitated triplets in the right hand against a bass descent through the chromatic tetrachord, D to A (see Example 3). In the triplets the alto voice descends in tenths against the bass, sandwiched between oscillating octave A♮s that seem locked in place. A memorable jolt in measure 3 disturbs the flow as the alto, having failed to move when the bass fell to C♮, sinks to D♯ against the bass B♮; it takes six beats before the chromatic descent can resume and move to a D-minor cadence. With the singer's entry the bass descent begins anew, passing over the C♮ that had threatened to inflect B♮ as a dominant in measure 3. When the pattern starts up again for strophe two ("Mir fehlt etwas"), the bass stalls almost immediately on C♯ for two bars while the vocal melody is jerked up a fifth before pushing a half step higher to F♮ on the word "Lieb" just as the bass and alto sink to octave C♮s and E♭ respectively. The resulting unstable dominant seventh echoes the disturbance in the piano introduction and "Lieb" is held out for five full beats before tension is released in two quick cadences to B♭ in the middle of the verse (B♮ is bypassed this time). This places an abrupt, utterly unexpected emphasis on the word. From this point forward the D-minor "lamento" pattern loses its grip on the remaining strophes—but note that it is a bass C♮ in measure 45 (not shown in the example) that turns the harmony to a sad A minor for the cadence-ending strophe three at "Die Thräne tritt mir wieder nah." Tears—a lament—step nearer again.

Example 3. *Sehnsucht*, D879, mm. 1–25.

Example 3. continued

Though the harmonic trajectory of each strophe is different, Schubert returns to the tonic for each new beginning—to D minor for strophes one, two, and four; D major for the apostrophe to the beloved star in three, and again when the star's glow touches the poet in strophe five. The first three strophes elide one into the next and the later ones close firmly. This is underscored by the words in the last line of each, which are always heard twice, followed by an echo of the formulaic cadence in the piano. The only exception to this pattern is in strophe three where the words "dich lieb' und brauch' ich ja" repeat instead. A casual translation of this line, "you know that I love and need you," would miss a crucial point expressed in the poet's word order: by placing *dich* at the head of the clause, *ich* at the end, a special emphasis is created: "You know 'tis *you* I love and need." Seidl's positioning of the deictic pronoun *dich* lays stress on the identity of the beloved, and Schubert has us linger over these words.

In the poem's cryptic final couplet the formulation "Wenn mich mein Loos vom Liebchen warf" is awkward, undoubtedly because the poet was constrained by the need for a rhyme with "singen darf." Words declaimed in song will sometimes rearrange themselves in our heads when musical forces gain the upper hand. To make a better fit with Schubert's buoyant, upbeat music my own mind strains to assemble a meaning to this effect: If my lot's been *thrown to* me by my love ("Wenn mir mein Loos das Liebchen warf") then I feel that I may sing. His "Liebchen" grants him permission to sing, in conformance, say, with the courtly love tradition whereby a lowborn singer takes commands from his lady. But the syntax won't allow this—"mich" is the accusative reflexive pronoun, not the dative "mir."

All these problems fall away if we take into account something external to the text. The song dates from the spring of 1826 and the poem was published that same year, just as tensions were mounting in Vienna.[44] The three words on which this politicized hearing turns (less so a song about absent love, which can run parallel to it until the trouble at the end) are "Lieb," so drastically underscored by Schubert; "darf"; and most inconspicuous of all, "fühl." Moreover, Schubert's setting does indeed perfectly take the last line at face value, only with a different mien than we may have first thought.

"Words are proscribed," Franz Grillparzer would observe in an April 1826 conversation with Beethoven, "it's a good thing that tones, the exponential representatives of words, still are free." This remark was entered into Beethoven's conversation book just a few days after the raid on the literary association and social club known as the Ludlamshöhle (which took place during the night of 18 April and continued into the wee hours of the next morning).[45] Grillparzer, who was placed under house arrest, and Seidl were both members; Schubert and Eduard von Bauernfeld (1802–1890), author of the libretto for Schubert's *Der Graf von Gleichen* (it would be banned in October) and a passionate advocate of free speech, were on the verge of joining. By chance, the whole affair landed on Bauernfeld's desk (he was an intern—*Konzepts-Praktikant*—in the department of the Lower Austrian Government that was expected to ratify such charges) and he was able to sweep it under a busy rug: "Had the police delayed their interventions by but a single day Schubert and I would also have become 'Ludlamites' and I might have had to assist at my own enquiry. What irony!"[46] Even before this incident, however, there was talk that the censors did not have control over music. The political meaning in *Sehnsucht* comes together by a counterintuitive accent and the realization that "Lieb" or "Liebchen" names the ideal: "Wenn mich mein Loos vom Liebchen warf, / Dann *fühl'* ich, daß ich singen darf" (If it is my lot to be cast away from my beloved Liberty then I truly *feel* that I may sing, that I *may* sing). The piano, all alone at the final cadence, has the last word: "singen." I may sing—but not declare my love openly. Perhaps it was here that the political and the personal merged (Example 4).

Tucked away in the new Schubert edition's typescript critical report for volume 5 of *Lieder* (1985) is mention of an intriguing autograph leaf in Seidl's *Nachlass* in which the poem appears outfitted with an alternate final couplet: "Muß ich, mein Lieb, dir ferne seyn, / Gleich stellt das Lied von selbst sich ein!" This is no less ambiguous. The antecedent clause is clear as "If I must be distant from you, my love," but the consequent "sich einstellen" can suggest numerous possibilities. Are we to understand "Then, promptly, the song does (my) duty all by itself"? If so: in love or in war? Or perhaps we hear "stellt . . . sich ein" as a form of "zusammenstellen" (to put together), allowing the meaning "Suddenly the song comes together all by itself"? Too many mixed signals fly for any one meaning, or even a pun, to spring into place.

Further small variants in the manuscript poem let us conclude that this was likely the earlier draft (see Figure 4). The second stanza's first line reads "Mir fehlt etwas, das *merk* ich gut." Beneath *merk* (to notice) we can just make out an erased *fühl* (to feel), the word that appears both in Schubert's song and in Seidl's 1826 publication, but this substitution was plainly made because *fühl* recurred in the last lines of the same stanza, "Und will ich in die Sterne seh'n, / Fühl ich die Augen übergeh'n" (When I wish to gaze into the stars, I feel my eyes brim over), a routine formula-

Example 4. *Sehnsucht*, D879, mm. 73–89.

Example 4. continued

tion next to the publication's "muß stets das Aug' mir übergeh'n" (again and again my eye must brim over). The excision of *fühl* at this point frees up this word for "Dann fühl ich, daß ich singen darf." The only other variants are minor (but telling) ones. The penultimate stanza ends "*Weil* nimmer sich erzwingen lässt / *Weil's* frei hinsäuselt wie der West" (in place of "Weil's nimmer sich erzwingen lässt / Und frei hinsäuselt wie der West" in the publication). In the manuscript poem, interestingly, the first of these two clauses floats free of any referent; for a brief instant we do not know what will not be forced.

Although the sense of the closing couplet in the manuscript poem is just as indeterminate as in the publication, its rhythm, sounds, and rhyme make better poetry than "Wenn mich mein Loos vom Liebchen warf." A political meaning is not impossible but it is more remote. How, when, or from whom the suggestion came to replace the final couplet we do not know. Only one thing is sure: the manuscript version cannot be sung to Schubert's music. His entire song is calibrated to be able to proclaim at the end: "daß ich *singen* darf."

Sehnsucht is only one song among many (*Der zürnenden Diana* is another) that must have delighted attentive listeners who recognized Schubert's virtuoso command of music's power to shape verbal meaning. In *Sehnsucht* the pleasing surface and understated rhetoric create emphases similar to the subtle verbal stresses that skilled actors like Nestroy employed on the stage to get around what censorship forbade.

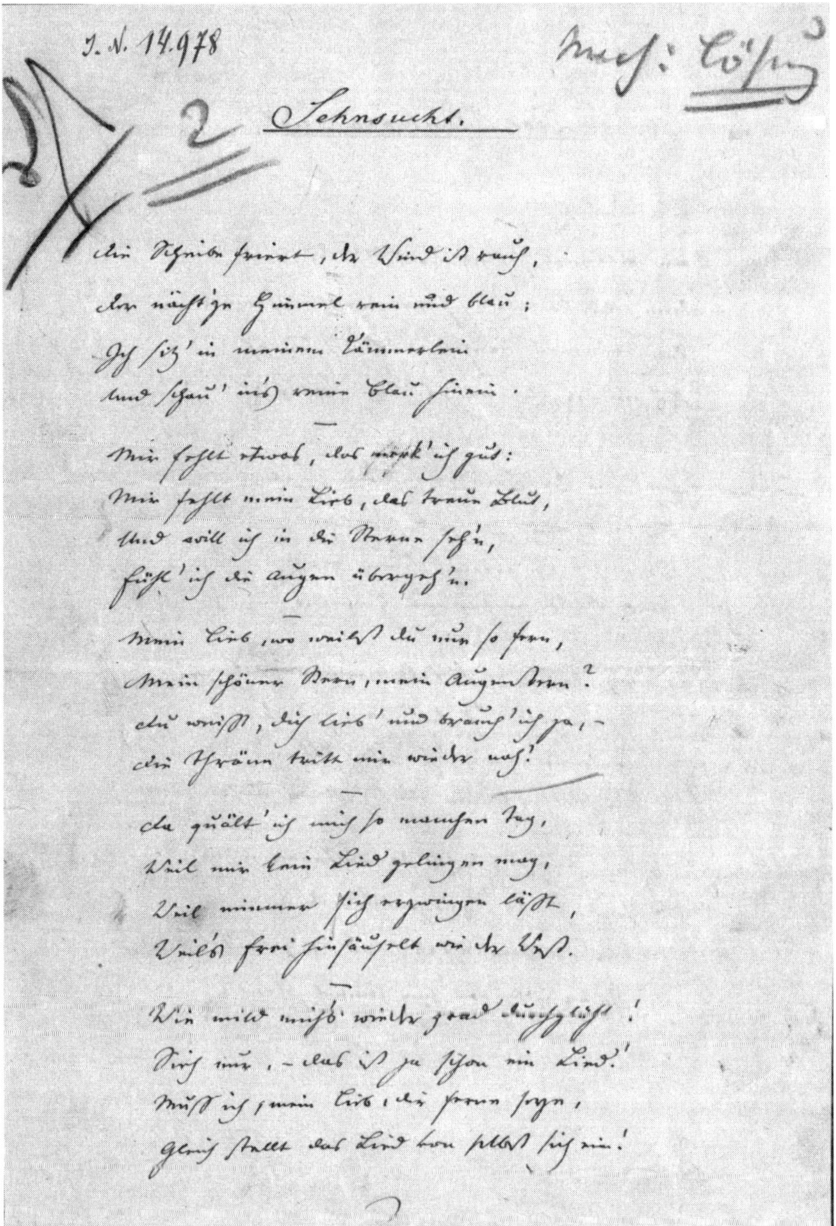

J. N. 14.978

Sehnsucht.

Die Scheibe friert, der Wind ist rauh,
der nächt'ge Himmel rein und blau;
Ich sitz' in meinem Kämmerlein
und schau' ins reine Blau hinein.

Mir fehlt etwas, das fühl' ich gut:
Mir fehlt mein Lieb, das treue Blut,
Und will ich in die Sterne seh'n,
fühl' ich die Augen übergeh'n.

Mein Lieb, wo weilst du nur so fern,
Mein schöner Stern, mein Augenstern?
Du weißt, dich lieb' und brauch' ich ja, –
die Thräne tritt mir wieder nah.

Da quält' ich mich so manchen Tag,
Weil mir kein Lied gelingen mag,
Weil's nimmer sich erzwingen läßt,
Und frei hinsäuselt wie der West.

Wie mild mich's wieder grad durchglüht!
Sieh nur, – das ist ja schon ein Lied!
Mußt ich, mein Lieb, dir ferne seyn,
gleich stellt das Lied von selbst sich ein!

Figure 4. Johann Gabriel Seidl, *Sehnsucht*, autograph ms., Wienbibliothek.

NOTES

1. Beethoven's own *Fidelio* is a case in point. Even at the 1805 premiere the French libretto's revolutionary-era story was displaced to sixteenth-century Seville to escape Viennese censorship (in contrast to adaptations of this story for other European stages). For the 1814 revival strategic revisions to the libretto and music made the story current, yet the freedom that Beethoven's *Fidelio* held out remained but a fervent hope and the historical mask was not lifted.

2. August von Kotzebue, *Ode an Napoleon* (Moscow, 1813), 12. My translation. "Mögen Tausende zu Grunde gehen, hingewürgt von Hunger, Pest und Schwert; Wenn nur siegreich Deine Fahnen wehen, und Dich nichts in Deinen Planen stört. Nenne dich die Welt entmenschter Tyger! Treu und Glauben schändender Betrüger! Immerhin, bist Du allein doch Sieger! Dieser Zweck ist jedes Mittel werth." One revision Georg Friedrich Treitschke made to Beethoven's *Fidelio* in 1814 was to add a dramatic recitative for Leonore (adapted from Ferdinando Paer's *Leonora*), "Abscheulicher! Wo eilst du hin?" In it, she excoriates the tyrant who no long feels pity, no longer hears humanity's voice, has but a "Tigersinn" (the mind of a tiger). The vast majority of publications listed in Ernst Weber's *Lyrik der Befreiungskriege (1812–1815): Gesellschaftspolitische Meinungs- und Willensbildung durch Literatur* (Stuttgart, 1991), 336–59, are poems and songs celebrating German emancipation and war heroes, but Weber also turned up two volumes apparently in praise of Napoleon "from one of his most avid followers and admirers" in Königsberg, ca. 1813–14 (343), and the above-mentioned ode attributed to Kotzebue (341).

3. A fuller biographical sketch of Körner may be found in Susan Youens, *Schubert's Poets and the Making of Lieder* (Cambridge, 1996), 51–150. Besides Schubert's settings of Körner she discusses settings by north German composers. Details about Körner's competing offers from Pállfy and Lobkowitz and his activity as a court poet are included in the narrative biography by Heribert Rau, *Theodor Körner: Vaterländischer Roman in zwei Theilen* (Leipzig, 1863).

4. Jonathan Sperber, "The Atlantic Revolutions in the German Lands, 1776–1849," in *The Oxford Handbook of Modern German History*, ed. Helmut Walser Smith (Oxford, 2011), 144–168, esp. 158. The picture he sketches is broad but Sperber believes that the early German nationalists were not concerned, as were their Atlantic revolutionary counterparts, with "the creation of a nation of equal citizens, repudiating the distinctions of the old regime society of orders" (157). Theirs was less a class struggle than an effort to forge a national identity, to which end they employed a range of scientific evidence, linguistic theories, and philosophical arguments.

5. Heinrich Heine, *Ludwig Börne: A Memorial*, translated with excellent commentary and an introduction by Jeffrey L. Sammons (Rochester, NY, 2006), xi.

6. The poet Wilhelm Müller fought in the war against Napoleon as well as in the Greek war of independence. In 1822 the journal *Urania* (the1823 issue contained the first twelve poems of his *Winterreise*) was given the Viennese censor's *damnatur*, hence it was not for sale in Austria. Susan Youens, *Retracing a Winter's Journey: Schubert's "Winterreise"* (Ithaca, NY, 1991), 10. Schubert originally set only these twelve poems. He kept intact their order in *Urania* even after composing part two of *Winterreise* (in the month following the poet's death) from the new poems Müller had interleaved before reissuing his poetic cycle.

7. Hans Sturmberger reports that as punishment for his free-thinking ideas C. E. Bauernschmied was appointed censor in Linz. The influence of Bavarian constitutionalism—Bavaria was under French stewardship—was even more pronounced there than in Vienna. Sturmberger, *Der Weg zum Verfassungsstaat: Die politische Entwicklung in Oberösterreich von 1791–1861* (Vienna, 1962), 29. Contemporary reports abound of Metternich's efforts to enlist dissident liberals as censors: Joseph Schreyvogel succumbed

in 1817; Charles Sealsfield resisted. In Johann Nestroy's 1848 play *Freiheit in Krähwinkel* the liberal Ultra replies to just such an offer from the Burgomeister with a brilliant tirade against censorship. Censorship restrictions finally were lifted in March 1848, only to be reinstated by year's end. Following the premiere in Vienna on July 1, *Freiheit in Krähwinkel* played nightly to a packed house until the end of the season. Johann Nestroy, *Stücke* 26.1, *Historisch-kritische Ausgabe*, ed. John R. P. McKenzie (Vienna, 1995), 1–2.

8. James J. Sheehan, *German History 1770–1866*, The Oxford History of Modern Europe, ed. Lord Bullock and Sir William Deakin (Oxford, 1989), 423–24.

9. Moriz Enzinger, "Zur Biographie des Tiroler Dichters Joh. Chrys. Senn," *Archiv für das Studium der Neueren Sprachen* 156 (1929): 169–83; letter of 24 February 1823 (176).

10. Werner Ogris, "Die Zensur in der Ära Metternich," in *Humaniora Medizin—Recht—Geschichte: Festschrift für Adolf Laufs zum 70. Geburtstag* (Berlin, 2006), 248. Gentz had already backed away from his early support of the French Revolution after reading and translating Edmund Burke's pamphlet *Reflections on the Revolution in France* ca. 1793.

11. Senn's story has often been told and Schubert's two songs on poems of Senn, *Selige Welt* (D743) and *Schwanengesang* (D744), have been richly explored in recent years. Suzannah Clark's analysis of the "transformational" voice leading in *Selige Welt*, for example, is in dialogue with Gottfried Wilhelm Fink's (we believe) observations on harmony and Charles Rosen's comments on rhythm, phrase structure, and the song's political implication. See Clark, *Analyzing Schubert* (Cambridge, 2011), 67–73. Fink's remarks appeared anonymously in the 24 June 1824 issue of the Leipzig *Allgemeine musikalische Zeitung*; Rosen's in "Schubert's Inflections of Classical Form," in *The Cambridge Companion to Schubert*, ed. Christopher H. Gibbs (Cambridge, 1997), 77–78. Susan Youens explores how Schubert revisited *Schwanengesang* in another A-flat minor-major piece belonging to the same genre in "Swan Songs: Schubert's 'Auf dem Wasser zu singen,'" *Nineteenth-Century Music Review* 5/2 (2008): 19–42. Philosophical (Hegelian) and political meanings in the Senn songs are taken up by Werner Aderhold in "Johann Chrisostomus Senn," in *Schuberts Lieder nach Gedichten aus seinem literarischen Freundeskreis: Auf der Suche nach dem Ton der Dichtung in der Musik. Kongreßbericht Ettlingen 1997*, ed. Walther Dürr, Karlsruher Beiträge zur Musikwissenschaft, vol. 1 (Frankfurt am Main, 1999), 97–111. Aderhold also contributed entries on these songs to the *Schubert Liedlexikon*, ed. Walther Dürr, Michael Kube, Uwe Schweikert, and Stephanie Steiner, in collaboration with Michael Kohlhäufl (Kassel, 2012), 591–92.

12. Christian Jansen, "The Formation of German Nationalism, 1740–1850," in *The Oxford Handbook of Modern German History*, ed. Helmut Walser Smith (Oxford, 2011), 234–59, 243.

13. Ibid., 244–48. Jansen carefully notes regional differences (Bavarian, Prussian) in the accelerating development of organized nationalism. To indicate the range of early German nationalisms he provides sketches of the thinking of five influential representatives. Friedrich Ludwig Jahn, the founder of gymnastic (paramilitary) societies with nationalist aspirations, and Ernst Moritz Arndt, Johann Gottlieb Fichte, Friedrich Daniel Schleiermacher, and Heinrich Luden, 245ff.

14. Sturmberger reports this in *Der Weg zum Verfassungsstaat* 27, citing G. Grüll, *Die Robot in Oberösterreich* (1952), 216ff.

15. Michael Kohlhäufl, *Poetisches Vaterland: Dichtung und politisches Denken im Freundeskreis Franz Schuberts* (Kassel, 1999), 260. Kohlhäufl's book sheds much light on political imagery in the poems that Schubert chose to set; he leaves others to explore how Schubert's music inflects those meanings.

16. I have discussed several such censorship incidents in the opening chapters of my book *Vanishing Sensibilities: Schubert, Beethoven, Schumann* (New York, 2012).

17. Six hundred thousand soldiers fought for three days in this bloody battle known as the *Völkerschlacht* before Napoleon's French army, supplemented by Italian, Polish, and

German troops from the Confederation of the Rhine, lost to the coalition of Russians, Prussians, Austrians, and Swedes.

18. *Ludwig Börne: A Memorial*, 75–76. My brief quotations are all from Sammons's translation. "Alt Deutsch" refers to the propensity of the early nationalist groups to trace their tribal roots back to the Middle Ages.

19. Ibid., 89. These remarks take aim at the conservative critic Wolfgang Menzel, who, to Heine's witty and earnest relief, "joyfully vaulted back into the old circle of ideas . . . after the air grew cooler."

20. Heinrich Heine, *Ludwig Börne: Eine Denkschrift und kleinere politische Schriften*, ed. Helmut Koopman, vol. 11 of *Historisch-kritische Gesamtausgabe der Werke,* ed. Manfred Windfuhr (Hamburg, 1978), 83–84, 97–98. Heine writes *Teutschthümler* when he speaks of Menzel (see 84 and 97), mimicking one such mannerism. For more examples see vol. 11's massive critical commentary. Members of a *Burschenschaft* in Linz also had distinctive paraphernalia, carrying gnarled walking sticks with friends' names carved into them or wearing unmarked white caps. Sturmberger, *Der Weg zum Verfassungsstaat,* 22.

21. Heinrich Heine, *Briefe aus Berlin*, ed. Jost Hermand, vol. 6 of Windfuhr, *Historisch-kritische Gesamtausgabe der Werke*, 43, 367. See also "The Formation of German Nationalism, 1740–1850," 247. Heine's readiness to name the names of political (nationalist) activists so soon after the Carlsbad Decrees was noted with surprise in the contemporary press.

22. *French Affairs: Letters from Paris,* vol. 7, bk. 1 of *The Works of Heinrich Heine,* trans. Charles Godfrey Leland (Hans Breitmann) (London, 1893), 14.

23. There is just one more Körner song from 1818. Ilija Dürhammer, "Deutsch- und Griechentum. Johann Mayrhofer und Theodor Körner," in *Schubert 200 Jahre, Schloß Achberg: Ich lebe und componiere wie ein Gott*," ed. Ilija Dürhammer and Till Gerrit Waidelich (Heidelberg, 1997), 21–24.

24. Ruth Melkis-Bihler, "Politische Aspekte der Schubertzeit," in *Schuberts Lieder nach Gedichten aus seinem literarischen Freundeskreis*, 1–96, quote at 92. Her information on Senn's and Mayrhofer's fraternity membership is drawn from Max Doblinger and Georg Schmidgall, *Geschichte und Mitgliederverzeichnisse burschenschaftlicher Verbindungen in Alt-Österreich und Tübingen 1816–1936*, with an introduction by Paul Wentzke, *Burschenschafterlisten*, vol. 1, ed. Paul Wentzke (Görlitz, 1940), 15. The full list of twelve is Franz v. Bruchmann; Graf Colloredo (formerly a "Prager Teutone"); Anton, Freiherr von Doblhoff-Dier; Alois Fischer; "Gerhardi . . . aus Göttingen"; Karl Hieber; Karl Kiesewetter; Johann Mayrhofer; Josef von Scheiger; Georg Schuster; Johann Senn (later a member of Libera Germania Innsbruck); Karl Stegmayer. Doblinger and Schmidgall report that the police broke up the group even before it could be formally constituted as a *Burschenschaft* but that its members had already undertaken outings called "Turnfahrten" (14). Senn was arrested following a party for Alois Fischer that Bruchmann and Schubert also attended on 20 January 1820. Gerhardi fled to Prague and shot himself before the police could catch up with him. See also Enzinger, "Zur Biographie des Tiroler Dichters Joh. Chrys. Senn," 172.

25. Goethe's poem about a furtive passionate liaison first appeared in the early 1770s. It was revised and republished in 1789 and reissued again in 1810 under the now familiar title "Willkommen und Abschied"—perhaps its imagery sounded differently in later political climates.

26. Theodor Körner, *Leyer und Schwert*, 3rd ed. (Berlin, 1815), 74ff.

27. Youens, *Schubert's Poets and the Making of Lieder*, 130.

28. Ibid., 154, citing Carl Glossy, "Aus den Lebenserinnerungen des Freiherrn von Spaun," in *Jahrbuch der Grillparzer-Gesellschaft*, 8 (Vienna, 1898), 275–303, quote at 295.

29. Otto Erich Deutsch, *Schubert: Memoirs by His Friends*, trans. Rosamond Ley and John Nowell (London, 1958), 14.

30. Ovid, *Metamorphoses*, books 1–8, trans. Frank Justus Miller, revised by G. P. Goold, Loeb Classical Library (Cambridge, MA, 1994), 135–39.

31. For more on discussions at the Congress of Vienna on the repatriation of artworks, see Bette W. Oliver, *From Royal to National: The Louvre Museum and the Bibliothèque Nationale* (Plymouth, UK, 2007), 65ff. The dispersal of the Orléans collection is discussed in Francis Haskell, *The Ephemeral Museum: Old Master Paintings and the Rise of the Art Exhibition* (New Haven, 2000), 22–29; and Nicholas Penny, *The Sixteenth-Century Italian Paintings*, vol. 2: *Venice, 1540–1600*, National Gallery Catalogues (New Haven and London, 2008), 461–70.

32. Michael Thimann comes to this conclusion in his study of Parmigianino's Actaeon frescos in Fontanellato where Latin didactic inscriptions frame the pictures on the ceiling of the Rocca Sanvitale. Michael Thimann, *Lügenhafte Bilder: Ovids "favole" und das Historienbild in der italienischen Renaissance* (Göttingen, 2002), 145, passim. I give thanks to Katelijne Schiltz for directing me to this stimulating study. The masculine Diana in the Orléans *Mort d'Acteon* is an intriguing obverse of Parmigianino's remarkably feminine Actaeon.

33. *Gedichte von Johann Mayrhofer* (Vienna, 1824). Schubert's text diverges from Mayrhofer's publication in minor details: Mayrhofer's published poem has "im zornigen Erröthen" and "am buschigen Gestade" whereas Schubert's song text reads "im zürnenden Erröthen" and" "am blühenden Gestade." Neither change is important for the present discussion. In addition, the first edition of the song is titled *Die zürnende Diana*, as it was in Schubert's composition manuscript, in which it was later corrected to *Der zürnenden Diana*.

34. The image remained in wide circulation. Beethoven, for one, "kept under glass on his writing desk during his later years" three sayings, two of them inscriptions said to be from a statue of Isis and a temple at Sais, apparently copied out from Schiller's 1790 essay "Die Sendung Moses": "Ich bin, was da ist" (I am that which is) and "Ich bin alles, was ist, was war, und was seyn wird, kein sterblicher Mensch hat meinen Schleier aufgehoben" (I am everything that is, that was, and that shall be. No mortal man has lifted my veil). Maynard Solomon, "Beethoven, Freemasonry, and the Tagebuch of 1812–18," *Beethoven Forum* 8 (2000): 117. Or see Solomon's *Late Beethoven: Music, Thought, Imagination* (Berkeley, 2003), 147.

35. *Entschlossen* was the marking in the first version of the song, notated a half step higher, also from December 1820. In the early version the dynamic scale of the introduction's crescendo was not yet so extreme, beginning *mezzo forte* not *piano*; dynamic intensity underwent revision at other points as well. Two autographs (and several copies) survive for the song. The early version, in A major, in the Gesellschaft der Musikfreunde, A 230, was once owned by Johannes Brahms. A *Reinschrift* in A-flat that belonged to the singer Karl Schönstein is housed in the Wienbibliothek, MH 96c: it is marked *Feurig* (Op. 36: *Risoluto*). Further details of the sources may be found in the critical report accompanying the new Schubert edition. The Wienbibliothek manuscript can be viewed digitally at: http://www.schubert-online.at/. A digital facsimile of the first edition of Opus 36 is accessible at Harvard University's library site, http://pds.lib.harvard.edu/pds/view/12640640.

36. I refer to Edward T. Cone's "Schubert's Promissory Note: An Exercise in Musical Hermeneutics," in *Schubert: Critical and Analytical Studies*, ed. Walter Frisch (Lincoln, NB, 1986), 11–30. His provocative essay on Schubert's *Moment Musical* in A-Flat, Op. 94, No. 6 was first published in *19th-Century Music* 5 (1982): 233–41. A probing critique of Cone's method by Leo Treitler is "Hermeneutics, Exegetics, or What?," in *Reflections on Musical Meaning and Its Representations*, Musical Meaning and Interpretation, Robert S. Hatten, series editor (Bloomington, IN, 2011), 234–52.

37. In the original, "mehreren der gewähltesten Privat-Zirkel." *Schubert: Die Dokumente seines Lebens*, ed. with commentary by Otto Erich Deutsch, series 8, supplement volume 5 of *Franz Schubert: Neue Ausgabe sämtlicher Werke* (Kassel, 1964), 274–75.

38. Clemens Höslinger, "Schubert, Schwind und die Göttin Diana: Eine Erinnerung an die Sängerin Catinka Buchwieser," *Schubert: Perspektiven* 10/1 (2010): 45–69. Schwind got to know Lacsny in 1825 after she had retired from the stage. Schubert had already

known her for some time but we do not know how or when they became acquainted. Theodor Körner, when he was in Vienna (around the time of the 1812 incident), wrote home enthusiastically about her performances.

39. The 29 March 1848 report in the *Wiener Zeitung* is quoted in Nestroy, *Stücke* 26.1, 119.

40. Just four years earlier, in 1815, Jesus's words from the cross had sounded in Beethoven's song for bass and chorus, *Es ist vollbracht*, the last number in Friedrich Treitschke's *Die Ehrenpforten*, written to celebrate Napoleon's defeat. Nicholas Mathew opens *Political Beethoven* (Cambridge, 2013) with some reflections on this piece and the political atmosphere within which it arose (1–16).

41. Nestroy was famous for the subversive meanings he conveyed by puns and comic understatement in performance and by the use of what Berthold Brecht called "slave language," coded messages that evaded the censors but were "fully grasped by the Viennese lower and middle classes who attended Nestroy's plays." Joel Schechter and Jack Zipes, "Slave Language Comes to Krähwinkel: Notes on Nestroy's Political Satire," *Theater* 12/2 (1981): 72–75.

42. For more on the place of the Memnon legend in nineteenth-century culture, see Marjorie W. Hirsch's *Romantic Lieder and the Search for Lost Paradise* (Cambridge, 2007), 41–53. Mayrhofer's Memnon longs to be united with the *Morgens Göttin* (goddess of the morning) so that he may shine down as a pale star from spheres of noble freedom, pure love ("Aus Sphären edler Freyheit, reiner Liebe, / Ein bleicher stiller Stern herab zu scheinen").

43. See the insightful study by Susanne Eckstein, "Die 'Aufstehgesellschaft oder Eos' und ihre Constitution: Gesetzgebung und Geselligkeit," *Schubert: Perspektiven* 9/2 (2009): 183–214. See also Kohlhäufl, *Poetisches Vaterland*, 251–67; and Ilija Dürhammer, *Schuberts literarische Heimat: Dichtung und Literatur-Rezeption der Schubert-Freunde* (Vienna, 1999), 68–77.

44. *Sehnsucht* can be found together with three other songs in an autograph manuscript split between the Library of Congress and the Wienbibliothek. The first song in the gathering, *Am Fenster*, D878, is dated March 1826. Both libraries have made digital facsimiles available online. The poem appeared among the "Lieder der Nacht" in *Johann Gabriel Seidl's Dichtungen*, part 2 (Vienna, 1826), 51. I have chosen to retain old spellings. A "Loos" may have meant something specific, perhaps a military lotto ticket.

45. *Ludwig van Beethovens Konversationshefte*, edited for the Deutsche Staatsbibliothek Berlin by Gritta Herre with Günther Brosche, vol. 9 (Leipzig, 1988), 219. For more on the Ludlamshöhle, see Horst Belke, "Ludlamshöhle," in *Handbuch literarisch-kultureller Vereine, Gruppen und Bünde 1825–1933*, ed. Wulf Wülfling, Karin Bruns, and Rolf Parr (Stuttgart, 1998), 311–20.

46. Deutsch, *Schubert: Memoirs by His Friends*, 241.

Schubert's *Tombeau de Beethoven*: Decrypting the Piano Trio in E-Flat Major, Op. 100

CHRISTOPHER H. GIBBS

For nearly two centuries now listeners have perceived, however dimly, a ghost haunting Schubert's Piano Trio in E-flat Major, Op. 100. Most of the attention has focused on the second movement, the principal cello melody of which in turn haunts the trio's finale through a threefold cyclic return. Indeed, the Andante con moto is often characterized as a funeral march—although it is not so marked. For Robert Schumann the publication of the trio in late 1828 "went across the ordinary musical life of the day like an angry thunderstorm" and he characterized the Andante as "a sigh intensified to the point of an anguished cry of the heart."[1]

Within weeks of Schubert's death on 19 November 1828, Schumann heard the piece played at a musical soirée given by Friedrich Wieck in Leipzig and wrote in his diary: "Enraptured by [Schubert's] Trio." After hearing it again four days later he noted: "Home at 3AM—excited night with Schubert's immortal Trio ringing in my ears—frightful dreams."[2] Attending those evenings as well was the editor of the august *Allgemeine musikalische Zeitung*, Gottfried Wilhelm Fink, who wrote the first extended review of the piece, which John Daverio has likened to "eavesdropping on the discussions prompted by readings of the work for the inner circle of Leipzig's musical elite."[3]

Of the second movement, Fink states that it "is equal to the first in beauty and harmony. The ever sad sensibility, as if torn from within, comes forth even more palpably in tones of melancholy. The heart of the listener, full of gentle pity, at times almost becomes uneasy, intimately attracted by the deep truth of the sentiment."[4] And in the third movement he finds "not only the profound, but rather more a ghost [*Geist*] restlessly fluttering from one path to the next that wants to catch the joy in flight again that he lost in rest, or rather, that he had driven away." About the return of the cello theme in the finale Fink comments:

> In a wondrously moving way, the lamenting Romance [*klagende Romanze*] of the second movement often enters into the wild bustle of pain and pleasure, and now and then we perceive the various voices of remembrance, whose echo is quickly drowned out by the restlessness of the present which, with its veiling mist, spreads over the otherwise amiable morning of the future. One sees that this work presents us with a very remarkable picture of the soul.

Such sentiments continued to be expressed. More than a century after Fink, J. E. Westrup observed that in the second movement "the curiously accented rhythm on the piano, like a march of ghosts, and the cello's nostalgic theme (said to be a Swedish air), combine to produce an atmosphere for which the word 'haunting' is, for once, appropriate."[5] More recently, Lawrence Kramer noted that the accompaniment of the second movement "has the air of a funeral march" and likened the cello theme to a "specter," a "ghost," stating that the finale is "haunted by a song." Echoing Fink's observation about the last movement's restlessness, Kramer considers all the more effective that into this "vacuous busyness" the lyrical cello theme brings "expressivity—rich, nostalgic, evocative—of a lost melody, an absent voice."[6] Leo Treitler uses the E-flat Trio as the principal musical example in his essay "Language and the Interpretation of Music." Like Kramer and other critics he too has little kind to say of the finale's opening themes, which makes the cyclicism all the more remarkable: "As if out of the depths of the unconscious, the cello steps forward to play the morose theme of the second movement *sotto voce*. It is as though the persistent memory of this is what all that patter had been meant to suppress. . . . The meaningfulness of this music is immensely enriched through this conspiracy of incompatible realms, producing as powerful a metaphoric effect as any that I can think of in language."[7]

In earlier writings I proposed a possible reason for the trio's haunted reception: that the piece, written in the aftermath of Beethoven's death on 26 March 1827 and premiered exactly one year later on the first anniversary of that death, is Schubert's "*tombeau de Beethoven*." It served as the centerpiece of the lone concert Schubert devoted entirely to his own music, given just eight months before he died at age thirty-one. One of the first reviews of the published trio invoked Beethoven's name, saying that in it Schubert "follows *Beethoven's* path." Many critics ever since have also perceived Beethoven's presence.[8]

In this essay I will explore the idea that Beethoven is in fact the ghost haunting Schubert's E-flat Piano Trio, and consider the implications of this for our understanding of Schubert. I will provide biographical and musical evidence to support my claim that the trio is Schubert's deliberate and significant homage to Beethoven, and try to account for various elements people have heard in the work and the stories they have told about it. As a *tombeau de Beethoven*, Schubert's trio joins a rich lineage of pieces composers have written over the centuries honoring earlier masters. This tradition includes *déplorations* of the fourteenth and fifteenth centuries (such as Ockeghem's for Binchois, Josquin's for Ockeghem, Gombert's for Josquin) through Baroque *tombeaux*, to Romantic tributes (Liszt's for Wagner and Tchaikovsky's for Nikolai Rubinstein).[9] Such pieces often allude in some way to the honored composer's music and though most homages, especially pre-Romantic ones, offer public testimony, some tributes have been private, the honor undeclared even if still sometimes perceived.[10]

In Schubert's case, he did not announce a memorial concert for 26 March 1828 nor did he dedicate any memorial piece to Beethoven. Nonetheless, I suspect that many at the time received his message—which I hope to recover here, at least in part. I will further suggest that the literal implications of a compositional *tombeau*—a musical tomb—resonate more richly than usual in Schubert's trio because its composition was intimately connected to Beethoven's death, burial, and gravestone dedication. The trio in uncanny ways connects the deaths of the two composers, not only in Schubert's initial reaction to Beethoven's passing, but also in contemporaneous perceptions of them as reflected in the famous funeral oration Franz Grillparzer wrote for Beethoven and the notorious gravestone epitaph he crafted not long afterward for Schubert.

"Who shall stand beside him?": Schubert at Beethoven's Grave

One month after the death of Beethoven on 26 March 1827 the *Allgemeine musikalische Zeitung* reported: "At 5:50 Beethoven passed into eternal rest, painless, after an hour of sustained agony. At that moment Schuppanzigh was playing the incomparable Adagio from his Piano Trio in G." The concert at which violinist Ignaz Schuppanzigh performed was part of his pathbreaking chamber music series held at Vienna's Musikverein. The program had opened with string quartets by Haydn and Mozart before Carl Czerny joined Schuppanzigh and cellist Josef Linke for Beethoven's Piano Trio, Op. 1, No. 2.[11]

We do not know whether Schubert attended Schuppanzigh's concert that stormy afternoon, as he usually did, but three days later he participated as a torchbearer in Beethoven's funeral.[12] Vienna had a reputation for lavish obsequies—it was something that Emperor Joseph II tried to reform during the 1780s—and Beethoven's on 29 March was formidable. Reports vary as to how many attended, with estimates ranging from ten to thirty thousand.[13] An account published two weeks later in the Vienna periodical *Der Sammler* lists some of the eminent cultural figures who participated:

> The splendidly ornate coffin was carried by the aforementioned singers and escorted by Kapellmeisters Eybler, Hummel, Seyfried and Kreutzer on the right, Weigl, Gyrowetz, Gänsbacher and Würfel on the left, all bearing white cockades. A row of torchbearers on both sides, among whom could be found Anschütz, Bernard, Blahetka, Jos. Böhm, Castelli, Carl Czerny, Signore David, Grillparzer, Konrad Graff, Grünbaum, Haslinger, Hildebrandt, Holz, Katter, Krall, Signore Lablache, Baron Lannoy, Linke, Mayseder, Mr. Meric (spouse of Mad. Lalande), Merk, Mechetti, Meier, Signore Paccini, Piringer, Radicchi, Raimund, Riotte, Schoberlechner, Schubert, Schickh, Schmiedl, Streicher, Schuppanzigh, Steiner, Weidmann, Weiss, Wolfmayer and many other friends of art and devoted friends of the departed. Everyone was dressed in black, with gloves of the same color and fluttering crepes on the left arm, except for the torchbearers, who had draped their torches with white sprays of lilies.[14]

The coffin was placed in a hearse drawn by four horses for transport to the parish church in Währing, where two priests blessed it and there was further singing of the *Miserere*, motets, and *Libera*. Schubert's older brother Ferdinand was allegedly the organist on this occasion.[15] As only priests were permitted to speak at the consecrated ground of the grave site, Vienna's foremost actor, Heinrich Anschütz, stood at the gates of the cemetery to deliver the funeral oration by Franz Grillparzer, Austria's leading literary figure.[16] For Grillparzer, Beethoven's death marked the conclusion of a magnificent musical age: "The last master of resounding songs, the gracious mouthpiece of music, the heir and enhancer of the immortal fame of Handel and Bach, of Haydn and Mozart, is now no more, and we stand weeping over the broken strings of an instrument now still." After welcoming Beethoven to this pantheon of great German composers, he posed a question: "He was an artist, and who shall stand beside him? . . . he traversed all, he comprehended everything. He who follows him cannot continue; he must begin anew, for his predecessor ended only where art ends."[17]

One can only try to imagine what Schubert might have thought as he heard the words of his literary friend proclaimed in honor of his musical hero. What did he make of this challenge about who would emerge as Beethoven's successor, a question so many others would also ask in the years to come? Some quarter-century later Schumann declared that he had found the answer in the young Johannes Brahms. Brahms himself would later contradict his mentor when he observed that "Schubert, not Mendelssohn or Schumann, is Beethoven's true successor."[18] It is not unreasonable to think this is the position that Schubert himself took as he assumed Beethoven's mantle.

Schubert had recently turned thirty, but had been in poor health for more than four years, since he contracted what was most likely syphilis in 1822. Letters suggest that he viewed himself as a marked man. A comment to his close friend Franz von Schober is typical: "I am fairly well. Whether I shall ever again be completely healthy I am inclined to doubt."[19] Schubert faced the death of Europe's preeminent composer knowing that his own health was precarious. His identification with Beethoven therefore concerned not only artistic stature, but also the fragility of life in the face of mortal illness. Schubert's lifelong friend Josef von Spaun recalled that Beethoven's "death shocked him very deeply. Did he, perhaps, have a premonition of how soon he would follow him and rest at his side?" (*SMF*, 137).

Schubert died barely twenty months later, on 19 November 1828.[20] Two days afterward Ferdinand wrote to their father saying that "very many people have expressed the wish that the body of our good Franz be buried in the sacred ground of Währing Cemetery. I am amongst these, because I believe Franz made this request to me." Ferdinand related that the delirious Schubert, shortly before he died, did not know where he was and said, "This is not where *Beethoven* lies." Ferdinand went on to ask his father, "Is this not an indication of his last wish to be buried beside Beethoven, whom he so revered?"[21] Schubert was buried just a few feet away from Beethoven.[22] Memorial concerts and publications were initiated as part of a fundraising effort to pay for a grave monument and a cast-iron bust of Schubert, completed in July 1830 (see Figure 1). Grillparzer's epitaph on the monument was the spark of a long controversy:

THE ART OF MUSIC HERE ENTOMBED A RICH POSSESSION,
BUT EVEN FAR FAIRER HOPES.
FRANZ SCHUBERT LIES HERE.
BORN ON XXXI JANUARY MDCCXCVII
DIED ON XIX NOVEMBER MDCCCXXVIII
XXXI YEARS OF AGE

Schubert's early death elicited considerable commentary and fueled much speculation as people marveled at the "riches" he had created during his brief career and wondered about the "far fairer hopes" that might have come given more time.[23] The nickname of his most beloved instrumental work—the "Unfinished" Symphony (1822)—captures his "unfinished" life.[24] Equally significant is that for more than forty years that magnificent composition lay buried in the Graz home of his good friend Anselm Hüttenbrenner, waiting to be discovered and finally premiered in December 1865. Most of Schubert's other mature instrumental works—piano sonatas, chamber music, and all of his symphonies—were released only gradually in the decades after his death, alongside the continuing publication of ever more vocal music. In 1862, Vienna's preeminent music critic Eduard Hanslick observed: "If Schubert's contemporaries rightly gazed astonished at his creative power, what shall we, who come after him, say, as we incessantly discover new works of his? For thirty years the master has been dead, and in spite of this it seems as if he goes on working invisibly—it is impossible to follow him."[25]

Schubert's grave monument, with its epitaph suggesting a not fully realized creative potential, became integral to his posthumous reception. His entire life was retrospectively interpreted through this early demise. Further, his achievement was consistently evaluated in counterpoint to the older master who lay nearby. In this constellation of dying, funerals, burials, memorials, and monuments, Schubert and Beethoven meet in fascinating and consequential ways: an alleged encounter at Beethoven's deathbed and the events soon to follow at his funeral; memorial poems, compositions, and concerts; the circumstances of Schubert's own illness, death, and burial; joint exhumations of their remains in 1863 and 1888; and a long critical and analytical tradition that has repeatedly compared and contrasted their music. Thus over the course of the nineteenth century, as Schubert's physical body was twice exhumed from its original

Figure 1. Schubert's grave in Währing Cemetery.

resting place near Beethoven, so too his figurative body of musical work was gradually being exhumed from oblivion, made public, and continually causing his stature to be reassessed.

Schubert's "immortal Trio," as Schumann called it, is the crucial composition in this nexus of death, dying, and commemoration. Together with the 26 March 1828 concert at which it premiered, the work offers Schubert's most public engagement with the challenge Grillparzer posed in his funeral oration for Beethoven as well as an ultimately joyous declaration of the "far fairer hopes" of which his contemporaries, including close friends, were not fully aware.

"We talked of nothing but Beethoven": The Master and Schubert

Except for a diary entry the teenage Schubert wrote in 1816 that has been interpreted as offering oblique criticism of the unnamed Beethoven, all the evidence points to a lifelong and passionate reverence on the younger composer's part.[26] Schubert declared it most publicly in the 1822 dedication of his Opus 10 piano variations: to Beethoven from "his worshipper and admirer Franz Schubert." There are plentiful accounts of his extraordinary devotion reported by family and friends, supplemented by a few documents from the composer himself.[27] Nicholas Temperley begins a widely cited article by proposing that "Beethoven's influence on Schubert was profound and pervasive, more so, perhaps, than in any other case of two composers of the first rank."[28] The many connections to Beethoven's music in his compositions is a well-studied area of inquiry that I will not explore in this essay except as reflected in the works Schubert presented at his concert on the exact first anniversary of Beethoven's death.

The nature and extent of any personal contact between the two composers has long been in dispute. There were ample opportunities for them to meet in the relatively self-contained city of Vienna, where various spheres of musical life and patronage overlapped. Beethoven is said, for example, to have held court for some years several mornings a week at S. A. Steiner & Company, a local publisher, and Anselm Hüttenbrenner, known as an acquaintance of Beethoven, states that "Schubert often used to accompany me there."[29] Yet the documentary evidence of a possible relationship is limited and contradictory. Two well-informed sources offered opposed accounts. Ferdinand Schubert stated: "Beethoven, whom [my brother] held sacred and who often expressed himself with great appreciation, especially about his songs, he met frequently, although he could not for that reason be called Beethoven's pupil, as has often been done" (*SMF*, 37). On the other hand, Spaun recounted that his friend "often lamented, especially at the time of Beethoven's death, how much he regretted that the latter had been so inaccessible and that he had never spoken to Beethoven" (*SMF*, 366).

There are likewise contradicting stories concerning interplay between the composers regarding the Variations on a French Theme for Piano Four-Hands, Op. 10 (D624), the work that carries Schubert's effusive dedication. (According to the law at the time Beethoven would have had to grant permission for the dedication.) Beethoven's erstwhile assistant and later biographer, the none-too-reliable Anton Schindler, claims that Schubert's shyness incapacitated him in Beethoven's presence, and that he "completely lost control of himself" when the senior composer gently pointed out a mistake in the harmony.[30] On the other hand, Josef Hüttenbrenner (Anselm's younger brother) related that Beethoven was not at home when Schubert attempted to deliver the piece. Nevertheless, he asserts that the variations "received Beethoven's full approval" and that he "played them almost every day with his nephew for a period of months" (*SMF*, 75). Although Hüttenbrenner's account dates from some three decades after Schubert's death, in 1822 Hüttenbrenner was actively involved in helping his friend with his business affairs. In August of that year, not long after the publication of Opus 10, he contacted the Leipzig publisher Karl Friedrich Peters saying, "Among the newer local composers Vienna once again possesses a talent that has already attracted general attention and enjoyed the public's favor—in short, and without exaggeration, we may speak of a 'second Beethoven.' Indeed that immortal man says of him: 'This one will surpass me.'"[31] Maynard Solomon rightly observes that such praise would have been unusual for Beethoven to offer concerning any young contemporary. Schubert's name is mentioned a few times in Beethoven's conversation books, but he makes no personal appearance.[32] In any case, the conflicting accounts about their relationship should remind us that so much of what we know (or think we know) about Schubert's biography comes from the distant memories of friends and family rather than from contemporaneous documents.[33]

A possible late connection between Beethoven and Schubert concerns the transmission of some poems that Beethoven was considering setting but were eventually passed on to Schubert. According to Schindler, Beethoven studied Schubert's Lieder during his final months and "with delighted enthusiasm he called out repeatedly 'Truly, in Schubert there dwells a divine spark!'" (*SMF*, 307; see also 66). Asking to see more, he "often spoke of Schubert and prophesied 'that he will still make a great stir in the world'" (*SMF*, 308). Spaun related similar information: "It certainly made him [Schubert] extremely happy when he learned that, during his last days, Beethoven had derived great pleasure from his songs" (*SMF*, 366). Although such benedictions, perpetuating a lineage of great composers, are the stuff of legends, there does seem to have been a practical consequence relevant to our story here: Schindler reports that in the summer of 1827, he gave Schubert poems from Beethoven's estate that had been sent by the critic and poet Ludwig Rellstab, some of which Beethoven had "earmarked" to compose (*SMF*, 319). Schubert eventually set ten of them—seven in *Schwanengesang* (D957), as well as two others, and *Auf dem Strom* (D943), which contains important musical connections to Beethoven that we will consider later.[34] In his memoirs Rellstab basically corroborates Schindler's account, stating that Beethoven had indicated the poems "he liked best and the ones that he had given Schubert to compose at that time, because he himself felt too unwell."[35] The discrepancies in these accounts, as Rufus Hallmark has observed, are "inessential to the simple, central point that Schubert became acquainted with Rellstab's poetry in a way that caused him to associate the poet with Beethoven."[36]

The most tantalizing tale of a meeting surrounds Beethoven's death. Anselm Hüttenbrenner stated that he knew "as an absolute fact, that Professor Schindler, Schubert and I visited Beethoven at his sickbed about a week before he died" (*SMF*, 66). Josef enlarged the cast: "When Beethoven was dying, Schindler invited me to take along my brother Anselm, Schubert, and the painter [Josef] Teltscher."[37] Schindler, however, recorded no such meeting, nor did anyone else, and the Hüttenbrenners' accounts are among the many that appeared decades later.[38] Another familiar anecdote concerns Schubert's activities following Beethoven's funeral: he allegedly went with his friends Franz Lachner and Benedikt Randhartinger to a local inn, where he filled two wine glasses. With the first, he toasted the memory of Beethoven, and with the second, whoever among the three of them was destined to die next (*SDB*, 623). Fritz von Hartmann's diary offers a less dramatic report actually written later that day: "Went to the Castle of Eisenstadt [a tavern], where I remained with Schober, Schubert, and Schwind until almost 1 AM. Needless to say, we talked of nothing but Beethoven, his works and the well-merited honors paid to his memory today" (*SDB*, 623).

Even if the deathbed encounter between Beethoven and Schubert never occurred, Schubert's participation in the funeral must have made a profound impression, as Spaun recalled Beethoven's death already had. In summary, however unclear the nature of their personal relationship, Beethoven's powerful legacy as man and musician had significant consequences for the remaining twenty months of Schubert's life, and beyond that vast implications for his posthumous reputation.

"Pave the way toward a grand symphony": Schubert's Career Strategy in the Mid-1820s

Schubert wanted to present a concert devoted entirely to his music—an *Akademie*, as such events were often called—at least as early as 1823, when his friend Moritz von Schwind mentioned in a letter to Schober hopes for "a musical academy" or "public Schubertiade" (*SDB*, 314). Schubert expressed this desire in what may be deemed the most revealing of the limited quantity of his surviving letters, sent in March 1824 to the artist Leopold Kupelwieser. At this crucial juncture in his life Schubert lamented his sorry state:

> I feel myself the most unhappy and wretched creature in the world. Imagine a man whose health will never be right again, and who in sheer despair over this ever makes things worse and worse, instead of better; imagine a man, I say, whose most brilliant hopes have perished, to whom the happiness of love and friendship have nothing to offer but pain, at best, whose enthusiasm (at least of the stimulating kind) for all things beautiful threatens to disappear, and I ask you, is he not a miserable, unhappy being? (31 March 1824; *SDB*, 339–40)

He proceeded to complain to Kupelwieser, who was living in Italy at the time, about the dissolution of their social circle—"Thus, joyless and friendless, I should pass my days, were it not that Schwind visits me now and again and shines on me a ray of those sweet days of the past"—and concluded with an update on his career and professional plans. His failure to get any operas produced (he mentions *Fierabras* and *Die Verschworenen*) meant that he seems "once again to have composed two operas for nothing." The quantity of Lieder had declined in favor of a new direction: "I have not written many new ones, but I have tried my hand at several instrumental works, for I wrote two string quartets and an octet, and I want to write another quartet; in fact, I intend to pave the way toward a grand symphony in that manner."

Schubert's letter reveals a determined career strategy, one that casts him in a quite different light from his prevalent image as a clueless clairvoyant effortlessly tossing off masterpieces who cared little what happened to them afterward. Of the two completed quartets he mentions, the A Minor (D804) and D Minor (D810), only the former was released during his lifetime, the first of "Trois Quatuors," Op. 29. Apparently Schubert intended to have his friend and publisher Maximilian Leidesdorf issue a set of three, which would inevitably have invited comparison with Beethoven's "Razumovsky" Quartets, Op. 59.[39] He dedicated the A-Minor Quartet to "son ami I. Schupanzigh [*sic*] membre de la chapelle de S. M. L'Empereur d'Autriche." Schuppanzigh's quartet premiered it at the Musikverein on 14 March 1824, the last concert of the violinist's first season back in Vienna after living abroad. The other work on that program was Beethoven's Septet, Op. 20, which clearly provided the model for Schubert's Octet (D803) that Schuppanzigh premiered on 16 April 1827, less than a month after Beethoven's death. This was another concert in which Beethoven was the only other composer featured (*FSD*, No. 476).

Schubert informed Kupelwieser that these ambitious chamber compositions were intended to lead to a "grosse Sinfonie."[40] And at this point in the letter, as if free associating immediately after discussing his own pieces and plans, Schubert informs his friend that "the latest in Vienna is that Beethoven is to give a concert at which he is to produce his new symphony, three movements from the new Mass, and a new overture. God willing, I too am thinking of giving a similar concert next year." He is referring to Beethoven's 7 May 1824 concert that featured the premiere of the Ninth Symphony, the first Viennese performances of the Kyrie, Credo, and Agnus Dei from the *Missa solemnis*, and the overture to *The Consecration of the House*. Schubert knew many of the musicians involved with this concert, which Schuppanzigh led.[41]

After his recent disappointments getting theatrical works produced, it made sense for Schubert to concentrate on large-scale chamber music and keyboard compositions.[42] Not only did such pieces stand a much better chance of being played and published, but they were the type most likely to be taken up by Beethoven's own performers and publishers, the group with which Schubert now sought closer contact. Schuppanzigh, the principal proponent of Beethoven's music in Vienna, played a key role.[43] The violinist's association with Beethoven went back decades and over the years he premiered many of his string quartets and piano trios. After an all-Beethoven farewell concert on 11 February 1816, Schuppanzigh spent nearly seven years abroad, primarily in Russia. His return to Vienna in 1823 offered new opportunities for both Beethoven and Schubert. Schuppanzigh formed a quartet with Beethoven's assistant Karl Holz, violist Franz Weiss, and cellist Josef Linke that offered either eighteen or twenty-four subscription concerts each season, most of which featured a quartet each by Haydn, Mozart, and Beethoven.[44]

During some concerts Schuppanzigh presented other composers and genres and enlisted additional performers, occasions that gave Schubert an unusually prestigious forum for his works. The participating instrumentalists included leading musicians in Vienna, such as pianists Carl Czerny and Karl Maria von Bocklet. The only prominent performer associated with Schubert's early career was the singer Johann Michael Vogl.[45] We tend to think of Schubert's supporters as primarily amateurs—family, friends, and musical dilettantes, a word that carried different, more positive connotations at the time—but the late promotion of his instrumental music by Vienna's outstanding professional musicians, largely Beethoven's, pointed in new directions and provided promising career opportunities. While Schubert's social life continued to revolve around the "Schobert" circle,[46] his professional ties expanded considerably in his final years.

As mentioned, Schubert's A-Minor Quartet and Octet were prominently featured at concerts that ended Schuppanzigh's 1824 and 1827 seasons, respectively, and were otherwise devoted entirely to Beethoven's music. It is therefore hardly surprising that Schubert should use Beethoven as a model in two senses: compositionally and professionally. Commentators in Schubert's own time observed how he modeled many of his compositions on Beethoven's, but that fundamental influence, as the letter to Kupelwieser and other evidence indicates, went well beyond the purely musical. Beethoven provided a model for building a career as a composer writing "for posterity," or for "strivings after the highest in art," as Schubert expressed it in a letter to a publisher.[47] Schubert was keenly aware of the illustrious musical tradition he was confronting and of the obstacles he faced, notably the increasing popularity of Rossini's music and the preference of publishers for "wretched fashionable stuff," as he once called it (*SDB*, 375). Schubert decided to engage ever more directly with Beethoven's genres, aesthetics, and ambitions. John M. Gingerich, who has studied Schubert's career trajectory, aptly calls this his "Beethoven Project."[48]

In any case, comparisons with Beethoven proved unavoidable, as Schubert repeatedly found in the criticism of his music. Although he was never mentioned in any contemporaneous review of Beethoven, the master's specter haunted his critical reception from the beginning.[49] The most prestigious music journal in German-speaking Europe, Leipzig's *Allgemeine musikalische Zeitung*, frequently mentioned Beethoven in its reviews of Schubert, beginning in 1820 when a critic remarked: "In this first dramatic essay [the Singspiel *Die Zwillingsbrüder*] he seems to attempt to fly as high as Beethoven and not to heed the warning example of Icarus" (*SDB*, 139). Comparisons could also work to Schubert's advantage, however, as in a review from 1826 that praised the "freedom and originality" of the Piano Sonata in A Minor, Op. 42 (D845), which can "probably be compared only with the greatest and freest of Beethoven's sonatas." The review called the scherzo "Beethovenian, without, be it understood, any intention to dispute the composer's originality" (*SDB*, 512, 514). In a later review of the Sonata in G Major, Op. 78 (D894), the journal stated that Schubert had a large following because of his "excellent songs" and that he "is capable of doing the same by means of pianoforte pieces," though this praise was followed by a word of caution against imitating the works of a unique genius: "Beethoven appears to us to be in a class by himself alone, as it were, especially as he showed himself in his middle and later period, so that in truth he should not by any means be chosen as an absolute model, since anyone who desired to be successful in that master's own line could only be he himself" (*SDB*, 694).

Thus in the mid-1820s Schubert confronted the Beethovenian legacy in both compositional as well as practical ways. Schubert's large-scale pieces, not just his successful songs, part-songs, dances, and small keyboard works, increasingly had to contend with the most elevated musical standards. His health temporarily improved and his productivity accelerated, finding expression not only in keyboard and chamber music, songs and dances, but also in orchestral, religious, and virtuoso pieces, as well as in another attempt at an opera. The twenty months that separate the deaths of Beethoven and Schubert saw the production of an astounding quantity and quality of work composed with a new intensity.

"A frenzy of admiration and rapture": Schubert's Concert of 26 March 1828

On the first anniversary of Beethoven's funeral, 29 March 1828, a ceremony was held in Währing Cemetery in which a chorus sang one of his Equale for trombones (WoO 30), fitted with a poem by Grillparzer.[50] Marie von Pratobevera described the scene in a letter to her fiancé:

> The day was heavenly fair, the music most touching, and sung among the graves it could not fail to make a deep impression. I was surprised only that not more people were there,

> and also at the simple monument, made of common stone. It represents a pyramid, at the top of which hangs a very clumsy lyre, and at the base is just his name in gilt letters. I admit that I so much like the idea of making no verses on him, but merely to set down his name, and yet making him immortal thereby; but I do think the stone and the workmanship unworthy. But enough of graves and death: I must tell you of fresh and blossoming life, which prevailed at the concert of Schubert on the 26th March. Only compositions by himself were given and gloriously. Everyone was lost in a frenzy of admiration and rapture. (*SDB*, 760)

Decades later Eduard von Bauernfeld claimed credit for urging his friend finally to undertake this long hoped-for concert.[51] On 5 March Schubert petitioned the Gesellschaft der Musikfreunde for permission to give it on 21 March in its hall at the Roter Igel (Red Hedgehog) in the Tuchlauben.[52] The time around the first anniversary of Beethoven's death was very busy musically in Vienna. On 20 March the third of the Concerts Spirituels presented Beethoven's Symphony No. 4 in B-flat, Op. 60, and oratorio *Christus am Ölberge*, Op. 85. There followed two historic events that framed Schubert's concert.[53] On Sunday, 23 March, Josef Linke gave an all-Beethoven program featuring the premiere of the String Quartet in F, Op. 135, the composer's final work. Figure 2 reproduces the program, which is particularly noteworthy as it shows that the final movement title "Der schwer gefasste Entschluss" (The Difficult Decision) was listed along with the musical mottos "Muss es sein" (Must it be) and "Es muss sein! Es muss sein!" (It must be! It must be!).[54] On Saturday, 29 March, Niccolò Paganini made his first appearance in Vienna, initiating an unprecedented series of fourteen concerts over the next four months.

The date of Schubert's concert changed at least once, and probably twice, for reasons that remain unclear but may relate to the quantity of musical activity at the time. As we know from Schubert's petition, and as is confirmed in the first of three lithographed versions of the program announcement, the event was initially scheduled for Friday, 21 March. A rare copy of the program, with the date hand-corrected to "26," is given as Figure 3. This first version included a number of editing and spelling errors that were eventually corrected in the third and final version: *österreichen Musickvereins* (later *österreich. Musikvereins*), an unnecessary period after Linke's name in No. 4, the misspelling of the poet Klopstock (not Klopfstock), and *Musickstücke* (later *Musikstücke*) after No. 7. Most import-

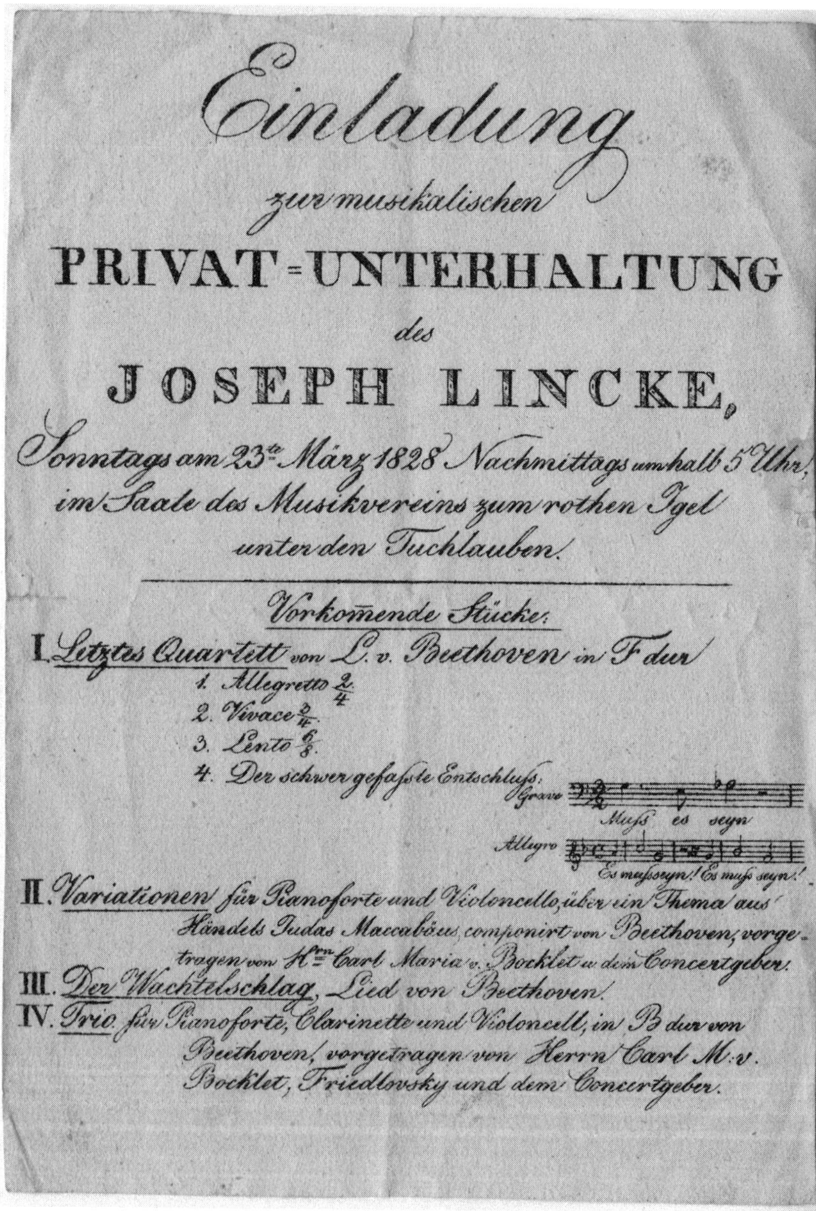
Einladung

zur musikalischen

PRIVAT=UNTERHALTUNG

des

JOSEPH LINCKE,

Sonntags am 23ten März 1828 Nachmittags um halb 5 Uhr,
im Saale des Musikvereins zum rothen Igel
unter den Tuchlauben.

Vorkomende Stücke:

I. Letztes Quartett von L. v. Beethoven in F dur
1. Allegretto $\frac{2}{4}$
2. Vivace $\frac{2}{4}$
3. Lento $\frac{6}{8}$
4. Der schwer gefaßte Entschluß. Grave — Muß es seyn — Allegro — Es muß seyn! Es muß seyn!

II. Variationen für Pianoforte und Violoncello, über ein Thema aus Händels Judas Maccabäus, componirt von Beethoven, vorgetragen von H.rn Carl Maria v. Bocklet u. dem Concertgeber.

III. Der Wachtelschlag, Lied von Beethoven.

IV. Trio für Pianoforte, Clarinette und Violoncell, in B dur von Beethoven, vorgetragen von Herrn Carl M. v. Bocklet, Friedlowsky und dem Concertgeber.

Figure 2. Program for Josef Linke's all-Beethoven concert, 23 March 1828.

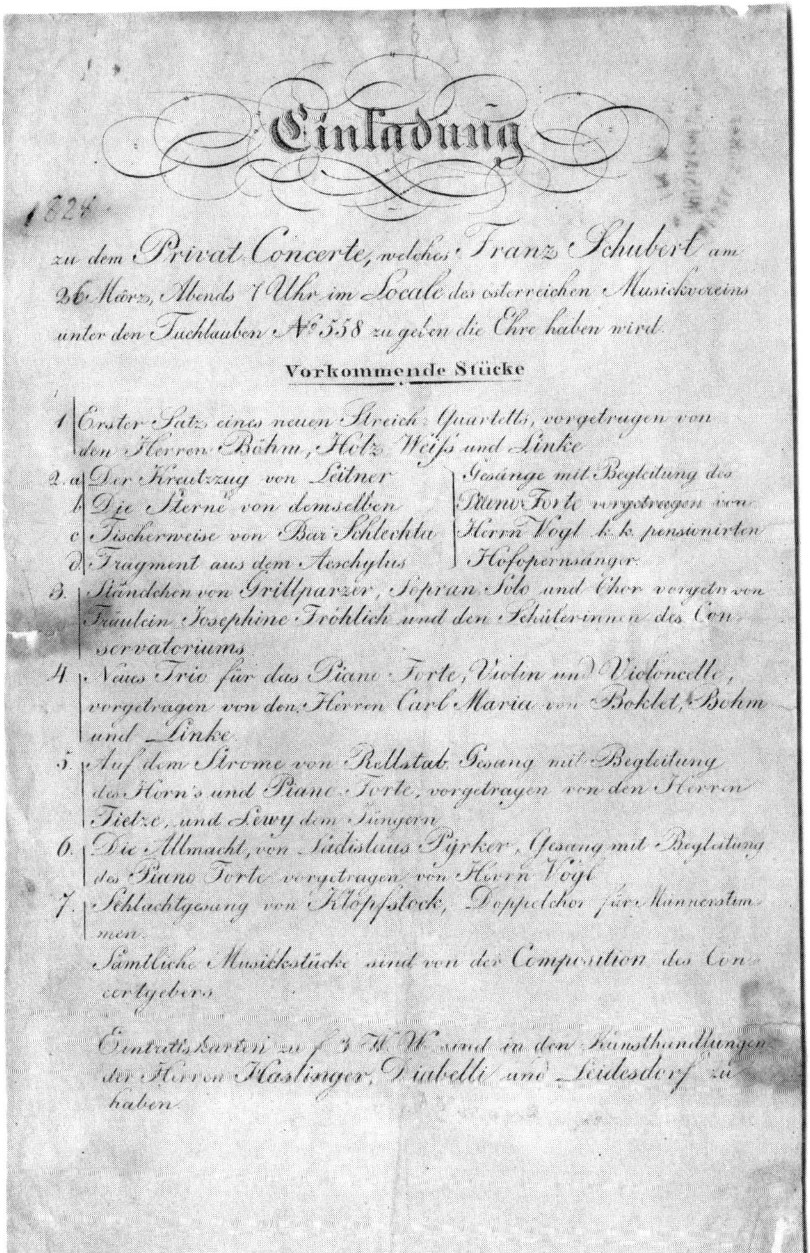
Einladung

1828

zu dem Privat Concerte, welches Franz Schubert am 26 März, Abends 7 Uhr im Locale des österreichen Musikvereins unter den Tuchlauben N.o 558 zu geben die Ehre haben wird.

Vorkommende Stücke

1 Erster Satz eines neuen Streich Quartetts, vorgetragen von den Herren Böhm, Holz, Weiß und Linke

2. a Der Kreutzzug von Leitner
b Die Sterne von demselben
c Fischerweise von Bar Schlechta
d Fragment aus dem Aeschylus
Gesänge mit Begleitung des Piano Forte vorgetragen von Herrn Vogl k. k. pensionirten Hofopernsänger.

3. Ständchen von Grillparzer, Sopran Solo und Chor vorgetr. von Fräulein Josephine Fröhlich und den Schülerinnen des Conservatoriums

4 Neues Trio für das Piano Forte, Violin und Violoncelle, vorgetragen von den Herren Carl Maria von Boklet, Böhm und Linke.

5. Auf dem Strome von Rellstab Gesang mit Begleitung des Horn's und Piano Forte, vorgetragen von den Herren Tietze, und Lewy dem Jüngern

6. Die Allmacht, von Ladislaus Pyrker, Gesang mit Begleitung des Piano Forte vorgetragen von Herrn Vogl

7. Schlachtgesang von Klopfstock, Doppelchor für Männerstimmen.

Sämtliche Musikstücke sind von der Composition des Concertgebers

Eintrittskarten zu f 3 W. W. sind in den Kunsthandlungen der Herren Haslinger, Diabelli und Leidesdorf zu haben.

Figure 3. Program for Schubert's Concert, 26 March 1828 (first version).

ant, there was a change in the repertory of the concert: No. 2c was originally to be the Lied *Fischerweise* (D881), but was ultimately replaced by *Der Wanderer an den Mond* (D870).[55] A second printed version of the program contains the same typographical errors and still lists *Fischerweise*, but gives the date exactly a week later, on 28 March. A surviving copy of this program also has the date hand-corrected to "26."[56] The third and final version of the lithographed program corrects the earlier errors, and now lists *Der Wanderer an den Mond*, but still prints the date as "28," once more hand-corrected to "26" in the surviving copy at the Wienbibliothek.[57]

In any case, Schubert did hold the event on the 26th, a Wednesday, which was somewhat unusual. Perhaps the changes of date were related to scheduling conflicts for the participating performers, vying for rehearsal and performance space, and concerns about competing for audiences. A large benefit concert on 28 March of Handel's oratorio *Jephtha*, presented by the Tonkünstler-Gesellschaft at the Hofburgtheater, might have played a role in avoiding that day. There is also the possibility that Schubert wanted his concert to fall on the first anniversary of Beethoven's death. Another mystery, perhaps related, is why Schuppanzigh did not perform at Schubert's concert—he had, it seems, already played the E-flat Trio with Linke and Bocklet at a private Schubertiade on 28 January 1828 at the home of Josef von Spaun.[58] Otto Erich Deutsch conjectured he was indisposed and contends that he did not participate in Linke's concert either, unsupported claims I find doubtful.[59]

On 25 March Schubert's concert was announced in articles that appeared in three Viennese journals.[60] In addition to listing the program and performers, the one in the *Wiener allgemeine Theaterzeitung* stated:

> Among the manifold musical art exhibitions that have been offered us in the course of this *saison* and still await us [i.e., Paganini], *one* should attract general attention the more because it offers enjoyment both new and surprising by the novelty and sterling value of the compositions and the attractive variety among the musical items, as well as the sympathetic collaboration of the most celebrated local artists. Franz *Schubert*, whose powerfully intellectual, enchantingly lovely and original tone-poems have made him the favorite of the whole musical public, and which may well secure their creator a more than ephemeral, nay an imperishable, name by their genuine artistic value, will perform on 26 March, at a private concert (in the Austrian Music Society's room), a series of the latest products of his mind. . . . May the glorious

> German tone-poet, then, be granted an attendance such as his modesty and unobtrusiveness would alone deserve, quite apart from his artistic eminence and the rare and great musical enjoyment that is to be expected.[61]

Although the event was not promoted as a Beethoven memorial, I believe the master was honored in two pieces premiered that evening. The concert began with the first movement of a "new string quartet," either the D Minor (D810) or the more recent G Major (D887), played by Holz, Weiss, and Linke, with Josef Böhm taking Schuppanzigh's usual place. Vogl next sang four Lieder—*Der Kreuzzug* (D932), *Die Sterne* (D939), *Der Wanderer an den Mond*, and *Fragment aus dem Aeschylus* (D450)—with Schubert at the piano. Schubert also accompanied Josefine Fröhlich and female students of her sister Anna at the conservatory in *Ständchen* (D920), a recent setting of a poem by Grillparzer.

The centerpiece came with Böhm, Linke, and Bocklet performing the E-flat Piano Trio, an unusually long composition to which Schubert subsequently made three cuts in the finale. The remainder of the program consisted of the premiere of *Auf dem Strom*,[62] the setting of Rellstab mentioned above, sung by Ludwig Tietze with the horn obligato played by Josef Rudolf Lewy.[63] As we will see, this work, composed especially for the concert, is important because, as Rufus Hallmark has persuasively argued, Beethoven was its "unnamed dedicatee."[64] Vogl and Schubert next performed *Die Allmacht* (D852), and the program ended with the rousing *Schlachtlied* (D912),[65] an unaccompanied double-male chorus setting of a poem by Friedrich Gottlieb Klopstock. Schubert was the pianist for all the Lieder, but not for the trio. In addition to Vogl, who made a rare public appearance at this late stage in his career, the distinguished performers of the chamber music were those who had premiered Beethoven's own late chamber music. Tietze as well had sung earlier in the week at Linke's concert and had previously premiered many Schubert Lieder.

Schubert's concert proved a great success, immediately prompting talk of repeating it and of doing comparable, or even more ambitious events in the future. Other admirers echoed Marie von Pratobevera's enthusiasm: Bauernfeld noted in his journal, "Enormous applause, good receipts" (*SDB*, 754; see also 893). Leopold von Sonnleithner later recalled, "The event was a success in every way and provided Schubert with a considerable sum of money" (*SMF*, 115). Ferdinand Schubert stated: "Never had this hall been crowded with more people" (*SDB*, 919). Franz von Hartmann wrote in his diary that he would "never forget how glorious" the concert was and that everyone afterward went to the Schnecke

(Snail), a favorite pub, "where we jubilated until midnight" (*SDB*, 754). Flush with cash, Schubert invited Bauernfeld to Paganini's debut three days later (*SMF*, 67; also 186, 228). A review in the Leipzig *Allgemeine musikalische Zeitung* likened Schubert's concert to Linke's and made a comparison with Beethoven, this time to the young composer's benefit: "If all these works [by Beethoven], performed to perfection, afforded an indescribable aural treat, the same must be said with hardly less emphasis in praise of that *soirée musicale* that the excellent Schubert held in the very same place on the 26th." The *Berliner allgemeine musikalische Zeitung* noted that "the numerous gathering of friends and patrons did not stint on resounding applause after each number and saw to it that several of them were repeated." The Dresden *Abendzeitung* was somewhat less enthusiastic because of comparisons, not with Beethoven in this instance, but rather with Paganini: "The minor stars paled before the radiance of this comet in the musical heavens" (*SDB*, 756–57).

Two weeks later Schubert informed a prospective publisher in Germany that the E-flat Trio had been "received at my concert by a tightly packed audience with such extraordinary applause that I have been urged to repeat the concert" (*SDB*, 764). Indeed, supporters had immediately written an article urging just that, which they submitted to the *Wiener Zeitschrift für Kunst, Literatur, Theater und Mode*, whose editor Johann Schickh passed it on to Schubert with an admiring letter (*SDB*, 762). In his 1829 memorial essay on Schubert, Josef von Spaun related that the "exceptional participation of the packed audience matched the rare enjoyment of this evening, which will certainly remain in the memories of all who had the good fortune to participate in this never to be repeated festival of music. It was Schubert's intention to give a similar concert each year, not suspecting that this first would also be his last and that the next public performance of his compositions would take place only in celebration of his memory."[66]

"I look forward to it longingly": The Path to Publication

The great importance Schubert attached to the E-flat Piano Trio is evident not only from its central position at his concert but also in his fervent wish to see it published as soon as possible, a desire that led to its rather complicated publication history.[67] As early as 9 February, some six weeks before the concert, two German publishers—Heinrich Albert Probst in Leipzig and B. Schott's Söhne in Mainz—independently approached

Schubert expressing interest in his music. The former hoped for smaller works (Lieder, part-songs, and piano music) that "without sacrificing any of your individuality, are yet not difficult to grasp" (*SDB*, 735). The latter stated that they had been wanting to publish his works for some time but have "been occupied by the works Opp. 121, 122, 123, 124, 125, 126, 127, 128, and 131 of the departed Beethoven, among which is many a very bulky *opus*"; they would now be interested in vocal and smaller keyboard pieces (*SDB*, 737). Once again Schubert found himself in a competition of sorts with Beethoven—and being admired for his domestic pieces rather than sought after for his "strivings after the highest in art," as he expressed it to Schott (*SDB*, 740).

Schubert had not yet officially published anything outside of Vienna.[68] He responded to Schott on 21 February, offering a variety of works, including a piano trio that had been "produced here with much success" (*SDB*, 739); Schott requested to see most of the pieces, including the trio (*SDB*, 744–45). No doubt preoccupied with preparations for his concert, Schubert took six weeks to respond, informing the publisher that he had had copies made of the "desired trio" and requesting 100 florins for it and 60 for four keyboard impromptus (D935) and a five-part male chorus (D875). He ended by saying, "All I should request is publication as soon as possible" (*SDB*, 764). He wrote a similar letter to Probst the same day, 10 April. Probst thought Schubert was offering the E-flat Trio, which he immediately accepted and dispatched 60 florins to secure (15 April; *SDB*, 767–68).

After various misunderstandings and problems juggling these negotiations, Schubert ultimately decided to accept Probst's offer: "In order, however, to make a beginning at last, I would only ask for the speediest possible publication, and for the dispatch of 6 copies." He concluded his 10 May letter: "In expectation of the earliest publication" (*SDB*, 774). Probst took more than two months to reply, at which point he inquired about the title, dedication, and opus number of the trio and promised publication in "about six weeks" (18 July; *SDB*, 793). Schubert responded on 1 August: "The opus number of the trio is 100. I request that the edition should be faultless and look forward to it longingly. This work is to be dedicated to nobody, save those who find pleasure in it. That is the most profitable dedication" (*SDB*, 796). When the piece had still not arrived as promised two and a half months later, Schubert wrote again: "I beg to inquire when the trio is to appear at last. Can it be that you do not know the opus number yet? It is Op. 100. I await it with longing." (2 October; *SDB*, 810). The trio was finally released in Leipzig near the end of October or beginning of November and was advertised for sale in Vienna on 11 December. It is unlikely that Schubert had received his copies of the piece he so longed to see before he died.[69]

"Not to be obliged to have recourse to plagiarism": The Piano Trio in E-flat, Op. 100

Unlike his extended engagement writing string quartets, which began as a family affair playing with his father and brothers, Schubert came late to the piano trio. He composed a single movement in B-flat (D28) in 1812, which apparently he initially scored for two violins and piano, and then ignored the genre for some fifteen years until producing what proved to be two of his longest and most ambitious chamber works: the Trio in B-flat, Op. 99 (D898) and the Trio in E-flat, Op. 100 (D929). It is not known exactly when he wrote the B-flat Trio, for which the manuscript is lost, although scholars generally agree that it is the earlier of the two.[70] A separate slow movement, an Adagio in E-flat (D897), first published in 1846 by Anton Diabelli with the spurious title "Nocturne," was perhaps originally intended for it. The manuscript survives for the E-flat Trio, along with sketches for the first three movements, all dated as begun in November 1827.

The chronology and early performance history of the trios have long been debated, but the best evidence is that Schubert composed the B-flat Trio in 1827 and that Schuppanzigh, together with Linke and Bocklet, premiered it as a "new" work during his 26 December subscription concert at the Musikverein.[71] One of the trios, more likely the E-flat, was performed by the same musicians at Josef von Spaun's house on 28 January 1828. (Spaun had recently returned to Vienna after years living in Linz and was engaged to be married; this special Schubertiade, apparently the last he hosted during the composer's lifetime, honored the occasion.)[72] The public premiere of the E-flat Trio was at Schubert's 26 March 1828 concert, when it was billed as a "new" work.

As with most of Beethoven's mature piano trios, which Schuppanzigh frequently performed and in some instances premiered, both of Schubert's are in four movements: fast, slow, scherzo, and lengthy finale.[73] The E-flat Trio is particularly formidable in the orchestral nature of the lengthy opening movement, the canonic intricacies of its third movement scherzando, and the cyclic structure and contrapuntal ingenuity of the finale. On first hearing the second movement, Andante con moto, may appear the most characteristically Schubertian, and it will be my focus here, along with the finale, which, as mentioned, is itself haunted by the cyclic return of the Andante's opening cello theme.

There is an important piece of background information about this theme that has fundamentally influenced discussion of the trio ever since the mid-nineteenth century. Schubert's first significant biographer, Heinrich Kreissle von Hellborn, stated in his influential 1864 biography of Schubert that the theme of the Andante "is a Swedish folksong."[74] He learned this, he said, from Leopold von Sonnleithner, an early supporter of Schubert.[75] Sonnleithner related that Schubert was enamored of Swedish melodies he heard sung by Swedish tenor Isaak Albert Berg, who visited Vienna from Copenhagen in 1827. Berg apparently met Schubert through the Fröhlich sisters—Anna (1793–1880), Barbara (1797–1879), Katharina (1800–1879), and Josefine (1803–1878)—who were active in the musical life of Vienna and play a continuing role in our story. Josefine ("Pepi") had been a fellow student with Berg in Copenhagen, studying with the Italian tenor Josef Siboni. Berg was in Vienna by at least 18 September 1827, when he performed at the Kärntnertor Theater.[76]

Grillparzer had intimate connections with this group: he was related to the Sonnleithner family through his mother's side and was very close to the Fröhlich sisters (Kathi was his "eternal bride," and although they never wed, he lived for most of his adult life in the same building as she and her two unmarried sisters). Berg met Grillparzer at the Fröhlichs' on 10 November and was in contact with Schubert around this time as well, exactly when the composer was becoming more involved with the poet.[77] Schubert set only a few of Grillparzer's poems, most importantly two multi-voice compositions: *Ständchen* (D920) and *Mirjams Siegesgesang* (D942).[78] The former, written in July 1827, was performed at Schubert's concert and it seems the latter, dating from March 1828, was intended for that event as well. Schubert's increased engagement with Grillparzer's poetry suggests greater contact during the months separating the deaths of Beethoven and Schubert.[79] There is good reason to believe that Grillparzer and Schubert had contact in early November, when Schubert began composing the trio and got to know one of Berg's songs, which he used in it. This was when Beethoven's tomb was dedicated in Währing Cemetery, an occasion for which Grillparzer wrote another speech that the actor Anschütz delivered, as he had eight months earlier at the funeral.[80] Although there is no documentation of Schubert attending, he did have a familial connection in that his brother Ferdinand supposedly designed Beethoven's monument.[81] It seems likely that Schubert, Grillparzer, and Berg were together exactly at the time when Beethoven's tomb was dedicated and when Schubert began his memorial piece to the master. The confluence of events may in fact have been what inspired Schubert to write the trio as a tribute to Beethoven.

Let us return to Berg and his role in the genesis of the trio. According to Sonnleithner:

> The famous singer, Josef Siboni, at that time director of the Conservatory in Copenhagen, had a pupil, Herr Berg, a young tenor of remarkable talent. . . . This Berg (who later on was Jenny Lind's first teacher) came to Vienna in the winter of 1827–28 and had an introduction to the Misses Fröhlich (former pupils of Siboni's) at whose house he often sang to a small circle. He sang Swedish folksongs extremely well, and Schubert, who heard him on one of these occasions, was quite enchanted with these Swedish songs. He asked for a copy of them and used the best of them as themes for the E-flat Trio. Schubert made no secret of it and, besides, he was rich enough in ideas not to be obliged to have recourse to plagiarism. And no one who knows the trio will regret that he was stimulated to write this composition by external influences. (*SMF*, 115)

Some further details about Berg's connection to Schubert come from information that Anna Fröhlich later related to Gerhard von Breuning, son of Beethoven's good friend Stephan von Breuning: "Berg had composed excellent Swedish songs. Schubert was so captivated by his music that, whenever we invited him to spend the evening with us, he always asked 'Is Berg coming? If so, you can absolutely count on my coming too.'" Fröhlich reported that "Schubert was so especially fond of one of his songs that he used the theme for one of his quartets."[82] To this, Breuning added a clarification of his own: "On the other hand, C. F. Pohl, the archivist of the Gesellschaft der Musikfreunde in Vienna and biographer of Josef Haydn, informed me that there was a reminiscence of a Swedish song by Berg in the Piano Trio, Op. 100" (*SMF*, 251). Scholar Gustav Nottebohm possessed further details: the song's key was D minor and its title *Se solen sjunker*.[83] Indeed, it seems that both Pohl and Nottebohm knew the song through a copy from the music collector Aloys Fuchs dated 1844 that is in the archive of the Gesellschaft but was overlooked or lost for a long time (see Figure 4).[84] The eminent Schubert scholars Otto Erich Deutsch and Maurice J. E. Brown did not know it, nor did Arnold Feil, who edited the trios for the *Neue Schubert-Ausgabe* in 1975.[85] In 1978 Manfred Willfort resolved the matter in an

Figure 4. Isaak Albert Berg, *Se solen sjunker.*

Figure 4. Continued

article titled "Das Urbild des Andante aus Schuberts Klaviertrio Es-Dur, D 929," which finally presented the music and text of *Se solen sjunker*.[86] Although it remained uncertain whether Berg himself composed the melody and/or the piano accompaniment, a score of the song was at last available, making it possible for the first time to determine its exact relation to Schubert's trio. After Kreissle's biography appeared in 1864, writers mentioned the alleged Swedish source without having access to the notated music, and thus it was widely assumed that the lyrical cello melody that opens the second movement was the Swedish tune. In fact, the first melodic borrowing only comes later, in measure 11. The inspiration for the lamenting opening theme, I believe, came from Beethoven.

"To celebrate the memory of a great man": The Keys to the Crypt

The opening two piano measures of the Andante con moto are processional, similar to the accompaniments of various Schubert's songs, notably *Gute Nacht* beginning *Winterreise*, composed early in 1827.[87] The cello, the singing instrument, enters to spin out an extended 18-measure melody (see Example 1). The strings and keyboard then reverse roles for the next twenty measures to produce a first theme group of a symmetrical forty measures that is often characterized as a funeral march. Some commentators have pointed more specifically to similarities with the second movement, the *marcia funebre*, of the *Eroica* Symphony, which Beethoven marked "composta per festeggiare il sovvenire di un grand Uomo" (composed to celebrate the memory of a great man); see Example 2.

Some of the initial similarities between the E-flat Trio and *Eroica* Symphony are generic ones associated with funeral marches, including others that both composers wrote. In addition to sharing the key of C minor and the hushed duple meter opening, the slow movements of the E-flat Trio and *Eroica* have a processional accompaniment that uses the same distinctive dotted sixteenth, thirty-second note rhythm. The plagal relationship that Schubert sets up in the first two measures echoes Beethoven's plagal cadence in measure 8. In both trio and symphony, a melody is presented twice to form balanced opening sections. In the trio, eighteen measures of the cello melody lead to eighteen featuring the piano; in the *Eroica*, eight measures of violins playing in a low register are followed by eight featuring solo oboe. In both pieces there is not only an immediate re-presentation of the same melodic material, but also a general brightening of the sound. In addition to the use of ornamental notes in the melodies, the contour is initially similar: beginning on the repeated pitch G, they move to C, ornamented by grace note(s), then up to E-flat before returning to C. It takes Schubert four measures to outline this tonic triad, whereas Beethoven does so in two.

Both movements relate to a long musical tradition, one particularly associated with French composers around the turn of the century.[88] Dotted rhythms appear in other funeral marches that Beethoven and Schubert composed, including the latter's "Marcia Funebre sulla morte d'un Eroe" (Funeral March on the Death of a Hero) from the Piano Sonata in A-flat Major, Op. 26, which he later orchestrated to use in the incidental music for *Leonore Prohaska* (WoO 96). The fifth variation of Beethoven's Piano Variations, Op. 34, written shortly before the *Eroica* and a work signaling his "new path," is also a funeral march, once again with dotted rhythms and in C minor. Schubert composed many more pieces connected with death, beginning with some of his earliest songs, and also wrote several explicit funeral marches. Both versions of the opera *Des Teufels Lustschloss* (D84) have a *Trauermarsch* in C minor. The fifth of his *Six Grandes Marches*, Op. 40 (D819), is a funeral march,[89] as is another piano duet, the *Grande Marche Funèbre*, Op. 55 (D859), which shares with the *Eroica* the C-minor tonality, dotted rhythm, and opus number. The musical associations with a funeral march in Schubert's trio thus encompass multiple parameters—tonality, meter, rhythm, cadence, melodic contour, affect, and tradition—all of which echo the *Eroica*.

Schubert ingeniously combined these funereal features with other elements he mined from *Se solen sjunker*, most obviously three melodic fragments. Schubert, of course, is famous for his transformative use of song materials in many instrumental compositions, usually drawn from his own Lieder, but occasionally from those by others or from a folk tradition. He deployed these songs in different ways, sometimes obvious, at other

Example 1. Schubert, Piano Trio in E-flat Major, Andante con moto, mm. 1–20.

Example 2. Beethoven, Symphony No. 3 in E-flat Major (*Eroica*), Adagio assai, mm. 1–8.

times hidden. Though few generalizations can be made about why he did this so often and in such varied manners, Sonnleithner understated the matter in observing that Schubert was "rich enough in ideas not to be obliged to have recourse to plagiarism." The issue points to larger ones concerning Schubert's working methods, career trajectory, social interactions, and outlets for personal expression. In some cases, such as the "Trout" Quintet, he capitalized on the popular success of one of his songs to enhance the appeal of a new instrumental work, similar to the countless variation sets on favorite opera tunes so many composers produced. In other instances his use of preexisting Lied material was brief and allusive—it seems to have carried some purely personal meaning for him or been meant to be appreciated only by a small group of friends. Scholars have long recognized the possible hermeneutic significance of unsung songs within instrumental works by Schubert and later Romantics.[90] We need to remember that many in Schubert's social sphere were highly musical individuals even if they were not professional musicians.[91] Amid such an intimate and musically sophisticated orbit, Schubert could count on people recognizing things that now go unnoticed.

Such was probably the case with *Se solen sjunker*, which he called upon for both its music and words. The song provided Schubert with various musical ideas, some quite subtle, that also affected parts of the trio besides the second movement.[92] The three melodic connections between *Se solen sjunker* and the cello melody of the Andante are given in Example 3, with the song transposed from D minor to C minor to facilitate comparison. The first fragment to appear in the cello part of the trio, the pitches E♭, D, G, with an expressive grace note before the falling fifth, comes from the "la, la, la" refrain near the end of the song. The second fragment is the most striking one: an unaccompanied octave leap, G to G, beginning in measure 14 that the piano echoes and is then repeated. These measures interrupt the steady accompanimental flow in both the trio and song, thus even more emphasizing the words "Farewell, farewell." The last quotation is a more extended melody from the middle of the song with a dramatic upward leap of a tenth on the word "bride."

When Schubert employed fleeting references such as he does here it is often revealing to consider the words attached to the melody he quotes, which may carry some personal meaning or have been intended to convey some kind of message. The text reads:[93]

Se solen sjunker ner back höga bergens topp,	See the sun is setting behind the high mountain peaks,
För nattens dystra skuggor du flÿr o sköna hopp,	You take flight before the gloomy shadows of the night, oh fair hope.
Farväl Farväl ack vännen glömde bort	Farewell, farewell, alas the friend forgets
Sin trogna väna brud sin trogna väna brud sin trogna väna brud lala, la . . .	His true sweet bride, his true sweet bride, his true sweet bride, la, la . . .

The brief poem can easily be interpreted with regard to Beethoven, whose death—the setting sun, a common literary metaphor, as in *Romeo and Juliet*, Act 3, scene 5—marks the end of an era, a sentiment that reso-

Example 3. Comparison of Schubert's Piano Trio in E-flat Major, Andante con moto, and *Se Solen sjunker*

nates richly with Grillparzer's funeral oration. Most noteworthy are the words "Farewell, farewell" set to the falling octave leaps that Schubert uses as the principal motive for the movement. This "farewell" motive later generates the second theme, is developed in the heart of the Andante, and ultimately ends the entire movement. The prominent "farewell" motive thus reveals a further part of Schubert's encrypted message to "celebrate the memory of a great man."

Se solen sjunker needs to be placed within the larger context of the second movement in which traces of the *Eroica* continue to appear. The structure of the movement elegantly combines aspects of variation, sonata, and rondo forms. Schubert's second theme, beginning in measure 41, unfolds over flowing triplets, adapts the rhythm of the "farewell" motive, and lyrically transforms the falling octaves into falling thirds, in this way suggesting a variation design. The movement is most often viewed as a rondo form (ABA'B'A"), similar to many other Schubert slow movements, including the "Great" C-Major Symphony, G-Major String Quartet, and several piano sonatas.[94] Although this form is different from the unusual one Beethoven employed for the *Eroica*'s funeral march, Schubert nonetheless forges striking connections to some of the most important tonal areas in the symphony while also creating a variety of textural, harmonic, dynamic, and affective commonalities.

After the double statement of the first theme, both movements move with little preparation to E-flat, the relative major (Schubert's sketch reveals that he originally had a sixteen-measure episode in C major that he cut and annotated "in Es"; that is, into E-flat). After the reprise of the opening theme in the tonic (measure 84), a deceptive cadence lands on an A♭ tremolo in the piano (measure 104). This jarring event has a similar effect as Beethoven's striking interpolation of A♭ at measure 158 of the *Eroica*, after the false reprise of the movement's opening theme in G minor. In the trio this initiates a semi-developmental section of considerable anguish, moving to C-sharp minor, to F-sharp minor, and reaching a climax at measure 122, marked *fortississimo* (a rare dynamic for Schubert). The violence and anger evoked here is a characteristic instance of what Hugh Macdonald has called the composer's "volcanic temper."[95] Repeatedly in his late instrumental music, including the "Great" C-Major Symphony, C-Major String Quintet, and A-Major Piano Sonata, Schubert interjects a violent passage that disrupts lovely lyricism. (I mentioned earlier Schumann's characterization of the Andante as "a sigh intensified to the point of an anguished cry of the heart.") Immediately following this terrifying passage ending in F-sharp minor the music abruptly shifts to the tonic major a tritone away for the return of the second theme, and all seems calm and well again (mm. 129ff). This second "B" section offers yet another formal similarity to the *Eroica*, which also has a luminous section in C major (mm. 69ff), where the oboe is accompanied by the same first-inversion arpeggiated triplets in the violins as Schubert has in the piano part (see Example 4).

By the midpoint of the movement, therefore, we have heard affective states common to many funeral marches: a slow procession in the minor mode with a dotted rhythm to begin, a contrasting lyrical section in a major key offering hope and consolation, and a passage of violent anger. Schubert's surviving sketches for the trio show that all three moods were part of his original conception, although initially their unfolding somewhat differed in a movement that was longer and more harmonically varied. These sketches are immensely revealing. Long before they were published as an appendix to the *Neue Schubert-Ausgabe*, Maurice Brown called those for the second movement "the most fascinating and import-

Example 4. Comparison of the C-major section of the second movement of Beethoven's *Eroica* (mm. 69–71) and the C-major section of Schubert's Piano Trio in E-flat Major, Andante con moto (mm. 129–31).

ant of all Schubert's manifold sketches" and expressed the hope that they would be made available so that people could appreciate "the marvelous—no less marvelous if partly unconscious—power of Schubert's genius."[96] Although Brown falls into the trap of thinking Schubert may not have been aware of what he was doing, the sketches show that he

Example 5. Sketch for a deleted passage in Schubert's Piano Trio in E-flat Major, Andante con moto (mm. 79–82), quoting Beethoven's Symphony No. 5 in C Minor.

initially intended, but ultimately withheld, an overt Beethoven quotation: the famous opening of the Fifth Symphony (mm. 79ff in the sketch).[97] Here the reference seems all too obvious, which is probably the reason Schubert cut the passage (see Example 5).

The initial echoes of the *Eroica* and the shared tonal areas might be viewed as either generic features of funeral marches or as coincidental, although in combination with the "farewell" motive from *Se solen sjunker* they are certainly suggestive of a conscious homage. At the end of the movement, moreover, Schubert becomes explicit (as can be seen in Examples 6a and 6b). Commentators have long remarked on the extraordinary way in which Beethoven concluded the funeral march of the *Eroica*. After the preceding storms, he softly reprises the opening material as a gradual disintegration. Maynard Solomon has observed that Beethoven used this strategy in other compositions as well, going back

Example 6a. Beethoven, Symphony No. 3 in E-flat Major (*Eroica*), Adagio assai, mm. 236–39.

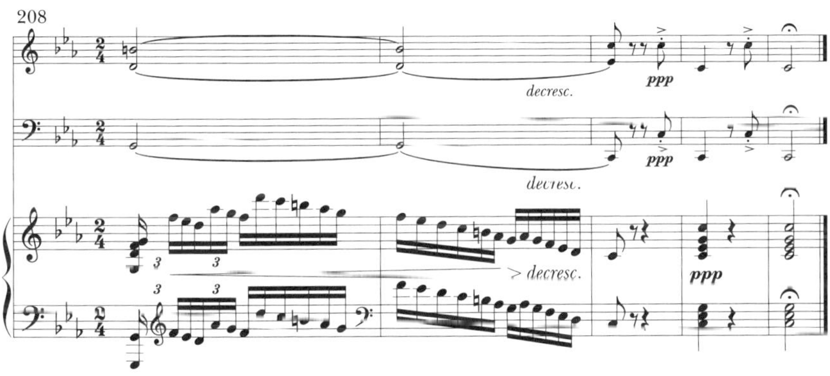

Example 6b. Schubert, Piano Trio in E-flat Major, Andante con moto, mm. 208–12.

as far as the teenage *Cantata on the Death of Emperor Joseph II* (1790), and argues that it reveals "Beethoven's association of certain ideas with the concept of death." For Solomon, the "extramusical meaning of the 'disintegrating' passage in the closing measures of the [*Eroica*'s] Funeral March movement is confirmed by the composer's use of a similar passage in the cantata to accompany the word 'Todt' (dead)."[98] Schubert not only copies Beethoven's procedure of dismantling the opening theme but also, exactly at this point, as if teasing those who may have already perceived his encrypted message, tips his hand: he quotes the *Eroica* by transferring, almost note for note, the triplet flute and violin passage from Beethoven's own concluding measures (mm. 236–38) to the piano accompaniment (mm. 208–10).[99] This triplet passage might seem an unimportant flourish, and here the sketches are once again helpful because they show the quotation was there from the outset (mm. 233–35 in the sketch).[100] The Beethoven quotation in the concluding measures leads to a *pianissimo* ending, with the falling octave motive as violin and cello twice intone a final "farewell, farewell" (see Example 6b).

"Like a march of ghosts": The Haunted Finale

But the farewells are not in fact final. The trio's most prominent Beethovenian procedure comes in the fourth movement when Schubert remarkably brings back the Andante's cello theme, an overt cyclic device such as Beethoven employed in his Fifth and Ninth symphonies, among other pieces.[101] Many recent critics have commented on the subtle cyclicism unifying the entire trio, but the threefold return of the cello theme in the last movement is not just obvious, it seems to be much of the point of the movement.[102] As Fink already hinted at in his 1828 review, and as we saw earlier in the complaints of recent critics about the quality of Schubert's finale, this movement has long come in for criticism on account of both its length and character. Brown argued that the first theme seems "all the more trivial against the sombre and passionate depths of the slow movement."[103] Leo Treitler calls the finale "one of those endless rondos of Schubert's that seem to modulate through more keys than there are, this one going on in an endless patter of mindless energy."[104] Lawrence Kramer characterizes the thematic material as "unusually neutral and colorless, especially for Schubert . . . [it is] entertainment music on a bad night."[105] John M. Gingerich points to the second theme's "perky banality" in contrast with the "dignified, stately, elegiac, introspective" Andante theme.[106]

The carefree opening theme is stated by the piano in E-flat major and is then taken up by the strings; it alternates with a perpetual-motion repeated note second theme, *l'istesso tempo* in C minor (mm. 73ff). This material sets up a sonata form with Schubert employing a popular style associated with some of his domestic music. The uncanny return of the Andante cello theme beginning at measure 279 disturbs this conviviality. After a four-bar introduction, the entire eighteen-measure melody is presented by the cello in the minor, an extraordinarily long cyclic return in comparison with what Beethoven usually did before and with what most other composers would do afterward.

I mentioned earlier that Schubert made three cuts to the final movement. The original version was the one played at his 26 March concert and survives in manuscript; it was published for the first time in 1975 in the *Neue Schubert-Ausgabe*.[107] Since this uncut version was what Schubert originally composed and performed, it will be my concern here—and, like the sketches already discussed, it reveals further aspects of Schubert's homage to Beethoven. Schubert brings the haunting cello theme back a second time at measure 477, again in its entirety, this time in B minor, a key that played an important function in the first movement. He decided to cut this passage, most critics now believe unfortunately. The excised section offers an impressive contrapuntal juxtaposition with the second theme, thus having the serious directly confront the convivial, a battle between death and life that furthers the psychological trajectory of the movement. Example 7 gives the initial part of this second return.

The Andante theme—what I propose can now be considered the ghost of Beethoven—appears a third time to end the movement (mm. 795ff). In contrast to the previous two complete statements, its final presentation is abridged. The octave "farewells" are omitted and the music turns to the major, with the last phrase repeated five times. Treitler describes the effect: "By the simple device of opening the third phase of the theme, which until now had always looped back to the beginning, into the major mode (changing G flat to G natural), he emancipates the piece from the sense of entrapment with which the second movement had closed."[108] Kramer, commenting on the published version of the trio, also remarks on the different effect produced this time: the Andante theme "returns not once but twice: the first time as disruption, and the second, incredibly, as resolution and closure."[109] John Daverio, who was aware of my argument that the trio was a *tombeau de Beethoven*, wrote that the "coda's overall affective progress from melancholy reflection to unbridled joy may well have had programmatic implications for Schubert."[110] Many critics, performers, and listeners have been struck by the optimistic and joyous conclusion of

Example 7. Deleted section from Schubert's Piano Trio in E-flat Major, Allegro moderato, mm. 477–88.

the trio, which in my view sees life win out over death. Following my reading of the haunting Andante theme as Beethoven's ghost, I am tempted to say that here Schubert, at the last moment, exorcises the spirit that has kept intruding in the finale, no longer says farewell, and ecstatically goes his own way. The E-flat Piano Trio is an homage, but also an assertion of Schubert's new position standing beside Beethoven.

Schubert's trio was a private *tombeau*. He did not announce a Beethoven memorial concert on 26 March 1828, nor did he dedicate any memorial piece to him. One might indeed wonder about the lack of a dedication for the trio—"To nobody, save those who find pleasure in it," as he told the publisher—and note that all of Schubert's other significant instrumental compositions, as well as most of his less significant ones and most of his Lieder, carry a public dedication, either to a friend, performer, patron, or hero (Goethe and Beethoven).[111] That Schubert deliberately withheld a dedication is therefore revealing and suggests there is a dedicatee, but one who must remain publicly unnamed—the music itself does that for those who can hear it. There were many memorial works published in the wake of Beethoven's death with public dedications, some of which alluded to his music.[112] Carl Czerny's *Marcia funebre sulla morte di Luigi van Beethoven*, in C minor and with dotted rhythms, for example, begins with a clear allusion to the *Eroica*'s funeral march. In the E-flat Trio Schubert chose to make the musical echoes to Beethoven subtle, omitting the too obvious quotation of the Fifth Symphony. This private homage may have helped him work through his mourning for the composer he most revered, with whom he increasingly identified, and whom he soon followed in death.

Though Schubert did not publicly declare his *tombeau*, he demonstrated his intention in ways that many listeners have heard over the years, even if unconsciously. For nearly two centuries many have heard a funeral march and echoes of the *Eroica* as well as of other works by Beethoven, yet the larger connections remained hidden. The first reason for this seems to have come from the determination of many to make Schubert clueless as to what he was doing; by ascribing any similarities with the *Eroica* entirely to his unconscious genius, such commentators are reenacting the cliché of his historical reception: that of a natural artist, unaware of his intentions, of why and how he creates, and of what the consequences of his actions might be for his immediate career or for his lasting image.[113] The perception that Schubert tossed off songs on the backs of menus, was incapable of self-promotion, and unconcerned about the unfolding of his career has been further complicated by the rudimentary understanding of his working methods, compositional aesthetic, and the context of musical life in Vienna during the 1820s. If we acknowledge that Schubert planned both his music and career to a far larger extent than generally recognized, then the trio assumes much greater importance in his professional trajectory, and we can better understand why he placed it at the center of his concert and longed so for its publication.

Another reason commentators have not fully realized the significance of Beethoven in the trio's Andante is because they were distracted by incomplete knowledge about the Swedish folksong, which became an excuse simply not to look any further. Most discussions, popular and scholarly, mentioned the folksong (not available until 1978) and, often, funereal or elegiac associations, then moved on to other issues. That the sketches and original version of the trio also became available only in the 1970s further hampered serious study of the genesis of the work. In recent years it has become increasingly clear that Schubert enjoyed experimenting with sophisticated musical games (such as an extended palindrome in *Rosamunde*) and with programmatic associations that he intentionally worked into many compositions.[114] Scholars have long known of the myriad connections between and among his vocal and instrumental music, but the search for more subtle allusions that might carry personal or hermeneutic import has received serious attention only in recent decades. What we have come to expect from Robert Schumann or Alban Berg seemed uncharacteristic for Schubert, but that view needs to be revised.

"Take these last farewell kisses": Another Homage to Beethoven

I have concentrated on musical evidence and reception to support my claim that the trio is Schubert's homage to Beethoven. The hermeneutic implications are enhanced when we go outside the work to its performance context and consider other pieces Schubert presented on his 26 March program, because the whole event was haunted by Beethoven's death. There is uncertainty about the first movement of a "new string quartet" that opened the concert, which had to be either the D Minor or G Major. Deutsch supposed it to be the latter, saying only that "if the D Minor had been chosen it is certain that the movement played would have been the second, the variations on 'Death and the Maiden'" (*SDB*, 752). Schubert scholar Christa Landon evidently had reason to believe it was the D Minor, but died in a plane crash before she could publish her findings.[115] The hidden memorial aspect of the concert would support the argument that it was the D-Minor Quartet, known as "Death and the Maiden" because it is based on Schubert's euphonious song (D531). Scholars have argued the entire quartet is permeated with the idea of death, culminating in a tarantella finale that alludes to *Erlkönig*.[116]

Schubert wrote one work specifically for his concert: *Auf dem Strom*.[117] As we saw earlier, Rellstab sent poems to Beethoven that were ultimately

a) Beethoven, Symphony No. 3: second movement.

b) Schubert, *Auf dem Strom.*

Example 8. Comparison of Beethoven's *Eroica* (mm. 1–4) and Schubert's *Auf dem Strom* (mm. 50–54).

passed on to Schubert, who set ten of them in 1828. In an article from 1982, Rufus Hallmark argued that *Auf dem Strom* quotes the *Eroica*, in fact the same passage opening the funeral march that I hear echoed in the trio's Andante.[118] The use of the horn obligato, the instrument with such a prominent role in the *Eroica*, is also suggestive (see Example 8).[119] Like the text of *Se solen sjunker*, Rellstab's poem concerns leave-taking and farewells. The first stanza reads:

Nimm die letzten Abschiedsküsse	Take these last farewell kisses,
Und die wehenden, die Grüsse	And the wafted greetings
Die ich noch ans Ufer sende,	That I send to the shore,
Eh' Dein Fuss sich scheidend wende!	Before your foot turns to leave!
Schon wird von des Stromes Wogen	Already the boat is pulled away
Rasch der Nachen fortgezogen,	By the waves' rapid current,
Doch den tränendunklen Blick	But longing forever draws back
Zieht die Sehnsucht stets zurück!	My gaze, clouded with tears![120]

Schubert set the five-stanza poem in an ABABA form with the B sections alluding to the funeral march of the *Eroica*. Hallmark explores other connections to Beethoven, notably to *An die ferne Geliebte*.[121] Commentators had noted the affective affinity to Beethoven long before concrete musical connections were suggested by Hallmark,[122] and since then Larry Hamberlin has identified an allusion in the horn part at the beginning of the song (mm. 2–9) that echoes the bridge passage in the finale of Beethoven's Fifth Symphony (mm. 26–36).[123] Hallmark argues that the musical and biographical evidence suggests "Schubert may have composed *Auf dem Strom* in memory of Beethoven. He wrote it for the concert on the anniversary of Beethoven's death, selected a genre which he knew had won Beethoven's hearty approval, chose an appropriate text by a writer whose poems had been intended for Beethoven to set, and paid homage to Beethoven by imitating and quoting his music."[124] Two works on Schubert's concert program therefore allude to the *Eroica*, specifically—and fittingly—to the *Marcia funebre*, both are connected as well with songs whose texts deal with farewells, and both reference the Fifth Symphony: in *Auf dem Strom* with an allusion, in the trio with an all-too-obvious quotation that Schubert therefore discarded.[125]

"Who shall stand beside him?": Franz Schubert Lies Here

Schubert lived eight more months after his concert. Grillparzer's question as to who would emerge as Beethoven's successor assumed unanticipated poignancy as he accelerated an already staggering pace of composition and furthered his ambitious "strivings after the highest in art." In a creative achievement with few parallels in music history, Schubert produced some of his greatest works, including *Schwanengesang*, the Mass in E-flat, the Fantasy in F Minor for piano duet, the String Quintet in C Major, the last three piano sonatas, brief sacred and keyboard pieces, and Lieder. He may have returned as well to his opera project, *Der Graf von Gleichen*. Volcanic outbursts continued to interrupt beautiful slow movements. He wrote more funereal laments and commentators have pointed to many Beethovenian connections in these pieces.[126] One of the most intriguing late works is relatively unfamiliar because it is incomplete: sketches for a Symphony in D Major (D936a), which may as well allude to Beethoven by referencing the trombone Equale that Schubert heard repeatedly at Beethoven's funeral.[127] Rita Steblin, after looking at a variety of evidence, has concluded that Schubert's late works "seem to be filled with hidden messages and secret tributes, in particular to Beethoven."[128]

As his compositions were posthumously unearthed over the course of the nineteenth century, many came to believe that in them Schubert came to stand by Beethoven and surpassed what Beethoven himself achieved at the comparable age. (Schubert died at 31 years, 9 months, and 19 days, close to Beethoven's age when he wrote his "Heiligenstadt Testament" and contemplated suicide.) Schubert not only stood figuratively next to Beethoven, but too soon lay literally buried nearby. Stories concerning his final days and the aftermath of his death frequently enlisted the figure of Beethoven, and biographers ever more often juxtaposed the two, causing Beethoven to haunt Schubert's posthumous reception in ways that increasingly defined his popular image.[129]

At the time of Beethoven's death, and extending through the summer after Schubert's concert, Schubert lived with Schober in the center of Vienna. He moved in September to his brother Ferdinand's apartment in the district of Wieden. An oft-repeated tale that comes from Beethoven's assistant Karl Holz, the violinist who played at Schubert's concert, has a piece by Beethoven as the last music the dying composer heard. According to Holz, Schubert requested that he arrange a private bedside performance of the String Quartet in C-sharp Minor, Op. 131: "Schubert was sent into such transports of delight and enthusiasm and was so overcome that [we] all feared for him. . . . The quartet was the last music he heard. The King of Harmony had sent the King of Song a friendly bidding to the crossing!"[130]

Schubert died on the afternoon of 19 November and the funeral was held two days later at the Parish Church of St. Joseph in the Margareten district. Among the works sung was his *Pax vobiscum* (D551), fitted with new words by Schober. The body was then transferred the considerable distance to the Church of St. Gertrud in Währing for a second service and the coffin interred near Beethoven in the cemetery. Within a week there was talk about raising funds for a monument. Schubert's friend Johann Baptist Jenger wrote to Josef Hüttenbrenner that Schober "believed it would be best if the Requiem cost as little as possible so that more money can be put toward the monument and purchase of the grave."[131] Jenger also wrote to Marie Pachler, a pianist Beethoven had admired and whom Schubert had visited in Graz in September 1827, about a subscription for the monument: "He has already been given a grave to himself, three graves away from Beethoven's, in the new Währing cemetery" (*SDB*, 831). Jenger mentioned preparations for a performance of a Requiem by Anselm Hüttenbrenner to be sung at the Court Chapel of St. Augustin on 23 December at eleven in the morning. An announcement of it in newspapers included an appeal to "friends of music" for donations leading to a monument to be constructed "at the side of the immortal composer Beethoven" (*SDB*, 845–46; *FSD*, Nos. 666–68). The service was even noticed in the French press, which commented: "A subscription was opened to erect a monument to him next to Beethoven, whose friend he was" (*SDB*, 850). The evening of the Requiem Mass a Schubertiade was held at Spaun's house at which Vogl sang some of Schubert's last songs, including *Der Doppelgänger* and *Die Taubenpost*.[132] Deutsch speculates that a long and personal memorial poem Bauernfeld wrote, published years later, was read that evening; it makes various oblique references to Beethoven, including lines that further suggest Schubert's reluctance to form a personal relationship with the "master":

For truly he'll outlast our deepest sorrows
In realms beyond which ever to us call,
Where earlier another master went,
Who now he may approach to his content. (*SDB*, 841)

Obituaries appeared in the Viennese and foreign press, the most illuminating of which were written by friends, including Spaun, Sonnleithner, Bauernfeld, and Johann Mayrhofer.[133] Many mentioned Beethoven and some, such as Spaun's, made a concluding remark about Schubert's grave and its proximity to Beethoven:

> That heart of his, so rich in benevolence as in music, now reposes in the cool of the grave prepared for the deceased next to Beethoven's. A memorial stone, erected by friends and admirers, will show posterity who reposes here and how much we loved him, so that we shall not be subjected to the same reproach as our forebears, who neglected to mark for us the grave which encloses the bones of Mozart.[134]

As in the aftermath of Beethoven's death the previous year, albeit to a lesser extent, memorial poems, compositions, and concerts commemorated Schubert's passing, with some of the honors used to raise money for the monument. A brief poem appeared in the *Wiener Zeitschrift für Kunst, Literatur, Theater und Mode*, written by Schubert's friend Franz Xaver von Schlechta, that began: "The Muses weep, one favorite joins another: Wherefore thou too, so young, so full of hope?"[135] Bauernfeld wrote a poem, beginning with the death dates of both composers and continuing: "Who gives us another *Eroica*? / Who fresh Miller songs? / The reign of glorious Music / is over and shall not return."[136] Diabelli released two keyboard fugues that used as a subject "the name of the too soon departed composer," one by Simon Sechter and the other by Abbé Stadler. Anselm Hüttenbrenner, who had published a musical obituary for Beethoven (*Nachruf an Beethoven*), now did the same for his friend, basing it on the opening of the Piano Sonata in B-flat.[137]

As we saw earlier, the success of Schubert's 26 March concert had led to plans for repeating it, but the event ultimately became a posthumous benefit, half of the proceeds going to the monument. Anna Fröhlich organized a concert held on the eve of what would have been Schubert's thirty-second birthday, 30 January 1829 (Figure 5). The Friday evening concert featured most of the performers involved with the original 26 March program, again took place at the Musikverein, and again fea-

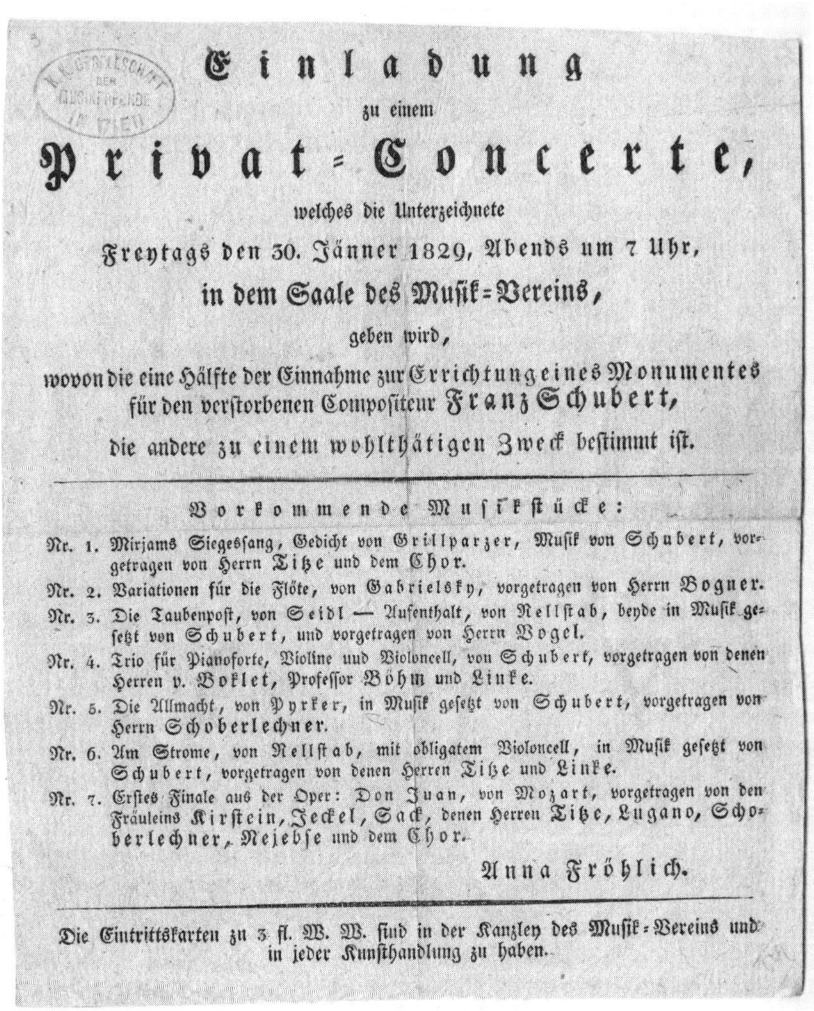

Einladung
zu einem
Privat-Concerte,
welches die Unterzeichnete
Freytags den 30. Jänner 1829, Abends um 7 Uhr,
in dem Saale des Musik-Vereins,
geben wird,
wovon die eine Hälfte der Einnahme zur Errichtung eines Monumentes
für den verstorbenen Compositeur Franz Schubert,
die andere zu einem wohlthätigen Zweck bestimmt ist.

Vorkommende Musikstücke:

Nr. 1. Mirjams Siegessang, Gedicht von Grillparzer, Musik von Schubert, vorgetragen von Herrn Titze und dem Chor.
Nr. 2. Variationen für die Flöte, von Gabrielsky, vorgetragen von Herrn Bogner.
Nr. 3. Die Taubenpost, von Seidl — Aufenthalt, von Rellstab, beyde in Musik gesetzt von Schubert, und vorgetragen von Herrn Vogel.
Nr. 4. Trio für Pianoforte, Violine und Violoncell, von Schubert, vorgetragen von denen Herren v. Boklet, Professor Böhm und Linke.
Nr. 5. Die Allmacht, von Pyrker, in Musik gesetzt von Schubert, vorgetragen von Herrn Schoberlechner.
Nr. 6. Am Strome, von Rellstab, mit obligatem Violoncell, in Musik gesetzt von Schubert, vorgetragen von denen Herren Titze und Linke.
Nr. 7. Erstes Finale aus der Oper: Don Juan, von Mozart, vorgetragen von den Fräuleins Kirstein, Jeckel, Sack, denen Herren Titze, Lugano, Schoberlechner, Rejebse und dem Chor.

Anna Fröhlich.

Die Eintrittskarten zu 3 fl. W. W. sind in der Kanzley des Musik-Vereins und in jeder Kunsthandlung zu haben.

Figure 5. Program for Anna Fröhlich's concert, 30 January 1829.

tured the E-flat Trio as the centerpiece. The program began with the premiere of *Mirjams Siegesgesang*, sung by Tietze and chorus with a two-piano accompaniment. There followed flute variations by Johann Wilhelm Gabrielsky, played by Ferdinand Bogner (Barbara Fröhlich's husband), *Die Taubenpost* (Schubert's last completed work), and *Aufenthalt*, sung by Vogl. The trio was again performed by Böhm, Linke, and Bocklet. Johann Karl Schoberlechner (rather than Vogl) sang *Die Allmacht*, and Tietze repeated *Auf dem Strom*, but this time with Linke playing the obbligato horn part on the cello. The evening ended with the first-act finale from Mozart's *Don Giovanni*. The successful concert was to be repeated on 21 February but due to Anna Fröhlich being ill was postponed until 5 March.[138]

These concerts, sales of Hüttenbrenner's *Nachruf an Schubert* and of a lithograph of Schubert by Josef Teltscher,[139] combined with other contributions, funded the memorial stone and a cast-iron bust of the composer, a rarity in Vienna at the time. The monument was based on a design by Schober and the bust sculpted by Josef Alois Dialer, a young artist who had known Schubert and who may have based the sculpture on the death mask.[140] Grillparzer sketched five epitaphs, one of which alluded to Beethoven: "He was placed near the best ones when he died, and yet he was still scarcely halfway in his career."[141] In collaboration with Schober and Jenger, the poet helped administer the project and in July 1830 wrote an announcement that was not published but may have been distributed: "All Schubert's friends and admirers, but especially those who have actively shown their feelings for him by contributions to his monument, are informed that this memorial, very successfully executed by a skilled hand and adorned with a good likeness of the deceased in the form of a cast-iron bust, has been completed and erected in the churchyard of Währing, where it is open to general inspection."[142] The Vienna *Allgemeiner musikalischer Anzeiger* published an image of the grave in November 1830, noting that the "tombstone is simple—as simple as [Schubert's] songs; but it conceals a profound soul, as they do" (*SDB*, 907; see Figure 1 above).

Währing Cemetery was destined to become a pilgrimage site (Figure 6). Schumann visited Vienna in the fall of 1838, the trip on which he received the music for the "Great" C-Major Symphony from Ferdinand. His deep love for Schubert's music grew as he learned more, prompting him to remark concerning the epitaph that it is "pointless to guess at what more [Schubert] might still have achieved. He accomplished enough; and let those men be praised who strove and accomplished as did he."[143] When he visited the cemetery he "gazed long on those two sacred graves, almost envying the person buried between them—a certain Count O'Donnell [*sic*]."[144] Earlier that year his future wife, Clara Wieck, had concertized in Vienna and he had asked her: "Will you not pay a visit to our Schubert? And Beethoven? And take with you some sprigs of myrtle, bind them together in two, and place them on the graves. Speak softly your name and mine as you do so—not another word. You understand me?"[145] Schumann had been aware of Schubert's music from a distance when the composer was still alive—the eighteen-year-old "cried all night" upon learning of his death,[146] and he became a great advocate in the decades to come as Schubert's fame grew. He continued to be particularly drawn to

Figure 6. Nineteenth-century photograph of the graves of Beethoven and Schubert in Währing Cemetery.

Schubert's "immortal Trio." He not only wrote a review of the piece but also offered a kind of criticism of the work in music through his own early Piano Quartet in C Minor (1829), Piano Quartet in E-flat, Op. 44, Piano Quintet in E-flat, Op. 47, and other compositions.[147]

All the while ever more of Schubert's unknown music was performed and/or published for the first time, including late works like the Piano Trio in B-flat (published in 1836), last piano sonatas (published in 1839 with a dedication to Schumann), C-Major Symphony (premiered in 1839), C-Major String Quintet (published in 1853), E-flat Mass (published in 1865), and "Unfinished" Symphony (premiered in 1865). This activity further enhanced Schubert's artistic stature, turning the screw yet again on Grillparzer's epitaph as "far fairer hopes" were realized. Even Grillparzer's funeral oration came to be reinterpreted: a passage about the other great German artist still living (Goethe), was over time reinterpreted by some as referring to Schubert.[148] Comparisons with Beethoven accelerated as their names became ever more wedded—an apt word that also registers the frequent gendered comparisons made between them.[149] David Gramit and Scott Messing have explored this aspect of Schubert's reception, so I will mention only a comment in connection with their graves. In October 1863 their bodies were exhumed so as to secure them in metal coffins, at which time their skulls were measured and compared.[150] Gerhard von Breuning, who had known them both, remarked that "it was extremely interesting physiologically to compare the compact thickness of Beethoven's skull and the fine, almost feminine thinness of Schubert's, and to relate them, almost directly, to the character of their music."[151] The comparisons were popularized in the biography of Schubert that was published in late 1864 (dated 1865) by Kreissle, who also weighed in on the epitaph:

> Nowadays, when the greater part of Schubert's treasures has been revealed to us, Grillparzer's epitaph, which gave offense so many years ago, sounds to our ears still more strangely, and we may hope that over Schubert's future resting place there will be nothing carved but the name of the composer. As does the simple "Beethoven" over that great man's grave, the word "Schubert" will speak volumes.[152]

And this, uncannily, is what happened. Währing Cemetery was deconsecrated and the bodies of Beethoven and Schubert were transferred in 1888 to the "Grove of Honor" in Vienna's new Central Cemetery. The monument there reads simply "Franz Schubert." The tombstones in Währing remain there as cenotaphs in what is now the Schubert Park—all the graves having long been removed, so that the monuments to Beethoven and Schubert now stand side by side.

NOTES

The genesis of this essay was a re-creation of Schubert's 26 March 1828 concert that I helped produce at the Schubertiade of New York's 92nd Street Y on 26 March 1997. It was in connection with this project that some of the implications of the works on the program and the importance of the anniversary date of Beethoven's death first struck me. In the years since I have had the chance to present versions of this essay at various universities and conferences, and I appreciate the many helpful responses I have received. I am particularly grateful to early suggestions from Scott Burnham and James Sobaskie. This current version, part of a larger project examining events surrounding the deaths of Beethoven and Schubert, benefited from comments by Byron Adams, Luis Garcia-Renart, John M. Gingerich, Dana Gooley, John Halle, Kristina Muxfeldt, and Irene Zedlacher. I am grateful to Dr. Otto Biba and the Archive of the Gesellschaft der Musikfreunde for providing some of the illustrations, previously unpublished.

1. *On Music and Musicians*, ed. Konrad Wolff, trans. Paul Rosenfeld (New York, 1946), 121.

2. John Daverio, *Crossing Paths: Schubert, Schumann, and Brahms* (New York, 2008), 20.

3. Ibid., 20; see also Marie Luise Maintz, *Franz Schubert in der Reception Robert Schumanns* (Kassel, 1995), 26–33.

4. Leipzig *Allgemeine musikalische Zeitung* 30 (10 December 1828), 837ff, reprinted in Till Gerrit Waidelich, ed. *Franz Schubert Dokumente 1817–1830*, vol. 1 (Tutzing, 1993), No. 654; hereafter cited as *FSD* and the number of the document, rather than the page number; a second volume of commentary and additional documents was published in 2003, edited by Ernst Hilmar. The translation concerning the fourth movement is adapted from Daverio, *Crossing Paths*, 20.

5. J. E. Westrup, "The Chamber Music," in *Schubert: A Symposium*, ed. Gerald Abraham (London, 1946), 104. Similar comments are abundant in popular biographies and program notes; for example, Robert Haven Schauffler remarks that "the Andante con moto begins with a long cello cantabile. Schubert is said to have taken it from a Swedish folk song. . . . This mournful melody, with its spectral, oddly accented accompaniment, suggests a funeral march," in *Schubert: The Ariel of Music* (New York, 1949), 209–10.

6. Lawrence Kramer, *Franz Schubert: Sexuality, Subjectivity, Song* (Cambridge, 1998), 152–72. See as well his chapter "Ghost Stories" in *Musical Meaning: Toward a Critical History* (Berkeley, 2002), 265.

7. Leo Treitler, "Language and the Interpretation of Music," in *Reflections of Musical Meaning and its Representations* (Bloomington, IN, 2011), 21. The chapter earlier appeared in Jenefer Robinson, ed., *Music and Meaning*, (Ithaca, NY, 1997), 23–56.

8. *Allgemeiner musikalischer Anzeiger* 6 (7 February 1829), 21, 24; repr. in *FSD*, No. 695.

9. See Michael R. Fling, *Musical Memorials for Musicians: A Guide to Selected Compositions* (Lanham, MD, 2001); and Alec Robertson, *Requiem: Music of Mourning and Consolation* (London, 1967).

10. Christopher Reynolds, *Motives for Allusion: Context and Content in 19th-Century Music* (Cambridge, MA, 2003).

11. Leipzig *Allgemeine musikalische Zeitung* 29 (25 April 1827), 289; hereafter cited as *AMZ*.

12. Beethoven's assistant, violinist Karl Holz, states that Schubert never missed a concert; see Otto Erich Deutsch, *Schubert: A Documentary Biography*, trans. Eric Blom (London, 1946), 536; hereafter cited as *SDB*.

13. See Christopher H. Gibbs, "Performances of Grief: Vienna's Response to the Death of Beethoven," in *Beethoven and His World*, ed. Scott Burnham and Michael P. Steinberg (Princeton, 2000), 227–85. The most detailed study concerning Beethoven's death and its immediate aftermath is Artemio Focher, *Ludwig van Beethoven, 26–29 marzo 1827* (Lucca, 2001).

14. *Der Sammler* 19 (14 April 1827), 179–80 (complete English translation in Gibbs, "Performances of Grief," 264–66); see as well the *Berliner allgemeine musikalische Zeitung* 4 (23 May 1827), 167–68. Eduard von Bauernfeld's diary states that he went to the funeral with Schubert (*SDB*, 622).

15. Ernst Hilmar, "Ferdinand Schuberts Skizze zu einer Autobiographie," in *Schubert-Studien: Festgabe der Oesterreichischen Akademie der Wissenschaften zum Schubert-Jahr 1978*, ed. Franz Grasberger and Othmar Wessely (Vienna, 1978), 94–95; and Gibbs, "Performances of Grief," 243.

16. Heinrich Anschütz, as well as his brothers Eduard and Gustav, knew Schubert. See Otto Erich Deutsch, *Schubert: Memoirs by His Friends*, trans. Rosamond Ley and John Nowell (London, 1958), 222–24; hereafter cited as *SMF*; and Rita Steblin, *Die Unsinnsgesellschaft: Franz Schubert, Leopold Kupelwieser und ihr Freundeskreis* (Vienna, 1998). Concerning Grillparzer's relationship with Schubert, see Otto Erich Deutsch, "Schubert und Grillparzer," *Österreichische Musikzeitschrift* 32 (1977): 497–505.

17. The oration exists in several slightly different variants and has been translated many times; see, for example, *Beethoven: A Documentary Study*, ed. H. C. Robbins Landon (New York, 1970), 395–96; Elliot Forbes, ed., *Thayer's Life of Beethoven*, rev. ed. (Princeton,

1967), 1057–58; Johann Aloys Schlosser, *Beethoven: The First Biography*, ed. Barry Cooper, trans. Reinhard G. Pauly (Portland, OR, 1996), 113–18 and 179–81; Gerhard von Breuning, trans. Henry F. Mins and Maynard Solomon, *Memories of Beethoven: From the House of the Black-Robed Spaniards*, ed. Maynard Solomon (Cambridge, 1992), 109–10 and 141–42. The last two sources discuss variants of the speech, as do the notes to *Franz Grillparzer: Sämtliche Werke*, ed. Peter Frank and Karl Pörnbacher, vol. 3 (Munich, 1964), 1325. Grillparzer objected to the publication of the address without his permission in the *Wiener allgemeine Theaterzeitung* and elsewhere, and published a notice to that effect in the *Theaterzeitung* (19 June 1827); see 3:883.

18. Quoted in Michael Musgrave, *The Music of Brahms* (New York, 1994), 78.

19. *SDB*, 286. Elizabeth Norman McKay's *Franz Schubert: A Biography* (Oxford, 1996) summarizes Schubert's medical history, 319–31.

20. *Franz Schubert: Todesmusik*, ed. Heinz-Klaus Metzger and Rainer Riehn, Musik-Konzepte 97/98 (Munich, 1997).

21. *SDB*, 825; a facsimile of the letter is in *Franz Schubert: Ausstellung der Wiener Stadt- und Landesbibliothek zum 150. Todestag des Komponisten*, ed. Ernst Hilmar and Otto Brusatti (Vienna, 1978), 93.

22. Schubert's grave was number 323 and Beethoven's 290; in between were the Hardtmuth and Schlechta families, and then that of Johann Count O'Donell (*SDB*, 828). Many illustrations depict the graves as side by side or with just one separating them, no doubt for symbolic reasons. See Otto Erich Deutsch, ed. *Franz Schubert: Sein Leben in Bildern* (Munich, 1913), 64–65.

23. Ernst Hilmar rightly notes that Grillparzer was echoing the view of many contemporaries, including some of Schubert's closest friends. See "Zu Grillparzers Inschrift auf Schuberts Grabdenkmal," *Schubert durch die Brille* 29 (2002): 125–28.

24. John M. Gingerich, "Unfinished Considerations: Schubert's 'Unfinished' Symphony in the Context of His Beethoven Project," *19th-Century Music* 31 (2007): 99–112.

25. *SMF*, 383; the comment is in a review in *Die Presse* from 11 March 1862, see *Eduard Hanslick: Sämtliche Schriften*, ed. Dietmar Strauss, vol. 1:6 (Vienna, 2010), 60.

26. *SDB*, 64. Although Schubert's comment is sometimes considered as reflecting a resistance to Beethoven, I have offered another view in Gibbs, "Writing Under the Influence? Salieri and Schubert's Early Opinion of Beethoven," *Current Musicology* 75 (2003): 113–40.

27. In comparison with most nineteenth-century composers, relatively few of Schubert's letters survive (most are in *SDB*). He rarely commented on other composers, but there are a few references to Beethoven, for example, in *SDB*, 265 and 339.

28. Nicholas Temperley, "Schubert and Beethoven's Eight-Six Chord," *19th-Century Music* 5 (1981): 142–54.

29. *SMF*, 66. Maynard Solomon has considered the evidence concerning their personal relationship in his article "Schubert and Beethoven," *19th-Century Music* 3 (1979): 114–25; see as well Walther Dürr, "Wer vermag nach Beethoven noch etwas zu machen? Gedanken über die Beziehungen Schuberts zu Beethoven," in *Franz Schubert*, Musik-Konzepte Sonderband (Munich, 1979), 10–25.

30. *SMF*, 325; see also 366. Schindler recounts the story in the 1860 third edition of his biography of Beethoven, but, as Solomon notes, did not report this information in the first two editions of his book ("Schubert and Beethoven," 121).

31. *SDB*, 232. As Solomon has observed, Hüttenbrenner is unlikely to have risked making up such a glowing recommendation when Peters could confirm the reference directly with Beethoven; but, Solomon adds, it still may not reflect what Beethoven actually said, only what Hüttenbrenner thought he had said ("Schubert and Beethoven," 115).

32. In 1823, for example, Beethoven's nephew Karl wrote in a conversation book: "They greatly praise Schubert, but it is said that he hides himself" (*SDB*, 288). The obser-

vation comes around the time of Schubert's illness and hospitalization. Three years later Karl Holz asked, "Do you know *Erlkönig*? [Schubert] always talked very mystically" (*SDB*, 536; also 341).

33. The only document that unequivocally places the two composers together may be a forgery: an 1822 letter written by the critic Johann Friedrich Rochlitz says that Schubert took him to an inn where Beethoven was eating (*SDB*, 228); published in Leipzig *AMZ* 30 (2 January 1828), 2; *FSD*, No. 552b; *SMF*, 303–4; and *Thayer's Life of Beethoven*, 800–801.

34. Rellstab's poems had recently been published when Schubert set them.

35. *SMF*, 303; Rellstab, *Aus meinem Leben* (Berlin, 1861), 244–45.

36. Rufus Hallmark, "Schubert's 'Auf dem Strom,'" in *Schubert Studies: Problems of Style and Chronology*, ed. Eva Badura-Skoda and Peter Branscombe (Cambridge, 1982), 44.

37. *SMF*, 192; Rita Steblin, "Schubert und der Maler Josef Teltscher," *Schubert durch die Brille* 11 (1993): 119–32.

38. Solomon observes that Anselm had not discussed this event in his 1854 reminiscence of Schubert ("Schubert and Beethoven," 122). As I have explored in an earlier article, there are good reasons to be skeptical about the Hüttenbrenners' later accounts, although it does seem that Anselm was in the room when Beethoven died. See Gibbs, "Performances of Grief," 232–35.

39. The D-Minor Quartet, "Death and the Maiden" (D810), written the same month as the letter to Kupelwieser, was published in 1831; the third quartet, the G Major (D887), was composed in 1826 and published in 1851.

40. John M. Gingerich suggests that what Schubert meant was that chamber music would make a name for him and thus open doors to orchestral performances in "Unfinished Considerations," 106.

41. Some of Beethoven's admirers wrote an open letter urging him to give the concert in Vienna. Beth Shamgar observes that many of these people were connected to Schubert as publishers, literary collaborators, performers, or patrons in "Three Missing Months in Schubert's Biography: A Further Consideration of Beethoven's Influence on Schubert," *Musical Quarterly* 73 (1989): 417–34. Josef Hüttenbrenner, Fritz von Hartmann, and Schuppanzigh were among those who performed at Beethoven's concert, which Leopold von Sonnleithner helped to organize.

42. See John M. Gingerich, *Schubert's Beethoven Project* (Cambridge, 2014).

43. Clemens Hellsberg, "Ignaz Schuppanzigh (Wien 1776–1830): Leben und Wirken" (PhD diss, University of Vienna, 1979).

44. See John M. Gingerich, "Ignaz Schuppanzigh and Beethoven's Late Quartets," *Musical Quarterly* 93 (2010): 450–513. Gingerich and I have identified the programs of almost all of Schuppanzigh's quartet concerts from the 1820s. In his subscription series there were twenty-four concerts (four groups of six) during seasons 1823–24, 1824–25, 1826–27; and 18 (three groups of six) in 1825–26, 1827–28, 1828–29.

45. Vogl's primary connection to Beethoven came from singing the role of Pizarro in the 1814 version of *Fidelio*, performances that deeply influenced the seventeen-year-old Schubert. The Credo of the Mass in G quotes the prisoners' chorus from the opera. Vogl performed in Schubert's *Zwillingsbrüder*, presented at the Kärntnertor Theater in June 1820.

46. See John M. Gingerich's essay in this volume.

47. See *Thayer's Life of Beethoven*, 586; Schubert's comment came in a letter to Schott (*SDB*, 740).

48. Gingerich, *Schubert's Beethoven Project*.

49. *SDB*, 694. Most published reviews of Schubert's music that appeared during his lifetime are collected in *FSD* and many are translated in *SDB*. There is what seems to be an oblique reference to Schubert in a review of Beethoven's Scottish folksongs—my thanks to Robin Wallace for this information.

50. Tobias Haslinger published the work as *Trauerklänge bei Beethoven's Grabe: Vierstimmiger Männer-Chor, nach einer Original-Melodie des Verewigten: Die Worte von Franz Grillparzer*, in a supplement to the *Allgemeiner musikalischer Anzeiger* 12 (21 March 1829); see also Leipzig *AMZ* 30 (7 May 1828), 310–11.

51. *SMF*, 237. Bauernfeld's earlier 1829 memorial article simply stated that Schubert had been "persuaded by his friends" to give the concert (*SDB*, 893).

52. See Otto Biba, "Franz Schubert in den musikalischen Abendunterhaltungen der Gesellschaft der Musikfreunde," in *Schubert-Studien*, 7–31; and "Franz Schubert und die Gesellschaft der Musikfreunde in Wien" in *Schubert-Kongress Wien 1978: Bericht*, ed. Otto Brusatti (Graz, 1979), 23–36.

53. Other events included a Gesellschaft-Concerts on 23 March, a concert by violinist Joseph Mayseder on 27 March, and one that day as well for violist Franz Xaver Glöggl, and a performance of Handel's *Jephtha* on 28 March. See *Chronologisches Verzeichniss aller auf den fünf Theatern Wien's gegebenen Vorstellungen; vom ersten November 1827 bis letzten October 1828* (Vienna, 1829), 56–57.

54. Since the quartet had been published a few months earlier it is conceivable the work had already been performed somewhere. The lithographed program given in Figure 2, which to my knowledge has not been published previously, does not list the piece as "new," which would have been expected. The other works on the concert were the Variations in G on a Theme from *Judas Makkabäus*, WoO 45; *Der Wachtelschlag*, WoO 129 (sung by Ludwig Tietze); and the Trio for Piano, Clarinet, and Cello, Op. 11.

55. When Schubert gave his concert he was living with Schober in the Tuchlauben next door to the Musikverein. At this time Schober was running a Lithographic Institute he had taken over from Count Pálffy and he no doubt produced the handsome program. The first version is reproduced in *FSD*, No. 599a and comes from a private collection; it was first published in Gerrit Waidelich, "Weitere Dokumente aus 1828 und 1833," *Schubert durch die Brille* 19 (1997): 58. Figure 3 is another copy of this same version, although at some point someone changed the date to 26—there is also an annotation of "1828." (When this was added is not known—it may have happened long after the event.) This copy of the program, now in the Gesellschaft der Musikfreunde, has not been previously discussed in the Schubert literature; it was reproduced in a 1928 program re-creating the concert at the Gesellschaft itself and in Heinrich Werlé, *Franz Schubert: Der Mensch und sein Werk* (Berlin, 1941), 288. Yet another copy of this first version (also with the date hand-corrected) is better known, having been reproduced in Hilmar and Brusatti, *Franz Schubert*, 86, and elsewhere. There has been a great amount of confusion about the different versions of the program largely because of mistakes Deutsch made in his collection of documents, where he was misled by a review of the concert. Margret Jestremski attempted to sort out the issue and reproduces what she states are three versions of the program—in fact, two of them are of the same first printed version and differ only in the hand-written change of date in one of them. There is, actually, a second printed version of the program, which is referenced in the following endnote. The issue of the different versions of the program is complicated by the limited access to the original documents and that they are not usually reproduced as high-quality photographs; see Jestremski, "75 Jahre 'Privatkonzert'—Eine längst fällige Korrektur," *Schubert durch die Brille* 29 (2002): 115–24.

56. *FSD*, No. 603 on page 295 of the commentary volume, No. 2—the document was incorrectly numbered in volume 1 of *FSD*, adding further to the confusion about the different printed versions of the program. The commentary states that the printed date for the program on p. 295 is "21," but "28" is clearly visible underneath the 26, as it also is in the third and final version of the program, noted by Deutsch (*SDB*, 754) and Waidelich ("Weitere Dokumente aus 1828 und 1833," 63), but disputed as well by Jestremski ("75 Jahre 'Privatkonzert,'" 120). This crucial printed alteration in the second version suggests the date of Schubert's concert was moved before the change of programming (the Lied in No. 2c).

57. *SDB*, 755; *FSD*, No. 603a. This is the most often reproduced version in the standard Schubert literature, beginning as early as Richard Heuberger, *Franz Schubert* (Berlin, 1902), 85; Walter Dahms, *Schubert* (Berlin, 1912), 105; and the next year in Deutsch, *Franz Schubert: Sein Leben in Bildern*, 178.

58. See Schubert's letter to Probst (*SDB*, 724f) and also Spaun's reminiscence (*SMF*, 138).

59. *SDB*, 752; Schuppanzigh played a concert on 9 March featuring Beethoven's String Quartet in A Minor, Op. 132, and conducted a concert for Josef Böhm on 16 March. He had performed at Linke's previous academies. Gingerich reasonably believes that had he not played on the 23rd that fact would have been mentioned in a review or on the program.

60. *SDB*, 751–52; and *FSD*, Nos. 600–602.

61. *SDB*, 751. Ernst Hilmar speculates that the announcement may have been written by Franz Xaver von Schlechta—see commentary for *FSD*, No. 600.

62. The title of the song was listed as *Auf dem Strome*, as it was in some of the concert announcements, but not in the manuscript or first publication.

63. Tietze had sung Beethoven's *Der Wachtelschlag* on Linke's concert and often performed Beethoven's music.

64. Hallmark, "Schubert's 'Auf dem Strom,'" 25.

65. The program listed the work as *Schlachtgesang*, which is not the title of the manuscript or first publication.

66. *SMF*, 28. Bauernfeld mentions "a larger concert the following winter," which suggests perhaps an orchestral concert—if we remember that Beethoven's 1824 concert was Schubert's model, then his 26 March concert, with its repertory of vocal and chamber music, was more modest (*SDB*, 893).

67. See Badura-Skoda, "The Chronology of Schubert's Piano Trios," 277–95.

68. Pirated editions of some Schubert Lieder had appeared abroad, as well as the Lied *Widerschein* in a Leipzig periodical. See Christopher H. Gibbs, "Einige Bemerkungen zur Veröffentlichung und zu den frühen Ausgaben von Schuberts *Erlkönig*," *Schubert durch die Brille* 12 (1994): 33–48.

69. The piece was announced for sale in the *Wiener-Zeitung* on 11 December 1828 (*FSD*, No. 656a). The work sold very well in the decade that followed.

70. The opus numbers of both trios are apparently Schubert's own—certainly the latter is. As the manuscript of Opus 99 is lost, there is no certainty about its dating, although most writers, beginning with Schumann, thought it the earlier of the two. The best arguments for the datings are in Badura-Skoda, "The Chronology of Schubert's Piano Trios."

71. The *Neue Schubert-Ausgabe* and Deutsch thematic catalogue make various mistakes concerning chronology and performances, which Eva Badura-Skoda has corrected; my findings concerning the E-flat Trio support her conclusions in "The Chronology of Schubert's Piano Trios."

72. See *SDB*, 724f and *SMF*, 138. Franz von Hartmann mentions this Schubertiade, where "we nearly all got tipsy" (*SDB*, 724–25).

73. Of Beethoven's six published piano trios with opus numbers (not counting the string version of Opus 11), all but Op. 70, No. 1 ("Ghost") are in four movements. The order of the slow movement and scherzo are switched in the "Archduke."

74. Heinrich Kreissle von Hellborn, *Franz Schubert* (Vienna, 1865), 552.

75. Sonnleithner had provided an earlier report to Ferdinand Luib for use in a biography the latter was intending to write but never completed, instead passing on his collected materials to Kreissle (*SMF*, 115).

76. *Chronologisches Verzeichniss aller auf den fünf Theatern Wien's gegebenen Vorstellungen; vom ersten November 1826 bis letzten October 1827* (Vienna, 1828), 66. Schubert scholarship has traditionally said that Berg arrived in October or November; at the concert he was identified as a student of Siboni.

77. Manfred Willford, "Das Urbild des Andante aus Schuberts Klaviertrio Es-Dur, D 929," *Österreichische Musikzeitschrift* 33 (1978): 278.

78. *Mirjams Siegesgesang* shows Schubert's interest in Handel and suggests another Beethoven connection as Schubert may have had access to the Arnold edition of the Baroque master's works, which had been sent to Beethoven from England. As with the Rellstab poems Schubert received from Beethoven's estate, the possibility of access to the Handel scores and perhaps to Beethoven's sketches for a string quintet and symphony, raise intriguing issues I hope to explore at a later time. When *Mirjams Siegesgesang* was premiered two months after his death, a critic perceptively observed that Schubert was able to "fuse the powerful seriousness of Handel with the fiery passion of Beethoven." *Der Sammler* 21 (21 February 1829), 92.

79. In late October 1827 Bauernfeld recorded in his diary that Grillparzer was helping him and Schubert with their opera project *Der Graf von Gleichen* by sending the libretto to the Königstadt Theater in Berlin (*SDB*, 682).

80. Grillparzer, *Sämtliche Werke*, 3:883ff. The service is described in the *Berliner allgemeine musikalische Zeitung* 5 (9 January 1828), 16.

81. This is what Ferdinand claimed in a later autobiographical sketch; see Hilmar, "Ferdinand Schuberts Skizze zu einer Autobiographie," 94; and Rita Steblin, "So wurde nach Ferd. Schubert's Entwurfe Beethovens Grabmahl aufgeführt," *Wiener Beethoven-Gesellschaft Mitteilungsblatt* 30 (1999): 9–16.

82. Fröhlich thought Schubert used the song in the Andante of the G-Major String Quartet, but that work was written well before Berg's visit to Vienna. Schubert did not compose any quartets after his arrival.

83. See Otto Erich Deutsch, *Schubert: Thematic Catalogue of All His Works* (London, 1951), 453, where the information is credited to Gustav Nottebohm (see also *SMF*, 257). Contrary to some claims, Nottebohm did not mention Berg's song in his *Thematisches Verzeichniss der im Druck erschienenen Werke von Franz Schubert* (Vienna, 1874).

84. *5 schwedische Original-Lieder für 1 Singstimme mit Clavierbegltg componirt von Mr. B.* Figure 4 is from the Archive of the Gesellschaft der Musikfreunde (VI 29868; Q 21109); see also the entry in the elegant exhibition catalogue *Schubert 200 Jahre*, ed. Ilija Dürhammer and Gerrit Waidelich (Heidelberg, 1997), 162.

85. Deutsch wrote that "the dates of these two works [G-Major Quartet and E-flat Trio] seem to bear out Sonnleithner [that Schubert used Berg's Swedish song in his trio]; but, to this day [1958], the theme has not been found. Anna [Fröhlich] may have been right [that the song was for a Quartet], if there is any truth in the story at all, inasmuch as she speaks of a song of Berg's, while Sonnleithner had spoken of a Swedish folksong" (*SMF*, 257). See also Brown, "Schubert and Some Folksongs," *Music and Letters* 53 (1972): 173–78. Although the song is not discussed in the *Neue Schubert-Ausgabe* (1975; see note 107), by the time of the 1986 critical report by Hans-Günther Bauer and Arnold Feil, it was acknowledged.

86. Manfred Willfort, "Das Urbild des Andante," 277–83.

87. See William Kinderman, "Wandering Archetypes in Schubert's Instrumental Music," *19th-Century Music* 22 (1997): 208–22. Hugh Macdonald explored the "steady tread" found in many of Schubert's compositions in "Schubert's Pendulum," in *Beethoven's Century: Essays on Composers and Themes* (Rochester, 2008), 16–27. Basil Smallman observes that the slow movements of both of Schubert's piano trios start "in an 'unclassical' manner with two preparatory bars before the entry of the main theme, and thereby set a precedent which was followed by numerous trio composers later in the nineteenth century." Smallman, *The Piano Trio: Its History, Technique, and Repertoire* (Oxford, 1990), 75. The sketches show that Schubert originally had three introductory measures for the piano, the last one having even eighth notes without the dotted rhythm.

88. Richard N. Burke, "The Marche Funèbre from Beethoven to Mahler" (PhD diss., City University of New York, 1991). In relation to the *Eroica* see as well a discussion of earlier works by various composers in Constantin Floros, *Beethoven's* Eroica, trans. Ernest

Bernhardt-Kabisch (Frankfurt, 2013), 58–63. Solomon discusses Beethoven's many death pieces, including his first published composition, WoO 63, written at age eleven; *Beethoven*, rev. ed. (New York, 1998), 70–72.

89. Leopold von Sonnleithner's obituary for Schubert explicitly calls it a funeral march (*SDB*, 873).

90. See Christopher H. Gibbs, "Beyond Song: Instrumental Transformations and Infiltrations from Schubert to Mahler," in *The Cambridge Companion to the Lied*, ed. James Parsons (Cambridge, 2004), 223–42.

91. There were various connections among this group: Leopold von Sonnleithner, a lawyer, composed, performed, and conducted—he was related to Grillparzer, who also composed; both were closely associated with the Fröhlich sisters.

92. After studying the surviving sketches for the trio, Brian Newbould argued that Schubert added a passage to the second theme of the first movement (mm. 72–74; 81–83) derived from the song; see *Schubert: The Music and the Man* (Berkeley and Los Angeles, 1997), 372.

93. The Swedish in Willfort's article differs in various respects from the manuscript in the archive of the Gesellschaft der Musikfreunde, reproduced here for the first time. Although I have normalized the spelling, there is good reason to believe that the person who wrote the manuscript, perhaps Aloys Fuchs, did not know the language. My thanks to Thorvald Daggenhurst for assistance with the Swedish.

94. Mozart used a similar formal plan in his C-Major String Quintet (which Schubert studied in 1824) and that served Beethoven in the second movement of his Seventh Symphony, one of his most popular works. Schubert quoted the opening theme in the fifth variation of his Eight Variations on an Original Theme (D813). See Temperley, "Schubert and Beethoven's Eight-Six Chord"; and Shamgar, "Three Missing Months in Schubert's Biography." Charles Fisk calls the form a "Schubertian specialty" and makes fascinating connections to Schubert's allegorical tale "Mein Traum" in *Returning Cycles: Contexts for the Interpretation of Schubert's Impromptus and Last Sonatas* (Berkeley, 2001), 278.

95. Hugh Macdonald, "Schubert's Volcanic Temper," *The Musical Times* 99 (1978): 949–52, an article elaborated on in "Schubert's Pendulum,"16–27.

96. Maurice J. E. Brown, *Essays on Schubert* (New York, 1966), 17.

97. The only scholar yet to address this aspect of the sketches, so far as I am aware, is Anselm Gerhard, "Franz Schuberts Abschied von Beethoven? Zur 'poetischen Idee' des Es-Dur-Klaviertrios von 1827," *Schubert: Perspektiven* 2/1 (2002): 1–21. A speculative reconstruction of the original conception of the movement based on the sketches has been most effectively recorded by the Abegg-Trio with spoken commentary written by Anselm Gerhard: *Schuberts Werkstatt (Ein Text von Anselm Gerhard mit Musikbeispielen)*, TACET 996 (Stuttgart, 2001).

98. Maynard Solomon, *Beethoven*, 69; also 71–72, 138, 263.

99. This quotation has been noticed at least once before by Stephen E. Hefling and David S. Tartakoff in "Schubert's Chamber Music" in *Nineteenth-Century Chamber Music*, ed. Stephen E. Hefling (New York, 2004), 119.

100. Since so few sketches for Schubert's music survive, it is hard to generalize, but he customarily did not include this sort of accompanimental detail in the sketching process, nor is he here presenting material that relates thematically to what has preceded, which suggests that the final quotation was planned from the outset.

101. Elaine Sisman, "Memory and Invention at the Threshold of Beethoven's Late Style," in *Beethoven and His World*, 51–87; and Janet Schmalfeldt, *In the Process of Becoming: Analytic and Philosophical Perspectives on Form in Early Nineteenth-Century Music* (New York, 2011), 143–46.

102. For discussions of cyclic aspects of the entire trio see Gerhard, "Franz Schuberts Abschied von Beethoven?"; James William Sobaskie, "A Balance Struck: Gesture, Form, and Drama in Schubert's E-flat Major Piano Trio," in *Le style instrumental de Schubert:*

Sources, analyse, contexte, évolution, ed. Xavier Hascher (Paris, 2007), 115–46; and Schmalfeldt, *In the Process of Becoming*, 144–57.

103. Maurice J. E. Brown, *Schubert: A Critical Biography* (London, 1958), 201.

104. Treitler, *Reflections of Musical Meaning*, 21.

105. Kramer, *Franz Schubert*, 157–58.

106. Gingerich, *Schubert's Beethoven Project*, 292–93.

107. Schubert told Probst that "the cuts indicated in the last movement are to be scrupulously observed" (*SDB*, 774). The first cut simply omits the repeat, the second omits mm. 358–407, and the third mm. 463–513. The complete original version of the trio was first published in 1975 and since then it has become increasingly common for musicians to play it; most scholars who have written about the original version feel it is superior to the abbreviated one published in 1828 and therefore best known; see Werner Aderhold, ed., *Neue Schubert-Ausgabe*, series VI, vol. 7 (Kassel, 1975); also Dietrich Berke and Dorothee Hanemann, "Zur formalen Organisation des Schlußsatzes aus Franz Schuberts Klavier-Trio in Es-dur op. 100 (D929)," in *Festschrift Arno Forchert zum 60. Geburtstag am 29. Dezember 1985*, ed. Gerhard Allroggen and Detlef Altenburg (Kassel, 1986), 200–207.

108. Treitler, *Reflections of Musical Meaning*, 22–23.

109. Kramer, *Franz Schubert*, 157.

110. Daverio, *Crossing Paths*, 28.

111. Schubert's dedications are given in *SDB*, 947–49.

112. See Gibbs, "Performances of Grief," 246–47.

113. See Christopher Gibbs, *Life of Schubert* (Cambridge, 2001).

114. Brian Newbould, "A Schubert Palindrome," *19th-Century Music* 15 (1992): 209–10.

115. It is usually assumed that the G-Major Quartet was played, most likely because of Deutsch's influential conjecture. Ernst Hilmar and Otto Brussati mention Landon's finding in *Franz Schubert*, 86.

116. See Christoph Wolff, "Schubert's 'Der Tod und das Mädchen': Analytical and Explanatory Notes on the Song D 531 and the Quartet D 810," in *Schubert Studies*, 143–71; and Gingerich, *Schubert's Beethoven Project*, 85–104.

117. Schubert's only other concerted Lied is the much more famous *Der Hirt auf dem Felsen* (D965) with clarinet, one of his last compositions.

118. Hallmark, "Schubert's 'Auf dem Strom,'" 25–46.

119. The song was published in 1829 specifying "Waldhorn oder Violoncelle (obligat)." The instrumentalist who performed the part, Josef Lewy, was with his brother Eduard one of the leading horn virtuosos in Vienna during the 1820s. Linke performed the piece on 30 January 1829 at one of the memorial concerts to raise money for Schubert's gravestone. Whether the cello scoring had Schubert's authority is not known, but when played on the string instrument the similarity to the E-flat Trio is of course more striking. Christopher Reynolds links the use of horn to Beethoven's trombone Equale played at his funeral in *Motives for Allusion*, 126.

120. Translation from Richard Wigmore, *Schubert: The Complete Song Texts* (London, 1988), 57–58.

121. The manuscript for *Auf dem Strom* reveals an alteration Schubert made to the poem that renders it more personal. Rufus Hallmark considers the change in text from *vom* to *zum*, making the line "no song can penetrate *from* the shore" become "no song can penetrate *to* the shore," thus "identifying the persona as the singer of the song, and thus as a composer whose creative life is at an end." "Schubert's 'Auf dem Strom,'" 46.

122. Ibid., 40. Hallmark cites Alfred Einstein's comment that "if any of Schubert's songs was inspired by the spirit and 'sentiment' of Beethoven's *An die ferne Geliebte*, it is this one." See Einstein, *Schubert: A Musical Portrait* (New York, 1951), 302–3.

123. Larry Hamberlin, "The Beethoven Allusions in 'Auf dem Strom' (D. 943)," in *The Unknown Schubert*, ed. Barbara M. Reul and Lorraine Byrne Bodley (Aldershot, 2008), 137–45.

124. Hallmark, "Schubert's 'Auf dem Strom,'" 45.

125. Schubert was apparently long enamored with the *Eroica* and commentators have remarked on other pieces of his that they feel owe it a debt. In this instance an anecdote concerning a lost "Eroica Fantasy" that he allegedly wrote in 1825, long dismissed as apocryphal, assumes more interest and should perhaps be taken more seriously. According to Albert Böhm, "One day I found, among the dust in the loft, a hitherto entirely unknown manuscript, bearing, on the front, the title 'Fantasie by Franz Schubert' and, as signature, the name 'Watzl.' Experts, like Professor [Julius] Epstein, Anton Bruckner and others, to whom I played the Fantasy, did not raise the least doubt as to the authenticity of the work, which revealed Schubert's individuality throughout, and they found it extremely interesting and attractive. It consists of three movements: Allegro vivace, Adagio assai and Presto, the two end movements being in E-flat Major and the middle in C Minor. Surprisingly, each of the three movements is built out of one of the main themes of Beethoven's *Eroica*, that is, it is Beethoven's *Eroica* translated, as it were, into Schubert's musical language" (*SMF*, 248).

126. Discussing the unexpected middle Andante sostenuto section of the C-Major Quintet's third movement, Martin Chusid remarks that the "impression . . . as a whole is that of a funeral march, not unlike the slow movement of the *Eroica* Symphony with which it shares an important melodic element"; see Chusid, "Schubert's Chamber Music" in *Cambridge Companion to Schubert*, ed. Christopher H. Gibbs (Cambridge, 1997), 185. See also Xavier Hascher, "Eine 'traumhafte' *barcarola funebre*: Fragmente zu einer Deutung des langsamen Satzes des Streichquintetts D956," in *Schubert und das Biedermeier: Beiträge zur Musik des frühen 19. Jahrhunderts (Festschrift für Walther Dürr zum 70. Geburtstag)*, ed. Michael Kube, Werner Aderhold, and Walburga Litschauer (Kassel, 2002), 127–38; and Christian Strehk, "Letzte Antwort auf Beethoven? Zur Entstehung von Schuberts Streichquintett C-Dur (D956)" *Schubert-Jahrbuch 1998* (Duisburg, 2000), 133–50.

127. Othmar Wessely, "Zur Geschichte des Equals," in *Beethoven-Studien: Festgabe der Oesterreichischen Akademie der Wissenschaften zum 200. Geburtstag von Ludwig van Beethoven*, ed. Erich Schenk (Vienna, 1970), 341–60. In an intriguing article, Daniel Jacobson and Andrew Glendening argue that Schubert, who as a torchbearer that day heard these Equale repeated again and again, was inspired to incorporate them into his haunting "Tenth" Symphony (D936A). See "Schuberts D.936A: Eine sinfonische Hommage an Beethoven?" *Schubert durch die Brille* 15 (1995): 113–26; although this was challenged by Brian Newbould, "Schuberts D.936A: Eine sinfonische Hommage an sich selbst?" *Schubert durch die Brille* 16/17 (1996): 123–29.

128. Steblin, "Hoechle's 1827 Sketch of Beethoven's Studio: A Secret Tribute to Schubert?" *Beethoven Forum* 8 (2000): 22.

129. See Scott Messing, *Schubert and the European Imagination* (Rochester, NY, 2006).

130. *SMF*, 299. The reading of the quartet allegedly took place on 14 November. Ferdinand Schubert reported that the last music his brother heard was Ferdinand's own Requiem on 3 November (*SDB*, 920). The cover of Ferdinand's Requiem, when it was published, included an illustration of Schubert's grave.

131. This letter is not in *SDB*, but is included in the German edition. Kreissle first published it in *Franz Schubert*, 460–61. On 27 November the Church Music Society in St. Ulrich presented Mozart's Requiem in Schubert's honor.

132. Walburga Litschauer, ed., *Neue Dokumente zum Schubert Kreis: Aus Briefen und Tagebüchern seiner Freunde*, vol. 2 (Vienna, 1993), 104.

133. Most are collected in *SMF*, 9–39, and *SDB*, 852ff.

134. *SDB*, 879. Bauernfeld's memorial article notes that "Schubert's frame lies in the grave prepared for the departed next to that of Beethoven, the master he so greatly venerated, and a modest memorial stone will show our descendants who reposes side by side with the great master, and who it was we deemed worthy of such a resting place" (*SDB*, 893).

135. *SDB*, 838. Schlechta's memorial poem for Beethoven was sung at his funeral, Leipzig *AMZ* 29 (25 April 1827), 290; Gibbs, "Performances of Grief," 247.

136. *SDB*, 829. For a list of the other poems, see *SDB*, 925, the German originals of which are given in *FSD*.

137. *FSD*, No. 456; this and other memorial pieces are reproduced in Deutsch, *Franz Schubert: Sein Leben in Bildern*, 236, 370, 478.

138. On the second concert Fanny Sallamon replaced Bocklet as the pianist in the trio (*FSD*, Nos. 705 and 723); Schuppanzigh still did not perform. The most complete report of the concert is *FSD*, No. 703 from the *Monatbericht der Gesellschaft der Musikfreunde* (March 1829), 41–46.

139. See Margret Jestremski, "Unveröffentlichte Dokumente aus dem Nachlass Anselm Hüttenbrenners," *Schubert durch die Brille* 15 (1995): 95–99.

140. Kreissle, *Franz Schubert*, 463. Josef Kenner states that Schober did the design (*SMF*, 89), working with architect Christian Friedrich Ludwig Förster, and it was executed by Anton Wasserburger (*SDB*, 848). Deutsch observes that such a bust was very unusual at the time (*SDB*, 907).

141. *SDB*, 899.

142. *SDB*, 907; see facsimile in *Franz Schubert: Ausstellung der Wiener Stadt- und Landesbibliothek*, 98.

143. Schumann, *On Music and Musicians*, 118.

144. Ibid., 107. As mentioned above, in between were the Hardtmuth and Schlechta families—Count O'Donell had died on 31 January 1828.

145. Letter of 7 February 1838, *Schumann Briefedition*, series 1, *Familienbriefwechsel*, 4:1, ed. Anja Mühlenweg (Düsseldorf, 2010), 215.

146. Daverio, *Crossing Paths*, 14.

147. Ibid., 13–46.

148. Deutsch, "Schubert und Grillparzer," 503; *SDB*, 822.

149. Gramit, "Constructing a Victorian Schubert: Music, Biography, and Cultural Values," *19th-Century Music* 17 (1993): 65–78; and Messing, *Schubert in the European Imagination*, vol. 1 (Rochester, NY, 2006), 8–102.

150. The results are reported in *Actenmässige Darstellung der Ausgrabung und Wiederbeisetzung der irdischen Reste von Beethoven und Schubert* (Vienna, 1863). The second disinterment is described in reports of Vienna's Anthropological Society; see *Bericht über die am 21. Juni 1888 vorgenommene Untersuchung an den Gebeinen Ludwig van Beethoven's gelegentlich der Uebertragung derselben aus dem Währinger Orts-Friedhofe auf den Central-Friedhof der Stadt Wien* (Vienna, 1888); and *Bericht über die am 22. September 1888 vorgenommene Untersuchung an den Gebeinen Franz Schuberts gelegentlich der Uebertragung derselben von dem Währinger Orts-Friedhofe nach dem Central-Friedhofe der Stadt Wien* (Vienna, 1888); excerpts from both 1863 and 1883 reports appear in Hans Bankl and Hans Jesserer, *Die Krankheiten Ludwig van Beethovens: Pathographie seines Lebens und Pathologie seiner Leiden* (Vienna, 1987), 89–101. See also Karl Adametz, *Franz Schubert in der Geschichte des Wiener Männergesangvereines* (Vienna, 1938), 49–58.

151. Breuning, *Memories of Beethoven*, 116.

152. Kreissle, *Franz Schubert*, 464; translation by Arthur Duke Coleridge in *The Life of Franz Schubert* (London, 1869), 2:150.

Schubert in History

LEON BOTSTEIN

When Franz Schubert died in 1828, the extent of his influence, fame, and popularity would have been hard to predict. His posthumous musical legacy in the nineteenth century and the controversies surrounding his biography in the twentieth would have astonished his contemporaries.[1] Our understanding of Schubert the man and his music represents a remarkable case of historical reassessment and scholarly revision.

The impetus behind twentieth-century revisionist Schubert scholarship was the double-edged image of Schubert bequeathed to posterity at the end of the nineteenth century. The Schubert who persisted well into the modern era of recording and cinema was as much a mid-nineteenth-century mythic construction as an authentic historical figure from the 1820s.[2] The myth-making was inspired only in part by posthumous discoveries of unknown major works, primarily in the 1850s and 1860s. Already in the 1850s, independent of these discoveries, Schubert's stature in music history had begun to rise as a function of political and cultural change. However, in the six decades between the publication of the "Unfinished" Symphony in 1867 and the 1928 centenary of Schubert's death, Schubert and his music achieved a status unique in the popular culture of German speaking Europe, particularly in Vienna.

Schubert contra Wagner

In the 1850s the critical reception of Schubert became a battleground for protagonists in the mid-century culture war within Europe over the character and destiny of music. This conflict is frequently reduced to a split between Wagnerians and anti-Wagnerians. But the issues in the cultural conflict in which Wagner would himself later play such a key role dated back to the 1830s, prior to his emergence as a major figure.

The origins of this debate can be found in widespread anxieties about a cultural decline that was, ironically, partially the result of a remarkable increase of interest in music.[3] Robert Schumann's polemics against philistinism were one of many critiques concerning the growth of musical dilettantism and amateurism. Such criticism registered the fear that musical art in the tradition of Bach, Haydn, Mozart, and Beethoven, once the nearly exclusive province of the aristocracy, was at risk. The new public appeared to favor a superficial expressive style: virtuosity detached from any higher aesthetic aspiration, facile theatricality (as in Meyerbeer), and a rather sterile Romantic music for the theater audible in the works of composers such as Heinrich Marschner.[4]

Music, however, was merely one barometer of a perceived general decline in cultural standards that resulted from rapid changes in economic and social conditions. In his 1841 book on Vienna, the theater and music critic Heinrich Adami (1807–1895) observed:

> The number of concerts and traveling virtuosi is increasing steadily—but not that of real artists . . . can we deny that concert music comes nearer to decline each year? . . . Is the fault with the audience or the virtuosi? . . . Or is the real reason for this tendency in all the arts to be found in our era's trend toward the material, toward sensual enjoyment, superficial pleasure, toward gain and industry? . . . As it is always with a calamity, one side assigns fault to the other . . . and we allow ourselves to be told a hundred times how much better it was in olden days, and every complaint seems true and just—but . . . in the end we allow everything to remain as it was.[5]

The cultural debate that began in the 1830s centered on a presumed conflict between contemporaries obsessed with the virtues of progress in industry and commerce and their beneficial impact on mores and culture, and those who viewed contemporary economic and social change as a threat to the ideal of a true aesthetic sensibility—an inheritance of the eighteenth century. In the 1830s and 1840s, music and musical culture came to be understood as a key marker in the trajectory of history—a symptom of the consequences of the rapid spread of literacy and education.

In music the question was framed in terms of the legacy of Beethoven, whose shadow seemed inescapable to subsequent composers in German-speaking Europe. Purely musical issues intersected, not always neatly, with sharp divisions about the unique character of things "German."

Music became representative of the connection between culture and politics, evidence of the essential relationship between aesthetics and ethics and the individual and the community.

German speakers widely agreed that music was the distinguishing and outstanding feature of their cultural singularity. As the composer Peter Cornelius exclaimed in 1867, in a review of a concert of string quartet music by Haydn, Beethoven, and Schubert, "This magical mirror of the German quartet, which reveals to the eye of the soul a world history of emotional life . . . this is entirely our possession . . . and all the most noble passions of sentiment drive us to these proud thoughts: to be a German, to be a musician, to understand this language, to possess citizenship in the nation [*Heimat*] of the spirit."[6]

Indeed, the history of music, as opposed to the history of other art forms, seemed to reveal a special connection to Germany's emergence as a preeminent power in modern history. The nineteenth-century cultural historian and music critic W. H. Riehl observed, "There is no antiquity for the musician."[7] Consequently, the work of German composers from Gluck (one of Riehl's favorites) to Beethoven had become widely acknowledged as representing universal aesthetic norms in music, the equivalents of Johann Joachim Winckelmann's idealization of Greek and Greco-Roman antiquity in the visual arts.[8]

Music was seen as well as exemplifying a uniquely contemporary German Romantic sensibility. In German hands music, it was said, had broken its inherited shackles as a trivial art form. It was not mere temporal entertainment and background distraction for the landed aristocracy. It had become an art of philosophical weight and spiritual profundity (both sacred and secular). It held a special key to the formation and expression of individuality and personality. Music possessed a formal capacity for the expression of the sublime and the beautiful; it was a means of communicating the intensity of life, and was tied to a stark psychological realism about suffering, love, joy, and death. But music also led, ultimately, to realism's transcendence. Under the Romantics it had become rooted in life, yet was capable of exceeding its limits and expressing the infinite—all in forms that mirrored the highest abstract aesthetic ideals.

Given this singular prestige, it is not surprising that after 1815 music became a marker of status in German middle-class life, primarily through the spread of amateur choral societies. As a domestic pastime and public activity, it became a defining feature in the formation of community among literate and educated individuals from a wide spectrum of society.[9] Consequently, the content, conduct, and meaning of an elevated musical sensibility—that uniquely German attribute—became a matter of contention. Was it on the decline? Was it being crushed by changes in the economy and society? Were its norms dependent on a slavish adherence to the past? Was it susceptible to progress? The young Wagner made his dramatic and commanding entrance into this already raging debate in the late 1840s and early 1850s, a debate in which Schubert took on an unexpectedly central, posthumous role alongside Wagner.

The challenge for a cultivated person wishing to maintain an elevated musical sensibility within the conditions of contemporary life after 1850 was eloquently expressed in 1869 by the twenty-four-year-old Florentine Galliny (1845–1913), a journalist and later editor of the *Wiener Zeitung* writing under the pseudonym Bruno Walden. She described the dilemma faced by a typical urban amateur music enthusiast in Vienna who was a member of a choral society:

> In every person . . . there is a dim desire for the ideal. In his youth, he displays heaven-storming airs, but the steeple-chase tempo slows as soon as he encounters and comes into contact with real life . . . it sinks below consciousness in the course of his fight for material survival. . . . This sort of opportunity-driven process gradually turns the arts from objects of sacred enthusiasm into mere means of entertainment. None of the arts suffers as much from this demeaning transformation from queen to chambermaid than our sweet, lovely Lady Musica. The holy shudder of awe vanishes and makes room for trivial familiarity. A voice that once sought to serve only the devout simplicity of Haydn and the noble Romanticism of Schubert, the delicacy bordering on gentleness of Mendelssohn and perhaps the bizarre energy of Schumann, now makes do with melodies [Walden cites a string of operetta titles]. . . . Certainly, the pursuit of the ideal can be bargained with . . . but the two driving forces, idealistic enthusiasm and the need for entertainment, do not need to be as separate as the sun and the moon. . . . Vienna owes much that is pretty in music, some that is beautiful, and that rare single extraordinary work to those who combine the two in their efforts. They serve our many musical societies, associations, and academies. These organizations have in turn created a new, sharply delineated type: the member of a choral society, an individual who differs considerably from all other useful and likable members of society.[10]

As musical culture spread at midcentury to an aspiring literate urban middle class, popular biographies of composers and music lexicons became a welcome genre. The rapidly growing audience was eager to find linkages between the music they admired and the lives of composers. Readers who were music enthusiasts sought clues to the connection between music and the expression of individuality. Precisely because music by nature differed so much from word and image, biography seemed to offer clues to meaning. And biography, per se, invites invention. The common nineteenth-century conceit that some illuminating coherence could be found in the way artists lead their lives (explaining how and why artists deviated from the restrictions and norms that ordinary people suffered) meant that biographies of composers were prone to embellishment. Few personalities invited and demanded as much invention as Schubert. His life and career had been local, if not provincial, and his life short, rendering the documentary evidence strikingly limited; fewer than a hundred letters survive, most fairly trivial.

At first, Schubert was identified primarily with the genre of the art song, the Lied, and therefore as a worthy but limited successor to Beethoven. At the same time, his music lent itself precisely to the participatory amateur activity that music had become. Yet Schubert, for all the accessibility of his vocal and choral music, still represented the noble aesthetic aspirations of Classicism. Not surprisingly, after 1850, an asymmetry became apparent between the scant historical record of his life and thoughts and the demand for his music (much of whose existence came as a surprise); between the circumscribed assessment of his importance on the one hand and the rapidly deepening popular adoration for it on the other. Schubert's surviving friends compensated for this imbalance by writing memoirs. A few dated from the period right after his death, but most, like those of the writer Eduard von Bauernfeld, were penned decades later. The first biography, by Heinrich Kreissle von Hellborn (who was unaware of the B-Minor "Unfinished" Symphony), was published in Vienna in 1864. Soon after, Franz von Suppé's fanciful operetta on the life of Schubert, *Franz Schubert*, opened at Vienna's Carltheater to great acclaim.

Nothing approaching the depth and complexity of Mozart's correspondence or Beethoven's sketchbooks, conversation books, and letters was left behind in Schubert's case. The astonishing industry of Otto Erich Deutsch (1883–1967), the pioneer Schubert scholar, accumulated little more than three volumes of documents, memoirs, and images, not all consistently illuminating. This explains why a handful of letters of Schubert and his prose sketch "Mein Traum" (My Dream) have experienced such close scrutiny. Remembrances without corroborating evidence in historical sources are hard to rely on; they are history that begs for archeological remains as justification. Memories of friends and colleagues inspire extreme caution in scholars, especially if the subject is an increasingly and unexpectedly famous, and dead, friend who in his short life span elicited more compassion than envy.

Deriving biography from music is itself a hazardous undertaking, and in Schubert's case working from the music led further away from history than otherwise might have been the case. So many of the works for which he ultimately became famous were discovered long after his death, and apart from references in the Lieder, musical clues fueled an ahistorical invention of Schubert the person. Fortuitously, the posthumous revelations brought Schubert's entire oeuvre more in line with that of Beethoven, challenging the notion of Schubert's limitations vis-à-vis the older master.

The posthumous revelations were indeed extraordinary. They started with Schumann's "discovery" of the "Great" C-Major Symphony in 1839. Then, beginning in the 1850s, works such as the C-Major String Quintet appeared. The high point was Johann Ritter von Herbeck's successful coaxing of the Symphony in B Minor, the "Unfinished," out of the aged composer and friend of Schubert, Anselm Hüttenbrenner, a trick the charismatic Viennese conductor accomplished in 1865, in time for its premiere in December of that year. This work, which became subsequently Schubert's most familiar and famous, was published in 1867. The discovery fueled hopes for more of the same. In 1868, Johannes Brahms, writing his friend Joseph Joachim, reported that he had been approached about completing the E-Major Symphony (D729). Ferdinand Schubert, the composer's older brother, had shown Felix Mendelssohn the manuscript in 1846, but it had subsequently disappeared only to resurface again. Brahms was inquiring whether Joachim, who had so successfully orchestrated the "Grand Duo" (D812) in 1855, might be interested in a second Schubert project.[11]

Brahms's suggestion echoed the history behind Joachim's earlier orchestration. The idea initially came from Schumann, who heard in the Sonata in C Major for four hands a latent symphony. Why was Schumann eager to find a new symphony by Schubert? Why did Joachim complete the project? Why was Brahms, in 1868, concerned to see the E-Major fragment completed? And why did Brahms perform the Joachim "Grand Duo" orchestration twice in the early 1870s in Vienna? The answers rest in Brahms's and Joachim's negative perception of the contemporary rage for music as a dramatic medium of sentiment, sensuality, theater, and spectacle. They viewed this trend as a symptom of the decline in musical standards away from a Classical ideal of musical thinking and its formal requirements, albeit tempered by an early Romantic sensibility. The challenge, as they would come to see it from the 1860s onward, was how to reconcile the legitimate demands of a growing participant and listening public for an accessible expressive Romanticism with an allegiance to the normative standards of musical beauty bequeathed by musical Classicism.

Wagner came to represent the most persuasive case for the novel approach to music as an easily grasped dramatic medium tied to text and narration. He was the apostle of the idea that music needed to be a progressive art form whose historical imperative rendered Classical traditions obsolete. As music historian, critic, and Wagner advocate Franz Brendel wrote in 1855, "Our age is not only one of decline and the disintegration of an inherited art . . . it is . . . one of a new creativity."[12] By 1855, Brendel promoted Wagner as the protagonist of a new musical art that "leaves the narrow, limited customary musical spheres behind, and in opera, puts aside the one-sided overemphasis on music." Wagner realized an historical imperative; he fulfilled the expectation that composition be justified by "a new spiritual substance." "Musical creativity is purposeless," Brendel wrote, "if it is not driven by a higher spiritual goal," by which Brendel meant inspiration and meaning garnered from the other arts.[13]

The currency of such notions, not the originality and striking brilliance of Wagner's music, caused the most concern among skeptics like Brahms and Joachim. What better antidote to Wagner's success in the theater than new, large-scale works in traditional genres by Schubert, an acknowledged and popular master who had already made his entrance on the historical stage alongside Beethoven. The Schubert of the "Great" C-Major Symphony, the orchestrated "Grand Duo," the "Unfinished," of the E-flat Mass, the String Quintet, late piano sonatas, and *Alfonso und Estrella*, which Liszt premiered in 1854, represented a powerful alternative to Wagner: music that revealed the ideal synthesis of the Classical with a new "spiritual substance."[14] Schubert's recently discovered works lent him a requisite if not exquisite expressive modernity. Wagner himself recognized Schubert as rising from the dead to challenge him. In 1869, at the end of his essay on conducting, he ridiculed Joachim and Brahms for "anticipating all sort of good things from a return to the new ballad-melody of Schubert."[15]

They were not so far off the mark. Schubert's music satisfied the public's expectation of profound meaning in a musical language of narrative realism that conveyed the sensibilities and intensity of emotion so evident in Wagner. Schubert's originality reflected a debt to Classical aesthetics in terms of melody, harmonic usage, formal structures, and conventional links between music and text. He undermined the claim by progressives that the logic of history rendered Viennese Classicism "narrow," and that the musical "spheres" represented by masterpieces from the past were either sterile or irrelevant (as items of mere luxury), and disconnected from the needs and aspirations of the new, educated public for music.

What made this use of Schubert plausible after 1850 was that the Schubert everyone had already come to love turned out to be more than a familiar composer of vocal and piano music played at home and, more importantly, sung in semi-public and public venues.[16] The surprise was that he was also the author of symphonies, masses, and operas—works for the concert stage. Furthermore, the music Schubert had written for amateur participation—primarily choral works absent in Wagner's oeuvre (with the exception of arrangements of a few operatic excerpts)—could not be dismissed as old-fashioned. Herbeck, writing in 1862 to the director of the Choral Society in Königsberg, expressed delight "like a child" at an inquiry "from the far north for a choral work by Schubert."[17] He exhorted his colleague "to make much propaganda for this artist of the heart and spirit. Only so can we make the many choruses of our great common fatherland understand that male choral singing has to look for its greatest treasures in Schubert and that Schubert alone is the best remedy against the unfortunate and increasing superficiality of choral programs."[18] Schubert was new music for a new national consciousness at the highest level of aesthetic merit.

Nonetheless, by the mid-1870s many observers, even in Vienna, conceded reluctantly that German national sensibilities were becoming inseparable from the Wagnerian. Just as Bismarck and the Prussian Monarchy eclipsed all other alternatives to German unification, including the Austrian dream of a grand German nation that encompassed the Habsburg Empire, Wagner, with the opening of Bayreuth in 1876, appeared close to victory on the cultural front. But if the Austro-German option had been already defeated decisively on the battlefield in 1866, in culture there was still a war to be won. Schubert, not Brahms, offered the distinct alternative popular vision.[19] Owing to Schubert's historical status as a contemporary of Beethoven, it seemed more plausible to temper the Wagnerian with him than attempting a counter-revolution with Brahms.

Herbeck himself sought valiantly to straddle both sides of the mid-century cultural conflict. An enthusiast for Wagner, he ran afoul of the Master of Bayreuth when the 1871 Vienna premiere of *Die Meistersinger* under his baton turned into a near catastrophe. For all his advocacy of Wagner, as a conductor in Vienna he also sought to defend the Classical tradition and even brought Handel's *Messiah* back into the concert repertory (in a performance that outraged the historically minded Brahms).

What made Schubert a perfect complement to Wagner in Herbeck's view was not only that he was an historical figure, but that he offered a contribution to German art and culture uniquely absent in Wagner. Schubert possessed an "openness to nature and life" in which a true ideal of beauty dominated. His work reconciled high aesthetic ideals with a sense for "natural enjoyment." He brought a "soft warm breeze from the south" into "the deep green German forest." "Yes," Herbeck wrote, "it is through the delightful marriage of the profound Germanic soul with southerly colorful passion that Schubert touches us so wonderfully."[20] Furthermore, Schubert justified the role of the amateur participant in public musical culture. "Schubert's music was not devoted purely and only to the art song," the conductor wrote as early as 1855 in the preface to a new edition of the works for chorus, noting that Schubert had produced the most original choral music of all composers. Herbeck ended his preface with the exhortation: "Sing Schubert! Schubert! And once more Schubert!"

The Schubert who rose to prominence in the public imagination and the repertoire of the concert hall after 1850 had first been "conceived" in 1839 when Schumann wrote about the newly discovered "Great" C-Major Symphony. This, his second life, lasted until 1867, when the "Unfinished" was published. Thus the Schubert inherited and embraced by the twentieth century as one of the great composers was born not in 1797 but rather in 1839, making him more a contemporary of Brahms and Wagner than of Beethoven and Weber. Brahms was keenly aware of this anomaly. He remarked to Adolf Schubring in 1863 that with Schubert "one has the sense that he is still alive."[21] Indeed, one cannot underestimate the astonishment at the novelty of the form and sound of the "Unfinished" at its first performance just two years after Brahms's comment.

Thus by the end of the nineteenth century, Schubert's music and personality came to be understood as a central representative of the German musical culture of late Romanticism rather than as a characteristic historical figure of the decade after the fall of Napoleon. The reinvention of Schubert in German-speaking Europe can be compared to the early nineteenth-century radical reassessment of Shakespeare by English literary critics. In Shakespeare, as one scholar has put it, "artistic achievement and national pride could be cemented together." The "most desirable traits of British identity" were to be found in Shakespeare, as Henry Crawford said in Jane Austen's *Mansfield Park*. "It is part of an Englishman's constitution."[22]

This refashioning of Schubert at midcentury was persuasive precisely because he possessed a twin identity. He was a familiar personage from a hallowed (and rapidly vanishing) past, the age of Beethoven and the *Vormärz*, the period before the revolutions of 1848. He was also a composer of spectacular works whose first appearance provided a fresh alternative to the allure of anti-historicist musical aesthetics. By the 1870s the foregrounding of a "new" Schubert based on the posthumous revelations gave renewed strength to anti-Wagnerian circles, to the allegiances shared by Brahms, Max Bruch, Joachim, and Hermann Goetz, and to a faith in the vitality and future potential of the Classical legacy: instrumental music, symphonic form, early-Romantic lyricism, and the conception of the expressive connection between music and text characteristic of the Lied.

Not surprisingly, Wagner had little to say about Schubert, who was at best a peripheral figure in the Wagnerian account of history. In 1841 he poked fun at German composers who sought to emulate Schubert's songs just to gain notoriety in Paris. In 1869, he ridiculed those who hoped for a "Messiah" on behalf of that aesthetic. Wagnerians (with the notable exception of Bruckner) often derided Schubert, as George Bernard Shaw did (citing Schubert's "thoughtlessness" and "brainlessness").[23] Even Richard Strauss confessed in the 1920s that for most of his career he had never given Schubert much thought.[24] The "New German" movement's debt to Schubert resided mostly in Franz Liszt's advocacy and enthusiasm—understandable given the influence that Schubert's expressive musical rhetoric had on Liszt's notions of the connection between instrumental music and literature, between word and tone, and thus on the idea and realization of the tone poem.[25] For example, Schubert entered Russia's musical life through Liszt's transcriptions of his Lieder in the late 1840s.[26] Yet by the 1870s ardent Russian Wagnerians like Alexander Nikolayevitch Serov had no difficulty in saying that they "detested" Schubert's symphonies.[27] Other Wagnerians, like Hugo Wolf, would come to distance themselves from the music and its growing popularity in the 1880s.[28]

Wagner's lack of interest was consistent with the prevalent critical opinion of Schubert held during the years of Wagner's youth. Prior to his appropriation as a legitimate popular alternative to things Wagnerian in the late 1850s, Schubert's place in history had been circumscribed. His achievement, according to Brendel (writing in 1855) was limited to the art song. Brendel dismissed the larger works but lauded Schubert's elevation of the Lied into a fully contemporary medium of the "German spirit," through his "expansion" of music's narrative power on behalf of "the expression of the blossoming of life," a "deepening of interiority," the insertion of "subjectivity" into musical drama, and the "nuanced" representation of poetic meaning. Schubert was placed historically as an inspiration for Liszt and Schumann, a remarkable but restricted genius cut short by an early death. His works, for all their virtues, lacked the "grandiose seriousness, the manner, the refined artistic understanding and controlled power" of Beethoven.[29]

The influential 1861 *Neues Universal-Lexikon der Tonkunst* edited by Eduard Bernsdorf concurred. The "Great" C-Major Symphony was dismissed on account of its "formal deficiencies." Schubert merited a place alongside the greatest German composers through his contributions to the Lied, since he brought that uniquely "German possession"—the art song—"to its highest fulfillment." By perfecting the Lied, he brought an antiquated traditional genre to the limits of its historical significance.[30] But it was a sidebar in the progressive march of music history.

This line of criticism would persist. In 1875 Heinrich Köstlin, while conceding that Schubert produced "important works in all musical genres," observed that his greatness remained tied to the Lied and to music of "profound and moving lyricism" rather than music as an "imposing force that emanates from an organic work of art." Schubert was akin to a Biedermeier landscape and genre painter who, though evoking charm within an aesthetic of naïve realism, mirrored almost despite himself "the overwrought sentimentality" of his times.[31] This argument found a peculiar variant as late as 1900 in the views of Gustav Mahler, for whom barely four chamber works and just forty songs by Schubert were truly great. Mahler deemed Schubert's melodies to be so "eternal" that they excused his lack of "technical skill" and reliance on an inherently deceitful strategy, repetition (so much so that many works could be cut in half). Nevertheless, for Mahler, the critical fact was that Schubert was unable to develop his material adequately.[32]

Such views left the way open for Wagner to claim the mantle of Beethoven, which he did most directly in 1870. The reinvention of Schubert as the composer of music capable of competing with the dramatic musical rhetoric of Liszt and Wagner was supported explicitly to blunt Wagner's claim. To the reinventors Schubert was not only the rightful heir to Beethoven as a matter of history, but also the proper model for the future of music. In Schubert one encountered profundity, organic logic, nobility, individuality and even drama—all without the transgression of norms or historical precedent. As Brahms observed in 1887, "Schubert, not Mendelssohn or Schumann, is Beethoven's true successor."[33]

Culture as History

Wagner's appropriation of the legacy of Beethoven was based on his own internalization of a mid-nineteenth-century philosophical conceit regarding the existence of an inexorable logic in history. The emergence of Schubert as a popular figure, with unknown major and defining works coming to light in the 1850s and 1860s, coincided with seminal developments in the study of history and culture in German-speaking Europe. Indeed, the strange ahistorical nature of Schubert's posthumous emergence into the mainstream of classical musical culture made him an awkward subject for late nineteenth-century historians, particularly those who were ardent Wagnerians.

Historians and theorists in the generation after Leopold von Ranke—W. H. Riehl, Jacob Burckhardt, Karl Lamprecht, and Wilhelm Dilthey—all sought to challenge Ranke's fundamental emphasis on the state and politics as decisive forces in history and as the proper sources for periodization in history. For Ranke, human history was, objectively, a sequence of distinct eras without a discernible overarching trajectory. Therefore, no era possessed a philosophical priority. At midcentury, particularly after the events of 1848, ideas of causality in history came under scrutiny, both the historicist conceit regarding the objective existence of distinct eras in the past, as well as the determinist teleological philosophical claims of Hegel and his followers, notably Marx.

The acquisition of literacy and culture—*Bildung*—had become a defining ambition of the increasingly dominant German middle classes, who, as Riehl observed in 1864, cultivated a self-conscious collective identity as bearers of a noble historic tradition of *Bürgertum*.[34] The Schubert revival coincided with the search for an objective legitimation of contemporary middle-class cultural practices through the study of history. Music as a shared medium of cultural expression and the rise in popularity of Schubert, seen as a harbinger of the distinctive character of German values, coincided with the wide popularity of programmatic realist novels, such as the spectacularly successful 1855 *Soll und Haben* by Gustav Freytag (himself an anti-Wagnerian), written to celebrate the distinction and historic role of the German middle classes.[35]

Notions of history and culture (in a proto-anthropological sense) became ideological battlegrounds in the process of German unification after 1848. How did culture, or rather, a unified cultural sensibility and habits emerge? How might culture—including mores—be understood as coherent? If identifiable as a separate force, was culture itself a causal factor in historical change in politics and economics? Or was culture—literature, music, the visual arts, and philosophical ideas—subordinate to, or contingent on, the "real" forces in history: political power and material, economic conditions? Might culture be a primary historical factor, not only independent of economics and politics, but itself a shaping element in history?

These were not idle academic questions. Both the controversy between Heinrich von Treitschke and Riehl at the end of the 1850s about whether culture and society could be studied properly apart from politics, and the more extensive controversy over methods (*Methodenstreit*) that engulfed the writing of history at the turn of the nineteenth century were tied to ongoing struggles over politics, including the character of the new German State—its legitimacy, its origins, its connection to German language and culture outside of the post-1870 empire, its political system, and its relationship to the competing claims of liberalism and monarchical conservatism.[36] Culture was seen as increasingly relevant to the sense of what Germany had become, and to its perhaps "special" path and unique destiny in history.

Herbeck's evocation of Schubert's "German" character as distinctly influenced by a gentle warm spirit characteristic of the south, in direct contrast to the dark forests of the north, was a transparent cultural metaphor that juxtaposed two norms, the Austrian and the Prussian. As the inevitability of a Prussian and North German political solution to unification became apparent in the 1860s, the fear of the loss of a German connection to the Italianate—visible in Goethe's and Mendelssohn's romance with Italy and the work of the "German Roman" school of painters, including Schubert's friend Leopold Kupelwieser, who studied in Rome—was palpable. In this sense the impetus behind the rediscovery of Schubert during the 1860s went beyond music. The intense debate over defining culture as a factor in the laws of historical change heightened the stakes surrounding the midcentury reevaluation of Schubert; as an Austro-German figure his ties to the south seemed inscribed in his music.

Riehl, Burckhardt, Lamprecht, and Dilthey each had a deep, active interest in contemporary musical culture. They were (not always approving) witnesses of the dramatic expansion of the audience for music after 1848, as evidenced by the growth in amateurism, music education, music publishing, instrument manufacture, and concert life. These developments helped confirm the perception that the rate and nature of change during the second half of the century was unprecedented and traumatic. Change ranged from population growth and migration to the transformation of agriculture and industry, the rise of cities and, for German-speaking Europe, the political resolution of a burgeoning nationalism through the creation of the *klein-deutsch* Prussian-dominated German Empire after the 1870 Franco-Prussian War.

Historians struggled to understand the present in terms of the past. Was there such a thing as progress? Was there an endpoint to human development? What were the causes of change? Was it possible to grasp, in a manner that approximated or emulated the methods of science, a logic and coherence in history that illuminated the origins of social habits and justified sensibilities regarding collective identity and allegiance? Was the objective study of humankind and history—the human sciences—possible? Could it explain the past and present, even if it did not offer, as Marx claimed, a determined pathway into the future? And central to all these questions for the post-Ranke generation was the issue of the autonomy of culture and therefore music in shaping historical change.

By the time Schubert and Beethoven were reburied in adjoining plots in Vienna's Central Cemetery with considerable pomp and circumstance in 1888, Schubert's place in the larger frame of history had shifted from the periphery to the center. What did Schubert reveal in terms of what was distinctive about modern life and culture? As a representative of Classical aesthetic norms that transcended historical change, he had been placed alongside Haydn, Mozart, and Beethoven, and in this sense he was a reminder of the dangers of modernity and the elusiveness of progress in aesthetics and mores. Yet he was also a unique forerunner, a legitimate symbol of a vital German spirit that existed beyond the terms set by Wagner. Schubert's status as part historical and part contemporary, linked to a Classical, high-art tradition yet also a widely popular cultural symbol, made him a fiercely contested figure. In Vienna, Schubert's dual resonance as reminder of the past and influential contemporary assumed particular urgency during the last decades of the Habsburg Empire and during the First Republic before the Anschluss.

The most significant contribution to the historical question of the origins and character of nineteenth-century modernity was the appearance in 1869 of Jacob Burckhardt's *The Culture of the Renaissance in Italy*, a work written in the very decade of renewed enthusiasm for Schubert. Burckhardt's central thesis was that modernity had its roots in the Renaissance, and his aesthetic sympathies and prejudices help explain why he became one of Brahms's favorite authors. According to Burckhardt, what characterized modernity was the emergence of the idea of individuality and the valorization of the private person as separate from a corporate or collective entity. Individualism, particularly in the arts, became a decisive marker of nineteenth-century culture; it had been nascent in the plastic arts and literature of the Renaissance, and had blossomed in the political theories of the seventeenth and eighteenth century. Although music became in Burckhardt's view a prominent cultural medium only after 1600, the role of singing in Renaissance music underscored for him the highlighting of the individual as a distinct actor in life and history; it provided a public "exhibition of the individual man in society."[37]

Burckhardt was an avid amateur. He played the piano, even composed, and wrote music criticism early in his career in Basel, although in his later years he retreated from taking a role in music as a critic or active amateur. His tastes were distinctly anti-Wagnerian. Writing to the distinguished German jurist Friedrich von Preen (1823–1894), he derided the passion for Wagner as an example of the "horrendous" contemporary taste for luxury and the allure of a spiritual "nervousness" in the music. He expressed the hope that the Italians would not fall prey to the Wagnerian enthusiasms that had spread through German-speaking Europe, and thereby lose their natural lyricism.[38]

Each evening when he could no longer work, Burckhardt turned to his vast music library of piano vocal scores of operas, Lieder, and oratorios. His tastes ranged from Bach to Mozart, Cherubini, Rossini, and Verdi (but not Bizet). Mozart, like Raphael, was his ideal. Individuality and a Classicist sense of form were perfectly balanced in their work; Schubert and Weber—both defining figures in Romanticism before 1830—were not far behind. They had the virtue of appealing to a contemporary sensibility. The sensibility Schubert shared with Beethoven was the capacity to translate into the realm of the beautiful—into musical moments of joy— the subjective temporal transfiguration of the mundane realities in an individual's life. As Burckhardt observed on New Year's Day in 1887, only composers were granted this moment, though perhaps Raphael might have been an exception.[39]

Music was the prime medium for communicating a highly individualized expression of subjectivity that corresponded with an element of shared truth about reality. It was the most personal and intimate art form, the one most capable of expressing the individual. Beethoven was akin to Michelangelo—an instance of unparalleled individuality—but an intemperate one, suggesting the danger posed to norms of aesthetic beauty by the nineteenth century's cult of originality. Schubert possessed, in contrast, a calm and economical intensity regarding the truth. His music did not decorate, deceive, or camouflage. Rather, it shared the intimate and gave voice to the individual, all through a command of beauty.

For Burckhardt, Schubert realized the essence of music. As Burckhardt observed:

> At the extreme frontier of art . . . we find music, which, if we wish to penetrate the essence of its being, must be taken

> as instrumental music, detached from words and, above all, apart from dramatic representation. . . . [Music] is a comet, circling round life in a vastly high and remote orbit, yet suddenly sweeping down closer to it than any other art, and revealing to man his inmost heart. Sometimes it is a kind of mathematics of imagination—then again just pure soul, infinitely far, yet close and dear. Its effect (where such effect is genuine) is so great and so immediate that the feeling of gratitude at once seeks for its creator and spontaneously proclaims him great. The great composers are among the most undisputed great men.[40]

Burckhardt's admiration and ambivalence regarding Beethoven reveals the extent to which he was overcome, like Brahms, with a sense that in the growing attachment to music as the medium of drama and radical individuality he was witnessing a decline in taste and standards. In 1878 he confessed to Preen his fear that the broadening of the public and the cheapening of taste over the past two decades might ultimately obscure from future historians' view all that was truly beautiful in the music of first half of the nineteenth century. Would the renewed interest in Schubert and the iconic status of the B-Minor Symphony succeed in retarding the widespread enthusiasm for mere dramatic effect, justified in the name of Beethoven? Was not the ideal contemporary synthesis of beauty in form and expression—what Cornelius called "the subjectively unstable"[41]—to be found in Schubert?

Karl Lamprecht's reputation among historians never rivaled that of Burckhardt, but in his day he was perhaps more widely read and influential. He developed a theory of history that suggested music could be a central factor in the trajectory of history, a vital human activity that had causal consequences. Music, according to him, was a catalyst within the psychological life of humanity. It mirrored and shaped humanity's inner life, its *Seelenleben*. In Lamprecht's view, a key to understanding history was human nature as revealed through the still young science of psychology. This methodology put him at odds with a tradition of historical writing that began with Ranke and would reach its finest moment in the work of Max Weber. Lamprecht focused particularly on the human "capacity for fantasy" (*Phantasiethätigkeit*), and therefore on aesthetic proclivities. Aesthetic ideals in history prefigured the formulation of a new moral code (*Sittenlehre*) and worldview (*Weltanschauung*). In short, music was a leading force in modern history.[42]

Unlike Burckhardt, Lamprecht was not a cultural pessimist. For him, the distinguishing feature of post-1870 modernity was the transition from an age of assertive individuality to the contemporary age of radical subjectivity. The "total work of art" of Wagner exemplified subjective modernity through its synthesis of sound and word into drama. The use of extended chromatic harmony to represent nuances of psychological feelings and the emphasis on "sensation"—color and effect—in the orchestra were markers of a subjectivist outlook, where the total experience of the individual, not external reality, held sway. Wagner's successors, notably Richard Strauss, went further with Wagner's epoch-making appropriation of music as an instrument of subjective expression. Music held the key to understanding the essence of modern culture. "So it is proper," wrote Lamprecht, "that the effort for a cultural historical understanding of the most recent past—and at the same time, our immediate present—begins with the retelling and elaboration of the great occurrences in musical art, and closes with the presentation of the most recent progress in worldview."[43]

At the same time Lamprecht grasped the unusual but pivotal place occupied by Schubert in history. Schubert represented the transition from the age of individuality to the modern age of the subjective. Lamprecht understood the paradox of Schubert's twin identity as an icon from the past and as a contemporary aesthetic force. "What better can be said," he wrote, "of the weighty philosophy of his apparently unfinished sublime B-Minor Symphony than that it is worthy of being contemporary with that greatest of the great, who died just one year before him, and yet appears related to the work born much later of a Brahms?"[44] Lamprecht located the impetus behind the midcentury embrace of Schubert not so much in Schubert as a historical figure, but in Schubert's role as a newly discovered antidote to Wagnerism.

Lamprecht's emphasis on the psychological as a historical force put him at odds with Burckhardt. The difference between them is revealed not only in their radically opposed view of Wagner, but in their differing accounts of the significance of musical culture in history. For Burckhardt, literature and the visual arts were far more significant, whereas music always seemed to vanish from view, with the new replacing the old. While art and literature remained as living constant historical factors, music (in an age before recording) had to be realized in performance, in real time and space. For Lamprecht, on the other hand, music, precisely on account of its temporal nature and psychological, non-linguistic power, was a primary factor in history.

But it was not only Wagnerians who privileged music as a historical force. W. H. Riehl, as skeptical about Wagner as Burckhardt, had argued a half century before Lamprecht that music, as a matter of cultural history, was an essential clue to understanding the past. If Burckhardt believed music to be more ephemeral and thus less promising than art and literature as a source of historical understanding, Riehl took the opposite view. For him "the cultural image of past centuries" was located in music. In music one could "hear chords once listened to by people long gone, just as they heard them." The "most secret, instinctive moods of a past world's emotional life . . . the natural sounds of their souls which were so different from ours" could only be revealed through music. Riehl concluded, "Image and word would be far more distant had they not found expression in music."[45]

The methodological dilemma was how to read the music of the past historically. Riehl understood that listening had a history, just as tuning did; the very frequencies of the pitches we assume to be identical had changed over time. In order to get the proper character of the culture of the past, the "musical ear of the age" had to be grasped.[46] For Riehl that historical insight was inaccessible except through the historical reimagining of the music of the past.

This methodological strategy concealed Riehl's powerful bias. He idealized the late eighteenth century, particularly Gluck and Haydn, and distrusted the modern enthusiasm for the piano to the exclusion of all other instruments, particularly those closely allied to the voice. To him, the ideal musical education required training on the violin and the piano—combining the instrument of absolute lyricism and the instrument of harmonic drama. Riehl's ideal of the string quartet as the highest form of music emerges in the short story "Das Quartett," set in the mid-eighteenth century.[47] Riehl, influenced by Schiller's notion of aesthetic education, argued that for music to communicate emotion, passion, and therefore the essence of a particular historical culture, it had to adhere to a set of objective criteria regarding beauty. Riehl, writing during the 1850s (before *Tristan* or the *Ring*), thought that Wagner had gone too far by discarding the inherently objective nature of musical art, particularly in his use of the voice and his reliance on color and orchestral effects. Modern music lacked both the naïve and the sentimental clarity of eighteenth-century norms.

Riehl did not doubt that music had to progress, particularly as the German-speaking community realized its own communitarian character through culture. But "the basic outlines of the basis of a musical aesthetic" rested in Viennese Classicism. "Understanding," a dimension of *Bildung*, was a requisite attribute for Riehl's beloved middle classes. That meant grasping the aesthetic and historically valid character of music. Wagner's abandonment of tradition devalued that understanding and rendered music meaningless. The critique of older music as sterile and academic was a function of ignorance: it showed the inability to sense the objective aesthetic values beneath the shifting surface of historical style. Wagner's appeal to modern expressivity was unpersuasive. His abandonment of the valid syntax and grammar of musical form resulted in the following paradox: "Modern music appears mostly to be passionate without being so; the Classical is, however, passionate without appearing to be so," Riehl concluded.[48]

Riehl countered the widespread notion that Wagner was the exemplar of the modern in music, a leading representative of using music as a means of nuanced subjective expression, by claiming that music, to carry any real meaning—even that of personal emotion—had to respect and adhere to the formal logic that exemplified the true nature of music. Only within that logic could content or meaning be differentiated. The promise of music in the future, therefore, rested on a synthesis of aesthetic norms and music as a mirror of history. Following Schiller's distinction between the naïve and sentimental, Riehl thought that modernity had gone to extremes in its embrace of the sentimental, abandoning the naïve. Pure naïve simplicity in beauty and expressiveness could be reclaimed on behalf of contemporary German culture through the disciplined immersion in musical Classicism. Riehl, like Herbeck, worried about the loss of an Italianate sense of the melodic.[49]

The promise and potential direction of modern music was therefore most audible for Riehl in the German Lied. Its purest naïve form was the folksong, since it represented the most direct and "unmediated" expression of the "mysteries" of feeling, and therefore the "interiority" of a people's "actions and doings." Beethoven, Mozart, and Johann Friedrich Reichardt (1752–1814)—the widely influential North German writer on music and composer)—had established the norms of the self-conscious "idealistic" adaptation of the song away from its "naturalistic" origins, just as Haydn had extracted the ideal terms of the symphony and sonata form from their roots in dance and folk tunes. Beethoven sought to expand beyond this, to break out of the confines within which Haydn worked. Schubert attempted to achieve the same progress with the Lied.[50]

Despite the undeniable greatness of Schubert's achievement in this form—his recasting of the song as a psychological drama—Riehl believed that Schubert also revealed the limits of the song form. In this, Riehl failed to take into account the formal and harmonic innovation of Schubert's instrumental music such as the "Wanderer" Fantasy that so attracted Liszt. Indeed, he found such innovation absent in those few larger-scale instrumental works by Schubert he knew. Schubert, by perfecting the song and realizing the expressive potential of the song form, was still trapped by its inherent naïveté. For Riehl, the task facing the modern composer was to find new means for idealistic, aesthetic expression as a way of sustaining the naïve values underlying modern culture. One had to deny one's own instincts and become self-consciously probing in an historical sense, Riehl noted, to get under the skin of a Reichardt song. In Schubert's Lieder "the spirit of the age is found complete; it penetrates and sings it entirely naturally."[51] At the same time Schubert honored Classical norms. Wagner, in a desperate attempt to be modern, sacrificed this search for naïve beauty in favor of superficial theatricality. Riehl's argument helps explain why Schubert was for many, including later anti-Wagnerians such as Felix Weingartner, more akin to Mozart than to Beethoven.

Riehl's critique of Wagner, which sought to redefine the challenge facing the contemporary composer in a manner that supported the notion that in Schubert an alternative viable path was discernable, found its echo at the turn of century in Wilhelm Dilthey. For Dilthey *Erlebnis,* experience (the conduct of daily life), generated the underlying values of an age. These can be found in the "inner relations" of "mental life" that in turn reveal shared, wide-ranging coherences. The evidence of the way individuals fashion a sense of meaning includes forms of autobiography (self-representation), but the shared values of a historical age find their most eloquent expression in the arts—in poetry and music. Like Riehl, Dilthey located the model origins of German modernity in the literature and music of the eighteenth century. Mozart and not Wagner was the model musical dramatist of life. Mozart's achievement was characteristic of the naturalness and simplicity inherent in musical Classicism.

In a manner reminiscent of Lamprecht, Dilthey observed that imitating Mozart was no longer possible on account of the "intensification of subjectivity, the renewed emphasis on expression" characteristic of the second half of the nineteenth century. Like Riehl, Dilthey allowed himself to render the following aesthetic judgment of contemporary taste: "Compare this all finally with Richard Wagner!"[52] By employing material from a mythic German past, insisting on using specific markers for every emotion and passions as metaphysical notions, Wagner ended up "preferring musical abstraction"—a tendency already evident in the selection of mythic subjects for his music dramas. "He knows no lower reality, in which all life is rooted," Dilthey concluded.[53] But Schubert's music (like Mozart's) was rooted in that "lower reality"—the real conditions of life in Vienna. It possessed the intense subjectivity of modernity as well as the command of an ideal mode of aesthetic expression. For Dilthey, the "substance" of music, from a historian's point of view, was in the way sound was organized by the composer's imagination—the connection between memory and experience realized in music. Instrumental music—the Classical patterns of melody and form—offered the finest means to express artistically the expanse and detail of human experience. The ideal of program music in Liszt and the music drama of Wagner subordinated and limited the power of musical expression.[54]

For anti-Wagnerians, even avowed cultural pessimists such as Burckhardt and Brahms, Schubert offered the most optimistic model for the future. Schubert's inspiration was drawn from individual experience, from a realistic account of life's struggles. He conveyed his subjective response using the inherited Classical legacy of musical logic and form, without suggesting an academic neoclassicism (which was Riehl's critique of Mendelssohn). Rather, he presented a viable synthesis of the historical imperative to be within the present moment and the aesthetic imperative to affirm and adhere to norms of musical beauty and form. The popularity Schubert achieved by the early 1900s only confirmed these notions. Schubert became a voice of the contemporary world. He was not merely Beethoven's immediate successor, the last exponent of a Viennese Classicism that began with Gluck, but an alternative within late Romanticism and a harbinger of the post-Romantic aesthetics later adopted by modernist composers in the 1920s.

Schubert and the Myth of Old Vienna

An explicit realist strategy lay behind Schubert's music. His realism resided in his use of music as a medium for individual self-expression in the face of the severe political, grim economic, and brutal physical circumstances that defined life in Vienna in the 1820s.[55] These circumstances emancipated Schubert from remaining a short-lived, brilliant, and somewhat peripheral contemporary of Beethoven and precursor of Romanticism. This recognition of the psychic and narrative realism in Schubert remained most apparent in the very local context in which he had lived and worked: Vienna.

Burckhardt, an outsider with respect to Vienna, welcomed the massive physical transformation the city experienced after the Imperial patent of 1859 that permitted the demolition of the walls surrounding the inner city, the building of the Ringstrasse, and the integration of communities previously regarded as suburbs into one major metropolis. Arriving there in 1884, Burckhardt exclaimed, "Vienna has become enormously magnificent . . . something like the distance on the Ring between the

Elisabeth Bridge and Schottenring can nowhere be found in Europe any longer." He raved about the "magical beauty" of the Burgtheater, "the jewel of the neighborhood," and of the "ravishing" Votivkirche.[56]

This enthusiasm for apparent progress was hardly universal among the Viennese, the majority of whom were ambivalent and discomforted by the city's changes: the massive historicist public structures and the palatial houses and apartment buildings that replaced the *Glacis*, the stretch of green that once separated the inner city from the suburbs. He likewise failed to see this physical transformation as the symbols of the massive demographic and political changes in the 1860s and 1870s. As the Viennese journalist Adam Müller-Guffenbrunn lamented in a 1915 volume titled *Old Viennese Journeys and Visions*:

> There are still people among us who have known the old Vienna. They are to be envied; they have seen perhaps one of the loveliest among major European cities. One hears tell of the hesitation with which the Emperor signed the patent of 1859 that resulted in the destruction of the old cityscape. How understandable. We younger people can hardly imagine the peculiar magic than emanated from this cityscape . . . the wide space of the Glacis, which was never to be built upon, kept all that was not in accord with an aristocratic character away from the inner city. . . . Old Vienna was a garden city despite its tall walls, and an evening stroll on its ramparts must have been an incomparable delight.[57]

The images and accounts of Schubert and his friends happily going out into nature for picnics and parties that accompanied the post-1850 cult of Schubert tell a true story of the topography and social structure of pre-1848 Vienna. A decade after Schubert's death, Adolf Schmidl published a two-volume guide to Vienna's surroundings, organized by round-trip journeys that took twenty hours or less. Schmidl was proud that recent improvements in the transportation system (not railroads) had made what was once the province of a few—the ability to avail oneself of a unique connection between urban life and nature—a reality for many:

> The advantages of Vienna—that it has pleasanter surroundings than any other imperial city—are too well known to bear repeating here in detail. But it has only been a few decades that the Viennese has been able to enjoy the charming setting of the city as it deserves, and he owes this in particular to

> the implementation of the omnibus. Before this truly social institution existed, most of the inhabitants of Vienna had to limit themselves to a few extended excursions into the countryside each year. . . . Only the rich could afford to spend the summer in the country. . . . Ten years ago a communal carriage to Hietzing was established . . . interest soon was so great that it had to go back and forth at all hours of the day. Soon more such conveyances to other neighboring villages followed, and at present no fewer than 60 carriages go daily to the various surrounding areas of Vienna, and 18 of those leave every hour. On Sundays in beautiful weather more than 140 carriages are busy and convey at least 10,000 people. Naturally, the Fiaker coaches were initially the greatest opponents of this undertaking and there was no lack of tensions of all kinds. . . .
>
> Because of these institutions, a stay in the country is no longer an unaffordable expense; for a few pennies each day, the businessman can come into the city, and a visit to the country is now so much easier for friends and acquaintances. . . . The situation benefited greatly from the limitation of office hours in most of the offices to 9am to 2pm and the abolition of afternoon hours instituted a few years back. . . . Because easier traffic connections have allowed them to live at a distance, more officials of small income, who previously were not able to support a family, have dared to marry and lead, however narrow, a life cheered by domestic joys.[58]

The nostalgia for an old Vienna framed by nature and green spaces was more than a convenient myth. The physical transformation of Vienna that began in 1859 altered the daily life of the inhabitants; it made the city more susceptible to a rationalized sense of work and the use of time. No wonder that the invocation of the good old days of "Alt Wien" became a prominent vehicle for the expression of resistance and ambivalence not only to the physical and demographic changes that Vienna witnessed between the 1860s and the 1890s, but also to the cultural habits they brought with them. Eduard von Bauernfeld, the friend of Schubert's and Schwind's, described in 1872 the era leading up to the post-1859 years this way: "One lived a sort of double life. The old Viennese sense for enjoyment remained intact, as before, and remained loyal to its Strauss and Nestroy, just as one also began to harbor doubts about all the new material ambitions, forerunners of a new spirit."[59]

The rhetoric of lament and loss was picked up not only by voices with deep roots in early nineteenth-century Vienna, but also by newcomers eager to display Viennese credentials. The nostalgia for the physical character of pre-Ringstrasse Vienna framed the basis of a critique of the contemporary attitude to culture. Ferdinand Kürnberger (1821–1879) was a key figure in the Viennese 1848 revolution, a great satirical writer whose 1855 novel on America, *Der Amerika-Müde*, remains a classic; he was admired by Ludwig Wittgenstein and Otto Erich Deutsch. Kürnberger reminisced in 1872 about the shift from a traditional and genuine Viennese wonderment at real talent and beauty, rendered simply, to the present habits of enthusiasm for appearances—a commercialized sense of fashion spellbound by mere fame:

> Instead of the old law, an entirely new and changed natural one has thus emerged; the old law no longer exists. When I still was carrying my books to school, I used to stop reverently in front of the window of an art shop then across from the Court Theater. There I saw Kriehuber's lithographs of portraits of Löwe, Anschütz, Fichtner, La Roche, of Rettich, Schröder, Neumann, Haitzinger—people known to the boy by their artistic reputation though he had not yet set foot into a theater, and whom he was interested in knowing, be it only by face, through the picture. That was the old style. Today I regularly see in this or that window a life-size headshot photograph in a garish golden frame and have to ask: who is that? Then I'm told: this is the new soubrette to be engaged by Stramper; that is the leading lady to be engaged by Ascher; it is the violinist, the singer who will come to Vienna soon! Nobody knows them yet; they have not yet impressed with their art, thus one cannot yet be interested in them, but yet . . . their person is the advertisement for their art. And before we owe them for one single artistic pleasure we know the worthy faces of people we may boo at next Sunday. That is a new style![60]

Comparing the Vienna of the day to the earlier era, the legendary and critical chronicler of all things local, Friedrich Schlögl (1821–1892), lamented the same changes. Writing in 1883, he noted that the worlds of theater and music had become dominated by fashion, pretentions, the economics of advertisement and newspaper criticism; the people had become humorless, overcome with an obsession for money. An authentic local aesthetic culture, marked by simplicity and decency, had vanished and with it a natural sense of humor and taste.[61] Schlögl was equally suspicious of a false nostalgia for Old Vienna, and lamented that those who longed for a relief from a culture dominated by the day's all-powerful "era of fraud" through nostalgia were perhaps the only genuine idealists left in a time of fools and "knaves." Where had Old Vienna's taste for morality, clarity, lightness, life-affirming and cheerful beauty gone? "Time and people have become different," he concluded. "One used to go to the theater as the one place for distraction and inspiration, but today people are buried in those evil newspapers. After all, we have become a 'politically educated' people."[62]

Kürnberger noted the irony, also perceived by Schlögl, that the admirable Viennese attitude to life encapsulated in the term *Gemütlichkeit* had been hijacked and undermined, if not perverted and destroyed, just as it had became world-famous. Furthermore, the Viennese, mostly newcomers who lacked Old Vienna's virtues, were the first to idealize it in a depoliticized form at odds with its true historical character—to praise it, imitate and glorify it as a civic virtue. As Kürnberger observed in a glowing 1873 review of Schlögl's most famous book, *Wiener Blut*, the real simplicity of mores and manners that once existed had little in common with any imitation mannerism and mythic redefinition by later generations. The myth of Gemütlichkeit in its modern form—which persists to this day—was a dishonor to the past, and a reflection of the philistinism of culture divorced from the engagement with an unvarnished account of daily life:

> Our locale for "Viennese Blood" is that place of south-German laxity, multiplied with Slav slovenliness and rounded out by the clerical and secular mismanagement of a centuries-old Dalai-Lama absolutism. Thus there is inevitably much corrupted blood in that "Viennese Blood," and the person who does not gloss over that fact is Friedrich Schlögl. He shows us indolence, frivolity, vulgarity, moral depravity, impotent childishness, sacrilegious lust, craving, smutty fanaticism, hatred of education and intellectuals, and the obdurate, absolute, self-affirmative roguishness with that firm German hand of a true Dutchman who does not falsify anything. He tells truth directly and dares to spit where there is no spittoon. But the compatriot who is in the know and is privy to this intimate material tells himself in astonishment: So you know all that too; you have seen it and have conjugated it like we do, yes,

> dissected it even more visually, and still, your love for the people and the country did not suffer a shipwreck on those countless and forlorn cliffs? Or vice versa: So much love did not blind you and your eyes stayed clear and open? It did not make you weak and your anger remained firm and your disgust healthy, precisely where a forceful repulsion remained in its proper place? And now we can sense something of the true meaning of "Gemütlichkeit." We see the golden pearl of its most fine-grained gold.[63]

Schubert, through his music, remained an honest witness and protagonist of the best of Old Vienna—a morality tale of its virtues. He was the era's "golden pearl"—not a dated relic from the past and not like Beethoven detached from the material and physical reality of the local. Three elements came forth in his work—a subjective emotional voice that responded to nature and life in Vienna with a disarming directness immediately evocative of local mores; a beauty of melody and musical logic transcending the local; and a profundity connected to the real experience of life that transfigured the harsh rootedness of the local.

At the core of this was a genuinely Viennese voice that through its aesthetic power could serve as an alternative model of the dominant modern German spirit. For this reason Kürnberger took aim at the modern enthusiasm for Schubert within the city that was most famously symbolized by the erection in 1872 in the Stadtpark of a Schubert monument. Kürnberger considered "the plague of monuments" dedicated to cultural heroes a reflection of the new elite of businessmen who were so self-conscious of their own apparent *Bildung* and discernment, so eager to display wealth and cosmopolitan pretense, that they sought to build garish public monuments rather than emulate the virtues of "the man whose name has been familiar to us for a long time." Kürnberger commented with disdain on subsequent plans for a Schiller monument; it seemed as if the Viennese in charge were concerned with appearances, "covering up" as a liar might "the conscience of truth" by creating a false synthesis between an idealized neoclassicism and modern realism, ending up with an impossible distortion of the true reason to honor Schubert and Schiller. But the rage for displaying civic enthusiasm for high culture was unstoppable. Kürnberger suggested, sarcastically perhaps, that a whole array of bases for future monuments be built to more quickly satisfy the needs of "the unknown, the men of the monument committee. The famous person is the means, but the unknown are their ends in themselves. Monuments are erected to make unknown quantities famous."[64]

The most prominent of this new elite, these "unknown quantities,"was no doubt Nikolaus Dumba (1830–1900), an industrialist and an amateur singer who was a fanatical Schubert admirer. He was instrumental in organizing the funding of the 1872 Stadtpark Schubert monument through his leadership in the Wiener Männergesangverein (Vienna Male Choral Society), a prominent civic organization founded in 1843 with a largely middle-class membership.[65] Dumba, who came from a Greek-Austrian family, was not only a music enthusiast but a collector and patron of the visual arts as well. He would later commission Gustav Klimt to do what has become an iconic mural of Schubert at the piano in 1898 for the music room in his Ringstrasse palace (destroyed in 1945).

The cult of Schubert in Vienna in which Dumba played such a leading role led in 1863 to the founding of the second major Viennese male choir made up of teachers—the Schubertbund.[66] Glorifying Schubert was inextricably tied to the appropriation by newcomers and a new generation of a traditional Viennese conceit of cultural discernment and grace rooted in local nostalgia—nostalgia for the remnants and reminiscences of the rural within the urban, the evocation of nature, the ideal of human modesty and simplicity, a way of life before the walls came tumbling down: more carefree, relaxed, humble, and warm. The nostalgia was for a city in which the population had been homogenous (*unvermischt*, as Schlögl put it)[67] and not polluted by the massive post-1867 emigration of Moravians, Bohemians, southern Slavs, Poles, and above all, Jews.

The affectation of Old Viennese mores and attitudes appealed to those who wished to prove how much they were truly Viennese. Authenticity took the form of a reimagined *Vormärz* Viennese sensibility. What better medium to embrace than Schubert, himself a reimagined witness of that very past? Franz Mair (1821–1893), the composer and teacher who founded and led the Schubertbund, was born and raised in Weikendorf, in Lower Austria. He became Schubert's devoted advocate after his career brought him permanently to Vienna. It was he who conducted the choir that accompanied the reburial of Schubert in 1888. He was an epigone as a composer, eager to be taken seriously. Liszt's praise for one of his works in 1855 remained the high point of his career.

The formation of the Schubertbund was about art as much as politics. Mair was a liberal in the 1848 context, and in the 1850s he joined his fellow teachers in a political movement to create a teacher's organization. As part of the planned teachers' association, he proposed the creation of a choral society to strengthen the sense of solidarity among teachers and increase the visibility of the profession and its members. Schubert offered the ideal name; after all, he and his father and brothers had been teachers.[68]

Before the founding of the Schubertbund, Mair had been part of the Männergesangverein, the organization that spearheaded the Schubert cult in the 1850s. Interestingly, the repertoire of the Männergesangverein in its first two decades was not particularly dominated by the music of Schubert.[69] Only a few works were done. Schubert came rather to represent to the members their own solid, Viennese middle-class virtues—education, aesthetic judgment, simplicity, and patriotism. That Schubert composed for friends, lived with them, and remained close to his family made him an apt symbol of friendship, family, and community—communal virtues which were institutionalized in the mission of the choral societies of German-speaking Europe. His loyalty to the local and his use of music to cement and define community were transformed into ideological emblems of a city once bound not by economic interests, but by organic cultural connections within the middle-class citizenry.

In this manner Schubert the man achieved more local fame than did Schubert's music. The myth of how his person was embodied in music became linked to the idealization of the authentic pre-1848 Viennese, the quintessential Austro-German. Above all, Schubert was the "man of the people"—a teacher and non-aristocrat of modest economic means who nonetheless rose to be the last exponent of the Viennese musical Classical tradition. This view of Schubert as representing the best in the mores and habits of the citizens of Old Vienna, who at the same time became a master equal to Mozart and Haydn, was endorsed by Viennese critics at the end of the century. Between the 1870s and the early 1900s Eduard Hanslick, Robert Hirschfeld, and the scholar Guido Adler, all endorsed the idea of Schubert as an ideal representative of local middle-class sensibilities, as an accessible populist icon.

Yet an inherent tension and paradox lay in this post-1848 cult of Schubert. As a historical representative of modest middle-class autonomy, he also was a reminder of a social and economic system that was being systematically undermined by the developments of late nineteenth-century finance and industry. The ardent defenders of Schubert as the finest flower of local Viennese virtues after 1860 were Kürnberger's "unknown quantities"—modern businessmen and newcomers, whose wealth came at the expense of the traditional *Vormärz* artisan guild economy of the city. For them, Gemütlichkeit was a pose, not a reflection of a way of life. The public celebration of culture—visible through the erection of monuments to surround the new historicist architecture of Vienna—was more a sign of a shift away from the actual mores and habits of the *Vormärz*. The Schubert who was enshrined—particularly in the 1872 monument—was put forward as an exemplar of an affirmative, depoliticized way of life in which culture played the central role.

Wagner's triumphant visit to Vienna in the mid-1870s underscored the extent to which the Wagnerian aesthetic fit in with the grandiosity of the architecture of the Ringstrasse and its monuments. The pretensions of Hans Makart's historicist canvases were equivalent to Wagner's heavy-handed pseudo "old" German rhetorical and poetic style. Wagner mirrored the modernity of industry, journalism, the machine age, and philosophically-minded discourse. The Schubert memorialized in 1872 fit in, even though the underlying factual premise of his posthumous fame was subversive. Beneath the bland compromise of history visible in the sculptor's idealization was a bittersweet nostalgia about a vanished past and an ambivalence if not resistance to the economic and social changes of the era.

Therefore, after 1873—the year of a catastrophic financial collapse and a controversial World's Fair—the facile glorification of Schubert in the previous two decades, exemplified by the 1872 monument, became unsustainable.[70] The subversive aspect caused a split. In the wake of the economic collapse and ensuing stagnation, Schubert became a rallying cry for a regressive reactionary politics, toward an assertive Austro-German patriotism and, by the 1880s, the anti-liberal and anti-Semitic agenda of Christian Socialism. Opposed to this was the liberalism associated with those who built the 1872 monument and a populism that would ultimately be linked to the Austrian socialist movement, heirs of an embattled liberal tradition of civic reform that sought, among other goals, the extension of suffrage. In the struggle in Vienna between liberals and conservatives and between pan-Germans and Habsburg dynastic patriots, Schubert emerged readily as an authentic Viennese contrast to things Prussian and Wagnerian. Schubert's status as teacher and middle-class man of the people made this ever more plausible to those Viennese who began to pierce the veil of a false nostalgia and Gemütlichkeit and question the facile claims of economic and social progress.

In the 1880s, liberals such as the critic Robert Hirschfeld (1857–1914) sought a way around Christian and Marxist Socialism through the substitution of culture for politics. Schubert became emblematic of a local spontaneity, a love of nature, and a simplicity that defied politics. Schubert more than any other figure could bind together a city divided by class, religion, and ethnicity and defined by rapid growth from emigration within the empire. Commenting on the official 1897 centenary celebrations, Hirschfeld (himself not a native Viennese) criticized the attempt by the Christian Social Party to appropriate Schubert as a populist symbol against aristocrats, liberals, and Jews. Rather, Schubert represented the power of art over politics. By spreading the musical culture that Schubert represented—an art of restrained elegance, beauty, and accessibility—music could ennoble the people and reconcile patriotism with cosmopolitan virtues, including tolerance. Even Schubert's religious music was for Hirschfeld rather more the "elegant expression of individual feeling through which all love streams" than the expression of Catholic piety.[71]

Schubert also represented the need to sustain music as an active participant activity. Inviting citizens to be more than spectator held promise for Hirschfeld as part of a platform for civic education. But as the Viennese male choirs became politicized, mostly to the right, the middle-class patriotic pride in singing Schubert was absorbed within either the pan-German movement, which called on the German part of the Austrian monarchy to ally itself with imperial Germany, or a loyal Habsburg conservatism based on a fiercely local idealization of the Austro-German.

By the late 1890s, and certainly by the 1920s, the connection between the myth of Old Vienna and the ideal of a distinct Austro-German sensibility whose center was Vienna was still intact in all the variants of Schubert appropriation. In 1911 Walter von Molo, writing in *Der Merker*, reversed Kürnberger's scorn, turning it on its head: "Franz Schubert is the monument that this city erected for itself." He declared (after repeating all the familiar virtues of a southern spirit, Gemütlichkeit, and humanism), "Vienna is the focal point of German culture, which is why Vienna gave birth to Franz Schubert . . . the artist from the people, the artist of the people, the artist of the everyday."[72] These powerful sentiments, expressed in part to deflect widespread criticism of the city and its fin-de-siècle rage for operetta—the derisive claim that Vienna was merely a place of superficial sensuality—explain why Vienna became the crucial foil in what emerged at the end of the nineteenth century as a real and symbolic contrast between Berlin and Vienna as models of urban modernity.

By the early twentieth century the reception of Schubert's music began to show signs of change. Schubert increasingly was seen through the lens of the historical, as evoking the authenticity of an earlier age—the penetrating simplicity of the language of Johann Nestroy and Ferdinand Raimund; the colorful and subtle landscape and genre painting of Ferdinand Waldmüller and Josef Danhauser; the sleek restraint, refinement, and elegance of Biedermeier architecture and design that eschewed decorative ornamentation and permitted materials, notably wood, to reveal their natural beauty, all on a human scale. After the death of Wagner in 1883 and of Brahms and Bruckner in the 1890s, Schubert lost his role as an alternative to Wagnerian Romanticism. Rather, he became a source of twentieth-century anti-Romantic, modernist, aesthetic convictions.

Art and Politics: Vienna, Berlin, and the 1928 Schubert Centenary

The rivalry between Berlin and Vienna—the two major cities of German Europe—was cultural. In political and economic terms Vienna had, by the outbreak of World War I, lost out. But to Berliners, Vienna represented competition in culture. Writing in his 1911 music history of Berlin, the critic Adolf Weissmann took aim at Vienna's conceits. He explained Beethoven's unhappiness with his circumstances after 1815 as emblematic of how "the joy in life" characteristic of Vienna was incompatible with the "dark" creations of Beethoven. There was, in the end, no "causal link" between Beethoven's creative genius and the city in which he resided for the most significant thirty-five years of his adult life. The "flattering" mores of the Viennese never seduced him in the way they did Mozart and Haydn.[73]

These were fighting words. After all, Beethoven's art represented the deepest and most profound aesthetic achievement in German history, second only to Goethe's. Beethoven's centrality to the world knew of no linguistic barriers. But he was profoundly German in a manner Vienna was not. Weissmann juxtaposed Berlin and Vienna, claiming that serious thought and ambition resided in the first, and superficiality and lightheartedness reigned in the other. This contrast had become so common in cultural criticism that it motivated the distinguished economist Werner Sombart to write an editorial in 1907 titled "Vienna," in which he took the opposite view.[74]

To Sombart, Berlin represented the worst of modernity; he dismissed it as a suburb of New York, itself a "cemetery of culture," the place where mere scale and quantity dominated over quality and individuality. Berlin was all about "traffic" and motion—commercial, industrial—as well as order, all qualities praised in the name of material progress. Berlin represented the victory of a heartless capitalism that had created fragments out of individual humans and the community as a whole. Vienna might seem backward and resistant to innovation to Berliners, but to miss the value of Vienna was to miss an object lesson as to how and why modernity dominated by technical rationality must be combatted.[75]

For Sombart, Vienna was above all a place of culture. "Vienna has culture. I do not even mean specifically 'old' culture. If one is seeking a modifier, an epithet, I would say 'aesthetic culture.'"[76] Sombart was reacting to an article by the writer (and *Bambi* author) Felix Salten, who, imitating a tradition of self-critical Viennese journalism that included Kürnberger, Daniel Spitzer, and Karl Kraus, offered a critique of Vienna that praised Berliners for their work ethic and concrete economic and scientific achievements. In reply, Sombart lauded the Viennese both for their humanity and their productivity. He urged readers who were concerned about German culture to "honor Vienna as holy," as a "symbol of that which we must preserve, and which we must seek to gain again for ourselves." For culture meant "human creativity, beauty, and harmony, a meaningful and reassuring life."[77] Culture meant Vienna.

Berlin and New York were widely considered emblems of modernity. The essence of that modernity, in terms articulated most famously by Max Weber, Sombart's contemporary and rival, was viewed with ambivalence. The domination of what Weber called "purpose rationality"—the hallmark of modern economic life—had shattered any inherited value system derived from religion and tradition. It had led to a collapse of any hierarchy of humanistic values. In the vacuum of values, modernity's "iron cage" of mere calculation and material progress dominated life.[78]

At the same time, modernist artists and architects who rejected Romanticism and the historicist aesthetics of the late nineteenth century saw in Berlin's and New York's material progress a way out of the grip of an aesthetic tradition that celebrated decoration and ornament and a surface sense of beauty. The efficient industrial structures of modernity—in their materials and in the rationality of a design that privileged structure—became new aesthetic inspirations for design. The work of architect Louis Sullivan (1856–1924) and the inherent beauty of functional, industrial designs in bridges and factories became emblematic of a new aesthetic to Viennese critics such as Adolf Loos.

This new aesthetic, rooted in the historical imperative of industrial progress and scientific reason, sought an alliance between the aesthetic and rational ethics and social reform—and a break from notions of beauty rooted in the connection between art and privilege, and the need to camouflage reality and hide the consequences of science and industry beneath a façade of historicism in art. Amid the enthusiasm for the materials and methods of modern industry within a new generation of artists, architects, and composers, particularly in Vienna, came a predictable conservative reaction: the widespread fear that traditional norms of beauty, and the autonomy of aesthetic values, would vanish and that valid hallmarks of aesthetic judgment would be set aside. The modernism represented by abstraction, cubism, constructivism, atonality and, ultimately, the twelve-tone system, would become identified with the harsh rationality of economic and technological progress—a sterility devoid of links to the past, particularly to eighteenth-century humanism and the expressiveness and emotionally accessible (and residually humanistic) fantasy of Romanticism. In defending Vienna against this reflexive fear of a radical, discontinuous aesthetic modernism remote from valid, inherited canons of taste, Sombart took pains not to limit his praise to mere tradition, but to Vienna's contemporary artistic culture.

His perception was not far off the mark. What emerged in Vienna between 1897 and 1914, amid the complex and often contradictory strains of modernist movements, was a distinctive variant of modernism and anti-historicism. Vienna displayed a unique approach to the embrace of modern materials, and the need to be truthful in design. The Viennese pioneered the belief that the substance of art should reflect a transformative synthesis of form and function, without purposeless ornamentation. In the realization of modernism, particularly in the work of Otto Wagner, Koloman Moser, Josef Hoffmann, the Wiener Werkstätte, and even Adolf Loos, a traditional pre-modern Viennese sensibility of grace and elegance was visible. The origins were local, and dated to the years of Schubert's brief life. (Compare, for example the designs, one from 1803, the other from 1905, in Figures 1 and 2.)

This distinctive quality in Viennese modernism may perhaps not have been so evident to Sombart, but it was nonetheless crucial. Its source was a special shared enthusiasm among Viennese modernists: a nostalgia for the aesthetic ideals of the Biedermeier period.[79] Viennese designers and architects adored Biedermeier furniture, fabrics, utensils, buildings, and clothes. The Viennese modernists who were most impressed by the local traditions of Biedermeier design produced an elegant variant of modernism, one that lent Viennese design, in the first decades of the twentieth century, its distinctly intimate and human character. The persistent glorification of "old Vienna"—this seemingly regressive taste for an old-fashioned simplicity—turned out to be fortuitous. Conservative nostalgia lasted long enough to be an impetus behind a novel progressive aesthetic and ideology in the visual arts.

Modernism in music in Vienna on the eve of World War I is best understood through the prism of the so-called scandal concert in March 1913. The music of Mahler, Schoenberg, Berg, and Webern was attacked as rejecting traditional aesthetic norms, for being pompous, grandiose, abstruse, abstract, and vulgar.[80] But most of all, their modernism in music was inaccessible to the participatory audience—the mass of amateurs. It was too advanced and complex. Much of the first wave of modernism—music

Figure 1. Silver teapot, Vienna, 1803. Franz Würth.

by Mahler, Alexander Zemlinsky, and the young Schoenberg—had been rather more Wagnerian in character. The extension and rejection of tonality, the fragmentation and condensation of form, and the eschewing of repetition seemed logical progressive advances beyond late Romanticism, but to the general public the music on the March concert, with the possible exception of Mahler, sounded radical indeed.

All the composers on that program venerated Schubert. But that respect and admiration for the very Biedermeier attributes of clarity and refinement celebrated by contemporary painters, artisans, and architects did little to solve the paradox. The progressive aesthetic ideology of musical modernism sought to reconcile itself with a progressive social and political agenda along lines pioneered by modern architects. But how could one justify music that only a few could comprehend and follow? The art, design, and architecture of Viennese modernism were comprehensible even when controversal and also useful and susceptible to being spread throughout all social classes. But the music was not. Liberal and progressive Viennese, inherently sympathetic to a new movement in the arts, understood this problem. They realized the imperative inherent in the nineteenth century cult of Schubert to reach a wide populace. A new music was needed that retained the norms of aesthetic beauty characteristic of Classicism and early Romanticism while emulating Wagner's

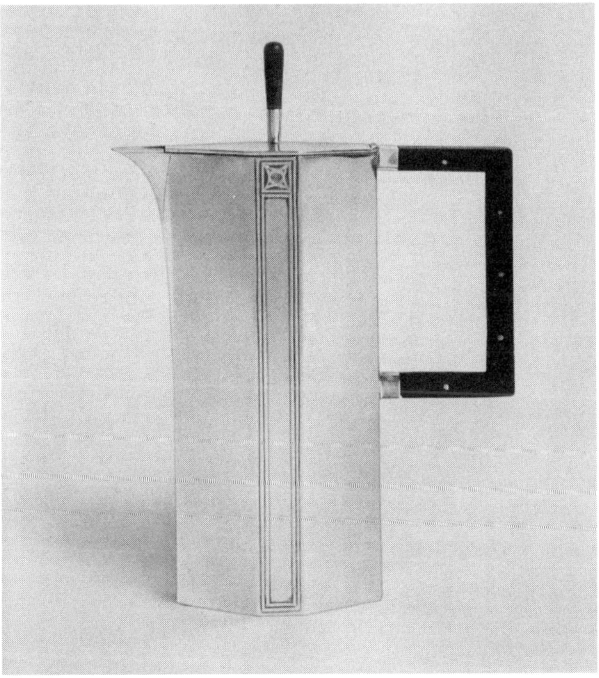

Figure 2. Coffee pot, 1905, Josef Hoffmann.

success in reaching a wide audience. In this context, Schubert emerged as a model for a progressive populist musical art. The question of how that might be realized remained unresolved.

For Viennese composers concerned with retaining the wide audience Schubert had amassed during the nineteenth century, he became a source of inspiration: the moral equivalent of Biedermeier design. Echoes of Schubert can be heard first in Zemlinsky's music, and later in that of Hanns Eisler (1898–1962), who grew up in Vienna. The public had been nurtured on Wagner as well as Schubert, and those on the left called for a modern music to which the masses could relate based on both or either—traditions once considered opposites. Among those who understood the relevance of Schubert for a populist modernism that merged an elegant Biedermeier-style beauty with contemporaneity was David Josef Bach (1874–1947), the music critic for Vienna's *Arbeiterzeitung*. The insight informed his ambivalent advocacy for Schoenberg.

Bach defended Schoenberg and his followers against the reactionary Christian Socialist and anti-Semitic cultural critique. But for all Bach's efforts to reconcile Schoenberg's music with his own commitments to socialism, he sensed contradictions. Like Schoenberg, Bach shared a belief in the autonomy of music, their mutual admiration for Wagner notwithstanding. Therefore the traditions of instrumental music remained ideal vehicles for the education of the masses. For Bach, new music had to be "understood plainly" and "respond to the basic needs of people." Music was not an "intellectual process" but one of sentiment, thereby making music an art form that could elevate the masses without inadvertently using art to beautify and justify economic and social injustice. Mahler's music suggested the accessibility of art for the masses, just as Schubert's did. Bach believed that succeeding generations of composers needed to do the same.[81]

Schubert therefore offered a mirror of how to respond to and elevate the aspirations of the working classes—the musical analogue to Biedermeier design. Bach developed Hirschfeld's dream of symphony concerts for the people with the production of Worker's Symphony Concerts in Vienna. They began in 1905, but were organized in earnest between 1919 and the early 1930s.[82] In June 1920, amid extreme postwar poverty and shortages, Bach announced a music festival devoted to "Great Performances of Viennese Music." He argued: "Viennese music is not a mere topographical concept, but an artistic one . . . this land, this air brought forth a particular kind of music . . . this landscape, that has its own music also has its saint: his name is Franz Schubert. This saint is also its martyr."[83]

A contradictory and competing appropriation of the myth of Old Vienna and the cult of Schubert also defined the character and politics surrounding the 1928 Schubert Centenary in Vienna. During the 1920s, Schubert had once again emerged as a contested figure. He was claimed by modernists like Bach with sympathies for the political left and by reactionary anti-modernists, protagonists of a renewed Austro-German cultural tradition in the neo-Romantic sense.

The revival of interest in the Biedermeier era in its local Viennese expression provided not only a more elegant and perhaps even humane path out of the labyrinth of eclecticism, density, and intensity of late Romanticism and historicism, but an impetus to scholarship. Otto Erich Deutsch's painstaking effort to reconstruct the historical Schubert reflected the need to emancipate the image of the composer from the sentimentalizing that had made him an emblem of privileged middle-class culture. The late nineteenth-century Schubert had entered popular literature and the operetta, but mostly as a tragic figure, a composer of songs, emblematic of romantic dreams of love. He was at one and the same time a symbol of local middle-class virtues and a tragic figure. Schubert was more local hero than a great composer in the tradition of Beethoven. Wagner had succeeded in diminishing his importance in music history. The impact of the kitsch glorification of Schubert in Vienna between 1897 and 1938 cannot be underestimated; it ranged from a cup and saucer from 1897 with a Schubert picture, to postcards and Schubert marzipan, to the use of Schubert's nickname "Schwammerl" as the title of Rudolf Hans Bartsch's 1912 wildly popular Schubert novel, to Heinrich Berté's legendary 1916 operetta *Das Dreimäderlhaus*. (As prime examples, see the illustrations in the portfolio commissioned by the Männergesangverein for the 1928 centenary, reproduced in Figures 3 and 4).

Deutsch sought to reconstruct Schubert and reassert his authentic historical roots as a *Vormärz* figure. Between 1905 and 1914, he immersed himself in Biedermeier culture with the intent to rescue Schubert from trivializing sentimentality—from the kitsch emblem of the Romantic that he had become—and from his place as an icon of local Viennese conservative middle-class provincialism. The garish sentimental cult of Schubert in fin-de-siècle Vienna thrived in the creation of tourist sites; Schubert was reduced to the Viennese cliché of the lighthearted, inspired, yet lovelorn hero. While seeking to puncture this image Deutsch also sought to strengthen, through research, Schubert's place as a sympathetic, populist figure. The intense realism audible within Schubert's music, as well as the trajectory of his life as outlined by Deutsch, could be readily associated with the profound alienation Marx described in his economic and philosophical manuscripts of 1844.

The pioneering research into the brutal details of Schubert's life, including his syphilis, the economic struggles of his father and brothers, and the difficulties posed by the absolutist tyranny of the pre-1830s era of Metternich, were dimensions of a cleansing of Schubert's image. In Deutsch's hands Schubert retained his singularity as a composer whose voice was motivated neither by the intent to amuse aristocratic patrons nor to please a bourgeois philistine audience. This reclaiming of Schubert as a Biedermeier figure and a spiritual forerunner of an egalitarian socialist ideal rooted in the authentic life of ordinary people caught in the web of nascent capitalism, laid the groundwork for the way in which Schubert would later be interpreted by T. W. Adorno as well as the eminent Viennese music historian Georg Knepler (1906–2003).[84]

The tension between two images of Schubert—the middle-class hero caught up by the personal search for love, master of songs and tunes uniquely expressive of local culture on one hand and, on the other, the troubled innovative genius, whose life experience inaugurated a new era in music history as a uniquely accessible composer in the tradition of Mozart and Beethoven—came to a head in 1928. Deutsch's scholarship

Figure 3. Cover from a portfolio commissioned by the Wiener Männergesangverein, 1928.

and the modernist Biedermeier revival in Vienna challenged the appropriation of Schubert as the exponent of local middle-class virtues by Austro-German nationalism and its successor, Austrofascism—heirs to Karl Lueger and the anti-Semitic Christian Socialists.

The contentious character of the 1928 centenary celebrations in Vienna stemmed as well from the politics of the moment. The Austrian Republic

Figure 4 Art by Karl M. Schuster, from a portfolio commissioned by the Wiener Männergesangverein, 1928.

was in the midst of civil strife, if not actual civil war. In July 1927, violence in the streets of Vienna between the *Heimwehr* on the right and the *Schutzbund* on the left, both paramilitary organizations, brought years of strife to a head; in these years of conflict the seeds of what would become the Austrofascism of the 1930s were sown. The Schubert centenary was planned to coincide with a massive gathering of German choral

Figure 5. Participants in the Tenth German Sängerbundfest, 1928.

societies, including German-American choral groups from New York, San Francisco, and Ohio: the tenth annual *Sängerbundfest*.[85] Pan-German choral society gatherings had been common since the mid-nineteenth century,[86] and 140,000 participants assembled in July 1928 in Vienna. The events included a pageant on the Ringstrasse (Figure 5) and a gathering in the Prater.

The 1928 Sängerbundfest was a symbol of pan-German sentiment in conflict with local Austro-German patriotism. The relentless public display of German cultural chauvinism and bourgeois pride (the Austrian Railroad Officials Chorus float in the parade featured a bust of Schubert), despite passing obeisance to a special "German-Austrian" tradition located in the Lied, fueled the Anschluss fantasies of the Austrian right (which were shared by some on the left during the early postwar years). It was an extremely tense moment in the history of the fragile First Republic.[87] Anton Wildgans (1881–1932), the playwright and poet who briefly directed the Burgtheater and was a fierce defender of postwar Austrian independence, took pains in his poetic prologue to the official memorial concert of the Gesellschaft der Musikfreunde on March 26 to stress Schubert's roots in Vienna, his role in bringing a different sensibility to the notion of the "German soul," his suffering in his own day, and his place as a "man of our times." Schubert, Wildgans proclaimed, embodied the hopes, dreams, and joys of Austria.[88]

The official Schubert celebration took place in Vienna, the home base of Austria's socialist movement, where the left was strongest, and the program became the object of severe criticism from that quarter. Key personalities were conspicuously absent, including Guido Adler, who, though associated with Mahler and Schoenberg, was nevertheless the nation's most distinguished music historian and a proud supporter of the Schubertbund and local Viennese musical traditions. Paul Pisk, the Schoenberg student and composer, writing in the socialist journal *Kunst und Volk*, argued that the centenary highlighted a "bourgeois" misunderstanding of Schubert as a bohemian and a superficial composer whose only real achievement was the Lied. Pisk averred that it was up to the working classes, the proletariat, to redefine Schubert as the great artist he was, whose inspiration came from the people and whose mastery of technique and form was both original and at the highest level.[89]

Pisk was taking aim at the lecture given by Robert Lach, an undistinguished musicologist who, through political maneuvering, had been named the successor to Guido Adler at the University of Vienna.[90] Lach's lecture on Schubert would become notorious, ridiculed by progressives as well as conservatives loyal to local Austro-German traditions. The historical revelations of Deutsch, the forging of a connection between Schubert and the harsh social realities (as opposed to a romanticized view) of Biedermeier Vienna—as well as its refined aesthetics—and the consequent link between Schubert and both modernism and socialism inspired Lach to assert a contrarian view. The old Romantic legend of Schubert as middle-class icon, bearer of stolid bourgeois virtues, and emblem of the ordinary Viennese of Old Vienna so cherished and exploited in the 1890s, was in his view no longer viable.[91] Modern scholarship had exposed it as a fiction, just as it had the legendary biographical connection between Schubert's *Die schöne Müllerin* and the mill at Höldrich.[92] Schubert actually led a dissolute life, as far as Lach was concerned. Schubert, the mythic albeit sentimental reminder of an outdated Austro-German middle-class ideal, had been exposed as a fraud. He had been an undisciplined genius whose personal habits, including drinking and carousing, prevented him from reaching the true heights of German music and what his own talent might have made possible.

Lach's critique of Schubert was both aesthetic and moral. He paved the way for what ultimately would become Schubert's ambiguous place in Nazi aesthetics. Lach put forward views on the connection between health, manliness, and art favored by many pan-German groups and ultimately by fascism. He outraged both the socialist left and the Austro-German Christian Social right. His speech was one unintended consequence of the strategy to lend the 1928 centenary a more conservative anti-socialist bent. Using the most recent research of Deutsch, Lach criticized Schubert's habits and exposed his shortcomings as a composer in a manner that echoed familiar criticisms in the nineteenth century by Brendel and Köstlin about the composer's inability to handle long forms and techniques of development. Beneath "a mask" of friendliness and lightheartedness, Schubert was possessed by demons he could not control: "burning longing, boundless thirst for love, and a heart filled with a nameless pain."[93] He was bewildered and lacked the chance to develop the disciplined personal attributes characteristic of greatness. Schubert's struggle did not lead to its transcendence and, owing to his early death, left his work a promise unfulfilled.

Lach's essential argument was that the most profound music and the highest "educative" mission to humankind in the German culture of music, the "ultimate transfigured heights," had been achieved by three figures: Bach, Beethoven, and Wagner.[94] His attempt to qualify and limit Schubert's historical significance and compare him unfavorably to Beethoven and the great German tradition of music was actually designed to undermine the viability of a distinct Austrian political and cultural existence, and to foreground the logic of an Anschluss that would render Austria subordinate.

Discarding the idealized late nineteenth-century version and highlighting moral and aesthetic shortcomings in Schubert, Lach confronted the conceits of local Viennese traditions. He maintained that Austrian and Viennese sensibilities needed to emulate the German tradition from the north. His 1928 Schubert speech is therefore best understood as a prophetic direct criticism of Chancellor Ignaz Seipel's attempt to appropriate the Schubert centenary on behalf of an independent albeit illiberal Austria.[95] Lach joined the Nazi Party early and became a vociferous and enthusiastic Austrian Nazi. Unlike other future fellow Austrian Nazis, in 1928 he had little sympathy with the idea or possibility of an autonomous Austrofascist state.

The serious historical research by Deutsch, the controversy sparked by Lach, and the potential of Schubert as a model for modernist art frame the context for T. W. Adorno's 1928 essay on Schubert (one of his earliest major publications on music)[96] and the place Schubert would occupy in Marxist historiography, notably in the much underestimated and brilliant work of Knepler.[97]

Adorno used to Schubert's advantage the invidious distinction between Schubert and Beethoven that had been a fundamental theme in Schubert criticism from Brendel to Lach. In Schubert's work "art" became an "image of reality." Schubert's music was understood in visual terms, as a landscape. In it an "image of truth" stood "within history." Schubert's lyricism was not "the blasphemous super-elevation of art" of the nineteenth century. Rather, "the paling images of existent objectivity" were combined in "cells of musical concreteness" with "the power of subjective inwardness." In Schubert's originality, in the "asymmetry" of his themes that challenge the "architecture of tonality," the "autonomy of the captured image" asserts "primacy" over the "abstract will to formal immanence." With its unique dialectical character as both an objective mirror of concrete experience and a rhetorical template for subjective expression, Schubert's music reaches where words cannot, into the regions of sorrow and hope.[98]

For Adorno, Schubert's joy is "unruly." Adorno used the true historical character of Schubert as revealed by Deutsch against both the sentimental Viennese mythologizing and against Lach's moralizing on behalf of a fascist construct of health and aesthetic greatness. Schubert is therefore removed from both "petty bourgeois music making" and "impoverished sentimentality." "Transcendental distance" through art "becomes attainable in the utmost proximity." The local realist aspect was the means Schubert used to achieve "a liberated music for a changed humanity" that could register "the message of humanity's qualitative change." The language of Schubert's music is, for Adorno, at once local and universal, "a dialect—but one that has no native soil. It has the concreteness of a homeland, yet its only homeland is one remembered." Schubert achieves aesthetic transcendence and subjective profundity by using nature and the mundane as the foundation of art. We "weep without knowing why" through music in which nature has "annulled itself" and a utopian hope is expressed, giving voice to a joy in the thought of a "promised state."

In stressing the metaphor of landscape and the visual imagery of music functioning as a crystal through which light shines, Adorno linked the modernist appreciation of Schubert, the affinity between modern design and Biedermeier precedents, and the ethical candor inherent in Schubert's realism. Simplicity and honesty in both musical content and form evoked a critical dimension (reminiscent of Nestroy and Raimund) rooted in human empathy that was absent from the affirmative art associated with the high capitalism of the late nineteenth century. Using music, Schubert articulated the inner suffering forced on him and others by the historical transformations of the 1820s, without manipulating the rhetoric of music into an act of masking truth through beauty. Adorno's theme of the close link between lived experience and aesthetic form set Schubert apart, rendering irrelevant the need to compare him to Beethoven as conventionally understood.

Georg Knepler took up Adorno's idea that Schubert's connection to concrete personal experience in history led to unique mechanisms of transcendence. Knepler's view of Schubert represents the most persuasive synthesis of the modernist and the many-sided populist strands of enthusiasm for Schubert in the history of German and Viennese reception. Schubert was certainly "German," but never in a political or nationalist sense. He was totally local in character, but never affirmative, more a critical realist than a Romantic: "In Schubert loneliness is not positive, and tears earn no praise. For him *Winterreise* is without purpose and filled with pain. In his presentation it becomes a bitter reproach against a world in which man must suffer."[99] In the great repertoire of songs, "desire, suffering, and despondency" predominate. Schubert's lyricism is distinctive since it reflects the encounter "with the social tensions of his era," which are transformed into "the emotions of his own heart." In this process, Schubert found a unique way to transcend the local and express the hope that "love and happiness" would be the inheritance of humankind.[100]

The post–World War II reception of Schubert, particularly among those committed to the ideals of socialism, held fast to a view of Schubert that was an amalgam of the historical Schubert and the late nineteenth-century object of mythic populist adulation. A Brahms-like aesthetic admiration and a populist veneration tempered by modern historical research were synthesized to render Schubert a voice of existential contradictions within the social and economic conditions of modernity. His music possessed a singular honesty, a focused realism rooted in the individual's encounter with the politics and landscape of Vienna. This had led Schubert to develop a distinctive new voice for Romanticism, in which a transcendent humanist idealism emerged from the concrete and the historical.

Subjective intimacy and progressive idealism about the power of music permitted Schubert to appropriate and extend the Classical heritage in music. At the same time, his work remained immune from the progressive critique of musical Romanticism as the self-serving, apolitical possession of a social and economic elite or as a voice of reactionary chauvinist nationalism. Schubert, in the twentieth century, appeared to redeem the autonomy and forward-looking power of music as a means of authentic, subjective, human freedom through aesthetic expression; his example suggested a path for an accessible musical modernism.

NOTES

1. See the important work by Scott Messing, *Schubert in the European Imagination*, vol. 1: *The Romantic and Victorian Eras*; vol. 2: *Fin-de-Siècle Vienna* (Rochester, NY, 2006 and 2007). Messing's impressive and detailed account focuses on aspects of Schubert reception in Vienna that are somewhat different but complementary to the argument in this essay. Another provocative and fine work is Andreas Mayer, *Franz Schubert: Eine historische Phantasie* (Vienna, 1997). The most radical biographical revision in recent memory was Maynard Solomon's controversial article on Schubert's sexuality, "Franz Schubert and the Peacocks of Benvenuto Cellini," *19th-Century Music* 12 (1989): 193–206. I would like to thank Irene Zedlacher, Christopher H. Gibbs, Morten Solvik, Anna Cafaro, and Lynne Meloccaro for their advice and assistance.

2. The literature on the popular reception of Schubert in modern times is immense. See David Schroeder, *Our Schubert: His Enduring Legacy* (Lanham, MD, 2009); and the essays by Cornelia Szabo-Knotik, "Franz Schubert und die österreichische Identität im Tonfilm der 1930er Jahre," and Manfred Permoser, "Der Schubert-Film nach 1950: Anmerkungen zur jüngeren Rezeptionsgeschichte," in *Schubert und die Nachwelt*, Kongressbericht: 1. Internationale Arbeitstagung zur Schubert-Rezension 2003, ed. Michael Kube, Walburga Litschauer, and Gernot Gruber (Munich, 2007), 309–19 and 321–28 respectively.

3. I do not wish to burden readers of this essay with extraneous historical background, but it is important to direct those interested in the historiography of the connection between culture and politics in the history of German-speaking Europe in the nineteenth and twentieth centuries to the peculiar and often troubled interaction between the oft discussed high value placed on *Kultur* and *Bildung* in the German middle classes after 1815 and especially after 1848 and 1870 and the direction of German politics. The concept of freedom, the individual, and citizenship—the whole complex of attitudes associated with liberalism in German-speaking Europe—was influenced by the prestige culture and learning assumed as surrogates for political activity as construed in the English and American sense. The sufficiency of an apolitical notion of individuality and freedom was bolstered by the huge emphasis on culture, including music, as was a pessimistic attitude to democracy. Within the massive literature on this subject, see the classic essays by Fritz Stern "The Political Consequences of the Unpolitical German," in *The Failure of Illiberalism: Essays on the Political Culture of Modern Germany* (New York, 1972), 3–25.

4. See Joseph Joachim's letter to Robert Schumann from 21 March 1853. Quoted in Beatrix Borchard, *Stimme und Geige: Amalie und Joseph Joachim* (Vienna, 2005), 121–22.

5. Heinrich Adami, *Alt- und Neu-Wien: Beiträge zur Beförderung lokaler Interessen für Zeit, Leben, Kunst und Sitte* (Vienna, 1841), 82–83.

6. Peter Cornelius, *Literarische Werke: Aufsatze über Musik und Kunst*, ed. Edgar Istel (Leipzig, 1904), 152. The review was originally published in the *Neue Zeitschrift für Musik* 51/52 (1867).

7. W. H. Riehl, *Kulturstudien aus drei Jahrhunderten* (Stuttgart, 1862), 391.

8. See Katherine Harloe, *Winckelmann and the Invention of Antiquity in the Age of Altertumswissenschaft* (Oxford, 2013), passim.

9. The members of the Männergesangverein were overwhelmingly from the middle class, with less than 3 percent of active members coming from the aristocracy. The bulk were professionals, civil servants, commercial employees, followed by bankers, merchants, industrialists, and a very small group of artisans, i.e. 60 percent upper-bourgeoisie, 30 percent comfortable middle-class Viennese, and 10 percent from the lower spectrum of the bourgeoisie. See Leon Botstein, "Music and Its Public," (PhD diss., Harvard University, 1985), 372–73 and Tables 17 and 18 in vol. 5: Appendix.

10. Bruno Walden, *Wiener Studien* (Vienna, 1869), 42–43.

11. Brahms to Joachim, December 1868, in *Johannes Brahms im Briefwechsel mit Joseph Joachim*, ed. Andreas Moser, vol. 2 (Berlin, 1912), 60–61.

12. Franz Brendel, *Geschichte der Musik in Italien, Deutschland und Frankreich*, vol. 2 (Leipzig, 1855), 335.

13. Ibid., 336–37.

14. The operas are still not much known and rarely performed. Liszt premiered *Alfonso und Estrella* in the 1850s. See a translation of his article on the opera in this volume.

15. Richard Wagner, "About Conducting," in *Richard Wagner's Prose Works*, vol. 4: *Art and Politics*, trans. William Ashton Ellis (New York, 1966), 363.

16. Herbeck, for example, premiered *Die Verschworenen* in Vienna in 1861.

17. Ludwig Herbeck, *Johann Herbeck: Ein Lebensbild* (Vienna, 1885), Appendix, 57.

18. Ibid.

19. On this subject see the essays in Celia Applegate and Pamela Potter, eds., *Music and German National Identity* (Chicago, 2002).

20. Herbeck, *Johann Herbeck*, 112–13.

21. Brahms to Adolf Schubring, 23 March 1863, in *Johannes Brahms: Briefe an Joseph Viktor Widmann, Ellen und Ferdinand Vetter, Adolf Schubring*, ed. Max Kalbeck (Berlin, 1915), 196.

22. Quoted in Charlotte Sussman, *Eighteenth-Century English Literature* (Cambridge, 2011), 36–40.

23. George Bernard Shaw, "Goetz über alles," in *Shaw's Music*, vol. 3: *1893–1950*, ed. Dan H. Laurence (New York, 1981), 39.

24. Richard Strauss, "Über Schubert: Ein Entwurf," in *Betrachtungen und Erinnerungen*, ed. Willi Schuh (Zurich, 1981), 112–13. Strauss's interest as a conductor was limited to the C-Major and B-Minor symphonies. On the general topic of the place of Schubert in the New German School, see Hans-Joachim Hinrichsen, "Der geniale Naive und der nachträgliche Progressive: Schubert in der Ästhetik und Politik der 'neudeutschen Schule,'" in *Schubert-Jahrbuch 1999*, ed. Dietrich Berke, Walther Dürr, Walburga Litschauer, and Christiane Schumann (Duisburg, 2001), 23–40.

25. The notion that the real recognition of Schubert came through Liszt was a widely held commonplace. The legendary cultural force during the Weimar Republic, Leo Kestenberg, even commented in 1956, "If I only think of what Liszt achieved for Schubert, how he was the one who brought Schubert to the world." *Leo Kestenberg and Franz W. Beidler: Complete Correspondence, 1933–1956*, trans. and ed. Philip A. Maxwell (Victoria, CA, 2013), 305.

26. See Thomas Kabisch, *Liszt und Schubert*, Berliner musikwissenschaftliche Arbeiten 23 (Munich and Salzburg, 1984).

27. Quoted in Vladimir Stasov, "Liszt, Schumann, and Berlioz in Russia," in *Selected Essays on Music*, trans. Florence Jonas, introduction by Gerald Abraham (London, 1968), 88–89. See also Robert Engel, "Schubert und Russland," *Die Musik* 21/2 (1921): 113–19.

28. Hugo Wolf, *Briefe*, vol. 1: *1873–1901*, ed. Leopold Spitzer (Vienna, 2011), 358 (to Emil Kauffmann) and 420 (to Melanie Köchert).

29. Brendel, *Geschichte der Musik*, 176–78.

30. Eduard Bernsdorf, *Neues Universal-Lexikon der Tonkunst*, vol. 3 (Offenbach, 1861), 513–18.

31. Heinrich Adolf Köstlin, *Geschichte der Musik im Umriss* (Tübingen, 1875), 282–83.

32. This is all according to Natalie Bauer-Lechner, in Herbert Killian, *Gustav Mahler: Erinnerungen von Natalie Bauer-Lechner* (Hamburg, 1984), 158.

33. Brahms is quoted saying this in 1887 in Max Kalbeck, *Johannes Brahms: 1856–1862* (Berlin, 1908), 220.

34. See W. H. Riehl, *Die bürgerliche Gesellschaft* (Stuttgart, 1851), passim.

35. See Maxim H. Botstein, "Popular History in an Age of Scholarship: Gustav Freytag's *Bilder aus der deutschen Vergangenheit*" (Senior thesis, Princeton University, 2014).

36. See Jasper von Altenbockum, *Wilhelm Heinrich Riehl, 1823–1897: Sozialwissenschaft zwischen Kulturgeschichte und Ethnographie* (Cologne, 1994), 85–90.

37. Jacob Burckhardt, *The Civilization of the Renaissance in Italy*, with an introduction by Hajo Holborn (New York, 1954), 291.

38. *Jacob Burckhardts Briefe an seinen Freund Friedrich von Preen, 1864–1893*, ed. Emil Strauss (Stuttgart and Berlin, 1922), 127 (scores), 63 (Wagner). The letter mentioning Wagner is quoted also in Max F. Schneider, *Die Musik bei Jacob Burckhardt* (Basel, 1946), 110–11.

39. Strauss, *Burckhardts Briefe an seinen Freund Friedrich von Preen*, 219.

40. Burckhardt, *Reflections on History*, with an introduction by Gottfried Dietze, trans. M. T. Hottinger (Indianapolis, 1979), 288–89.

41. Cornelius, *Aufsätze über Musik und Kunst*, 153.

42. See Karl Lamprecht, *Deutsche Geschichte*, 10 vols. and supplements (Freiburg im Breisgau, 1903–5), Zweiter Ergänzungsband: 3–10, and 10:3–5, 118–22, and 126–30. English readers can consult Karl Lamprecht, *What is History? Five Lectures on the Modern Science of History*, trans. E. A. Andrews (London, 1905; repr. 2012). The best short introduction to Lamprecht in English can be found in Karl J. Weintraub, *Visions of Culture* (Chicago, 1966), 161–207.

43. Karl Lamprecht, *Deutsche Geschichte*, 8/2:314; also 10:288–307.

44. Ibid., *Deutsche Geschichte*, Erster Ergänzungsband: 434–56, and 8/1:18–25, 30–33, 192–93.

45. Riehl, *Kulturstudien aus drei Jahrhunderten*, 101.

46. Ibid., 374–78, 399–400.

47. W. H. Riehl, "Das Quartett," in *Neues Novellenbuch* (Stuttgart, 1899), 190–240.

48. Riehl, *Kulturstudien aus drei Jahrhunderten*, 377.

49. Ibid., 377–81.

50. See W. H. Riehl, "Das Volkslied," in *Die Gegenwart: Eine enzyklopädische Darstellung der neuesten Zeitgeschichte für alle Stände*, vol. 3 (Leipzig, 1849), 680–81.

51. Ibid.

52. Wilhelm Dilthey, *Von deutscher Dichtung und Musik* (Leipzig and Berlin, 1933), 282.

53. Ibid.

54. Wilhelm Dilthey, *Gesammelte Schriften*, vol. 7: *Der Aufbau der geschichtlichen Welt in den Geisteswissenschaften* (Stuttgart and Göttingen, 1961), 220–24.

55. See Leon Botstein, "Realism Transformed: Franz Schubert and Vienna," in *The Cambridge Companion to Schubert*, ed. Christopher H. Gibbs (Cambridge, 1997), 15–35.

56. Jacob Burckhardt to Gustav Stehelin, 2 August 1884, in *Jacob Burckhardt: Briefe*, vol. 8: *1882–1885*, ed. Max Burckhardt (Basel, 1974), 218.

57. Adam Müller-Guffenbrunn, *Altwiener Wanderungen und Schilderungen* (Vienna, 1915), 191.

58. Adolf Schmidl, *Wiens Umgebungen auf zwanzig Stunden im Umkreise*, 2 vols. (Vienna, 1838), 1–3.

59. Eduard Bauernfeld, *Erinnerungen aus Alt-Wien*, ed. Josef Bindtner (Vienna, 1923), 221–22.

60. Ferdinand Kürnberger, "Ein Aphorismus zur Denkmal-Pest," in *Literarische Herzenssachen*, vol. 2 (Munich and Leipzig, 1911), 289–90.

61. See Friedrich Schlögl, *Wiener Luft! Kleine Culturbilder aus dem Volksleben der alten Kaiserstadt an der Donau* (Vienna, 1876), vii–xvi.

62. Schlögl, *Vom Wiener Volkstheater; Erinnerungen und Aufzeichnungen* (Vienna, [1883]), 10–13; see also 24–25 and 165–66.

63. Kürnberger, "Friedrich Schlögls 'Wiener Blut,'" 2:258.

64. Kürnberger, "Ein Aphorismus zur Denkmal-Pest," 290.

65. See Botstein, "Music and Its Public," passim; and *Jahresbericht des Männergesang-Vereines in Wien 1847–1874* (Vienna, 1848–74).

66. Anton Weiss, ed., *Fünfzig Jahre Schubertbund* (Vienna, 1913), 3–9.

67. Quoted by Kürnberger, "Friedrich Schlögls 'Wiener Blut.'" See also Friedrich Schlögl, *Wienerisches* (Vienna, 1883), vii–x and 240–41.

68. *Aus meinem Leben: Erinnerungen eines alten Schulmannes und Tonkünstlers nach Franz Mairs Mittheilungen und Aufzeichnungen* (Vienna, 1897), 25–28, 33–39, 50–59.

69. The repertoire was dominated by Mendelssohn, Kalliwoda, Kreutzer, Weber, Spohr, Lachner, Marschner, and a host of minor figures; see the lists in *Jahresbericht des Männergesang-Vereines in Wien 1847–1874*; e.g. for 1874: 93–106.

70. There has been a great deal written about this 1872 monument, its design by Carl Kundmann on a base by Theophil Hansen, the architect of the 1870 Musikverein. Schwind, Schubert's friend, advised Kundmann on the design. The discussion about creating a monument dates from the 1850s; the Männergesangverein played the decisive role in getting the project done. The design was as controversial as the whole enterprise, but Schubert was the first of the Classical composers to be so honored in Vienna: the Beethoven monument was erected in 1880, the one for Haydn in 1887, and the Mozart monument was completed in 1896. Hugo Wolf was not alone in his ambivalence toward the sentimental and idealized image. As he explained to his parents in 1878, every time he walked by the monument, it forced him to confront his own views; see Wolf, *Briefe*, 1:39. On the monument, see Ludwig Speidel's 1872 essay "Das Schubert Denkmal," in *Wiener Frauen und anderes Wienerisches* (Berlin, 1910), 120–25.

71. Robert Hirschfeld, "Die Schubert-Feier," *Wiener Abendpost* (Beilage zur *Wiener Zeitung*), 6 February 1897, 5–6. On Hirschfeld, see Elisabeth Riz, "Robert Hirschfeld: Leben–Wirken–Bedeutung," in *Biographische Beiträge zum Musikleben Wiens im 19. und frühen 20. Jahrhundert*, ed. Friedrich C. Heller (Vienna, 1992), 1–80.

72. Walter von Molo, "Schubert und Wien," *Der Merker* 2 (10/11 February 1911): 449–51.

73. Adolf Weissmann, *Berlin als Musikstadt* (Berlin and Leipzig, 1911), 121.

74. Werner Sombart, "Wien," *Morgen* 6 (1907), repr. in *Début eines Jahrhunderts: Essays zur Wiener Moderne*, ed. Wolfgang Pircher (Vienna, 1985), 35–40.

75. Ibid., 37.

76. Ibid., 36.

77. Ibid., 39.

78. See Max Weber, *The Protestant Ethic and the Spirit of Capitalism*, trans. Talcott Parsons (New York, 1958), 181.

79. See the catalogue *Moderne Vergangenheit: Wien 1800–1900* (Vienna, 1981) by Peter Pawerka for the 1981 exhibition at the Vienna Künstlerhaus.

80. See Botstein, "Vienna and Its Public," 1018–36.

81. Henriette Kotlan-Werner, *Kunst und Volk: David Josef Bach, 1874–1947* (Vienna, 1977), 21, 42–45.

82. David Josef Bach, "Arnold Schoenberg," *Arbeiter-Zeitung*, 17 February 1905; see also Botstein, "Music and Its Public," 1208–10.

83. Quoted in Kotlan-Werner, *Kunst und Volk: David Josef Bach*, 74.

84. Another fine example of the Marxist interpretation of Schubert can be found in the work of Harry Goldschmidt in *Franz Schubert: Ein Lebensbild* (Berlin, 1960).

85. For a sense of this anniversary, see *Offizielles Erinnerungsalbum an das 10. Deutsche Sängerbundesfest Wien 1928* and *Festblätter für das 10. Deutsche Sängerbundesfest Wien 1928* (both Vienna, 1928).

86. See *Der Deutsche Sängerbund 1862–1912: Aus Anlass des fünfzigjährigen Bestandes* (1912), 2–67.

87. Richard Strauss wrote *Die Tageszeiten*, Op. 76, a work for male choir and orchestra, for the Schubertbund for the 1928 festival. See Roland Tenschert, *Richard Strauss und Wien: Eine Wahlverwandschaft* (Vienna, 1949), 121.

88. Anton Wildgans, *Briefe*, vol. 3: *1925–1932*, ed. Lilly Wildgans (Vienna, 1947), 556–58; see also 207–8.

89. Paul A. Pisk, "Schubertfeiern," in *Volk und Kunst* 25 (June 1928): 1–2; see also Piero Violante, *Eredità della musica* (Palermo, 2007), 147.

90. On Robert Lach and Georg Knepler, see Gerhard Oberkofler, "Über das musikwissenschaftliche Studium von Georg Knepler an der Wiener Universität," *Mitteilung der Alfred Klahr Gesellschaft* 3 (2006); available at http://www.klahrgesellschaft.at/Mitteilungen/Oberkofler_3_06.html. There is some controversy about the fact that a street in Vienna is named for Lach. See the Viennese newspaper *Der Standard*, July 2012. The lecture, delivered on 19 November 1928 at the University of Vienna, can be found in Robert Lach, *Das Ethos in der Musik Schuberts* (Vienna, 1928).

91. An example of this reception pattern—glorifying Schubert as emblematic of the essence of Viennese middle-class cultural values and practices, produced after Deutsch's research—is the volume on Schubert in *Jugendhefte für Literatur und Kunst* published by the Lower Austrian Division of Youth right after World War I.

92. See Ludwig Speidel's 1894 essay, "Franz Schubert in der Höldrichsmühle," in his *Wiener Frauen und anderes Wienerisches*, 126–32.

93. Lach, *Das Ethos in der Musik Schuberts*, 22. On the 1928 Vienna celebrations, see Gabriele Johanna Eder, "Das Schubert-Jahr 1928 in Wien und anderen Städten des deutschen Sprachraumes," in *Schubert und die Nachwelt*, 297–307.

94. Lach, *Das Ethos in der Musik Schuberts*, 28–30.

95. See *Festblätter für das 10. deutsche Sängerbundesfest*, 241, and Eder, "Das Schubert-Jahr 1928," 302. On Seipel, see Klemens von Klemperer, *Ignaz Seipel: Christian Statesman in a Time of Crisis* (Princeton, 1972).

96. T. W. Adorno, "Schubert," in *Night Music: Essays on Music, 1928–1962*, ed. Rolf Tiedemann, trans. and introduced by Wieland Hoban (London and New York, 2009), 19–46; quotes at 22, 20, 23, 31, 37, 44, 45, 46. The original in German is in *Die Musik* 21/1 (1928): 1–12.

97. See Georg Knepler, *Musikgeschichte des 19. Jahrhunderts*, vol. 2: *Österreich, Deutschland* (Berlin, 1961), 591–656.

98. See the issue devoted to Adorno's 1928 Schubert essay: *19th-Century Music* 29/1 (2005).

99. Knepler, *Musikgeschichte des 19. Jahrhunderts*, 2:642.

100. Ibid., 2:634.

Index

Page numbers followed by n indicate notes. Page numbers in italics indicate figures and excerpts from musical works.

Index of Franz Schubert's Compositions

Index of Names and Subjects

Notes on Contributors

Leon Botstein is president and Leon Levy Professor in the Arts of Bard College, author of several books and editor of *The Compleat Brahms* (1999) and *The Musical Quarterly*. The music director of the American Symphony Orchestra and conductor laureate of the Jerusalem Symphony Orchestra, he has recorded works by, among others, Szymanowski, Hartmann, Bruch, Dukas, Foulds, Toch, Dohnányi, Bruckner, Chausson, Richard Strauss, Mendelssohn, Popov, Shostakovich, and Liszt.

Lisa Feurzeig is professor of music at Grand Valley State University in Michigan. Her research emphasizes German-language vocal music: Lieder, opera, and operetta. She is the author of *Schubert's Lieder and the Philosophy of Early German Romanticism* (2014) and of articles on Wagner, Fauré, and Schubert; she is drawn to interdisciplinary connections and to traditions where the arts mingle. As a singer, she has performed art song and chamber music ranging from the twelfth to the twentieth century.

Christopher H. Gibbs is James H. Ottaway Jr. Professsor of Music at Bard College, coartistic director of the Bard Music Festival, and executive editor of *The Musical Quarterly*. He edited *The Cambridge Companion to Schubert* (1997), co-edited *Franz Liszt and His World* (2006), and is the author of *The Life of Schubert* (2000), which has been translated into four languages. He is the co-author, with Richard Taruskin, of *The Oxford History of Western Music, College Edition* (2013). Since 2000 he has been the program annotator for the Philadelphia Orchestra.

John M. Gingerich has published articles on Schubert's cello quintet, his Latin Masses, his "Unfinished" Symphony, and on Ignaz Schuppanzigh and Beethoven's late quartets. His book, *Schubert's Beethoven Project*, was published in 2014 by Cambridge University Press. Before embarking on his musicology studies he spent several years playing in the cello section of the Baltimore Symphony Orchestra. He is currently working on a book on Ignaz Schuppanzigh.

David Gramit is professor of musicology at the University of Alberta. In addition to research and publications on the culture of German musical life in the late-eighteenth and early-nineteenth centuries and on music in the colonization of western North America, he received the AMS-50 Dissertation Fellowship and the Alfred Einstein Award of the American

Musicological Society for his work on the intellectual and aesthetic context of Schubert's circle.

Allan Keiler is professor of music at Brandeis University. He has a PhD in linguistics from Harvard University. He did his graduate work in musicology and music theory at the Universities of Michigan and Chicago, and did a lay traineeship at the Boston Psychoanalytic Institute. His work in semiotics, the history of music theory, and Liszt has appeared in many journals and collections including *Journal of Music Theory*, *19th-Century Music*, *Music and Perception*, *The Musical Quarterly*, and *Perspectives in New Music*. His biography, *Marian Anderson: A Singer's Journey*, was published by Scribner in 2000.

Kristina Muxfeldt is a music historian on the faculty of the Jacobs School of Music, Indiana University. She writes about European music and culture in those turbulent years before 1800 and in the decades after, when centuries-old social orders tottered and radical equalities became thinkable, reshaping our world in lasting ways. Novel perspectives on society, censorship, and gender in her book *Vanishing Sensibilities: Schubert, Beethoven, Schumann* complement the political focus of her essay here.

Morten Solvik holds degrees from Cornell University (BA) and the University of Pennsylvania (PhD in musicology). His publications on Schubert, Mahler, and others focus on the tantalizing connections between music and culture in nineteenth- and early twentieth-century Austria. While this work includes scholarly articles, editions, and edited books, it also extends to engaging wider audiences at festivals and in radio and television productions as a commentator and author. Solvik serves as the Center Director of IES Abroad Vienna, where he also teaches music history.

Rita Steblin earned degrees in musicology at the universities of British Columbia, Toronto, and Illinois at Urbana-Champaign, and studied harpsichord in Vienna. Her dissertation on the history of key characteristics was published by the University of Rochester Press in 2002. Other publications include articles in Canadian, American, British, and European musicology journals and the volume *Die Unsinnsgesellschaft: Franz Schubert, Leopold Kupelwieser und ihr Freundeskreis* (1998). Since 1991 she has worked full-time on research in Vienna's archives, concentrating primarily on Beethoven and Schubert.